Paper Action Figures of the Imagination

Clip, Color and Create

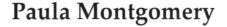

Paula Montgomery

A Teacher Ideas Press Book

Libraries Unlimited
An Imprint of ABC-CLIO, LLC

A B C ⬥ C L I O

Santa Barbara, California • Denver, Colorado • Oxford, England

Copyright 2009 by Teacher Ideas Press

Library of Congress Cataloging-in-Publication Data

Montgomery, Paula Kay.
  Paper action figures of the imagination : clip, color and create / Paula Montgomery.
    p. cm.
  "A Teacher Ideas Press Book."
  Includes edited portions from articles originally published in Crinkles, volumes I-IX.
  Includes bibliographical references and index.
  ISBN 978-1-59158-751-4 (hard copy : alk. paper) 1. Paper dolls. 2. Teaching—Aids and devices.
  3. Education, Primary—Activity programs. I. Crinkles. II. Title.
  NK8553.M66   2009
  741.6′5—dc22   2009017269

13 12 11 10 9   1 2 3 4 5

This book is also available on the World Wide Web as an eBook.
Visit www.abc-clio.com for details.

ABC-CLIO, LLC
130 Cremona Drive, P.O. Box 1911
Santa Barbara, California 93116-1911

This book is printed on acid-free pape ∞™
Manufactured in the United States of America

Contents

Introduction

Whether we call them paper action figures or paper dolls, we know they can bring hours of joy and satisfaction in play and in the act of creating. With the availability of inexpensive paper, crayons, and scissors, they have become ubiquitous in the marketplace. Today there are hundreds of adult collectors, and thousands young children color, paint, cut, and create paper dolls. We have chosen to call them paper action figures in the title of this collection because the paper dolls become something more when children play. It takes fine motor skills to make and dress them. It requires creative thinking and role playing.

Paper dolls have captured the imagination of authors for years. They can be found in some children's books. Perhaps one of the most poignant is *The Hundred Dresses*, written by Eleanor Estes and illustrated by Louis Slobodkin. In the story, a Polish American girl wears the same blue dress to school every day, but claims to have a hundred dresses. She is teased and treated cruelly. Only after she leaves the school does the truth come out, when the girl wins a design contest.

The paper action figures in this book first made their debut in *Crinkles* magazine beginning in 1998. In articles about imaginary or fantasy topics, the figures were included for children to actively incorporate ideas from their reading into their play. This collection represents the work of artists and authors who enjoyed their own creative acts. A special thanks is owed to Greenwood Press and acquisitions editor Sharon Courtney, who loved and played with paper dolls and used them when she was a teacher and library media specialist in Kansas.

In these pages the reader will find animals anthropomorphized; storybook characters from novels and picture books; characters from folktales, fables, myths, and legends; and many imaginary figures. All can be used to re-create the stories and tales or to provide a visual form for daydreams. The intent is for those who open and read these pages to clip, color, and create!

Chapter 1

History of Paper Dolls and How to Use Them in Instruction

Paper dolls seem a simple concept. They take up very little space in comparison to other toys, but can offer hours of occupied fun. Although they may seem to be passive, the play is usually imaginative and inventive. Making paper dolls requires some manual dexterity. It also requires relatively inexpensive materials. Even "store-bought" paper dolls are not usually budget breakers for parents and can be found in most toy and mass-market magazine stores and bookstores.

What are paper dolls, and how did they evolve into toys for children? According to Judy Johnson in *History of Paper Dolls* at the OPDAG Web site,

> [A] paper doll is a two-dimensional figure drawn or printed on paper for which accompanying clothing has also been made. It may be a figure of a person, animal or inanimate object. The term may be extended to include similar items made of materials other than paper, such as plastic, cloth or wood. The term also may include three-dimensional dolls and their costumes that are made exclusively of paper.

These figures may serve many functions, and have done so over time. These functions also help explain the evolution of the paper doll into a most favored toy, especially for young girls.

Early Paper Figures

Paper dolls are dependent on the major raw material—paper. The Egyptians made paper using papyrus, from which the name comes. The *tapa* technique, which dates back to about 3000 BC, involved using cooked bark or pulp and spreading it on a screen to dry. The making of paper as we know it is credited to Cài Lún (or Ts'ai-Lin), a Chinese eunuch from Lei-yang, in AD 105, during the reign of Emperor He of Han. It was made by pounding the inner bark of the mulberry tree and hemp, rags, and bamboo fibers in water to form a paste. This solution was poured over a flat piece of coarsely woven cloth to let the water drain through. The thin layer on the cloth dried and became sheets of paper. It isn't known if there were dolls made of papyrus or if the first dolls, as we know them, were made in China. We do know that paper figures were used in Japan and China for religious ceremonies.

Religion

Some of the earliest reported uses of paper figures come from Japan around AD 900. For purification rituals, paper human figures with folded kimonos were put to sea in boats in the spring. In 1280 Marco Polo reported seeing the Chinese burn painted-paper human and animal figures at funerals. Leather and paper shadow puppets were used by the Chinese and the Balinese for retelling myths and religious tales. In Mexico, paper figures were used by Otomi Indians in ceremonies. Paper art has been used to decorate, especially for the holidays, in China (Hua Yang), Japan (Kirigami), Poland (Wycinanki), and Germany and Switzerland (Scherenschnitte). In the 1700s the French used *pantins*, moveable paper puppets, not for religious purposes, but rather to satirize the aristocracy in plays.

Fashion

The first "true" paper dolls are believed to have been the fashion dolls found in Paris, London, Berlin, and Vienna in the nineteenth century. Wealthy adults were able to purchase hand-painted figures with costumes. These may have been made by dressmakers to showcase their fashions. They may also have been made as satires of well-known figures of the day.

In November 1859, *Godey's Lady's Book* was the first magazine to print a paper doll, in black and white, followed by a page of costumes for children to color. It was the only time the magazine published a doll, but other magazines followed. From 1908 to 1915, *Ladies' Home Journal* published Sheila Young's Lettie Lane, whose costumed family, friends, and servants often graced its pages.

Magazine artists produced many characters. Sheila Young produced Polly Pratt for *Good Housekeeping* from 1919 to 1921. *Good Housekeeping* continued to introduce artists and paper doll characters. Grayce Drayton introduced Dolly Dingle in *Pictorial Review* in March 1913, and the character was continued from 1916 to 1933. Kewpies were created by Rose O'Neill in *Woman's Home Companion* in 1912. In a fashion magazine from Butterick Publishing and Pattern Company, *The Delineator*, Carolyn Chester introduced three-dimensional, wraparound dolls in 1912 and 1913.

For most women over age forty, a favorite is Betsy McCall, who debuted in *McCall's Magazine*. Kay Morrissey created her in 1951. The doll continued with an unknown artist and then later Ginnie Hoffman. She was created to wear the fashions that could be made from McCall's patterns. Although Betsy is best remembered, other dolls were published in *McCall's* from 1904 onward.

Model Katy Keene first appeared in the *Archie Comics Suzie* from 1945 to 1954. Bill Woggon created this beloved comic book paper doll. Katy went on to appear in her own comics, *Katy Keene Charm*, *KK Annual*, *KK Glamour*, and *KK Fashions*. This was one of the many and varied comic book paper dolls that came on the market between the 1930s and 1950s. There was a revival of Katy in reprints from 1983 to 1990.

Of course, there is Barbie. It is difficult to know whether to consider Barbie a toy, entertainment, or fashion. Barbie and her friends appeared in books published by Whitman beginning in 1962 and are still published today, by Golden. Barbie has changed with the times, but her outfits mirror fashions of the contemporary adult world.

Instruction and Child's Play

In 1810 S & J Fuller of London printed the moral tale *The History of Little Fanny*. This was a fifteen-page book with seven figures and five hats. Fanny's head was separate and could be fitted onto each of the figures to match the outfits described in the tale. In 1812 American J. Belcher of Boston printed *The History and Adventures of Little Henry*, beginning a tradition of printing paper dolls, either hand-painted or black and white for children to color.

Magazines followed. Paper dolls could be found in *Golden Magazine, Jack and Jill* (1938–1974), and *Children's Playmate* (1929–1961). *Golden Magazine* featured paper doll artists like Hilda Miloche and L. M. Edens. Not only human figures, but also animals and stuffed toys in costumes, appeared. Teachers found paper dolls useful in instruction. Certain issues of such magazines as *The Grade Teacher* (1929–1951); *Junior Instructor* and *Junior Home Magazine* (1919–1931); *Normal Instructor, Primary Plans* and *The Instructor* (1913–1936); and *Primary Education* and *Popular Educator* (1924, 1928–1929) contained paper dolls that could be used in instruction.

For play and education, the modern American Girls paper dolls can be found in the bimonthly *American Girls Magazine*. The dolls began a phenomenon that captured young girls' and their mothers' attention.

Entertainment and Child's Play

The entertainment industry was quick to understand the value of paper dolls, and celebrity paper dolls made their debut. P. T. Barnum Circus characters were featured in the 1830s. Founded in 1828, McLoughlin Brothers was the largest manufacturer of paper dolls in the United States, with early favorites Dottie Dimple and Lottie Love. The company was sold to Milton Bradley in 1920. Other companies began making paper dolls during this period, including Dennison Manufacturing and Frederick A. Stokes and Company.

In 1866 Raphael Tuck was founded, "by appointment to her Majesty Queen Elizabeth II, Fine Art Publishers, London," and published its first paper doll, which was a baby with a nursing bottle. Fine Arts' major style was a set of paper dolls with many costumes and interchangeable heads. Tuck created many series, including *Prince Charming, Fairy Tale*, and many more.

In the early 1900s Selchow and Righter published a large envelope set called "Teddy Bear," which has been reproduced by B. Shackman/Merrimack and Co. The renowned artist Queen Holden began with Whitman Publishing, making paper dolls of children, families, and movie stars/characters from 1929 to 1950, such as Snow White and the Dionne Quints. Today, artists such as Tom Tierney continue creating dolls of the stars, historical people, and presidents. A major publisher of reprints and new paper dolls today is Dover Press.

Marketing and Advertising

One of the more successful ways paper dolls were used was in advertising. Because paper dolls were popular with children, mothers bought products that had paper dolls with them and gave the dolls to their children as treats. Children wanted all of the dolls offered in a series. The dolls were die-cuts or cards that could be cut out. Some were already in color, while others could be colored by the child. Thousands were printed and distributed with various products. Lion Coffee issued several well-known paper doll series. The Palmer Brownies Series and Mother Goose Nursery Rhyme Series were among the more popular make-believe items. Many other companies produced dolls, including Clarks thread, Diamond Dye, Singer sewing machines, Shaker salt, Pillsbury flour, Swift's meats, Baker's chocolate, McLaughlin coffee, Hood's Sarsaparilla, and None Such Mince Meat. The trend continued throughout the 1950s, with companies often publishing paper dolls as part of their magazine ads.

Making and Using Paper Dolls in Instruction

Manufactured paper dolls come in a variety of forms. In addition to individual boxed sets, printed booklets contain dolls that children or their parents can cut out. They may be made of thick cardboard, wood, or various thicknesses of paper. Some are die cut. In today's digital age, paper dolls found on the Internet can be copied onto any available medium. Digital photography makes it possible for children to make dolls with their own faces. Such freedom can allow for exploring different textures. The outfits can be made of bond paper, semigloss paper, tissue, fabric, and even other multimedia forms. For example, magnet paper, available in office supply stores, can be used. Dolls and clothes can be printed and pasted on these sheets. When the dolls are cut out, they may be dressed and attached to a cookie sheet or metal lunch box. Children can take the cookie sheet or lunch box and clothes with them in the car.

Making paper dolls is now considered a simple instructional technique. It requires few materials and is inexpensive. Paper, pencils, scissors, paints, crayons, and markers and a little bit of imagination are all students need. If paper dolls will be part of an instructional project, it would be wise to collect all the necessary items and set them up in a work area. Such a station would include

Paper supplies—heavy cardboard (old manila envelopes for backing, file folders), bond paper, tracing paper (tissue)

Pencils and erasers

Scissors appropriate to student level

Crayons

Colored markers

Colored pencils

Watercolor paints

Fabric scraps

Wallpaper scraps

Construction paper scraps

Mixed media items (feathers, braid, etc.)

Glue

Tape

Most people today see paper dolls as toys, especially for young girls. In this case, dolls are play. Setting collectors aside, adults as educators use paper dolls for instruction, hoping to capitalize on the element of play as a way to instruct. Educators often use paper dolls to make a point, make connections, and reinforce ideas. This book includes paper dolls that are nonhuman or imaginary figures. Such dolls may be used easily with both girls and boys. Each chapter includes information about the figures, a sample lesson for using the paper dolls, and paper doll figures and clothing, which may be reproduced and used in instruction. The lessons are examples only. The outfits accompanying each doll may be put directly on the dolls, or be used as models or ideas when students expand and create on their own, depending on what other lessons might be done.

Bibliography and References

Ackley, Edith Flack. *Paper Dolls: Their History and How to Make Them.* Philadelphia: J. B. Lippincott, 1939. 107p.

Combatalade, Barbara. "When Mother Goose Sold Coffee." *Doll Reader* (May 2004): 28–29.

Drawe, Judith Anderson. *Lithographic Paper Toys, Books, and Games: 1880–1915.* Atglen, Pa.: Schiffer Publishing Company, 2000. 192p.

Fawcett, Clara Hallard. *Paper Dolls: A Costume Guide.* New York: H. L. Lindquist Publications, 1951. 225p.

Ferguson, Barbara Chaney. *The Paper Doll: A Collector's Guide with Prices.* Des Moines, Iowa: Wallace-Homestead, 1982. 151p.

Garrett, Debbie Behan. *The Definitive Guide to Collecting Black Dolls.* Grantsville, Md.: Hobby House Press, 2003. 176p.

Gilbert, Anne. "Before Barbie, Kids Dressed Up Dolls." *Cincinnati Enquirer*, May 10, 2003.

Howard, Marian B. *Those Fascinating Paper Dolls: An Illustrated Handbook for Collectors.* New York: Dover, 1981. 307p.

Huff, Vivian. *Let's Make Paper Dolls.* New York: Harper & Row, 1978. 28p.

Johnson, Judy. *History of Paper Dolls.* http://www.opdag.com/History.html (accessed June 30, 2007).

Johnson, Steve. "Paper Dolls." *American Printer* 124, no. 7 (July 2007): 49.

Kinsey, Angie. "Kids Can Learn from the Simple Toys, Too." *Paducah Sun*, July 15, 2007.

La Du, Karen Herbert. "Beyond Betsy McCall." *School Arts: The Art Education Magazine for Teachers* 107, no. 5 (January 2008): 49.

Mieszala, Lorraine. *Collector's Guide to Barbie Doll Paper Dolls: Identification and Values.* Paducah, Ky.: Collector Books, 1997. 143p.

Musser, Cynthia Erfurt. *Precious Paper Dolls.* Cumberland, Md.: Hobby House Press, 1985. 238p.

Nichols, Carol. *Paper Dolls of the 1960S, 1970S, and 1980s: Identification & Value Guide.* Paducah, Ky.: Collector Books, 2004. 319p.

Rainey, Rhonda. *Creative Paper Dollmaking.* New York: Sterling, 2003. 128p.

Rogers, Dorothy. *French Provincial Costumes: Paper Dolls.* London: Hachette, 1944. 32p.

Ryan, Edward. *Paper Soldiers: The Illustrated History of Printed Paper Armies of the 18th, 19th & 20th Centuries.* London: Golden Age Editions, 1995. 528p.

Taliadoros, Jenny. *Paper Doll Artists Gallery: 22 Original Paper Dolls by 22 Artists.* Kingfield, Me.: Paper Studio Press, 2005. 48p.

Wallach, Anne Tolstoi. *Paper Dolls: How to Find, Recognize, Buy, Collect, and Sell the Cutouts of Two Centuries.* New York: Van Nostrand Reinhold, 1982. 164p.

Yamanashi, Taeko. *Paper Dolls of Old Japan.* Rutland, Vt.: Charles E. Tuttle, 1961. 49p.

Young, Mary. *A Collector's Guide to Paper Dolls*. Paducah, Ky.: Collector Books, 1984. 205p.

Young, Mary. *Tomart's Price Guide to Lowe and Whitman Paper Dolls*. Dayton, Ohio: Tomart Publications, 1992. 168p.

Young, Mary. *Tomart's Price Guide to Saalfield and Merrill Paper Dolls*. Dayton, Ohio: Tomart Publications, 2000. 152p.

Videos and the Internet

One source for learning more about making paper dolls isn YouTube. These video presentations were accessed March 23, 2009.

Blonde Hair for Your Paper Doll: Arts & Crafts for Kids—http://www.youtube.com/watch?v=vUFYennQuVQ

How to Make Art Journal Pages—Playing Printable Paper Dolls—http://www.findinternettv.com/Video,item,3813529463.aspx

How to Make Paper Dolls: Free Online Arts & Crafts for Kids : How to Make a Face for Your Paper Doll: Arts & Crafts for Kids—http://www.youtube.com/watch?v=nGJ58MvLrgM&NR=1

How to Make Paper Dolls: Free Online Arts & Crafts for Kids : How to Make Purses for Paper Dolls : Arts & Crafts for Kids—http://www.youtube.com/watch?v=kMfWgnCQbxU&feature=related

Paper Dolls/Make Paper Dolls—http://www.youtube.com/watch?v=kQnQecBSmXY&feature=related

Associations and Groups

Original Paper Doll Artists Guild (OPDAG)
PO Box 14
Kingfield, ME 04947
Phone:(207) 265-2500
Fax: (207) 265-2500
E-mail: info@opdag.com
URL: http://www.opdag.com

Chapter 2

Cat Tales

Since cats first agreed to live with people, authors and illustrators have recorded their many adventures and characteristics. There were times when cats were the victims of superstition and ignorance, so not all the stories celebrated their unique approach to life. Too bad! Cat lovers would probably be the first to tell you that cats have distinct personalities.

Historians believe that cats were probably first domesticated in ancient Egypt. In the rich valleys of the Nile, grain was plentiful and often stored in warehouses. As you might expect, mice and rats were attracted to this banquet, and feral or wild cats were attracted to the banquet of tasty rodents. As the cats became accustomed to people going to and from the warehouses, they stayed closer and closer to villages and towns. Finally, they became pets who enjoyed human bounty but maintained their ability to hunt and survive on their own if they so desired. Their aloof personality, their purrs and meows, and their wondrous control of the pest population earned them an important place in daily and religious life in Egypt. Cats are recorded on tomb frescoes, papyri, and pottery. The goddess Bastet was represented as a cat, and household cats were mummified in order to accompany their masters on the voyage to the afterlife.

Nearly 2,000 years later, domesticated cats made a strange journey to Greece. Overrun with varmints such as weasels and snakes, the Greeks sent expeditions to Egypt to steal cats. This was risky business indeed! Anyone caught taking a household cat faced terrible punishment, because by that time cats were considered sacred throughout most of Egypt.

Aesop, a slave of the Greeks, may have told the first stories about cats. Certainly he found them resourceful and clever, but did Aesop like cats? Read a selection of his feline fables at *Cat Stuff: Aesop's Fables of Cats* (http://www.xmission.com/~emailbox/fables; accessed March 23, 2009).

Aesop rarely recorded his fables, but they were so timeless and entertaining that they traveled worldwide by word of mouth. In the 1600s they were finally adapted and written down by a French poet, La Fontaine. However, the ability to read was not common, and many stories were presented on murals or in theatricals. Very popular among these performances were the stories of Puss in Boots (a devious trickster) and Dick Whittington's cat. (Read them for yourself at *Cat Stuff: Dick Whittington's Cat*, http://www.xmission.com/~emailbox/whittington.htm; accessed March 23, 2009.) These cats brought good fortune to their masters!

By the late nineteenth century, cats were appearing in a number of books. Some remained very independent, like Rudyard Kipling's *The Cat That Walked by Himself*. Others seemed to live almost human lives, with homes and families and adventures of all kinds. Kathleen Hale's marmalade cat, Edward Lear's pussycat, and Beatrix Potter's kittens are some you will want to meet.

Hale, Kathleen. *Orlando the Marmalade Cat: A Camping Holiday*. New York: Penguin UK, 2003. 32p. ISBN 9780723236481.

> Originally published between 1983 and 1972. Other titles are *Orlando the Marmalade Cat: A Trip Abroad; Orlando's Evening Out, Orlando's Home Life; Orlando the Marmalade Cat Buys a Farm; Orlando the Marmalade Cat: His Silver Wedding; Orlando's Invisible Pajamas; Orlando the Marmalade Cat Keeps a Dog, Orlando the Judge; Orlando: A Seaside Holiday; Orlando's Zoo; Orlando the Marmalade Cat: The Frisky Housewife; Orlando's Magic Carpet; Orlando the Marmalade Cat Buys a Cottage; Orlando and the Three Graces; Orlando the Marmalade Cat Goes to the Moon;* and *Orlando the Marmalade Cat and the Water Cats*.

Kipling, Rudyard. *The Cat That Walked by Himself*. Illustrated by Teresa O'Brien. New York: Childs Play, 1990. 32p. ISBN 10: 0859533093; ISBN 13: 9780859533096.

Lear, Edward. *The Owl and the Pussycat*. Illustrated by Jan Brett. New York: Putnam, 1991. 32p. ISBN 10: 0399219250; ISBN 13: 978-0399219252.

Potter, Beatrix. *The Tale of Tom Kitten*. New York: Frederick Warne, 2002. 64 p. ISBN 10: 0723247773; ISBN 13: 978-0723247777.

> In more recent times, stories and books about cats abound. In the United States alone, more than seventy-six million cats are household pets (from *Pet Cat Population* at http://www.mapsofworld.com/world-top-ten/countries-with-most-pet-cat-population.html; accessed March 23, 2009), and people love to read about them. Authors address cats in several thematic ways. It is often fun to look at cat books in this way to see similarities and differences.

Cats Who Use Their Nine Lives

Cats are said to have nine lives. This idea may date back to the combination of nine, an important number in Egyptian religion, and the deity of cats. However it began, the idea gained great popularity in the 1800s and is often perpetuated in literature. Check out these nine-lived characters.

Bacon, Peggy. *The Ghost of Opalina; or Nine Lives*. Boston: Little, Brown, 1967. 120p. ISBN 10: 0316075027; ISBN-13: 978-0316075022.

> An opal-eyed ghost cat shares the stories of her other eight lives in the old house, from early 1700 to the current day, to Phillip, Ellen, and Jeb Finley, the new residents. Grades 4–7.

Bailey, Carolyn Sherwin. *Finnegan II, His Nine Lives*. Illustrated by Kate Seredy. New York: Viking Press, 1953. 95p. ISBN 7277198654.

> Finnigan objects to only having nine lives, as he struggles to keep them from slipping away. Grades 2–4.

Balian, Lorna. *Amelia's Nine Lives*. Nashville, Tenn.: Abingdon Press/Humbug Books, 1986. 32p. ISBN 0687012503.

> Nora weeps because her beloved cat Amelia is lost. Friends and relatives bring cats into the house, but none is like Amelia. Nora is in for a surprise. Grades K–3.

Brett, Jan. *Comet's Nine Lives*. New York: Putnam, 1996. 32p. ISBN 10: 0399229310; ISBN 13: 978-0399229312.

> The loss of his first life inspires Comet to find a safe home on Nantucket. Pay close attention to the side panels!
>
> A sound cassette of the story is available from Scholastic Inc. (1997). Grades K–3.

Briggs, Katharine Mary. *Nine Lives: The Folklore of Cats*. Illustrated by John Ward. New York: Pantheon Books, 1980. 222p. ISBN 10: 0880292873; ISBN 13: 978-0880292870.

> Cats can be mysterious, affectionate, and more, in these tales from around the world. Grades 3–8.

Clymer, Susan. *The Nine Lives of AdventureCat*. New York: Scholastic Inc., 1994. 57p. ISBN 10: 059047149X; ISBN 13: 978-0590471497.

> When AdventureCat is sent out on his own by MomCat, he shows his bravery after running up a tree when chased. Grades 2–4.

DeSpain, Pleasant. *Tales of Cats*. Illustrated by Don Bell. Little Rock, Ark.: August House, 2003. 75p. (Books of Nine Lives Series; Volume 9). ISBN 10: 0874837138; ISBN-13: 978-0874837131.

> Included in this volume are the stories "The King of Cats," "A Kind Woman," "The Magnificent Cat," "Hunter Cat," "Three Children of Fortune," Why Cats Live with Women" "The House of Cats" "The Boy who Drew Cats," and "The Holy Cat." Grades 4–8.

Harjo, Joy. *The Good Luck Cat*. Illustrated by Paul Lee. Harcourt Brace, 2000. 32p. ISBN 10: 0152321977; ISBN-13: 978-0152321970.

> Woogie has used eight of his nine lives but has a magical quality: when her owner pets her, good things happen. Grades K–2.

Hess, Lilo. *A Cat's Nine Lives*. New York: Scribner, 1984. 47p. ISBN 10: 0684180731; ISBN 13: 978-0684180731.

> Misty, a purebred Persian cat, lives through many owners, from her birth in a cattery, to a cat show life, to an animal shelter and homelessness, until she finds an owner who loves her. Grades K–2.

King-Smith, Dick. *The Nine Lives of Aristotle*. Illustrated by Bob Graham. Cambridge, Mass.: Candlewick Press, 2003. 75p. ISBN 10: 0763622605; ISBN-13: 978-0763622602.

> A witch, Bella Donna, adopts a little white kitten, Aristotle, who falls through the chimney, nearly drowns, falls from a tree into a stream, is almost killed by a freight train, is chased by a dog, and is almost run over by a delivery truck. Grades 1–4.

Moncomble, Gaerard. *The Nine Lives of the Cat*. Illustrated by Andreei Arinouchkine. New York: Milk & Cookies Press, 2001. 32p. ISBN 10: 159687189X; ISBN 13: 978-1596871892.

> A black cat, Bottom-Pit, is rescued from a well and begins several lives as a cat bandit, witch's companion, and more, until he escapes with only one life left of the nine. Grades K–3.

Priceman, Marjorie. *My Nine Lives by Clio*. New York: Atheneum, 1998. 48p. ISBN 10: 0689811357; ISBN 13: 978-0689811357.

> Clio's journal records life in Egypt, China, Italy, and finally, Wisconsin. Grades 2–4.

Rifkin, L. *The Nine Lives of Romeo Crumb: Life One*. Beverly Hills, Calif.: Stratford Road Press, 2004. 311p. ISBN 10: 0974322105; ISBN 13: 978-0974322100.

> Romeo Crumb is a New York cat who learns the ways of the streets, attends cat school at the factory, and tries to stay clear of Fidel, a tough leader of a gang. Romeo eventually learns the truth about his parents. Grades 4–7. See the sequels for his subsequent lives:

Rifkin, L. *The Nine Lives of Romeo Crumb: Life Two*. Beverly Hills, Calif.: Stratford Road Press, 2005. 277p. ISBN 10: 0974322121; ISBN 13: 978-0974322124.

Rifkin, L. *The Nine Lives of Romeo Crumb: Life Three*. Beverly Hills, Calif.: Stratford Road Press, 2006. 300p. ISBN 10: 0974322121; ISBN-13: 978-0974322124

Cats Who Have Dog Friends

The relationship between cats and dogs has often made for a good story. Young children delight in the story of the Gingham Dog and the Calico Cat. See *CatStuff: The Gingham Dog and the Calico Cat* at http://www.xmission.com/~emailbox/gingham.htm (accessed March 23, 2009). The following titles capitalize on this relationship.

Adoff, Arnold. *Daring Dog and Captain Cat*. Illustrated by Joe Cepeda. Simon & Schuster, 2001. 32p. ISBN 10: 0689825994; ISBN 13: 978-0689825996.

In poetic free verse, Irving Dog and Ermine cat shed their obedient demeanor and chase bad guys. Grades 1–5.

French, Vivian. *Space Dog Meets Space Cat*. Illustrated by Sue Heap. New York: Little Apple, 2000. 64p. (Space Dog Series No. 3). ISBN 10: 0439130859; ISBN 13: 978-0439130851.

Space Dog is off into the universe to see what all the howling is about. Grades K–2.

Fry, Sonali. *Best in Show!* New York: Simon Spotlight, 2003. 24p. (Bob the Builder Series No. 8). ISBN 10: 0689857209; ISBN 13: 978-0689857201.

Scoop is not allowed to enter his cat Pritchard in the dog show. Grades K.

Potter, Beatrix. *The Tale of Ginger and Pickles*. New York: Frederick Warne, 1987. 59p. ISBN 10: 0723247870; ISBN-13: 978-0723247876.

A cat and a terrier run a general store for mice and rabbits. Grades K–2.

Sargent, Dave, and Pat Sargent. *The Cat Who Barked*. Illustrated by Laura Robinson. Prairie Grove, Ark.: Ozark Publishing, 2004. 18p. (Learn to Read Series No. 18). ISBN 10: 1567638317; ISBN-13: 978-1567638318.

Just because a cat barks and scratches, that doesn't make him a dog. Grades K–1.

Soto, Gary. *Chato Goes Cruisin'*. Illustrated by Susan Guevara. New York: Putnam, 2005. 32p. ISBN 10: 039923974X; ISBN-13: 978-0399239748.

When Chato and Novio win a cruise, it never occurs to them that they will be among dogs. They find themselves being of help to the partying sick mutts. Grades K–4.

Soto, Gary. *Chato's Kitchen*. Illustrated by Susan Guevara. New York: Putnam, 1995. 32p. ISBN 10: 0399226583; ISBN 13: 978-0399226588.

Chato can't believe his good luck when a mouse family moves into his Los Angeles neighborhood. He thinks of them as dinner. Imagine his surprise when he finds the mice have a dog friend! (A 24-minute videotape and audiotape are available from Weston Woods. Mac and Windows CDs are available from Scholastic Inc.). Grades K–4.

Cats Who Live in France

Do the French especially like cats? Certainly, authors seem to like Paris and the French countryside as settings for books about cats.

Arnold, Marsha Diane. *Metro Cat*. Illustrated by Jack E. Davis. New York: Golden Books, 2001. 40p. ISBN 10: 0307102130; ISBN 13: 978-0307102133.
 The fluffy-tailed cover girl for *Fancy Cat* magazine discovers a wonderful world and a new friend in the subways of Paris. Grades K–2.

Baker, Leslie A. *Paris Cat*. Boston: Little, Brown, 1999. 32p. ISBN 10: 0316073091; ISBN 13: 978-0316073097.
 Annie's cat chases a Parisian mouse around the city before she finds her way home. Grades K–2.

Butler, Jill. *Paintbrush in Paris: The Artistic Adventures of an American Cat in Paris*. New York: Workman Publishing, 1992. 96p. ISBN 10: 1563055244; ISBN 13: 978-1563055249.
 Paintbrush the Cat leaves his home in the Midwest to follow his dream of painting in Paris. Grades 4–6.

Edwards, Julie Andrews. *Little Bo in France*. Illustrated by Henry Cole. New York: Hyperion Books, 2001. 96p. ISBN 10: 0786806583; ISBN 13: 978-0786806584.
 Bo and her owner find adventure as they travel through France. But will they find the good fortune they seek? (Also read *Little Bo: The Story of Bonnie Boadicea*, a tale of Bo's seafaring days!). Grades 3–6.

McLaren, Chesley. *Zat Cat! A Haute Couture Tail*. New York: Scholastic Trade, 2002. 40p. ISBN-10: 0439273161; ISBN 13: 978-0439273169.
 A stray cat playfully rips and pounces through a famous fashion designer's show. The result will delight you! Grades K–2.

Cats Who Love Music

If you've ever heard a cat howling, you probably didn't think it was very musical! Cats and music are a bit more compatible in these titles.

Austin, Patricia. *The Cat Who Loved Mozart*. Illustrated by Henri Sorenson. New York: Holiday House, 2001. 32p. ISBN 10: 082341535X; ISBN-13: 978-0823415359.
 Amadeus remains aloof until he hears his new master playing Mozart! Grades K–2.

Crimi, Carolyn. *Tess's Tip-tapping Toes*. New York: Scholastic Inc., 2002. 32p. ISBN 10: 0439317681; ISBN 13: 978-0439317689.
 A rollicking time is had by a mouse who likes to dance and a cat who likes to sing. Grades K–1.

Weaver, Tess. *Opera Cat*. Illustrated by Andrea Wesson. New York: Clarion Books, 2002. 32p. ISBN 10: 0618096353; ISBN-13: 978-0618096350.
 Alma, the singing cat, must save the day when her owner, Madame SoSo, a star of the Milan opera, develops laryngitis. Grades K–3.

Wood, David, and Gaston Leroux. *The Phantom Cat of the Opera*. Illustrated by Peters Day. New York: Watson-Guptill. 2001. 40p. ISBN 10: 0823040186; ISBN-13: 978-0823040186.

> The mystery and magic of the Byzantine Paris Opera House is re-created with a cast of feline characters and a story told in four acts. Grades K–3.

Cats Who Flirt with Magic

Cats have a long affiliation with magic. This flirtation is often accompanied by curiosity and cleverness. In the 1400s in parts of Europe, it was believed that witches took the form of their animal helpers when they went about Satan's business, and people were actually put to death for owning a cat! In other times and places, cats have been considered good luck. Today in Japan, nearly every business displays Manki-Neko (Beckoning Cat) figures to attract success. These titles associate magic and cats to create interesting reading.

Alexander, Lloyd. *Time Cat: The Remarkable Journeys of Jason and Gareth*. New York: Henry Holt, 2003. 224p. ISBN 10: 0805072705; ISBN 13: 978-0805072709.

> Gareth, a talking, time-traveling cat, leads his master, Jason, through nine historical adventures. Grades 5–7.

Carter, Angela. *Sea-Cat and Dragon King*. Illustrated by Eva Tatcheva. New York: Bloomsbury Children's Books, 2002. 93p. ISBN 10: 074754882X; ISBN 13: 978-0747548829.

> His mother knits Sea-Cat bejeweled suits to keep him warm in their home below the sea, but his splendid attire attracts the jealousy of the not-too-handsome Dragon King. Grades 1–4.

The Cat Who Wished to Be a Man. New York: Dutton, 1973. 107p. ISBN 10: 0525275452; ISBN-13: 978-0525275459.

> In order to free the town of Brightford from a cruel leader, Lionel (a talking cat) begs his master, a wizard, to change him into a man. The cast of nine characters will amaze and amuse you! Grades 5–7.

Cregar, Elyse. *Feline Online: What Happens When a Smart Cat Surfs the Internet?* Salem, Mass.: Tamerac, 2001. 150p. ISBN 10: 0962129216; ISBN 13: 978-0962129216.

> Tarzan, Amanda's energetic house cat, is given the ability to read by a cat from ancient Egypt that visits him in his dreams. Mysterious events follow! Grades 5–7.

Deary, Terry. *The Magic and the Mummy*. Illustrated by Helen Flook. Minneapolis, Minn.: Picture Window Books, 2006. 64p. (Read It! Chapter Books Series). ISBN 10: 1404812717; ISBN 13: 978-1404812710.

> It is a great responsibility that Neria has been given—to mummify Pharaoh's cat. There is just one problem—the cat is still alive. Grades 2–4.

Jarvis, Robin. *The Alchemist's Cat*. San Francisco, Calif.: SeaStar Books, 2004. 304p. (The Deptford Histories Series; No. 1). ISBN 10: 1587172577.

> Young Will Godwin has been orphaned and arrives in London in 1664, where he ends up serving wicked alchemist Elias Theophratus Spittle. One night Will is pursued and hides in an overgrown graveyard, where he finds a mother cat and three kittens. Grades 5–8.

Johnson, Jane. *The Secret Country*. Illustrations by Adam Stower. New York: Simon & Schuster Books for Young Readers, 2005. 323p. (Eidolon Chronicles, No. 1). ISBN 10: 1416907122; ISBN-13: 978-1416907121.

    A talking cat, Iggy, tells twelve-year-old Ben Arnold that he and his sisters are half-elfin royalty from a parallel world, Eidolon, and must stop his evil uncle from smuggling magical creatures from that other universe.

Lattimore, Deborah Nourse. *The Winged Cat: A Tale of Ancient Egypt*. New York: HarperCollins, 1992. 45p. ISBN 10: 0060236353; ISBN 13: 978-0060236359.

    A young Egyptian servant girl is guided by the spirit of her sacred cat to discover the cat's killer. Grades 2–4.

Le Guin, Ursula K. *Catwings*. Illustrated by Steven D. Schindler. Scholastic Inc., 1990. 40p. ISBN 10: 0531057593; ISBN-13: 978-0531057599.

    "Fly to the countryside," Mrs. Jane Tabby tells her four winged kittens. But which will be more dangerous, country living or city streets? (Don't miss the other titles: *Catwings Return*; *Wonderful Alexander and the Catwings*; and *Jane on Her Own: A Catwings Tale*.). Grades 3–6.

Maccarone, Grace. *Magic Matt and the Cat*. Illustrated by Norman Bridwell. New York: Scholastic, 2003. (Scholastic Reader Series. Level 1). ISBN-10: 0613635558; ISBN-13: 978-0613635554.

    By using the "at" sound, Magic Matt tries to conjure up a cat, but finds himself with a bat, a dog, and other animals. Grades K–1.

Perrault, Charles. *Puss in Boots*. Illustrated by Fred Marcellino. New York: Farrar, Straus & Giroux, 1998. 32p. ISBN 10: 0374460345; ISBN 13: 978-0374460341.

    In this classic folktale, the youngest son is left with nothing but a cat, and a clever one at that. (This is a Caldecott Honor book. Many other versions of "Puss in Boots" are available.) Grades K–4.

Sampson, Fay. *Shape-shifter: The Naming of Pangur Ban*. Oxford: Lion Children's Books, 2002. 160p. ISBN-10: 074594762X (pb.); ISBN-13: 978-0745947624 (pb.).

    In this medieval tale, a white shape-shifting kitten travels with a monk named Niall to find his Welsh origin and has many harrowing adventures. Grades 6–9.

Seuss, Dr. *The Cat in the Hat*. New York: Random House, 1957. 61p. ISBN 10: 0717260593; ISBN 13: 978-0394800011.

    Dick and Sally are stuck indoors because of the rain, and their mother is out. Cat has just the remedy and transforms the day! (Video and audio editions are available as well as dolls and other media.) Grades K–2.

The Town Cats and Other Tales. Illustrated by Laszlo Kubinyi. New York: Dutton, 1977. 126p. ISBN 10: 0525414304; ISBN-13: 978-0525414308.

    A collection of stories about cats who save the day and tickle your funny bone! Grades 5–8.

Wahl, Jan. *Dracula's Cat/Frankenstein's Dog/Two Books in One*. Illustrated by Kay Chorao. New York: Simon & Schuster, 1990. 64p. ISBN 10: 0671708201; ISBN-13: 978-0671708207.

    Share a pet's eye view of two very unusual masters. Grades K–3.

Willard, Nancy. *The Tortilla Cat*. Illustrated by Jeanette Winter. San Diego: Harcourt Brace, 1998. 48p. ISBN 10: 0152895876; ISBN 13: 978-0152895877.

> When a magical cat cures each of his five children from a terrible fever, Dr. Romero thinks he must be dreaming. But what will happen when the fever strikes the doctor himself? Grades 1–3.

Williams, Ursula Moray. *Gobbolino the Witch's Cat*. Illustrated by Paul Howard. New York: Larousse Kingfisher Chambers, 2001. 220p. ISBN 10: 0753406306; ISBN-13: 978-0753406304.

> What adventures Gobbolino must survive in his quest to become an ordinary kitchen cat! Grades 4–7.

Cats Who Are Heroes

Of course, an animal as clever and self-reliant as a cat has often been called upon to help we poor humans. Meet these cat heroes.

Averill, Esther Holden. *The Fire Cat*. New York: Harper & Row, 1960. 63p. ISBN 10: 0060201967.

> A yellow-furred cat with black spots becomes famous for his firefighting exploits. Grades K–2.

Barber, Antonia. *The Mousehole Cat*. Illustrated by Nicola Bayley. Macmillan, 1990. 37p. ISBN-10: 0027083314; ISBN 13: 978-0027083316.

> The old fisherman's cat must soothe the great Storm-Cat that threatens the village of Mousehole. (Don't miss the videotape distributed by Goodtimes Home video. 25 min.). Grades K–3.

Bauer, Steven. *A Cat of a Different Color*. Illustrated by Tim Raglin. New York: Delacorte Press, 2000. 197p. ISBN 10: 0385327102; ISBN-13: 978-0385327107.

> The nasty mayor of Felicity-by-the-Lake makes the villagers' lives miserable. How can a strange cat and an orphan girl possibly help? Grades 3–6.

Goodhart, Pippa. *Fire Cat*. Illustrated by Philip Hurst. New York: Crabtree Publishing, 2002. 48p. (Go Bananas Series). ISBN 10: 0778726754; ISBN 13: 978-0778726753.

> Samuel Pepys's diary reveals the story of the Great Fire of London. Grades K–1.

Holm & Hamel. *The Postman Always Brings Mice: a Novel*. Illustrated by Brad Weinman. New York: HarperCollins, 2004. 129p. (Stink Files; Dossier 001).

> London cat James Edward Bristlefur's master is poisoned, and he is shipped off to the United States, where he helps his new family with a bully. Grades 2–5.

Price, Robin. *I am Spartapuss*. Mogzilla, 2004. 193p. (Spartapuss Tale Series). ISBN 10: 0954657624; ISBN 13: 978-0954657628.

> The only way that Spartapuss can free himself from allegations that he is responsible for a nasty poem about Catligula's mother that was written on a wall is to fight as a gladiator in the arena. Grades 3–6.

Rumford, James. *Calabash Cat: And His Amazing Journey*. Boston: Houghton Mifflin, 2003. 32p. ISBN 10: 0618224238; ISBN 13: 978-0618224234.

> A Calabash Cat leaves Africa to search for where the world ends. Grades 1–4.

Woelfle, Gretchen. *Katje, the Windmill Cat.* Illustrated by Nicola Bayley. Cambridge, Mass: Candlewick Press, 2001. 32p. ISBN-10: 0763613479; ISBN 13: 978-0763613471.

> When the dike breaks, it is up to Katje to save the miller's beloved baby daughter. (Inspired by a true story.)

Cats Who Are Mysterious

These mysteries are as intriguing as a cat! Problem solving and curiosity seem to blend, whether it is the cat itself or the plot that includes a cat.

Cushman, Doug. *Space Cat.* New York: HarperCollins Publishers, 2004. 32p. ISBN 10: 0060089679; ISBN 13: 978-0060089672.

> A space rock crashes into their rocket as Space Cat and Earl the Robot are headed home to Earth. They must figure out a way to fix the tank. Grades 1–3.

Freeman, Martha. *Who Is Stealing the Twelve Days of Christmas?* New York: Scholastic, 2003. 200p. ISBN 10: 0823417883; ISBN 13: 978-0823417889.

> Alex must figure out who is stealing the neighborhood yard decorations one at a time. Grades 3–6.

Gregory, Valiska. *The Mystery of the Grindlecat.* Illustrated by Claire Ewart. Guild Press/Emmis Publishing, 2003. 32p. ISBN-10: 1578601428; ISBN 13: 978-1578601424.

> What was the mystery behind the scraggly, snaggle-toothed grindlecat that must be solved by three children?

Hanson, Dave. *What Now, Puss?* Illustrated by Jonathan Langley. North Mankato, Minn.: Sea-to-Sea, 2006. 24p. (Reading Corner Series). ISBN 10: 1597710016; ISBN 13: 978-1597710015.

> A young boy does his best to understand what his cat wants.

Keene, Carolyn. *The Kitten Caper.* Illustrated by Jan Naimo Jones. New York: Aladdin Paperbacks, 2005. 72 p. (Nancy Drew Notebooks, No. 69). ISBN 10: 1417743336; ISBN 13: 978-1417743339.

> When two stray kittens are taken in by neighbor, Terry Smith, Nancy, and her friends must solve the mystery. Grades 2–5.

Kehret, Peg. *Cat Burglar on the Prowl.* New York: Pocket Books, 1995. 113p. ISBN10: 0671891871; ISBN 13: 978-0671891879.

> The theft of Grandma's silver tea set is followed by the disappearance of Webster, Kayo's beloved cat. Rosie and Kayo set out to investigate, only to find themselves in great danger. (Listen to this one on audiotape from Recorded Books. 150 min.) Grades 4–6.

Kehret, Peg. *Don't Go Near Mrs. Tallie.* New York: Pocket Books, 1995. 131p. ISBN 13: 9780141312378.

> Rosie and Kayo volunteer to find Mrs. Tallie's cat a new home, but they get a phone call warning them to leave the elderly, and suddenly very ill, woman alone. Could someone be trying to kill their neighbor? (Check out the audiotape by Recorded Books. 165 min.) Grades 5–8.

Kehret, Peg. *The Stranger Next Door.* New York: Dutton, 2002. 160p. ISBN 10: 0525468293; ISBN 13: 978-0525468295.

> A suspenseful story about two twelve-year-old boys who must learn to trust each other after terrible events happen in their neighborhood. The heroism of clever Pete, Alex's cat, leads the way. Grades 4–6.

Murphy, Elspeth Campbell. *The Mystery of the Coon Cat*. Illustrated by Joe Nordstrom. Minneapolis, Minn.: Bethany House, 1999. 61p. (Three Cousins Detective Club Series; No. 25). ISBN 10: 0613877454; ISBN 13: 978-0613877459.

> While taking a neighbor's Maine Coon cat to the blessing of the animals, Titus discovers a note in his pocket. Who could have put it there? Grades 4–6.

Naylor, Phyllis Reynolds. *Carlotta's Kittens*. Illustrated by Alan Daniel. New York: Atheneum, 2000. 144p. ISBN 10: 0689832699; ISBN-13: 978-0689832697.

> The members of the Club of Mysteries have to keep Carlotta and her babies safe from Bertram the Bad and Steak Knife until the kittens can be placed in a permanent home. Enjoy Elvis's lullabies! Grades 3–6.

Naylor, Phyllis Reynolds. *The Grand Escape*. Illustrated by Alan Daniel. New York: Yearling, 1994. 160p. ISBN 10: 1417740515; ISBN-13: 978-1417740512.

> Marco and Polo, two spoiled housecats, must complete three dangerous missions to win membership in the cat gang known as the Club of Mysteries. Grades 2–5.

Naylor, Phyllis Reynolds. *The Healing of Texas Jake*. Illustrated by Alan Daniel. New York: Aladdin Paperbacks, 1998. 128p. ISBN 10: 0689811241; ISBN 13: 978-0689811241.

> Marco and Polo encounter a rival gang led by Steak Knife as they seek the medicinal herb that will help the chief of the Club of Mysteries recuperate from injuries sustained in a fight with a villainous dog. And Elvis and Boots are having adventures of their own, too! Grades 3–6.

Naylor, Phyllis Reynolds. *Polo's Mother*. Illustrated by Alan Daniel. New York: Aladdin Paperbacks, 2005. 162p. ISBN 10: 0689874049; ISBN 13: 978-0689874048.

> In the final book, Polo is reunited with his mother and is sent out to solve mysteries by Jake. Grades 3–6.

Stewart, Linda. *The Big Catnap: A Sam the Cat Mystery*. New York: Cheshire House, 2000. 136p. ISBN 10: 0967507359; ISBN 13: 978-0967507354.

> A romp with this feline detective. Grades 3–6.

Stewart, Linda. *Sam the Cat: Detective*. New York: Cheshire House, 2000. 128p. ISBN 10: 0967507340; ISBN 13: 978-0967507347.

> Sam is a hard-boiled, tough-guy detective whose adventures will make you laugh! A cat caper you can share! Grades 3–6.

Stine, R. L. *Cry of the Cat*. New York: Apple Paperback/Scholastic, 1998. 119p. (Goosebumps Series 2000, No. 1). ISBN 10: 0613047826; ISBN-13: 978-0613047821.

> A nightmare begins when Alison accidentally runs over and kills Rip. He seems to come to life. (A forty-four-minute videotape of the story was produced by Protocol Entertainment and Scholastic Productions.) Grades 3–6.

Cats as Playful and Curious

Cat and kitten playfulness motivates and inspires some authors and illustrators. This turns into rollicking times in many titles. *The Cat in the Hat* set the tone, with many other book characters taking up the cause for good times.

Beardsley, Martyn. *Five Naughty Kittens*. Illustrated by Jacqueline East. North Mankato, Minn.: Sea-to-Sea, 2006. 23p. (Reading Corner Series). ISBN 10: 1597710067; ISBN13: 978-1597710060.
      One at a time, the kittens' uproar causes them to disappear after play. Grades K–1.

Capucilli, Alyssa Satin. *Mrs. McTats and Her Houseful of Cats*. Illustrated by Joan Rankin. New York: Aladdin Paperbacks, 2004. 30p. ISBN 10: 0689831854; ISBN 13: 978-0689831850.
      Mrs. McTats loves her cats and fills her rooms with more and more cats, until a puppy named Zoom moves in and the play begins. Grades K–2.

Newman, Leslea. *Cats, Cats, Cats!* Illustrated by Erika Oller. New York: Simon & Schuster Books for Young Readers, 2001. 27p. ISBN 10: 0689830777; ISBN 13: 978-0689830778.
      After Mrs. Brown has fed her sixty cats, she goes off to bed. While she snores, the cats go wild, throwing confetti, dancing, and leaving a mess. Grades K–3.

Soto, Gary. *Chato and the Party Animals*. Illustrated by Susan Guevara. New York: Putnam, 2000. 32p. ISBN 10: 0399231595; ISBN 13: 978-0399231599.
      Novio Boy has never had a birthday party, so Chato decides to throw a "pachanga." (A 12-minute sound disk is available from Live Oak Media, 2005.) Grades K–4.

More and More Cats!

Some authors seem completely involved with cats in many of their books. Here are several other authors whose work features felines. When students enjoy one title or character, they will want more by the same author. This is an opportunity to introduce authors with suggestions for how to access information in library media catalogs.

Mary Calhoun

This Iowa-born author wanted to be an author early in life. One of her characters is Henry. Whether attending a Christmas pageant, competing in a country fair, sailing a sloop, traveling on cross-country skis, or flying in a hot air balloon, Henry is a friendly cat, appealing to early readers.

Blue-ribbon Henry. Illustrated by Erick Ingraham. New York: Morrow Junior Books, 1999. 40p. ISBN 10: 0688146740; ISBN 13: 978-0688146740.

Cross Country Cat. New York: Mulberry, 1986. 40p. ISBN 10: 0688221866; ISBN-13: 978-0688221867. (A sound recording is available from Listening Library.)

Henry the Christmas Cat. Illustrated by Erick Ingraham. New York: HarperCollins, 2004. 32p. ISBN 10: 0688165605; ISBN 13: 978-0688165604.

Henry the Sailor Cat. Illustrated by Erick Ingraham. New York: HarperCollins, 1994. 40p. ISBN 10: 0688165605; ISBN 13: 978-0688165604

Hot Air Henry. Illustrated by Erick Ingraham. New York: Morrow, 1981. 40p. ISBN 10: 0688005012; ISBN 13: 978-0688005016. (A sound recording is available from Listening Library.)

Earlier titles included cats who were associated with witches. The cats have a hand in turning the witches around!

The Witch of Hissing Hill. Illustrated by Janet McCaffery. New York: Morrow, 1964. 32p. ISBN 10: 0688317626; ISBN 13: 978-0688317621.

The Witch Who Lost Her Shadow. Illustrated by Trinka Hakes Noble. New York: Harper & Row, 1979. ISBN 10: 0060209461; ISBN 13: 978-0060209469.

Wobble, the Witch Cat. Illustrated by Roger Duvoisin. New York: Morrow, 1958. 32p. ISBN 10: 0688316212; ISBN 13: 978-0688316211.

Mary Calhoun has shown the more affectionate side of cats in other titles, as only a cat lover could.

Audubon Cat. Illustrated by Susan Bonners. New York: Morrow, 1981. 32p. ISBN 10: 0688222536; ISBN 13: 978-0688222536

Tonio's Cat. Illustrated by Ed Martinez. New York: Morrow Junior Books, 1996. 32p. ISBN 10: 0688133142; ISBN 13: 978-0688133146.

Jack Gantos

Only Sarah could love such a mean, rotten cat! Well, actually, readers have loved him since the first book in a series of more than ten. Ralph has a *Happy Birthday*, *Goes Back to School*, and has a *Rotten Christmas* and a *Halloween Howl*.

Rotten Ralph. Illustrated by Nicole Rubel. New York: Houghton Mifflin, 1976.

Rotten Ralph Helps Out. Illustrated by Nicole Rubel. New York: Farrar Strauss & Giroux, 2001. 48p.
In Ralph's first reader, he builds pyramids of books in the library, fills the living room with sand as he attempts to re-create the Egyptian desert, and, as always, manages to do at least one thing right.

Read more about author Jack Gantos at http://www.jackgantos.com/ (accessed March 23, 2009).

Leigh Hobbs

Born April 18, 1953, Leigh Hobbs hails from Australia. He is best known for Old Tom, a lazy maker of mischief who does not seem to know that he is a cat. He has one bad eye and carries a fish bone with him. He drives Angela Throgmorton to distraction because he is so messy, while she is extremely neat. For all his bad manners, Angela considers him her precious baby. To read more about Hobbs and Old Tom, visit http://www.leighhobbs.com.au/ (accessed March 23, 2009).

Old Tom. New York: Hyperion Paperbacks for Children, 1994. 112p. ISBN 10: 1417677619; ISBN 13: 978-1417677610.

Old Tom Goes to Mars. New York: Hyperion Paperbacks for Children, 1997. 112p. ISBN 10: 0786855142; ISBN-13: 978-0786855148.

Old Tom, Man of Mystery. Atlanta, Ga.: Peachtree, 2005. 32p. ISBN 10: 1561453463; ISBN 13: 978-1561453467.

Old Tom's Holiday. Atlanta, Ga.: Peachtree, 2004. 32p. ISBN 10: 1561453161; ISBN 13: 978-1561453160.

Erin Hunter

The secret is out: Erin Hunter is a pseudonym for four British authors, Kate Cary, Cherith Baldry, Victoria Holmes, and Tui Sutherland. They take turns deciding on the story and writing a book in the *Warrior* series. The original series began in 2003, and titles are added yearly. More titles can be found at http://www.warriorcats.com/ (accessed March 23, 2009).

There are several related series: <u>Warriors: The New Prophecy</u>; <u>Warriors: Manga</u>; <u>Warriors: The Power of Three</u>; and <u>Warriors Field Guide</u>.

The first series includes six books, beginning with Rusty, a young house cat, who is taken into ThunderClan and becomes Firepaw, because his fur is the color of fire. Firepaw becomes a warrior to defend his clan.

Book 1: Into the Wild

Book 2: Fire and Ice

Book 3: Forest of Secrets

Book 4: Rising Storm

Book 5: A Dangerous Path

Book 6: The Darkest Hour

Once older readers become hooked, they will want to read all of the *Warrior* titles published by HarperCollins.

Cynthia Rylant

Cynthia Rylant's Mr. Putter and Tabby books are amusing and always pleasant; the illustrations by Arthur Howard add to the fun. Sound recordings narrated by John McDonough (Prince Frederick, Md.: Recorded Books) can also be useful in motivating and reinforcing reading. These hit the spot for young readers in grades 1–3.

Mr. Putter and Tabby Paint the Porch. Orlando, Fla.: Harcourt, 2001. 44p. ISBN 10: 0152017879; ISBN-13: 978-0152017873.

Tabby is chasing a squirrel across fresh pink paint; Zeke the next-door dog is chasing a chipmunk across blue! What will Mr. Putter's porch look like when they are through?

Mr. Putter and Tabby Pick the Pears. Orlando, Fla.: Harcourt, 1994. 44p. ISBN-10: 0152002456; ISBN-13: 978-0152002459.

Mr. Putter is too creaky to climb the pear tree, so he fashions a slingshot of old underwear elastic and tries to knock the pears down with fallen apples. There's a wonderful feast, but not what you might expect!

Other books by Cynthia Rylant are *Mr. Putter and Tabby Bake the Cake*; *Mr. Putter and Tabby Catch the Cold*; *Mr. Putter and Tabby Feed the Fish*; *Mr. Putter and Tabby Fly the Plane*; *Mr. Putter and Tabby Make a*

Wish; *Mr. Putter and Tabby Paint the Porch*; *Mr. Putter and Tabby Row the Boat*; *Mr. Putter and Tabby Spin the Yarn*; *Mr. Putter and Tabby Stir the Soup*; *Mr. Putter and Tabby Take the Train*; *Mr. Putter and Tabby Toot the Horn*; *Mr. Putter and Tabby Walk the Dog*; and *Mr. Putter and Tabby Write the Book.*

Illustrators, too, seem to fall in love with drawing and painting cats! Nicola Baylet, who illustrated two of our "hero" cat titles, has created numerous cat books. Most libraries have titles by Lesley Anne Ivory, especially *Cats in the Sun*, *The Birthday Cat*, and *Meet My Cats*. Books by Anne Mortimer are also favored, including *A Pussycat's Christmas*, *Santa's Snow Cat*, *Tosca's Christmas*, and *Tosca's Surprise.*

No list would be complete without these wonderful titles, all too good to miss. Library catalogs make this an easy topic to find books for by checking the subject "Cats Fiction." It is difficult to end the list when there are several hundred fictional cat books, but it would be remiss not to suggest Marion Dane Bauer's *Ghost Eye*, Beverly Cleary's *Socks*, Paula Fox's *One-eyed Cat: A Novel*; Patricia Lakin's *Clarence the Copy Cat*, Janette Okin's *The Prodigal Cat*, and Maggie Smith's *Desser, the Best Cat Ever.*

Published Cat Paper Dolls

Cats and dogs are favorite pets. They can become part of the family and take on "human" characteristics. It is not surprising that cat paper dolls to dress are found in the publishing world. In the late 1800s, McLoughlin Brothers published <u>Comic Series</u>, in which Tabby was included. The 3⅛-inch cat doll was cut and dressed with three costumes. In the early 1900s American Colortype Company published a set of Dressing Dolls called "Pretty Kitty." These were used for advertising until World War I by companies such as the bakery, Aunt Sally. Every wrapped loaf of bread included an envelope with a doll, an outfit, and a hat inside. Figures measured 5¼ inches. Another example from the early 1900s is "Funny Folks in Fur and Feather: Cat," published by Samuel Gabriel Sons & Co. It was a sheet to be cut out on which there was a standing cat with clothes. The names and outfit numbers were printed on the back of the figures and housed in a 5½-by-8½-inch box. In 1938 Merrill published "15 Puppy Kitty" with an advertised 116 pieces to cut out for play. Whitman followed with "Puppies and Kittens" in 1939. Later E. I. Horsman Company printed "New Puss in Boots Paper Doll," which showed Perrault's Puss and four outfits. Other examples are "Shuffle on Catsy" from Children's Workshop. This was more unusual; it was a book with a pop-up cat doll on the front. Six folded pages included clothes.

In the past fifty years, other cat figures have made their appearance. Samuel Lowe Publishing produced a *Lace and Dress Kitty* in 1975. Several cat paper dolls are available in bookstores and on the Internet. Once one has caught the fever, these cat paper dolls are difficult to resist.

Books

Drayton, Grace. *Die Cut Kitty Cat Paper Doll Set*. New York: B. Shackman & Co. Inc., 1994.

Gathings, Evelyn. *Victorian Cat Family Paper Dolls in Full Color*. Mineola, N.Y.: Dover, 1984 32p. ISBN 10: 0486247023; ISBN-13: 978-0486247021.

Sarnat, Marjorie. *Cat Family Sticker Paper Dolls*. Mineola, N.Y.: Dover, 1998. 4p. ISBN 10: 0486401987; ISBN 13: 978-0486401980.

Internet

Animal Friends in Color—http://www.makingfriends.com/friends/f_animcolsor.htm (accessed on March 23, 2009).

The Art Cat Paperdoll—http://www.geocities.com/SoHo/Gallery/3684/paperdoll1.htm (accessed on March 23, 2009).

Cats—http://www.paperdolls.org/cats1.jpg (accessed on March 23, 2009).

Clarence—http://www.gallimauphry.com/clarence/clarence.jpg (accessed on March 23, 2009).

The Kiki Paper Doll—http://www.geocities.com/SoHo/Gallery/3684/paperdoll2.htm (accessed on March 23, 2009).

Original Purrfect Paper Doll Set by "Cricket"—http://www.angelfire.com/country/dancin/Paperdolls12.html (accessed on March 23, 2009).

Puss and Boots—http://www.gallimauphry.com/clarence/clarence.jpg; http://www.gallimauphry.com/clarence/puss.jpg; http://www.surlalunefairytales.com/illustrations/pussboots/index.html (accessed on March 23, 2009).

Lesson Plan:
Dress up Your Favorite Cat!

Library Media Skills Objectives:

The student will select a book or story, determine what a cat character in the story might be wearing, and create a costume to go with the book character.

Curriculum (Subject Area) Objectives:

This lesson may be used in reading/language arts or be adapted to other subjects.

Grade Level: 2–5

Resources:

After a theme or subject is selected, titles such as those suggested in this chapter may be given to students. Each student will need his or her own copy of the paper dolls included in this chapter. Provide crayons or markers. Markers are more colorful in most cases, and fine line markers will help in defining patterns on the clothing. School safety scissors, paper, and pencils are also needed. For students who wish to expand on the project later, fabric, beads, glitter, and other scrap bits of paper may be provided along with glue. Books from which students may select costume examples should be pulled and within easy reach of the students.

Instructional Roles:

Library media specialists, teachers, or art teachers may work with students. Students should be divided into small groups for discussion during design. Allow 15 minutes for the story read-aloud and questions, 15 minutes for book selection and reading (if picture books), 20 minutes for design, and 10 minutes for coloring and display. Materials may be set out before students begin, to allow the full time for design and preparation. The time needed will vary depending on the level of students, the type of books being selected, and the level at which the designs are to be executed.

Activity Procedure for Completion:

Begin the small group session by reading or sharing at least one of the books listed on the paper doll clothing pages (24–25). After reading the story aloud, discuss the character and the clothing the character is wearing. How does the clothing fit the story? Why do the clothes fit the character? Why did the illustrator outfit the characters in the manner shown?

Provide materials and suggest that students cut out either a male or female doll and decorate the costumes from the story that was read and discussed.

Show students the books, which they may want to review. Students will need time to self-select and read.

When the students appear to be ready, ask them to consider which character they plan to design a costume for. In the case of picture books, the students will have clues from the artwork. Use the paper dolls provided as examples. Ask them to consider what the story is about. Where does it occur? What will the character be doing? What will the character need (accessories)?

Demonstrate how to lay out the figure on a sheet of paper. Lightly trace where the clothes will be. Suggest putting tabs at the top, sides, and arms to secure the outfit to the figure. After the students trace a light outline, they may complete the figure and add items such as fabric patterns, jewelry, etc.

Students may decide on the colors they will use and complete the coloring of the outfit. When the coloring is finished, the students may cut out the outfit and place it on the doll.

Provide time for students to explain what they made and why. This will include the telling something about the story and how they decided on the outfit they prepared.

Evaluation:

Each student will select one book and create an outfit to correspond to the cat character in the book.

Follow-Up:

Display the created outfits with the books. Students may write a brief explanation of what they designed.

Prepare a more elaborate wardrobe for the character or a character from another book.

Paper Dolls:
Cats

Instructions: Color and cut out the cat figures on these two pages. Dress each one as a favorite character. Which costumes might be used by the cat characters described in the books listed with the figures?

Arnold, Marsha Diane. *Metro Cat.*

Wells, Rosemary. *Yoko.*

Soto, Gary. *Chato's Kitchen.*

Wood, David, and Gaston Leroux. *The Phantom Cat of the Opera.*

Chapter 3

Who Goes Moo?

What makes cows the topic of so many funny books? Could it be their big brown eyes and quiet nature? Cows seem to be "cool" and very relaxed, like the television ads for cheese from California cows. Maybe people wish they could be more laid back, like cows. Or perhaps they wish they could spend time grazing and sunning themselves in a green meadow, like cows.

Whatever the reason, there are lots of great books written about these animals, often humorous. Doreen Cronin's 2001 Caldecott Honor book, *Click, Clack, Moo: Cows That Type* (Simon & Schuster Books for Young Readers, 2000. 32p. ISBN 10: 0689832133; ISBN 13: 978-0689832130), features Farmer Brown's hilarious cows. (A twenty-five-minute videotape is available from Weston Woods.) The cows get their hands on an old typewriter and decide to make some demands of their farmer. The riotous plot continues when the farmer doesn't meet their demands. Children may be able to add other demands that they might make. This spoof will bring laughter to parents and children. Betsy Lewin, the award-winning illustrator of the book, always wanted to be an artist. She loved the pictures that she saw in the books that her mother read to her and her brother every night, especially those by Beatrix Potter. After she graduated from Pratt Institute, she created drawings for greeting cards and stories in children's magazines. Then she turned to making picture books. *Araminta's Paint Box* and *Snake Alley* are two of her other award winners. She now lives in Brooklyn with her husband, Ted Lewin, who is also an illustrator, and their two cats.

Minnie and Moo, Two Crazy Cows

Minnie and Moo get themselves into all kinds of crazy situations. They are always cooking up another scheme for something to do. Whether it is a trip to the moon or to the farmer's house, Oakland, California-born author and illustrator Denys Cazet brings zest to the characters in these books. The titles are the best clues to what is to come from these zany bovines and would work well in any lesson on book titles for children in grades 1–3. (Live Oak Media has produced audio recordings of these stories.)

Minnie and Moo and the Musk of Zorro. New York: DK Ink, 2000. 48 p. ISBN 10: 0789426528; ISBN 13: 978-0789426529.

Minnie and Moo decide to save the world by dressing up in masks and wave their weapons of lipstick and deodorant spray hanging from swords.

Minnie and Moo and the Potato from Planet X. New York: HarperCollins, 2002. 48p. ISBN 10: 0066237505; ISBN 13: 978-0066237503.

> An alien crashes his ship and needs help from Minnie and Moo.

Minnie & Moo and the Seven Wonders of the World. New York: Atheneum, 2003. 144p. ISBN 10: 0689853300; ISBN 13: 978-0689853302.

> When they hear that the farmer might have to sell the farm because he needs money, the two crazy cows begin a fund-raising scheme that involves a barnyard version of sightseeing the seven wonders of the world.

Minnie and Moo and the Thanksgiving Tree. New York: DK Ink, 2000. 48p. ISBN 10: 0789426544; ISBN 13: 978-0789426543.

> Minnie and Moo begin by trying to hide turkeys, but guess who ends up hiding in a tree so they won't be eaten for Thanksgiving dinner?

Minnie and Moo Go Dancing. New York: DK Ink, 1998. 48p. ISBN 10: 0789425157; ISBN 13: 978-0789425157.

> The farmer has a party, and Minnie and Moo dress up to go.

Minnie and Moo Go to Paris. New York: DK Ink, 1999. 48p. ISBN 10: 0789425955; ISBN 13: 978-0789425959.

> The cows take a bus on a crazy, mixed-up trip as they start out to go to Paris.

Minnie and Moo Go to the Moon. New York: Dorling Kindersley, 1998. 48p. ISBN 10: 0789425165; ISBN 13: 978-0789425164.

> How in the world can two crazy cows drive a tractor to the moon?

Minnie and Moo Meet Frankenswine. New York: HarperCollins, 2002. 48p. ISBN 10: 0066237483; ISBN 13: 978-0066237480.

> It seems a monster is on the farm, and Minnie and Moo must solve a mystery.

Minnie and Moo Save the Earth. New York: DK Ink, 1999. 48p. ISBN 10: 0789425947; ISBN 13: 978-0789425942.

> The cows manage to relax in a hot tub and help save the earth.

Minnie and Moo: The Attack of the Easter Bunnies. New York: HarperCollins, 2004. 48p. ISBN 10: 0060005068; ISBN 13: 978-0060005061.

> When the farmer says he is too old to be the Easter Bunny, the cows try to do it.

Minnie and Moo: The Case of the Missing Jelly Donut. New York: HarperCollins, 2006. 48p. ISBN 10: 0060730099; ISBN 13: 978-0060730093.

> Moo is determined to catch the thief that Minnie believes is stealing her donuts.

Minnie and Moo the Night before Christmas. New York: HarperCollins, 2002. 48p. ISBN 10: 0066237521; ISBN 13: 978-0066237527.

> When the farmer loses the Christmas gifts, Minnie and Moo transform themselves into Santa and Mrs. Claus.

Minnie and Moo: The Night of the Living Bed. New York: HarperCollins, 2004. 48p. ISBN 10: 006000505X; ISBN 13: 978-0060005054.

> It's Halloween, and Minnie has a horrible dream and awakens to find the bed rolling down the hill.

Minnie and Moo: Will You Be My Valentine? New York: HarperCollins, 2002. 48p. ISBN 10: 0066237556; ISBN 13: 978-0066237558.

   The cows decide to write valentine poems to everyone in the barnyard, but the messages are misdirected, which causes chaos.

The Cow Who Jumped Over the Moon and Other Cows Who Fly

Hey diddle diddle, the cat and the fiddle,
The cow jumped over the moon.
The little dog laughed to see such sport
And the dish ran away with the spoon.

Nursery rhymes may have been invented to spread gossip about rulers such as kings and queens. Some think that the rhyme, "Hey Diddle Diddle" was about Queen Elizabeth I, who was thought to be like a cat who fiddled with her cabinet ministers as if they were mice. We don't know for sure today. The cow who jumped over the moon can be found in many picture books. In fact, authors and illustrators seem to revel in portraying the silly combination of cows, flying, and the moon!

Babcock, Chris. *No Moon, No Milk*! Illustrated by Mark Teague. New York: Knopf Books for Young Readers, 1993. 32p. ISBN 10: 0517587793; ISBN 13: 978-0517587799.

   Martha won't give milk until she can visit the moon like her great-great-grandmother did. Grades K–4.

Brown, Paula. *Moon Jump: A Countdown*. New York: Viking, 1993. 32p. ISBN 10: 0670842370; ISBN 13: 978-0670842377.

   Cows try to win the first Moon Jump Contest. Grades K–1.

Burnard, Damon. *Pork and Beef's Great Adventure*. Boston: Houghton Mifflin, 1998. 48p. ISBN 10: 0618070370; ISBN 13: 978-0618070374.

   Pork and Beef, a pig and a cow, cover themselves with frosting and feathers and fly to the moon. Grades 2–4.

Choldenko, Gennifer. *Moonstruck: The True Story of the Cow Who Jumped over the Moon*. Illustrated by Paul Yalowitz. New York: Hyperion Books for Children, 1997. 32p. ISBN 10: 0786801581; ISBN 13: 978-0786801589.

   The horse comes to respect the cow when she really does jump over the moon. Grades K–2.

Eagle, Kin. *Hey Diddle Diddle*. Illustrated by Rob Gilbert. Boston: Whispering Coyote Press, 1997. 31p. ISBN 10: 1879085976; ISBN 13: 978-1879085978.

   Don't miss the zany new verses for this rhyme. Learn what happened to the cow. Grades K–2.

Hillert, Margaret. *The Cow That Got Her Wish*. Illustrated by Krystyna Stasiak. Cleveland, Ohio: Modern Curriculum Press, 1981. 32p. ISBN 10: 0813651212; ISBN 13: 978-0813651217.

   Brownie tries as hard as she can to jump over the moon. Grades 1–2.

Johnson, Paul Brett. *The Cow Who Wouldn't Come Down*. New York: Orchard Books, 1993. 32p. ISBN 10: 0531086313; ISBN 13: 978-0531086315.

> Gertrude the cow takes to flying one day, and Miss Rosemary can't get her to come down. Grades K–1.

Kent, Jack. *Mrs. Mooley*. New York: Golden Press, 1993. 32p. ISBN 10: 0307106861; ISBN 13: 978-0307106865.

> Mrs. Mooley is determined to jump over the moon! Grades K–1.

Milgrim, David. *Cows Can't Fly*. New York: Viking, 1998. 32p. ISBN 10: 0670874752; ISBN 13: 978-0670874750.

> After a young boy draws cows flying, they actually start to fly. Grades K–2.

Roland, Timothy. *Come Down Now, Flying Cow!* New York: Random House, 1997. 32p. ISBN 10: 0679881107; ISBN 13: 978-0679881100.

> In this easy to read book, Beth the cow escapes from her pen in a hot air balloon and has quite an adventure. Grades K–2.

Smith, Linda. *When Moon Fell Down*. New York: HarperCollins, 2001. 32p. ISBN 10: 0060283017; ISBN 13: 978-0060283018.

> Moon comes down from the sky and finds a friendly cow to help him see the earth. See how they view the world together. Grades K–3.

Speed, Toby. *Two Cool Cows*. Illustrated by Barry Root. New York: Putnam, 1995. 32p. ISBN 10: 0399226478; ISBN 13: 978-0399226472.

> Millie and Maud are two cool cows who fly to the moon in Huckabuck boots.

Stevens, Janet, and Susan Stevens Crummel. *And the Dish Ran Away with the Spoon*. Illustrated by Janet Stevens. San Diego: Harcourt, 2001. 32p. ISBN 10: 0152022988; ISBN 13: 978-0152022983.

> When the dish and spoon don't return, the cat, cow, and dog venture forth to find them. (A twenty-four-minute audio recording is available from Spoken Arts.) Grades K–2.

Vail, Rachel. *Over the Moon*. Illustrated by Scott Nash. New York: Orchard Books, 1998. 32p. ISBN 10: 0531300684; ISBN 13: 978-0531300688.

> In a stage production of the nursery rhyme "Hey Diddle Diddle," the other actors try to persuade the cow to jump over the moon—not under, next to, or through it. Grades K–2.

> Check out these Web sites for cows to color:

> *Hey Diddle Diddle*—http://www.niteowl.org/kids/diddle2.html (accessed March 23, 2009).

> *Hey Diddle Diddle*—http://www.teachersandfamilies.com/nursery/heydiddle.html (accessed March 23, 2009).

Christmas Cows

Cows, at Christmas? Christmas is not limited to reindeer. Cows can be found among the many reading packages offered by authors and publishers, which are usually whimsical, especially for grades K–3. Blossom the cow invites Maggie to go on a trip to find Santa Claus in Henrik Drescher's *Looking for Santa Claus* (Lothrop, Lee & Shepard Books, 1984. 36p. ISBN 10: 068802999X; ISBN 13: 978-0688029999).

Meet cows in Cooper Edens's *Santa Cows*, illustrated by Daniel Lane (Green Tiger Press, 1991. 28p. ISBN 10: 0671748637; ISBN 13: 978-0671748630). In *Santa Cows*, it may be a surprise to find out who brings the tree and baseball equipment at Christmas. In *Santa Cow Island* (Green Tiger Press, 1994. 32p. ISBN 10: 0671883194; ISBN 13: 978-0671883195), the cows take the Schwartz family on a New Year's vacation. Can cows really surf? The cows take a grand tour of the Santa Cow Movie Studio in *Santa Cow Studios Tour* (Simon & Schuster, 1995. 32p. ISBN 10: 0689800304; ISBN 13: 978-0689800306).

What's in a Cow's Name?

What is the best name for a cow? Does the name fit the character? What are the characters like? What are their traits? Cows' names vary widely. It is difficult to know whether the farmer or author has more fun naming them.

Minnie and Moo aren't the only cows with names or adventures. The following sampling suggests the variety. After sharing books that have cows with names, children may enjoy reading and naming cows in books where the creatures are anonymous.

Africa

Rassmus, Jens. *Farmer Enno and His Cow.* New York: Orchard Books, 1998. 32p. ISBN 10: 0531300811; ISBN 13: 978-0531300817.

Farmer Enno dreams of boating on the ocean. When he awakens, the boat in his dream is there. He and his cow, Africa, set out for the city to try to find Africa's namesake. Students may understand Africa's name from the markings on her coat!

Bluebell

Ernst, Lisa Campbell. *When Bluebell Sang.* Macmillan/Aladdin, 1992. 32p. ISBN 10: 0027335615; ISBN 13: 978-0027335613.

Bluebell has talent but must get away from her greedy manager to use it. Grades K–2.

Cassie

Arkin, Alan. *Cassie Loves Beethoven.* New York: Hyperion Books for Children, 2000. 176p. ISBN 10: 0786805641; ISBN 13: 978-0786805648.

Cassie won't give milk, so her owners play classical music for her. The music moves her to speak and play the piano! Grades 3–6.

Clarissa

Talley, Carol. *Clarissa.* Illustrated by Itoka Maeno. Kansas City, Mo.: MarshMedia, 1992. 32p. ISBN 10: 1559420146; ISBN 13: 978-1559420143.

Clarissa the cow learns that even though she is an ordinary brown cow, she has special traits, to be valued.

Cora

Phylliss Adams, Eleanore Hartson, and Mark Taylor. *Stop the Bed!* Illustrated by John Sandford. New York: Children's Press, 1982. 32p. ISBN 10: 0516097199; ISBN 13: 978-0516097190.
>> Cora the cow goes off on a ski rescue.

Readers may also like other Cora adventures:

Time Out! Cleveland, Ohio: Modern Curriculum Press, 1982. 32p. ISBN 10: 0813654017; ISBN 13: 978-0813654010.
>> Cora helps out when two skunks stop a baseball game.

Jump in! Now! Cleveland, Ohio: Modern Curriculum Press, 1982. 32p. ISBN 10: 0813654025; ISBN 13: 978-0813654027.
>> Cora rescues two children on the beach. Grades K–2.

Daisy

Woodworth, Viki. *Daisy the Firecow*. Honesdale, Pa.: Boyds Mills Press, 2001. 32p. ISBN 10: 1563979349; ISBN 13: 978-1563979347. Grades K–2.
>> Daisy leaves the pasture and becomes the firehouse mascot because of her black and white spots.

Floramel

Buchwald, Emile. *Floramel and Esteban*. Illustrated by Charles Robinson New York: Harcourt Brace Jovanovich, 1982. 72p. ISBN 10: 0152286780; ISBN 13: 978-0152286781.
>> Floramel, a lonely cow, meets Esteban, a migrating egret, and persuades him to stay so she won't be lonely.

Laloo

Matthew, Judith. *There's Nothing to D-o-o-o!* Illustrated by Kurt Cyrus. New York: Harcourt Brace, 1999. 32p. ISBN 10: 0152016473; ISBN 13: 978-0152016470.
>> Laloo the calf gets bored and slips through the fence; she is missed by her mother.

Moozie

Morton, Jane. *Moozie's Kind Adventure*. Breckenridge, Colo.: Best Friend Books, 1999. 32p. ISBN 10: 096622681X; ISBN 13: 978-0966226812.
>> Moozie the cow turns a whole stampede of cattle around to save some ducklings that were in their path.

Do Cows Drink Milk or Eat Cookies?

Picture a cold glass of milk and Oreo cookies. It could be chocolate chip or oatmeal, too. Do cow characters snack on milk and cookies? There are many titles good for reading aloud before or after such a snack. (No eating while reading, please!)

Bulla, Clyde Robert. *Dandelion Hill.* Illustrated by Bruce Degan. New York: Dutton, 1982. 32p. ISBN 10: 0525451013; ISBN 13: 978-0525451013.
> Violet "marches to her own drum" and has a hard time finding her place in the herd. Grades 2–4.

Clements, Andrew. *Who Owns the Cow?* Illustrated by Joan Landis. New York: Clarion Books, 1995. 32p. ISBN 10: 0395701457; ISBN 13: 978-0395701454.
> Takes this question beyond the obvious answer of the farmer and leads the reader on an interesting journey.

Cole, Babette. *Supermoo!* New York: Putnam, 1992. 32p. ISBN 10: 039922422X; ISBN-13: 978-0399224225.
> Supermoo is a heifer hero unafraid to fight filth and pollution. Grades K–3.

Duffield, Katy. *Farmer McPeepers and His Missing Milk Cows.* Illustrated by Steve Gray. Flagstaff, Ariz.: Rising Moon, 2003. 32p. ISBN10: 0873588258; ISBN 13: 978-0873588256.
> The cows want a day out on their own, so they borrow the farmer's glasses. Grades K–2.

Egan, Tim. *Metropolitan Cow.* Boston: Houghton Mifflin, 1996. 32p. ISBN 10: 0395730961; ISBN 13: 978-0395730966.
> Bennett Gibbons becomes good friends with Webster, a pig who moves in next door to their art deco apartment. Bennett shares museums and urban life, and Webster shares a roll in the mud. Bennett's parents are not pleased! Grades 1–3.

Fajerman, Deborah. *How to Speak Moo!* Hauppauge, N.Y.: Barron's, 2002. 32 p. ISBN 10: 0764122851; ISBN 13: 978-0764122859.
> This is made for acting out; the book explains how cows make high, low, and even bumpy moos. Grades K–2.

Greenstein, Elaine. *Emily and the Crows.* Saxonville, Mass.: Picture Book Studio, 1992. 32p. ISBN 10: 0887082386; ISBN 13: 978-0887082382.
> There is a reason why Emily the cow is always surrounded by crows. Grades K–1.

Harrison, David L. *When Cows Come Home.* Illustrated by Chris L. Demarest. Honsdale, Pa.: Boyds Mills Press, 1994. 30p. ISBN 10: 1563971437; ISBN 13: 978-1563971433.
> A rhyming, fun book about what the cows do when the farmer isn't watching. Grades 1–4.

Horstman, Lisa. *Fast Friends: A Tail and Tongue Tail.* New York: Knopf, 1994. 32p. ISBN 10: 0517165155; ISBN 13: 978-0517165157.
> A chameleon and a cow become roommates in the city until they stop "seeing eye to eye." Grades K–2.

Hurd, Thacher. *Moo Cow Kaboom!* New York: HarperCollins, 2003. 32p. ISBN 10: 006050501X; ISBN 13: 978-0060505011.
> Zork, an alien cowboy, abducts Moo Cow, who although usually gentle, reacts with a fearless vengeance. (A sound recording is available from Live Oak Media.) Grades K–2.

Kirby, David, and Allen Woodman. *The Cows Are Going to Paris*. Illustrated by Chris L. Demarist. Honsdale, Pa.: Boyds Mills Press, 1991. 32p. ISBN 10: 1878093118; ISBN 13: 978-1878093110.

> French cows decide the countryside is boring and board a train to Paris, leaving the frightened people who fled the train in their place. Those familiar with art will smile at the poses that resemble Seurat's *Sunday Afternoon on the Island of the Grande Jatte*. Grades 1–3.

Krasilovsky, Phyllis. *The Cow Who Fell in the Canal*. Illustrated by Peter Spier. New York: Dell, 1985. 36p. ISBN 10: 0385077408; ISBN 13: 978-0385077408.

> A Dutch cow falls into the canal and floats down the stream. (Weston Woods produced a sound recording and Wood Knapp Video produced a 28-minute videocassette.)

Macaulay, David. *Black and White*. Boston: Houghton Mifflin, 1991. 32p. ISBN 10: 0395521513; ISBN 13: 978-0395521519.

> One of the four stories in this book, "Udder Chaos," begins with a cow who is licking a man in a convict suit. See how cows camouflage themselves. Grades 2–6. (Caldecott Award Winner)

Moers, Hermann. *Camomile Heads for Home*. Illustrated by Marcus Pfister. New York: North-South Books, 1987. 26p. ISBN 10: 0805002804; ISBN 13: 978-0805002805.

> A calf is left behind at the market and gets into mischief while coming home. Grades K–1.

Most, Bernard. *Cock-A-Doodle-Moo!* San Diego: Harcourt Brace, 1996. 33p. ISBN 10: 0152012524; ISBN 13: 978-0152012526.

> A rooster looses his voice and needs the help of one of the cows to wake up the farm. (A computer program by Greene Bark Press is available.) Grades K–2.

Pellowski, Michael. *Clara Joins the Circus*. Illustrated by True Kelley. New York: Parents Magazine Press, 1981. 48p. ISBN 10: 0819310581; ISBN 13: 978-0819310583.

> Clara Cow joins the circus but fails at most of the jobs she tries. Grades K–2.

Phillips, Mildres. *And the Cow Said Moo!* New York: Greenwillow Books, 2000. 32p. ISBN 10: 0688168027; ISBN 13: 978-0688168025.

> A young cow tries to persuade other animals to moo, until an owl makes him realize they are best off being who they already are. Grades K–2.

Root, Phyllis. *Kiss the Cow*. Illustrated by Will Hillenbrand. Cambridge, Mass.: Candlewick Press, 2000. 32p. ISBN 10: 0763602981; ISBN 13: 978-0763602987.

> Annalisa sneaks off and milks her mom's magic cow, but forgets to give her a kiss. The cow won't give any more milk until Annalisa kisses her. Grades K–3.

Schertle, Alice. *How Now, Brown Cow?* Illustrated by Amanda Schaffer. San Diego: Voyager Books, Harcourt Brace, 1994. 32p. ISBN 10: 0152017062; ISBN 13: 978-0152017064.

> Beautifully illustrated poems invite reading out loud. Grades K–5.

Spinelli, Eileen. *Something to Tell the Grandcows*. Illustrated by Bill Slavin. Grand Rapids, Mich.: Eerdmans Books for Young Readers, 2004. 32p. ISBN 10: 080285236X; ISBN 13: 978-0802852366.

> Admiral Byrd is accompanied on his 1933 expedition to the South Pole by none other than Emmadine. Grades 2–4.

Van Laan, Nancy. *The Tiny, Tiny Boy and the Big, Big Cow*. New York: Knopf, 1993. 32p. ISBN 10: 0679820787; ISBN 13: 978-0679820789.

> A little boy offers a cow many things to stand still. Finally, she stands still to be milked when he asks her NOT to stand still. Grades K–3.

Wheeler, Lisa. *Sixteen Cows*. Illustrated by Kurt Cyrus. San Diego: Harcourt, 2001. 32p. ISBN 10: 0152026762; ISBN 13: 978-0152026769.

> When the fence gets blown down, Cowboy Gene and Cowgirl Sue's cows get all mixed up. Grades K–3.

Wildsmith, Brian. *Daisy*. New York: Pantheon Books, 1984. 47p. ISBN 10: 0394959752; ISBN 13: 978-0394959757.

> A cow dreams of seeing the world. Grades K–4.

Young, James. *The Cows Are in the Corn*. Scholastic Inc., 1995. 32p. ISBN 10: 0590130927; ISBN 13: 978-0590130929.

> An easy-to-read book about a farm whose animals are out of control until the mother enters the scene. (Students may listen to the audiotape by Scholastic.) Grades 1–3.

Zidrou. *Ms. Blanche, the Spotless Cow*. Illustrated by David Merveille. New York: Henry Holt, 1993. 32p. ISBN 10: 0805025502. ISBN 13: 978-0805025507.

> Ms. Blanche wants spots like all the other cows have. Farmer Goodfellow introduces her to his liveliest bull. Grades 1–3.

Published Cow Paper Dolls

Advertising figures like Borden's Elsie the Cow have been in existence for over 150 years. Cows can be found as toys representing common nursery or children's stories in the early 1900s. George W. Jacobs and Company produced cow figures without clothing for *Hey Diddle Diddle, the Cat and the Fiddle* on a sheet in an envelope. Shortly afterward, in 1932, McLoughlin Brothers put out *Farm Yard Friends*, which included a cow. McLoughlin was sold to Milton Bradley in 1920. *Suzie Sweet*, a paper doll complete with her animal friend, Minnie Moo, was printed by Grinnell Lithographics in 1940.

These are two examples of paper dolls that can be found in stores today:

Cow—Clarabel. New York: The Original Magnetic Paper Dolls.

> The paper dolls are eight inches long and include clothes to be cut out. They are described in the catalog as "original refrigerator dress-up dolls" to be used on "metallically adherent appliance such as a filing cabinet, refrigerator, washer or dryer."

> 180 W. 93rd St., 4F
> New York, NY 10025
> Phone: 775-278-8684
> Fax: 775-310-4636
> E-mail: info@magneticpaperdollsinc.com

Sarnat, Marjorie. *Cow Sticker Paper Doll*. Mineola, N.Y.: Dover, 2001. 4p. ISBN: 0486418456.

Lesson Plan:
"More Milk and Cookies, Please," Said the Cow

Library Media Skills Objective:

The student will analyze a book character.

Curriculum (subject areas) Objectives:

This lesson may be incorporated into a social studies unit on manners and proper behavior in social situations.

Grade Level: K–2

Resources:

> Books about cows
>
> Cow paper doll handouts
>
> Paints, markers, crayons, and pencils
>
> Scissors
>
> Snacks (real or paper)
>
> Dishes (real or paper)

Instructional Roles:

The library media specialist or teacher may plan this activity alone or as a team. It is suitable for whole classes or small groups if small conversation tables are set up. It involves students planning for the party as well as reading the book and preparing the paper doll character. The teacher may make the table settings, or students may do it, depending on time available and the emphasis the library media specialist or teacher wants to place on reading and character analysis. The introduction and initial planning take about 45 minutes to an hour. Students will need to select and read a cow book, decide on a cow character, and color and cut out the paper doll on their own, all of which may take an hour or two. A follow-up session may take half an hour for review and making paper dolls. The milk and cookie party and cleanup take about 30 minutes.

Activity and Procedures for Completion:

Begin the sessions with a read-aloud. There are many cow books from which to select, preferably choose one that will make students laugh or at least chuckle. Discuss the story. What made it funny? Why were cows in the story silly or funny? Did they do zany things? Were some actions incongruous? Was there a play on words that was funny?

Be a little silly and suggest that you were moo-o-v-ed to have a milk and cookie party (or a similar approach). To have a milk and cookie party, students need to plan. They could come as cow characters that they read about in books. Allow time for students to select books. Pull the books or display whichever are available. Prepare a short bibliography with annotations using the materials listed in this chapter. Discuss when the party might be held and where. Also discuss what the students could bring and how they might behave at such a party.

Before the next session, send an invitation to each student with his or her name on it, listing all the things that were discussed (time, place, food, etc.). With the invitations, send two or three questions that the students must think about when they have read their books. (What is the cow character like? How does she talk and dress? What kinds of activities does he do? Does the cow have an obvious characteristic, like being curious, stubborn, lonely, etc.?

At the next session, review the party and discuss the books and some of the silly characters. Explain that students must bring a cow paper doll character for the book they have read. Distribute the paper dolls and allow time for students to color, cut out, and create new costumes if necessary. They must make the proper costumes for their dolls. They should be prepared to talk about their books. Review simple rules, such as listening to others when they are talking about the books, giving everyone a chance to talk, and using good manners when eating.

If the students are helping with the menu, this must be done ahead of time. Either real food or paper food may be used. Use paper plates and cups, and make paper cookies (trace and copy cookie cutters on paper). The school cafeteria or parents may be willing to help with the cookies. Set up the tables with four or five children at each. Put name cards by each setting with the student's name and a blank for the cow character's name.

When students arrive with the cow paper dolls, they must write the names of their characters on the name cards at their settings. Place the costumed paper dolls on the table with the name cards. Let the party begin with another cow read-aloud, followed by eating (real or pretend). (Children will most likely enjoy "real" more.) While eating, students should take turns telling about their paper dolls. When there appears to be a lull, end the party and thank everyone for coming. Cleanup may be necessary.

Evaluation:

Each student will select a cow book, read it, and respond to the questions about the cow character in the book before making a cow paper doll of the character. Each student will participate in conversation about his or her character at a milk and cookie party.

Follow-Up:

Display the cows with costumes and party name place cards.

Paper Dolls:
Cows

Instructions: Color the two cow figures. Select an outfit that fits one of the characters. Color it. Cut the pieces out and put the clothes on your character. Have an imaginary adventure or retell your favorite story.

Which cow character is your favorite?

Could you be Daisy the Firecow?

Perhaps you might be a cow tourist in Paris?

Could you be Minnie or Moo? Go to the pampas as a gaucho or go dancing?

Chapter 4

Dinosaurs Everywhere!

Imagine working in a nursery of Maiasaurus mothers soothed by a pipe organ. Making fashion jewelry for a Stegasaurus bedecked with silver caps on her spines. Cleaning the teeth of a Camarasaurus. Attending a summer camp designed to prepare young people and dinosaurs to coexist in a land of woodlands and forests, glaciers and high meadows, swamps, beaches, and bays.

James Gurney discovered the journals of Will and Arthur Denison on a dusty shelf in the library. In the journal, the father and son recorded their time spent in just such a land, the land of Dinotopia. Were their travels through the Canyon City to the Forbidden Mountains real? In his introduction to the journals, Mr. Gurney writes, "Honestly, I have my doubts, being skeptical by nature. But I offer you the facts of the case so you can form your own conclusions." Read more of the adventures in James Gurney's books.

Dinotopia: A Land Apart from Time. New York: HarperTrophy, 1992. 159p.

Dinotopia: The World Beneath. New York: HarperTrophy, 1995. 158p.

Dinotopia: Journey to Chandara. Toronto: Andrews McMeel, 2007. 160p. ISBN-10: 0-7407-6431-4; ISBN-13: 978-0-7407-6431-8.

Hallmark Entertainment produced a television miniseries of these books that received an Emmy for best visual effects, *Dinotopia: The Series* (2002. 240 min.).

To see more about this world and the art from the books, visit the Web site Gurney, James, http://dinotopia.com (accessed March 23, 2009).

Dinosaurs with Us

We may only have fossil records of dinosaurs, but they have captured our imagination. Many authors love to write about the creatures. Sometimes authors portray them as animals, and at other times the dinosaurs take on the same characteristics as people, complete with houses and clothes. As readers, children will find that some are pure fantasy, while others may have some basis in scientific facts. It can be a challenge to bridge the gap between reality and fantasy.

A series of books that includes a visit to the land of dinosaurs is *Dinoverse*. Four junior high students find themselves transported back in time. They are transformed into dinosaurs. Try these page-turners, all written by Scott Ciencin and illustrated by Mike Fredericks.

I Was a Teenage T. Rex. New York: Random House, 1999. 158p. (Dinoverse Series, No. 1). ISBN 10: 0679888438; ISBN 13: 978-0679888437.

The Teens Time Forgot. New York: Random House, 1999. 192p. (Dinoverse Series , No. 2). ISBN 10: 0679888446; ISBN 13: 978-0679888444.

Raptor Without a Cause. Random House, 2000. 208p. (Dinoverse Series, No. 3). ISBN 10: 0679888454; ISBN 13: 978-0679888451.

Please Don't Eat the Teacher. Random House, 2000. 224p. (Dinoverse Series, No. 4). ISBN 10: 0679888462; ISBN 13: 978-0679888468.

Beverly Hills Brontosaurus, New York: Random House, 2000. 173p. (Dinoverse Series, No. 5). ISBN 10: 0375805958; ISBN 13: 978-0375805950.

Dinosaurs Are My Homework. New York: Random House, 2000. 192p. (Dinoverse Series, No. 6). ISBN 10: 0375805966; ISBN 13: 978-0375805967.

Could dinosaurs have imagined that someday they would be captured on video? Here are just a few of the videos that feature the adventures of Littlefoot, an orphaned dinosaur, and the friends he makes as he looks for a safe and happy home.

The Land before Time. Universal Studios, 1988. 69 min.

The Land before Time: The Great Valley Adventure. Universal Studios, 2003. 74 min.

The Land before Time: The Time of the Great Giving. Universal Studios, 2003. 71 min.

To find out more about the characters and other videocassettes, DVDs, and music, visit http://www.landbeforetime.com/index.html (accessed March 23, 2009).

Dinosaur Adventurers

Just the mention of dinosaurs makes the mind race to adventure and mystery. Whether going back in time or finding clues about the past, dinosaur adventures provide a sense of intrigue.

Adler, David A. *Cam Jansen: The Mystery of the Dinosaur Bones*. Illustrated by Susanna Natti. New York: Viking, 1981. 64p. ISBN 10: 0670200409; ISBN 13: 978-0670200405.
> By using her photographic memory, Cam figures out who stole the dinosaur bones from the museum. Grades 2–4.

Alphin, Elaine Marie. *Dinosaur Hunter*. Illustrated by Don Bolognese. New York: HarperCollins, 2003. 48p. ISBN 10: 0060283033; ISBN 13: 978-0060283032.
> Ned finds triceratops fossils on his father's Wyoming ranch and is able to fend off a scheming collector. Grades 2–5.

Calhoun, B. B. *On the Right Track*. Illustrated by Daniel Mark Duffy. New York: W. H. Freeman, 1994. 127p. ISBN 10: 0716765306; ISBN 13: 978-0716765301.

    Fenton Rumplemayer must leave New York City to go to Wyoming with his father, a paleontologist. He is the only one who can solve the puzzle of dinosaur tracks. (Read *Fair Play*, *Bite Makes Right*, and *Out of Place* also.) Grades 4–6.

Cole, Joanna. *The Magic School Bus in the Time of Dinosaurs*. Illustrated by Bruce Degen. New York: Scholastic, 1994. 48 p. ISBN 10: 0780751744; ISBN 13: 978-0780751743.

    Ms. Frizzle and the gang want to find a Maiasaura nesting ground, so they are off in the school bus time machine visiting the Late Triassic Period, the Late Jurassic Period, the Late Cretaceous Period, and, finally, the Cretaceous Period. Grades 2–4. (A sound recording of the book is available from Scholastic. The book was adapted for television in 1995, and a software game package was produced by Microsoft in 1996 for PC and Mac.)

Hoff, Sid. *Danny and the Dinosaur*. New York: HarperTrophy, 2003. 64p. ISBN 10: 0060290374; ISBN 13: 978-0060290375.

    When Danny visits the museum, guess what follows him home! (An audio recording and a video recording are available from Wood Knapp Video. A computer program is available from Fox Toons Interactive.) Grades 1–3.

Hoff, Syd. *Danny and the Dinosaur Go to Camp*. New York: HarperTrophy, 1998. 32p. ISBN 10: 0064442446; ISBN 13: 978-0064442442.

    Danny and his pet share their first time at sleepaway camp. (A sound recording is available from Weston Woods.) Grades 1–3.

Hoff, Syd. *Happy Birthday, Danny and the Dinosaur*. New York: HarperTrophy, 1997. 32p. ISBN 0060264381.

    You are invited to a birthday party, and so is Danny's big friend. (A sound recording is available from HarperCollins.) Grades 1–3.

Hope, Laura Lee. *The Mystery of the Dinosaur in the Forest*. Illustrated by Larry Ruppert. New York: Little Simon, 2005. (Bobbsey Twins). ISBN 10: 141690705X; ISBN 13: 978-1416907053.

    The twins are on the lookout for a dinosaur that may be living in the forest. Grades 2–4.

Lampman, Evelyn Sibley. *The Shy Stegosaurus of Cricket Creek*. Illustrated by Hubert Buel. Keller, Tex.: Purple House Press, 2001. 219p. ISBN 10: 1930900090; ISBN 13: 978-1930900097.

    A wonderful story about Joey and Joan and the prehistoric friend they discover.

Marsh, Carole. *The Mystery of the Missing Dinosaurs*. Peachtree City, Ga.: Gallopade International/Carole Marsh Books, 2003. 150p. ISBN-10: 0635016605; ISBN 13: 978-0635016607.

    Four children head off to see the dinosaur bones at Chicago's Field Museum and end up solving a mystery. Grades 2–5.

McMahon, P. J. *The Mystery of the Disappearing Dinosaurs: Secret File # 5*. New York: Aladdin Paperbacks, 2005. 128p. ISBN 10: 1416900497; ISBN 13: 978-1416900498.

    The gang has a mystery to solve and the bookstore figures prominently. Grades 2–4.

O'Malley, Kevin. *Captain Raptor and the Moon Mystery*. Illustrated by Patrick O'Brien. New York: Walker, 2005. 32p. (Freaky Joe Club Series). ISBN 10: 0802789366; ISBN 13: 978-0802789365.

> When aliens are reported on Jurassica's moon, the shiny, armor-plated hero sets off with his crew. Grades K–3.

Osborne, Mary Pope. *Dinosaurs before Dark*. Illustrated by Sal Murdocca. New York: Random House, 1992. 80 p. (Magic Tree House Series, No. 1). ISBN 10: 0679924116; ISBN 13: 978-0679924111.

> In a <u>Magic Tree House</u> adventure, Pteranodon comes to Jack and Annie's rescue, but is he in time? Grades 4–6.

Richler, Jacob. *Jacob Two-Two and the Dinosaur*. Illustrated by Norman Eyolfson. New York: Tundar, 1997. 96p. ISBN 10: 0394987047; ISBN 13: 978-0394987040.

> A wild tall tale about a small boy who battles the Prime Minister to save his friend, a Diplodocus. Grades K–1.

Wilson, John. *Weet*. Illustrated by Janice Armstrong. Toronto: Napoleon Publishing, 1996. 160p. (The Weet Trilogy, Book 1). ISBN 978-0929141-40-4.

> Twelve-year-old Eric, his sister, and his dog time travel back sixty-five million years, where they meet Weet, who guides them through his world. Grades 4–7.

Wilson, John. *Weet Alone*. Illustrated by Janice Armstrong. Toronto, Ontario: Canada: Napoleon Publishing, 1999. 152p. (The Weet Trilogy, Book 3). ISBN 978-0929141-68-8.

> Weet's life changes when a great meteor strikes Earth. How will the young people survive this great catastrophe? Grades 4–7.

Wilson, John. *Weet's Quest*. Illustrated by Janice Armstrong. Toronto: Napoleon Publishing, 1997. 156p. (The Weet Trilogy, Book 2). ISBN 978-0929141-68-8.

> Eric, Rose, and Sally, their dog, help Weet as he travels beyond the foreboding Fire Mountain. Grades 4–7.

Zindel, Paul. *Raptor*. New York: Hyperion, 1999. 170p. ISBN 10: 078680338X; ISBN 13: 978-0786803385.

> This exciting adventure features teenager Zack, who finds a dinosaur egg. Mutant dinosaurs, a half-crazed paleontologist, and gory scenes will keep older readers in suspense. Grades 6-8.

> Although not within the parameters of this book, there are a number of computer and video games related to dinosaur hunting. These should be researched and evaluated carefully. Several companies have produced programs for Windows and Mac as well as for Nintendo. Examples are *Dinosaur Hunter* (DK, 2005); *Turok: Dinosaur Hunter* (Acclaim Entertainment Inc.); and *Paraworld* (Aspyr Media).

Dinosaurs in Your Home or Just Next Door

A theme repeated in a number of books is the dinosaur that appears at a human's home. The home aspect varies, especially with the age of reader. In some cases, as in William Joyce's Lazardo family, they choose to bring Bob, a dinosaur, back to their hometown with them. The books in this selection make dinosaurs seem like pets or friends.

Butterworth, Oliver. *The Enormous Egg*. Illustrated by Lois Darling. Boston: Little, Brown, 1956. 187p. ISBN 10: 0316119040; ISBN 13: 978-0316119047.

> Nate found an egg in the family hen house that eventually hatches into a dinosaur. Problems abound! (A sound recording is available from Listening Library.) Grades 2–5.

Carrick, Carol. *Patrick's Dinosaur*. Illustrated by Donald Carrick. Boston: Houghton Mifflin, 1985. 32p. ISBN 10: 0899191894; ISBN 13: 978-0899191898.

> Patrick's brother tells him a lot about dinosaurs but neglects to say that they are extinct. Suddenly, Patrick discovers the huge beasts everywhere! Grades K–2.

Carrick, Carol. *What Happened to Patrick's Dinosaurs?* Illustrated by Donald Carrick. Clarion, 1988. 32p. ISBN 10: 0899197973; ISBN 13: 978-0899197975.

> Patrick shares the secret with his brother Hank while they are raking leaves. Grades K–2.

Chausse, Sylvie. *The Egg and I*. Illustrated by Francois Crozat. Parsippany, N.J.: Silver Burdett, 1997. 32p. ISBN 10: 0382392841; ISBN 13: 978-0382392849.

> A picture book for older readers, Matthew's elderly uncle dies and leaves him with only the instructions, "Go cook an egg." The results are astounding. Grades 1–4.

Daniels, Teri. *G-Rex*. Illustrated by Tracey Pearson. New York: Scholastic, 2000. 32p. ISBN 10: 0531302431; ISBN 13: 978-0531302439.

> Gregory is tired of his brother Mark getting the better of him, so he becomes a dinosaur to take control. Grades K–2.

Grambling, Lois. *Can I Have a Stegosaurus, Mom: Can I Please?* Illustrated by H. B. Lewis. Mahwah, N.J.: BridgeWater Books, 1995. 32p. ISBN 10: 0816733864; ISBN13: 978-0816733866.

> Can you imagine having a dinosaur for a pet? Would your Mom say "Yes?" Grades K–3.

Hennessy, B. J. *The Dinosaur Who Lived in My Backyard*. Pictures by Susan Davis. New York: Viking, 1988. 32p. ISBN 10: 067081685X; ISBN 13: 978-0670816859.

> A little boy wishes that the dinosaur who lived in almost the same spot he does, only millions of years ago, would return. Grades K–2.

Joyce, William. *Dinosaur Bob and His Adventures with the Family Lazardo*. New York: HarperCollins, 1995. 48p. ISBN 10: 0382392841; ISBN 13: 978-0382392849.

> Bob is a great dinosaur, whether he is playing his trumpet or scaring off burglars. Grades 1–4.

Krasny, Julie, and Marc Brown. *Dinosaurs Divorce*. Boston: Little, Brown, 1988. 31p. ISBN 10: 0316112488; ISBN 13: 978-0316112482.

> Lizardy-looking dinosaurs help readers understand why parents sometimes divorce and how the process works. Grades 1–3.

Most, Bernard. *If the Dinosaurs Came Back*. San Diego: Harcourt Brace, 1978. 32p. ISBN 10: 0152380205; ISBN 13: 978-0152380205.

> A little boy imagines the many jobs and uses for dinosaurs in his modern city. (An audiocassette is available.). Grades K–2.

Nolan, Dennis. *Dinosaur Dream*. New York: Simon & Schuster, 1990. 32p. ISBN 10: 0027681459; ISBN 13: 978-0027681451.

> Wilbur, clad in his bright red pajamas, sets out to return Gideon, a young dinosaur, back to his proper place and time. Grades K–2.

Pfister, Marcus. *Dazzle the Dinosaur*. Translated by J. Alison James. New York: North South Books, 2000. 32p. ISBN 10: 1558583378; ISBN 13: 978-1558583375.

    Newly hatched Dazzle and his friend Maia share dino adventures. Grades K–1.

Schwartz, Howard. *How I Captured a Dinosaur*. Illustrated by Amy Schwartz. New York: Orchard, 1989. 32p. ISBN 10: 0531057704; ISBN 13: 978-0531057704.

    Young Liz uses leftover hamburgers to lure a live Albertosaurus to her campsite. Grades 1–4.

Shields, Carol Diggory. *Saturday Night at the Dinosaur Stomp*. Illustrated by Scott Nash. Cambridge, Mass.: Candlewick, 2002. 32p. ISBN 10: 1564026930; ISBN 13: 978-1564026934.

    Triassic Twist and Raptor Rap! It's a rocking good time! Grades K–2.

Sierra, Judy. *Good Night, Dinosaurs*. Illustrated by Victoria Chess. New York: Clarion Books, 2002. 32p. ISBN 10: 039565016X; ISBN 13: 978-0395650165.

    A happy way to end the day! Grades K–2.

Wahl, Jan. *The Field Mouse and the Dinosaur Named Sue*. Illustrated by Bob Doucet. New York: Scholastic, 2000. 32p. ISBN 10: 0439099846; ISBN 13: 978-0439099844.

    When the bone that has provided him with shelter disappears, Field Mouse goes looking for it. Based on the true story of the largest T. rex ever found. Grades K–2.

Yolen, Jane. *How Do Dinosaurs Say Goodnight?* Illustrated by Mark Teague. New York: Blue Sky Press, 2000. 32p. ISBN 10: 0590316818; ISBN 13: 978-0590316811.

    Young readers will recognize the very tricks they use to avoid going to bed in this dinosaur tale. (A videotape is available from Weston Woods.) Grades K–2.

Dinosaur Tongue Trickery!

Perhaps in a rhyme
You may visit another time,
With poets funny
And others serious
Or some, pun-ny.
There'll be dinosaur riddles
To stump your teacher,
And plenty of jokes
To enjoy. Okey-doke?

    Poetry can be overlooked, but the offerings in this subject area will bring readers running. Books in the joke section of libraries are often well worn. These titles are well worth sharing with children of all ages.

Hopkins, Lee Bennett, ed. *Dinosaurs: Poems*. Illustrated by Murray Tinkelman. San Diego: Harcourt Brace Jovanovich, 1987. 46 p. ISBN 10: 0517158051; ISBN 13: 978-0517158050.

    Eighteen poems about giants of long ago show a range of feelings and thoughts.

Horsfall, Jacqueline. *Giggle Fit: Dinosaur Jokes*. Illustrated by Steve Harpster. New York: Sterling, 2003. 48p. ISBN 10: 1402704410; ISBN 13: 978-1402704413.

> Silly-saurus!

Moss, Jeff. *Bone Poems*. Illustrated by Tom Leigh. New York: Workman Publishing Company, 1997. 96p. ISBN 10: 076110884X; ISBN 13: 978-0761108849.

> A remarkable amount of scientific information is presented in amazing poems, such as the one that's only three words long (with a twenty-word title!).

Phillips, Louis. *Wackysaurus: Dinosaur Jokes*. Illustrated by Ron Barrett. New York: Viking, 1991. 58p. ISBN 10: 0140386483; ISBN 13: 978-0140386486.

> Pie-in-the-face silliness permeates the pages.

Prelutsky, Jack. *Tyrannosaurus Was a Beast: Dinosaur Poems*. Illustrated by Arnold Lobel. New York: Greenwillow, 1988. 31p. ISBN 10: 0590424912; ISBN 13: 978-0590424912.

> Chuckles and great illustrations make a great combination.

Wise, William. *Dinosaurs Forever*. Illustrated by Lynn Munsinger. New York: Dial Books, 2000. 40p. ISBN 10: 0803721145; ISBN 13: 978-0803721142.

> The author and illustrator team up to present dinosaurs soaking in bubble baths, playing ball, and attending tea parties.

Yolen, Jane. *How Do Dinosaurs Get Well Soon?* Illustrated by Mark Teague. New York: Blue Sky Press, 2003. 32p. ISBN 10: 1579822185; ISBN 13: 978-1579822187.

> Do they pout? Do they throw their tissues about? These pleasant poems and cute pictures will throw some light on the subject.

Published Dinosaur Paper Dolls

Dinosaurs haven't always been featured as paper dolls. This phenomenon probably began with the popularity of dinosaurs among children. The following dinosaur paper dolls are more current.

Barbaresi, Nina. *Fun with Dinosaur Sticker Paper Doll*. Mineola, N.Y.: Dover. 8p. ISBN-10: 0486262243; ISBN-13: 978-0486262246

Brownd, Elizabeth King. *Dinosaur Family Sticker Paper Dolls*. Mineola, N.Y.: Dover. 32 p. ISBN 10: 0486284751; ISBN 13: 978-0486284750.

David the Dinosaur. Dinosaur Pattern for Paper Dolls. http://www.scrappershaven.com/creativersity/dinosaur.htm (accessed March 7, 2008).

Durbin, Lucinda C. "Dino Saurus" and "Dino Saurus Clothes." *Archived Paper Dolls*. 2002. http://www.paperdolls.org/ (accessed March 23, 2009).

Lesson:
Journal Writing for Archaeology News

Library Media Skills Objective:
The student will read and record details.

Curriculum (Subject Areas) Objectives:
This activity may be incorporated into a reading/language arts unit on mystery, or it may be part of a general lesson on journal writing and recording.

Grade Level: 2–4

Resources:

> Dinosaur books
>
> Paper doll handouts
>
> Paper and pencil

Instructional Roles:
The teacher and library media specialist may coordinate this set of lessons. After the library media specialist introduces the many fiction dinosaur books available and models reporting an observation from a book, the teacher may instruct students in writing journals. The set of lessons will take approximately 40 minutes for an introduction and for modeling a journal report. Allow 20 minutes for book selection and reading as a group. The time students require for reading books and writing in the journals on their own will vary. Teacher monitoring of journals during this time will be beneficial. A 20-minute follow-up will bring closure and allow students to write in the journals on other topics.

Activity and Procedures for Completion:
The library media specialist should pull and display dinosaur fiction works before the first session with students. During the introduction, the library media specialist should select one or two books to use as examples. James Gurney's books lend themselves to reading sections aloud. Students can listen to the observations and view the illustrations. Another selection might be a book in which a clothed dinosaur character appears. Share an observation about the book as if standing far off and reporting on what is seen. Describe what might be recorded or reported in a journal entry. Show a sample if you wish.

The teacher explains that students should select a dinosaur book, read it, and then write about it as if they were reporting or recording what they observe. They have a couple of options. They may pretend that they are dinosaur characters and dress themselves as the paper doll to accompany their journal reports. Or, they may locate a book in which the dinosaur character is dressed and use the paper doll of the character and its clothes to accompany the journal writing. Distribute the paper doll sheets.

From *Paper Action Figures of the Imagination: Clip, Color and Create* by Paula K. Montgomery. Santa Barbara, CA: Libraries Unlimited. Copyright © 2009.

The dinosaur paper dolls are fairly simple and can be elaborated on to fit many of the characters found in the easy to read and shorter chapter books.

While students are reading, the teacher may model making observations during read-aloud class time and talk about how one might write or report on what has been read or seen. How can you describe what has been read? What are the characters doing? What do the characters look like? How do they act? As students write in their journals, the teacher may monitor the work and make suggestions. Allow time for students to color and play with the paper dolls they have selected to accompany the journals.

When the students have completed their reading, paper doll dressing, and journal entries, they may share their work. Display entries on a bulletin board entitled "Archaeology News." Put journal excerpts and dolls on the board.

Evaluation:

The student will select a book and write an account, as if a reporter, of what was encountered in the book. The journal entries will vary according to the ability and level of the students. Journal entries may be one or two entries of two or three sentences each or more involved descriptions.

Follow-Up:

Display a section of a newspaper or the journals with the dressed dolls.
Scan images and writings for an online version of "Archaeology News."

Paper Dolls:
Dinosaurs

Instructions: Color each of the dinosaur paper dolls and his or her clothing. Cut them all out and read the books. Make your own clothes for the dolls and write your own story. You can find other dinosaur paper dolls in the sources listed on the following pages.

Which character would you like to be?

From *Paper Action Figures of the Imagination: Clip, Color and Create* by Paula K. Montgomery.
Santa Barbara, CA: Libraries Unlimited. Copyright © 2009.

Edwards, Pamela Duncan. *Dinorella: A Prehistoric Fairytale*. Illustrated by Henry Cole. New York: Hyperion, 1999. 32p.

The Fairydactyl saves the day when the lovely fushcia Dinorella wants to dance with a duke. A feast of fun and words that begin with D!

Being a detective has its ups and downs, especially if you are a dinosaur.

Dress the paper doll and pretend to be a character in a dinosaur detective story. Try these stories:

Skofield, James. *Detective Dinosaur.* Illustrated by R. W. Alley. New York: HarperTrophy, 1996. 48p. ISBN 10: 0060249072; ISBN 13: 978-0060249076.
    Three short stories about a cute but clumsy detective that will make you chuckle. Grades K–2.

Skofield, James. *Detective Dinosaur Lost and Found.* Illustrated by R. W. Alley. New York: HarperCollins, 1998. 48p. ISBN 10: 0060267844; ISBN 13: 978-0060267841.
    With the help of Officer Pterodactyl, cases are solved, but guess who gets lost! Grades K–2.

Goode, Diane. *The Dinosaur's New Clothes: A Retelling of the Hans Christian Andersen Tale.* New York: Blue
Sky Press, 1999. 40 p. ISBN 1: 0590383604; ISBN 13: 978-0590383608.
The T. rex is in his "all-together," but who is going to tell him? Grades K–3.

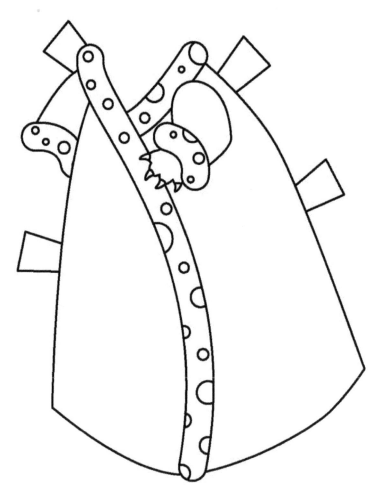

Kastner, Jill. *Dinosaur Princess*. New York: Greenwillow, 2001. 32p. ISBN 10: 0688170455; ISBN 13: 978-0688170455.

When a Dalmation takes the toy dinosaur princess from the playroom and buries it in the backyard, it seems like the end. Grades K–2.

Clement, Rod. *Just Another Ordinary Day.* New York: HarperCollins, 1997. 32p. ISBN 10: 0060276665; ISBN 13: 978-0060276669.

The text suggests an ordinary day for Amanda, but the pictures say otherwise!

Peek into the world of Mama Rex and T. In two of Rachel Vail's books, you will find Mama in her robe.

Vail, Rachel. *The (Almost) Perfect Mother's Day*. Illustrated by Steve Bjorkman. New York: Orchard, 2003. 32p. ISBN-10: 0439407184; ISBN 13: 978-0439407182.
T. Rex planned for a perfect Mother's Day breakfast in bed, but the kitchen is a mess. Grades 1–3.

Vail, Rachel. *Mama Rex and T Stay Up Late*. Illustrated by Steve Bjorkman. New York: Orchard, 2003. 32p. ISBN 10: 0439466822; ISBN 13: 978-0439466820.
Mama must stay up late to work on a project, and T stays up, too. Grades K–2.

Don't miss Mama Rex and T in their other titles: *Lose a Waffle*; *Shop for Shoes*; *Run Out of Tape*; *Turn Off the TV*; *The Horrible Play Date*; *Homework Trouble*; *Halloween Knight*; *The Sort-of-Super Snowman*; *The Prize*; and *The Reading Champion*. Visit Rachel Vail at http://www.rachelvail.com/ (accessed March 23, 2009).

Most, Bernard. *A Trio of Triceratops*. San Diego: Harcourt, 1998. 32p. ISBN 10: 0152014489; ISBN 13: 978-0152014483.

Three triceratops jump, ride tricycles, and have a good time. Bernard Most is an author and illustrator who likes to feature dinosaurs in his work. Visit him at http://www.bernardmost.com/ (accessed March 23, 2009).

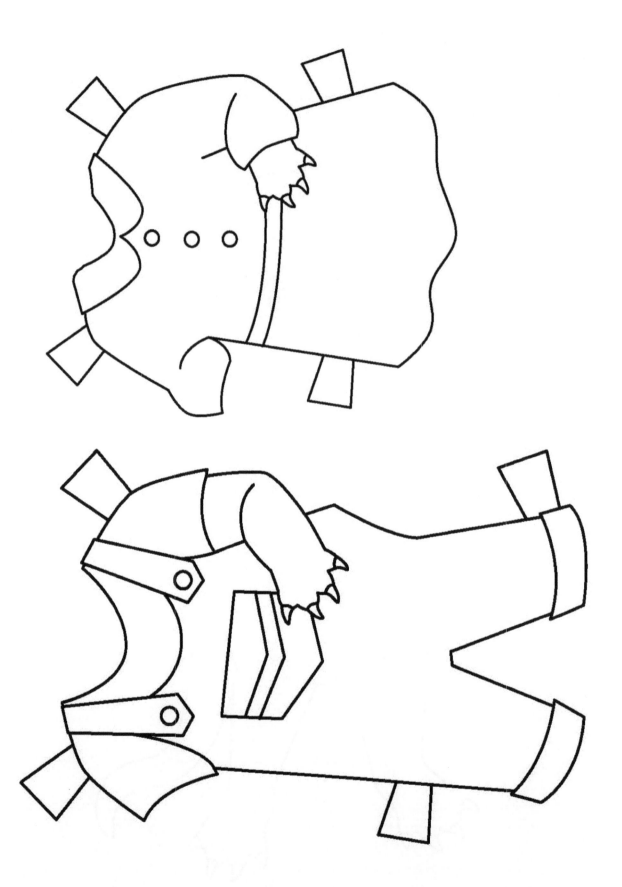

From *Paper Action Figures of the Imagination: Clip, Color and Create* by Paula K. Montgomery.
Santa Barbara, CA: Libraries Unlimited. Copyright © 2009.

Chapter 5

Elephants on Parade

Why did the elephant wear sunglasses?
She didn't want to be noticed!

Because of their huge size, it is difficult not to notice elephants. Elephants are the largest creatures on Earth. A newborn baby elephant weighs about 200 pounds. Depending on whether the elephant is African or Asian, an adult can weigh up to 13,000 pounds!

You have heard the expression, "An elephant never forgets." It is true! An elephant's brain is about four times the size of a human's. The elephant's brain is the largest known brain of any living animal. Believe it or not, elephants will recognize human and animal friends after being separated for years.

Elephants are easy to find in books, too. Many fiction stories have been written about elephant characters. In elephant stories, size and sometimes memory are often important elements of the story.

Here are some famous elephant "tails" to whet the appetite of any young reader. Pack a few into the storytelling trunk!

Base, Graeme. *The Eleventh Hour: A Curious Mystery.* New York: Harry N. Abrams, 1988. 32p. ISBN 10: 0810932652; ISBN 13: 978-0810932654.

> Horace the Elephant planned a clever party in celebration of his eleventh birthday. He invited eleven guests, fixed eleven sorts of food, and set up eleven games for everyone to play. The eleventh hour arrives, and it is time to eat. What has happened to the birthday feast? The food has disappeared! The reader must look for picture clues to figure out which guest stole the feast. Can you solve the mystery of the missing party food? No peeking at the answers!

Brunhoff, Jean de. *The Story of Babar, the Little Elephant.* New York: Random House, 1933. 48p. ISBN 10: 0440841739 (pb.); ISBN 13: 978-9562824576 (pb.).

> Introducing Babar the Elephant. Babar begins his life in a great forest. While still a young elephant, a wicked hunter kills Babar's mother! Scared and alone, Babar runs away to a town. What adventures await Babar in the city? What happens to Babar when two of his cousins find their way to the city, too? Life is a whirlwind of adventures for Babar in this first of many entertaining stories. (Sound and video recordings are available from Random House.)

Kipling, Rudyard. *The Elephant's Child*. Illustrated by Lorinda Bryan Cauley. San Diego: Harcourt Brace Jovanovich, 1983. 46p. ISBN 10: 083351752X; ISBN 13: 978-0833517524.

> Far away in Africa in far-off times lived the Elephant's Child. He was full of 'satiable curiosity and asked lots of questions. However, whenever he asked his relatives questions, they would spank him. One day he asked everyone, "What does the Crocodile have for dinner?" "Hush!" cried everyone and spanked him for a long time. The Elephant's Child, determined to find out the answer to his question, sets out to find the Crocodile. When he finally meets the Crocodile, the Elephant's Child gets a longer answer than he bargained for! (There are other editions and multimedia materials for the Kipling story.)

Noble, Kate. *The Blue Elephant*. Illustrated by Rachel Bass. Chicago: Silver Seashore Press, 1994. 32p. ISBN 10: 0963179837; ISBN 13: 978-0963179838.

> Sassi and Lina are two Indian elephants. They love their zoo home. They adore the children, the food, and the zookeepers. But unlike their old home in Africa, this one has no big muddy pond in which to play. Lina has a secret plan. Will the zookeepers understand Sassi's plea for a water wallow? Lina's plan backfires, and Sassi is locked up in a cage. Has Sassi turned into a wild elephant?

Seuss, Dr. *Horton Hatches the Egg*. New York: Random House, 1940. 64p. ISBN 10: 039480077X; ISBN 13: 978-0394800776.

> Good-for-Nothing Maysie convinces Horton to watch her egg when she flies off to vacation in Palm Springs. Poor Horton waits and waits for her return. He endures teasing, insults, and bad weather. Horton's patience is rewarded with a surprise.

Introducing Elephant Books

In 1874 a rumor circulated that animals had escaped from the New York City Zoo. At the same time, there were worries about a possible third-term presidential run by then Republican President Ulysses S. Grant. It was around this time that the symbol of the elephant was created for the Republican Party. Thomas Nast, a famous illustrator and cartoonist for *The New Yorker* magazine, drew the elephant symbol to represent the Republican Party. Why an elephant? Nast chose to draw Republicans as elephants because they were clever, steadfast, and controlled when calm, yet they were unmanageable when frightened. This bibliography, which may be shared with students, includes books with elephant characters in their many emotional forms.

Long-Trunk Elephant Fiction Chapter Books

"Long-trunk" translates into many pages of good reading. Each book focuses on at least one of the elephant's characteristics.

Campbell, Eric. *Papa Tembo*. San Diego: Harcourt Brace, 1996. 288p. ISBN 10: 0152017275; ISBN 13: 978-0152017279.

> For fifty years the poacher and the elephant have been enemies. The poacher vows revenge after suffering for years with an injured leg caused by an elephant calf running from gunfire. Grades 5–8.

Carrick, Carol. *The Elephant in the Dark*. Illustrated by Donald Carrick. New York: Clarion Books, 1988. 135p. ISBN 10: 0899197574; ISBN 13: 978-0899197579.

     Will's mother dies of consumption, leaving him an orphan in the 1800s in Massachusetts. He is chosen to train a huge elephant and moves to the stables, where his sense of worth is slowly restored by his work with the animal. Grades 3–6.

Croskery, Beverly F. *Shamir, the White Elephant: A Rain Forest Adventure*. Illustrated by Bonny Bregante. Cincinnati, Ohio: Bell-Forsythe Publishing, 1996. 120p. ISBN 10: 0965761940; ISBN 13: 978-0965761949.

     In sixteenth-century India a young elephant longs for his life before he was captured by a Burmese trainer. The white elephant is much valued, and it isn't easy to think of escape or learn to live with the trainer. Grades 3–6.

Cross, Gillian. *The Great American Elephant Chase*. New York: Holiday House, 1992. 193p. ISBN 10: 0823410161; ISBN 13: 978-0823410163.

     In 1981, fifteen-year-old Tad helps a girl take a mighty Indian elephant, Krush, from Pennsylvania to her friends in Nebraska, while being pursued by two villains who want to take the elephant from her. Grades 4–7.

Fleischman, Sid. *The White Elephant*. Illustrated by Robert McGuire. New York: Greenwillow Books, 2006. 95p. ISBN 10: 0061131369; ISBN 13: 978-0061131363.

     Young elephant trainer Run-Run and his old charge, Walking Mountain, anger the prince and are sent a white elephant, Sahib, as punishment. Sahib learns to work and helps Run-Run find his freedom. Grades 3–6.

Hamilton-Merritt, Jane. *Boonmee and the Lucky White Elephant*. Illustrated by Phongsun. New York: Scribner, 1972. 86p. ISBN 10: 0684126842; ISBN 13: 978-0684126845.

     It is the Loy Kathong festival, and a ten-year-old Thai boy is worried about the fate of a white elephant. Grades 2–5.

Kraus, Robert. *The Hoodwinking of Mrs. Elmo*. New York: Delacorte Press, 1987. 109p. ISBN 10: 0385295774; ISBN 13: 978-0385295772.

     Mrs. Elmo is a wealthy elephant who has an evil cousin bent on stealing all she has. Her mice servants soon deal with the cousin. Grades 3–6.

Morris, Judy K. *Nightwalkers*. Illustrated by Angelo. New York: HarperCollins, 1996. 144p. ISBN 10: 0060272007; ISBN 13: 978-0060272005.

     Ten-year-old James becomes attached to Daisy, an orphaned African elephant, and accompanies her on several nighttime searches. Grades 3–6.

Price, Reynolds. *A Perfect Friend*. Illustrated by Maurice Sendak. New York: Atheneum Books for Young Readers, 2000. 176p. ISBN 10: 0689830297; ISBN 13: 978-0689830297.

     When Ben's mother dies, it is Sala, an elephant, who helps him resolve his grief. Grades 4–7.

Pullman, Philip. *The Firework-Maker's Daughter*. New York: Arthur A. Levine Books, 1999. 97p. ISBN-10: 0590187198; ISBN 13: 978-0590187190.

     Lila receives help from Chulak and his talking white elephant, Hamlet, when she goes to the sacred volcano because she wants to be a master maker of fireworks. Grades 2–5.

Seuss, Dr. *Horton Hears a Who*. New York: Random House, 1954. 72p. ISBN 10: 0394800788; ISBN 13: 978-0394800783.

Horton proves his kindhearted nature as he does his best to protect the creatures living on a speck of dust. Grades K–6.

Short-Eared Elephant Picture Books

"Short-eared" translates into short but great picture books. There are "oodles" of short-eared elephant pictures books available. Some are listed here.

Appelt, Kathi. *Elephants Aloft*. Illustrated by Keith Baker. San Diego: Harcourt Brace Jovanovich, 1993. 32p. ISBN 10: 015225384X; ISBN 13: 978-0152253844.

Elephants Raja and Rama pack up their trunks and baggage, crawl into a hot air balloon, and are off across the world to visit their aunt in Rwanda. Grades K–2.

Bates, Ivan. *All By Myself*. New York: HarperCollins, 2000. 32p. ISBN 10: 0060285850; ISBN 13: 978-0060285852.

Every day a mother elephant picks juicy tree leaves for her and her daughter, Maya. Maya soon wants to pick the leaves all by herself. There is just one problem: she is too short! Maya is determined to reach the leaves and comes up with some interesting ideas for reaching those tasty treats. Can Maya accomplish her goal all by herself? Sometimes two heads are better than one! Grades K–2.

Bildner, Phil. *Twenty-one Elephants*. Illustrated by LeUyen Pham. New York: Simon & Schuster Books for Young Readers, 2004. 40p. ISBN 10: 0689870116; ISBN 13: 978-0689870118.

Hannah's father is convinced that the Brooklyn Bridge is safe to cross when twenty-one elephants cross over. Grades 1–4.

Brown, Ken. *Nellie's Knot*. New York: Four Winds Press, 1993. 32p. ISBN: 0027149307 ISBN: 9780027149302.

Nellie tied her trunk in a knot to remember something special, but unfortunately it isn't working. Grades K–1.

de Brunhoff, Jean. *Babar and Father Christmas*. New York: Random House, 1982. 40p. ISBN 10: 0375814442; ISBN 13: 978-0375814440.

Babar wants Father Christmas to come to elephant country. (Sound and video recordings are available.)

de Brunhoff, Jean. *Babar and His Children*. New York: Random House, 1954. 48p. ISBN 10: 0394805771; ISBN 13: 978-0394805771.

Babar and his queen await the birth of their first child, only to be surprised with three children. (A sound recording is available.) Grades K–3.

de Brunhoff, Jean. *Babar the King*. New York: Random House, 1986. 48p. ISBN 10: 0394882458; ISBN 13: 978-0394882451.

Babar is crowned king and builds a city called Celesteville. (Video is available.) Grades 1–4.

de Brunhoff, Jean. *The Travels of Babar*. New York: Random House, 1937. 56p. ISBN 10: 0394805763; ISBN 13: 978-0394805764.

Babar and Celeste are married and depart for their honeymoon in a hot air balloon, which crashes in the sea. (Babar and Celeste bendable dolls are available as well as a video.) Grades 1–4.

de Brunhoff, Laurent. *Babar á New York*. Paris: Hachette Jeunesse, 1965. 28p. ISBN 10: 2010025520; ISBN 13: 978-2010025525.
> Babar travels to New York and takes in the sights, with his usual adventures. Grades K–3.

de Brunhoff, Laurent. *Babar and the Ghost*. New York: Random House, 1986. 48p. ISBN 10: 0810943980; ISBN 13: 978-0810943988.
> When Babar returns to Celesteville, he finds that the ghost of Black Castle has followed him. Grades K–2.

de Brunhoff, Laurent. *Babar and the Succotash Bird*. New York: Harry N. Abrams, 2000. 32p. ISBN 0810957000.
> In the evening, when he can't sleep, Babar's son Alexander meets a wizard disguised as a succotach bird. When he meets the bird the next day, things turn ugly. Grades K–4.

de Brunhoff, Laurent. *Babar and the Wully Wully*. New York: Random House, 1975. 40p. ISBN 0810943972.
> Pom, Flora, and Alexander discover a strange new being, a wully wully. Grades K–3.

de Brunhoff, Laurent. *Babar Goes to School*. New York: Harry N. Abrams, 2003. 32p. ISBN 10: 0810945827; ISBN 13: 978-0810945821.
> Babar spends the day at school with his children and realizes how much work it is. Grades K–2.

de Brunhoff, Laurent. *Babar Loses His Crown*. New York: Harry N. Abrams, 2004. 32p. ISBN 10: 0810950340; ISBN 13: 978-0810950344.
> Babar's luggage gets mixed up with that of another passenger, and he loses his crown. Grades K–2.

de Brunhoff, Laurent. *Babar Visits Another Planet*. New York: Harry N. Abrams, 2003. 40p. ISBN 10: 0810942445; ISBN 13: 978-0810942448.
> Babar and his family are abducted by aliens and must find a way back to Celesteville. Grades 1–4.

de Brunhoff, Laurent. *Babar's Little Girl*. New York: Harry N. Abrams, 2001. 38p. ISBN 10: 0810957035; ISBN 13: 978-0810957039.
> Isabelle is the new addition to King Babar and Queen Celeste's family. Grades K–3.

de Brunhoff, Laurent. *Babar's Little Girl Makes a Friend*. New York: Harry N. Abrams, 2002. 30p. ISBN 10: 0810905566; ISBN 13: 978-0810905566.
> Isabelle and Vic, a rhino, show that they can be friends even in frightening adventures. Grades K–3.

de Brunhoff, Laurent. *Babar's Mystery*. New York: Alfred A. Knopf, 1978. 32p. ISBN 10: 0810950332; ISBN 13: 978-0810950337.
> Babar and his family are on vacation when a piano goes missing, Babar's car disappears, and a statue isn't in the right place. Babar becomes a detective. Grades K–3.

There are many other Babar stories, written by Jean's son Laurent and later by other writers. See *Babar Saves the Day; Babar's ABC; Babar's Battle; Babar's Birthday Surprise; Babar's Book of Color; Babar's Bookmobile; Babar's Busy Year; Babar's Counting Book; Babar's Cousin; Babar's French Lesson; Babar's Little Circus Star; Babar's Rescue; Babar's Museum of Art; Babar's World Tour; Isabelle's New Friend;* and *Meet Babar and His Family.*

Burns, Diane L. *Elephants Never Forget!* Minneapolis, Minn.: Lerner Publications, 1987. 32p. ISBN 10: 082250992X; ISBN 13: 978-0822509929.

> A collection of elephant jokes appeals to the silliness in everyone. Grades K–2.

D'Amico, Carmela, and Steve D'Amico. *Ella Takes the Cake.* New York: Arthur A. Levine Books/ Scholastic, 2005. 48p. ISBN 10: 043962794X; ISBN 13: 978-0439627948.

> Ella wants to help her mother in the bakery, but the job given to her is delivering a cake. (Ella has other adventures in *Ella the Elephant* and *Ella Sets the Stage*.) Grades K–1.

Day, Alexandra. *Frank and Ernest.* New York: Scholastic Inc. 1988. 32p. ISBN 10: 0590415573; ISBN 13: 978-0590415576.

> Bear Frank and Elephant Ernest run businesses while the owners are away and agree to take care of a diner for three days. Grades K–3.

Day, Alexandra. *Frank and Ernest on the Road.* New York: Scholastic Inc. 1994. 32p. ISBN 10: 0590450484; ISBN 13: 978-0590450485.

> Frank and Ernest take over a truck driver's business in this episode. Grades K–2.

Day, Alexandra. *Frank and Ernest Play Ball.* New York: Scholastic Inc., 1990. 32p. ISBN 10: 0590425498; ISBN 13: 978-0590425490.

> Frank and Ernest take over the management of a baseball team, but they don't know the language. Grades K–2.

Delacre, Lulu. *Nathan & Nicholas Alexander.* New York: Scholastic Inc., 1986. 32p. ISBN 10: 0590415735; ISBN 13: 978-0590415736.

> Elephant Nathan finds that a mouse has moved into his toy chest. Grades K–2.

Geraghty, Paul. *The Hunter.* New York: Crown, 1994. 32p. ISBN 10: 0517596938; ISBN 13: 978-0517596937.

> A young girl who wants to be a hunter wanders into the bush and finds a baby elephant whose mother has been killed by a hunter. Grades 1–4.

Giannini, Enzo. *Zorina Ballerina.* New York: Simon & Schuster Books, 1992. 32p. ISBN 10: 0671747762; ISBN 13: 978-0671747763.

> Zorina is the smallest elephant and wants to perform, but is told she is too young. The story is based on an actual event in 1942, in which George Balanchine choreographed "The Circus Polka" for Ringling Brothers Circus using Igor Stravinsky's music. Grades K–4.

Goodman, Joan E. *Bernard's Nap.* Illustrated by Dominic Catalano. Honesdale, Pa.: Boyds Mills Press, 1999. 32p. ISBN 10: 1563977281; ISBN 13: 978-1563977282.

> Bernard refuses to take a nap, and family members try various things, from reading him a story to singing lullabies. They succeed in putting themselves to sleep. Grades K–2.

Maestro, Betsy, and Giulio Maestro. *Around the Clock with Harriet: A Book about Telling Time.* New York: Crown, 1984. 32p. ISBN 10: 0517551187; ISBN 13: 978-0517551189.

> Harriet the elephant shows her activities from hour to hour. (Other Harriet concept books are *Dollars and Cents for Harriet: A Money Concept Book; Harriet Goes to the Circus; Harriet Reads Signs and More Signs* and *Through the Year with Harriet: A Time Concept Book*.) Grades K–1.

McKee, David. *Elmer*. New York: HarperCollins, 1989. 32p. ISBN 10: 0688091717; ISBN 13: 978-0688091712.

Elmer is a patchwork of color elephant who tries to hide among the herd. (Other books about Elmer are *Elmer Again*; *Elmer and the Kangaroo*; *Elmer and the Lost Teddy*; *Elmer and Wilbur*; *Elmer in the Snow*; *Elmer Takes Off*; *Elmer's Weather*; and *Hide-and-Seek Elmer*.) Grades K–1.

McNulty, Faith. *The Elephant Who Couldn't Forget*. Illustrated by Marc Simont. New York: Harper & Row, 1980. 62p. ISBN 10: 0060241454; ISBN 13: 978-0060241452.

This elephant learns that holding a grudge is different from having a good memory. Grades 1–3.

Paxton, Tom. *Engelbert the Elephant*. Illustrated by Steven Kellogg. New York: William Morrow, 1990. 32p. ISBN 10: 0688089356; ISBN 13: 978-0688089351.

Engelbert is invited to a ball and surprises everyone with his dexterity and dancing ability. Grades K–3.

Paxton, Tom. *Engelbert Joins the Circus*. Illustrated by Roberta Wilson. William Morrow, 1997. 32p. ISBN-10: 0688099874; ISBN 13: 978-0688099879.

Engelbert come to American to visit his cousin and ends up as the main attraction in a circus. Grades K–2.

Pearce, Philippa. *Emily's Own Elephant*. Illustrated by John Lawrence. New York: Greenwillow Books, 1987. 32p. ISBN 10: 0688076785; ISBN 13: 978-0688076788.

A zoo can no longer care for Jumbo, so Emily and her family find a place for him. Grades K–2.

Peet, Bill. *Ella*. Boston: Houghton Mifflin, 1978. 32p. ISBN 10: 0808526464; ISBN 13: 978-0808526469.

Ella is very sorry after she runs away from the circus. Grades K–2.

Peet, Bill. *Encore for Eleanor*. Boston: Houghton Mifflin, 1981. 32p. ISBN 10: 0808535749; ISBN 13: 978-0808535744.

Eleanor is retired from the circus ad learns she has a new career at the zoo. Grades K–3.

Prince, April Jones. *Twenty-one Elephants and Still Standing*. Illustrated by François Roca. Boston: Houghton Mifflin, 2005. 32p. ISBN 10: 061844887X; ISBN 13: 978-0618448876.

P. T. Barnum is a mastermind; he think of taking twenty-one elephants across the new Brooklyn Bridge to show its strength. Grades 1–5.

Sadler, Marilyn. *Alistair's Elephant*. Illustrated by Rober Bollen. New York: Simon & Schuster, 1983. 32p. ISBN 10: 0130227560; ISBN 13: 978-0130227560.

It is a great day for Alistair when an elephant follows him home. Grades K–1.

Steig, William. *Doctor De Soto Goes to Africa*. New York: HarperCollins, 1992. 32p. ISBN 10: 0062059017; ISBN 13: 978-0062059017.

Doctor De Soto, a world-renowned dentist, receives an unusual cablegram from West Africa. He has been asked to visit an elephant named Mudambo, who suffers from a terrible toothache. Soon after Doctor De Soto and his wife arrive in Africa, Doctor De Soto is kidnapped by an evil monkey! (It isn't hard to kidnap a famous dentist when he is a mouse!) Will poor Mudambo get his painful tooth fixed without the doctor's help? Grades K–4.

Tompert, Ann. *Just a Little Bit*. Illustrated by Lynn M. Munsinger. Boston: Houghton Mifflin, 1993. 32p. ISBN 10: 039577876X; ISBN 13: 978-0395778760.
> Mouse needs more help than Elephant in getting down from the swing. Grades K–1.

Weinberg, Larry. *The Forgetful Bears Meet Mr. Memory*. New York: Scholastic Inc., 1987. 32p. ISBN 10: 0590407813; ISBN 13: 978-0590407816.
> The Forgetful Bear family has problems, until they meet Mr. Memory, a wise elephant. Grades K–2.

Willems, Mo. *My Friend Is Sad; Today I Will Fly!* New York: Hyperion Books for Children, 2007. 57p. ISBN 10: 1423102959; ISBN 13: 978-1423102953.
> Elephant is skeptical that Piggie can fly.

Elephant Films

Children may watch these big, lovable creatures on film.

Babar and Father Christmas. Hi-Tops Video, 1987. 30 min.
> King Babar takes a journey in search of the legendary Father Christmas. But lurking along Babar's trail is Babar's archenemy, Rataxes the Rhinoceros, who wants all of Santa's toys for himself.

Dumbo. Walt Disney Home Video, 1941. 63 min.
> A baby elephant with oversized ears is ridiculed by all the circus animals and is finally befriended by a mouse. Dumbo becomes the world's only flying elephant.

Horton Hatches the Egg; If I Ran the Circus. Random House Home Video, 1992. 30 min.
> Horton the Elephant endures terrible snowstorms, jeering friends, and frightening hunters while egg sitting for Mayzie the lazy bird.

Horton Hears a Who! Random House Home Video, 1992. 30 min.
> Horton the Elephant must prove that his miniature friends the Whos exist. He attempts to rescue the tiny inhabitants, who live on a small speck of dust. (A movie starring Jim Carey was in theaters in 2008.)

Poky and Friends. Sony Wonder, 1999. 30 min.
> Saggy Baggy Elephant recognizes that each and every one of us is special, including little elephants and all their ele-friends!

Uncle Elephant. Golden Book Video, 1991. 30 min.
> Uncle Elephant comes to the rescue when his nephew's parents are lost at sea, then cares for them until the parents are found again.

Elephant-Sized Web Sites!

Elephanteria—http://www.himandus.net/elephanteria/ (accessed March 23, 2009).
> This fun-filled elephant site has tons of elephantine delights! The site also has lots of links to other elephant sites.

The Elephant's Child, Free Audio Story—http://storynory.com/2006/01/24/the-elephants-child/ (accessed March 23, 2009).

Just So Stories, Rudyard Kipling—http://www.boop.org/jan/justso/ (accessed March 23, 2009).

Just So Stories, by Rudyard Kipling—http://www.gutenberg.org/etext/2781 (accessed March 23, 2009). Read the stories as published in 1902.

Just So Stories, Free Audio Download—http://www.freeclassicaudiobooks.com/audiobooks/JustSo/mp3/ (accessed March 23, 2009).

Thurston the Smallest Elephant—http://eugelon.com/ (accessed March 23, 2009).

Published Elephant Paper Dolls

There are few examples of paper dolls from bygone times that feature elephants, but those that do, focus on the circus. In the very early 1900s, George W. Jacobs and Sons published *Tommy Goes to the Circus* as a single-sheet paper cut out. A cut-out book called *Circus Day*, published in 1946, included an elephant. Whitehall Publishing produced a pop-up paper doll book with foldout pages of clothes in 1950, *Jumbo and Bunny*, which featured an elephant and a rabbit.

In 1945 the comic book figure Katy Keene, created by Bill Woggin, appeared. Readers soon had paper dolls to cut out. Katy was relaunched in 1983 by John Lucas and Dan DeCarlo. Lucas created many fashion dolls, but also introduced a lively elephant in *Tooter's Trunkful of Togs* (http://the-jazzman. com/elephants/tooter.htm; accessed March 23, 2009). *Alfie*, from Samuel Lowe Publishing, appeared in 1956.

More recently, Judy Johnson's *Elephant Pinafore Paper Dolls* (Dover Press, 1992. 8p. ISBN 10: 0486264335; ISBN 13: 978-0486264332) allows the young elephant to come into her own. She is described as "petite." Perhaps the description comes from the fashionable outfits, including a ballet dress, a gardening ensemble, a nightgown, school slacks and a sweater, and a sunsuit.

Lesson Plan:
Elephants on Parade Game

Library Media Skills Objective:

The student will read for detail.

Curriculum (Subject Areas) Objectives:

This activity may be incorporated into a reading/language arts unit.

Grade Level: 1–4

Resources:

Selected chapter or picture elephant books

Paper slips for writing questions

Paper doll handouts

Crayons and scissors

Markers

Construction paper to make game board

Adhesive putty removable and reusable tape (Scotch)

One die or spinner

Instructional Roles:

The library media specialist or teacher may engage children in this lesson and activity. Book selection, booktalking, and introduction to the activity may take 45 minutes. Student reading time and composing of questions on their own will take an hour or more. Paper dolls will take about 30 minutes to cut out and decorate or to add other outfits on selected characters. The time needed depends on the book selected and the number of questions required. Monitoring of questions and review will take 30 minutes. The game may be played in an hour.

Activity and Procedures for Completion:

Begin with an introduction to elephants with pictures or nonfiction materials. Discuss elephants as we know them. What are their characteristics? What have animal behaviorists learned about them?

Share information about a number of elephant fiction and picture books. Display these and provide a book list or review the best way to find such materials in the library media center.

Challenge students to an elephant parade game. In this game, students will be grouped with several others who agree to read the same books (three or four books per group). Students will read the books and select one detail for a question on each book. Discuss how details might be selected. They could be things about the costume or character that help bring the character to life or make the plot move ahead. Students will dress a paper doll to serve as their game piece, which they will move on a parade board. There will be two ways to win the game. The first is to finish the parade first. The second is to have the best-dressed character matching a particular book, preferably one of the books being read for the game.

Students will select the books and agree to play with other players. Provide students with paper doll sheets to color and cut out. Students should review their questions and answers with the library media specialist. They may also agree to share their questions with other players before the game. Discuss possible answers and explain that students must be ready to support their answers when the questions are reviewed. They may keep notes on the page number of the answer if they so desire.

To make the game board, use 30 colored paper sheets. Line them up in a hallway or room on the floor. Place the colored construction paper sheets end to end so that they form one long parade route. Use adhesive putty such as Scotch brand to hold the paper in place. Add variety to the parade game by making one or two sheets that have the player "lose turn," "stop," or "gain a space." (For example, "Wheel on float broke; lose one turn." "Elephant got tired and needs a rest; lose one turn." "Elephant saw melons and sped ahead; move ahead one space." "Change clothes of paper doll; lose one turn.") Be creative. Label the rest of the construction paper sheets with one book title each.

Students should color and cut out the elephant character paper dolls. Provide small cards or paper slips on which students may write their questions. They will need about seven to ten questions for each of the three or four books they have agreed to read. For each question, make one card with the question and a second card with the question and the answer. (Or keep a master answer sheet.)

Each player puts his or her elephant paper doll at the beginning of the parade set. Players roll the die. The player rolling the lowest number goes first, rolling the die again. The player moves forward the number of spaces indicated on the die. The title on the space where a player's marker lands determines which question will be read to the player.

Questions are to be read aloud by someone who is not playing. Each player has 30 seconds to answer the question after it is read. If a player answers correctly, his or her paper doll remains on the spot where he or she landed, and the turn passes to the next player. If the player does not answer a question correctly, the player must return to the previous spot where his or her paper doll was. Play passes to the next player. If the 30-second period expires, play automatically passes to the next player.

Play continues until the first player reaches or crosses the finish line and correctly answers the winning question. The winning question can be read from an elephant character card of the player's choice.

After the game is done, nonplayers may judge the paper dolls and vote on the best dressed of the parade.

Evaluation:

Each student will complete at least one detail question and answer for three or four book questions in order to play the elephant parade game. The quality of the questions and answers will be determined by the library media specialist and will be discussed with the student.

Follow-Up:

Set up a display of paper dolls appearing in the parade, naming the books the dressed up characters were taken from.

Paper Dolls:
Elephants

Instructions: Color these figures and the clothes on the next page. When they are dressed in these outfits, the elephant paper dolls can become Babar characters or others from many other elephant reading choices. Select a book and dress the elephant as a character from that book.

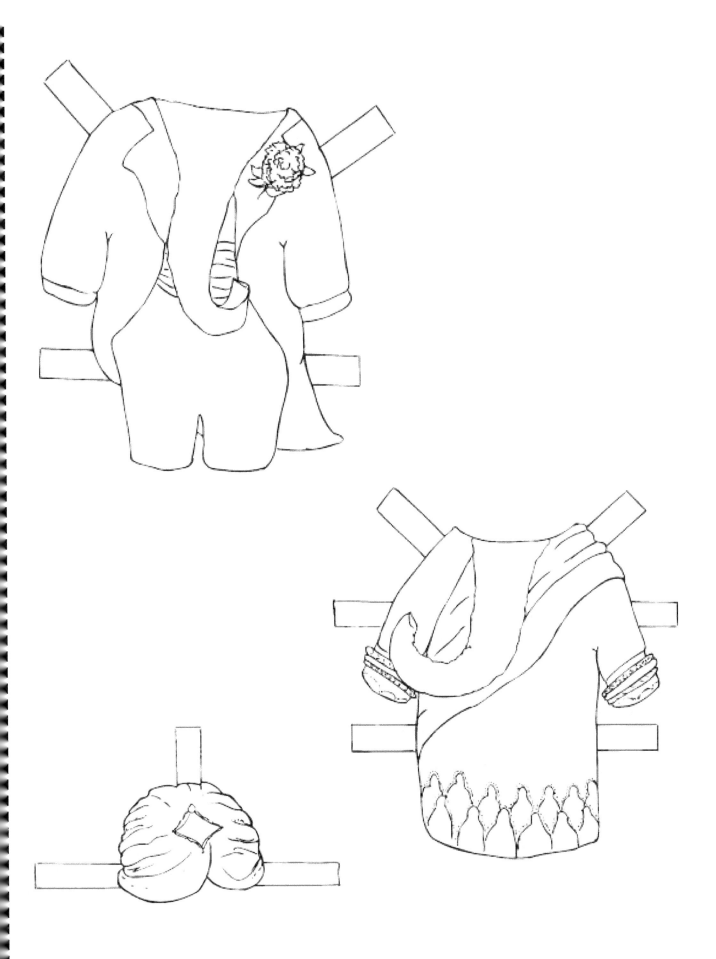

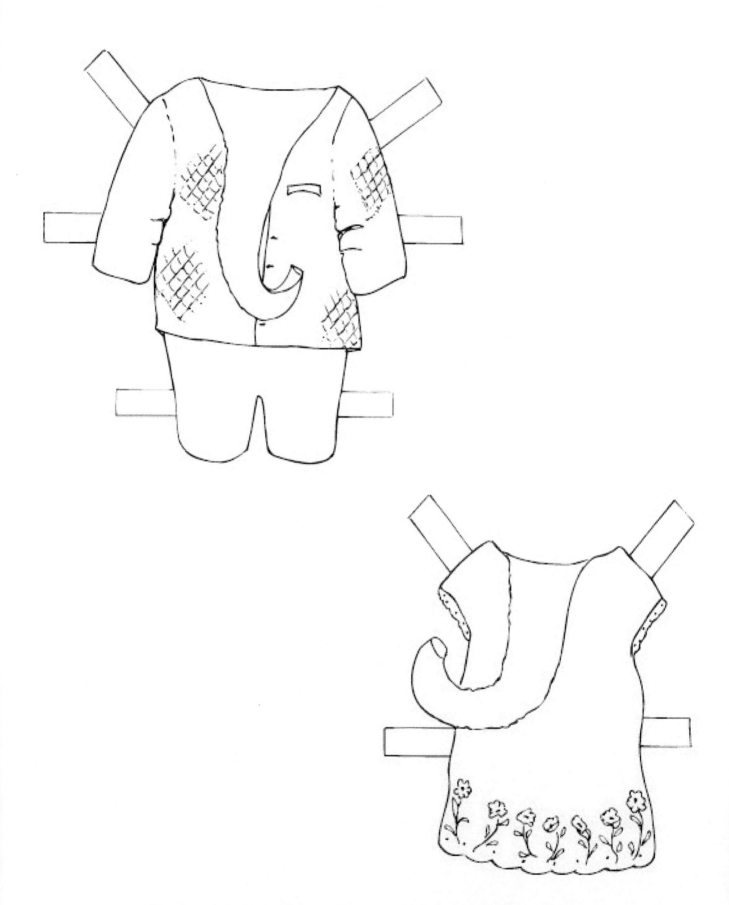

From *Paper Action Figures of the Imagination: Clip, Color and Create* by Paula K. Montgomery.
Santa Barbara, CA: Libraries Unlimited. Copyright © 2009.

Chapter 6

Kiss a Frog? Frogs in Fiction and Folklore

Have you ever kissed a frog? If you have, were you hoping for a prince? This is the theme in "The Frog Prince." Versions of this story or fairy tale are found in many countries, but the original tale, as we know it, was recorded by the German Grimm brothers. In this version, a prince is turned into a frog by a spell. In order for the frog prince to be turned back into a prince, he must be kissed by a beautiful princess. One day a beautiful princess is near a well when her golden ball falls in. The frog returns her golden ball on the condition that she will take him home with her. He returns the ball, but she fails to uphold her part of the bargain. Her father makes her take the frog in and treat him the way she promised. Her father also makes her kiss the frog. Guess what happens!

This story has appeal at many levels. Trickery, justice, redemption, and hope for love are all found in a few short paragraphs. Many authors and illustrators have retold the Grimms' tale. Each has his or her take on the characters and events. Because there are so many versions, it is easy for adults and children to read several and then pick a favorite. Collections of Grimms' fairy tales will usually include this story. Compare these selected illustrated versions of the tale for variety and style.

Blair, Eric. *The Frog Prince: A Retelling of the Grimms' Fairy Tale.* Illustrated by Todd Ouren. Minneapolis, Minn.: Picture Window Books, 2004. 32p. ISBN 10: 1404803130; ISBN 13: 978-1404803138.

Galdone, Paul. *The Frog Prince.* New York: McGraw-Hill, 1975. 32p. ISBN 10: 0070226881; ISBN 13: 978-0070226883.

Isadora, Rachel. *The Princess and the Frog; Adapted from the Frog King and Iron Heinrich by the Brothers Grimm.* New York: Greenwillow Books, 1989. 32p. ISBN 10: 068806373X; ISBN 13: 978-0688063733.

Kincaid, Lucy. *The Frog Prince.* Illustrated by Eric Kincaid. Windermere, Fla.: Rourke Corp., 1983. 24p. ISBN 10: 0865921865; ISBN 13: 978-0865921863.

Lewis, Naomi. *The Frog Prince, or Iron Henry.* Illustrated by Binette Schroeder. New York: North-South, 1998. 26p. ISBN 10: 1558580158; ISBN 13: 978-1558580152.

McKay, Sindy. *The Frog Prince.* Illustrated by George Ulrich. Redwood City, Calif.: Treasure Bay, 1997. 32p. ISBN 10: 189132702X; ISBN 13: 978-1891327025.

Ormerod, Jan. *The Frog Prince.* New York: Lee & Shepard Books, 1990. 26p. ISBN 10: 0688095682; ISBN 13: 978-0688095680.

Tarcov, Edith H. *The Frog Prince.* Illustrated by James Marshall. New York: Scholastic, 1987. 32p. ISBN 10: 0785711457; ISBN 13: 978-0785711452.

   A kit is available from Lakeshore Learning Materials (1994), which includes this book, a frog finger puppet, a princess doll, a golden ball, a well, a ring, and a pillow.

Trussell-Cullen, Alan. *The Frog Prince.* Illustrated by David Preston Smith. Carlsbad, Calif.: Dominie Press, 2000. 16p. ISBN 10: 0768504139; ISBN 13: 978-0768504132.

Wang, Mary Lewis. *The Frog Prince.* Illustrated by Gwen Connelly. New York: Children's Press, 1986. 32p. ISBN 10: 0516439839; ISBN 13: 978-0516439839.

Wargin, Kathy-Jo. *The Frog Prince.* Illustrated by Anne Young. Ann Arbor, Mich.: Ann Arbor Media Group, 2007. 32p. ISBN 10: 1587262797; ISBN 13: 978-1587262791.

Read It on the Internet . . .

   Copies of the story are easily shared using these versions on the Internet. Pulling the text from such versions can be useful for printing and editing a group or choral reading for students. (All sites accessed on March 23, 2009.)

   The Annotated Frog King—http://www.surlalunefairytales.com/frogking/index.html

   BBC—Cbeeies Stories and Rhymes—http://www.bbc.co.uk/cbeebies/stories/colour/frogprince.shtml

   The Frog King—http://www.fln.vcu.edu/grimm/frog.html

   Frog Kings—http://www.pitt.edu/~dash/frog.html

   Frog Prince—http://www.frogprince.ca/

   The Frog Prince—http://childhoodreading.com/Edmund_Dulac_and_Gus/Magic_Jewel.html

   The Frog Prince—http://www.frogsonice.com/froggy/tales/frogprince1.shtml, http://www.frogsonice.com/froggy/tales/frogprince2.shtml

   The Frog Prince—http://www.gwu.edu/~folktale/GERM232/frogp/FP_Main_Page.html

   The Frog Prince—http://www.yesicankids.gov/bedtime/princess.html

   Frog Prince by Jacob and Wilhelm Grimm—http://www.4literature.net/Jacob_and_Wilhelm_Grimm/Frog_Prince/

   The Frog Prince, Free Audio Stories for Kids, Storynory—http://storynory.com/2007/06/16/the-frog-prince/

   The Frog Prince and Other Stories by Anonymous—http://www.gutenberg.org/etext/20437

   Froggie Tales from Around the World—http://www.captainfrog.com/FT/index.html

   Short Stories—The Frog Prince by the Brothers Grimm—http://www.eastoftheweb.com/short-stories/UBooks/FrogPrin.shtml

Listen to the Story . . .

Listening to others read or tell a story helps in making one's own interpretation. Many books have accompanying audio recordings; these recordings are not part of book kits.

The Frog Prince. Read by Julie Harris. New Rochelle, N.Y.: Spoken Arts, 1987. 8½ min.

The Frog Prince. Confetti Entertainment, 1992. 13 min.

Watch the Movie . . .

Faerie Tale Theatre: The Tale of the Frog Prince. Playhouse Video, 1982. 55 min.

The Frog Prince. Encyclopaedia Britannica, 1982. 7 min.

The Frog Prince. Hi-Tops Video, 1989. 30 min.

The Frog Prince. Random House Home Video, 1995. 25 min. (closed captioned).

Or, Play with the Toy

Toys and puppets are also available from companies such as Caltoy, Inc., Fiesta Crafts, Imaginarium, and others.

Frog Prince Glove Puppet. Alex Toys.

Frog Prince Book and Puppet Theater. Straight Edge Press, 2004.

All Frog Princes Are Not the Same

Many authors enjoy writing different versions of this story. They write fiction based on folklore. What if the prince was lying? Sometimes the frog in the story is symbolic only. This allows children to explore other possibilities and delve into the deeper meanings or themes of folk stories.

Adler, C. S. *Willie, the Frog Prince.* New York: Clarion Books, 1994. 176p. ISBN 10: 039565615X; ISBN 13: 978-0395656150.

>Willie has many shortcomings, as pointed out almost constantly by his father. However, Willie manages to convince and a young neighbor, Marla, to be his friend, even if it is only for a short time. Grades 4–6.

Bear, John B. *The Frog and the Princess and the Prince and the Mole and the Frog and the Mole and the Princess and the Prince.* Illustrated by Charlie Powell. Berkeley, Calif.: Tricycle Press, 1994. 32p. ISBN 10: 1883672074; ISBN 13: 978-1883672072.

>In this version, the frog is kissed and turned back into a prince, but the princess is turned into a mole, and on and on. Grades K–3.

Berenzy, Alix. *A Frog Prince.* New York: Henry Holt, 1989. 32p. ISBN 10: 0805004262; ISBN 13: 978-0805004267.

>The frog is spurned and sets out on his own quest to find a better princess. Grades K–3.

Bos, Burny. *Prince Valentino.* Illustrated by Hans de Beer. New York: North-South Books, 1990. 26p. ISBN 10: 1558580891; ISBN 13: 978-1558580893.

> Because his mother calls him her "little prince," a frog thinks that he is one. He sets off to find a princess. Grades K–2.

Davidson, Susanna. *The Frog Prince.* Illustrated by Mike Gordon. London: Usborne Publishing, 2005. 48p. ISBN 10: 0794519172; ISBN 13: 978-0794519179.

> The princess is furious at being made to keep her promise and becomes violent. Grades 1–4.

Griffith, Helen V. *Emily and the Enchanted Frog.* Illustrated by Susan Condie Lamb. New York: Greenwillow Books, 1989. 32p. ISBN 10: 0688084834; ISBN 13: 978-0688084837.

> Emily kisses a frog that turns into a prince. But he doesn't want to be a prince, he liked being a frog. Fun!

Gwynne, Fred. *Pondlarker.* New York: Simon & Schuster Books for Young Readers, 1990. 32 p. ISBN 10: 0671708465; ISBN 13: 978-0671708467.

> Pondlarker wants to be a prince, until he meets a princess, who is about to kiss him, and realizes he likes being a frog. Grades 1–4.

Horwitz, Elinor Lander. *The Strange Story of the Frog who Became a Prince.* Illustrated by John Heinly. New York: Delacorte Press, 1971. 32p. ISBN 10: 0440084199; ISBN 13: 978-0440084198.

> A frog would rather be happy in the pond than be a prince. Grades K–3.

Lamm, C. Drew. *The Prog Prince, a Mixed-up Tale.* Illustrated by Barbara McClintock. New York: Orchard Books, 1999. 32p. ISBN 10: 0531301354; ISBN 13: 978-053130135.

> Jane goes off to market to get a muffin and finds a frog wearing a dime for a hat. Grades 1–3.

Napoli, Donna Jo. *Gracie, the Pixie of the Puddle.* Illustrated by Judy Schachner. New York: Dutton Juvenile, 2004. 160p. ISBN 10: 0525472649; ISBN 13: 978-0525472643.

> In the third book of the series, Gracie is enamored with Jimmy, who claims to have a human prince as a father, and she goes off to rescue him when he is taken to the palace. Grades 3–6.

Napoli, Donna Jo. *Jimmy: The Pickpocket of the Palace.* Illustrated by Judy Byron Schachner. New York: Dutton's Children's Books, 1995. 166p. ISBN 10: 0613825144; ISBN 13: 978-0613825146.

> Jimmy, the froglet son of the frog prince, must journey to the castle to save his pond from the evil hag. He finds himself turned into a human boy. A sequel to *The Prince of the Pond.* Grades 3–6.

Napoli, Donna Jo. *The Prince of the Pond: Otherwise Known as De Fawg Pin.* Illustrated by Judy Schachner. New York: Dutton's Children's Books, 1992. 151p. ISBN 10: 0525449760; ISBN 13: 978-0525449768.

> A small female frog helps a prince who is turned into a frog learn to survive and even have a frog family. Grades 3–6.

Schumacher, Claire. *Brave Lily.* New York: Morrow, 1985. 32p. ISBN 10: 0688049621; ISBN 13: 978-0688049621.

> Freddy wants to be kissed and become a prince; instead he is taken home by a little boy who thinks he is sick. His sister, Lilly, saves him. Grades K–3.

Scieszka, Jon. *The Frog Prince, Continued*. Illustrated by Steve Johnson. New York: Viking, 1991. 32p. ISBN 10: 0670834211; ISBN 13: 978-0670834211.

> The frog turns back into a prince, but he and the princess have some difficulties living happily ever after. (A sound recording is available from Live Oak Media.) Grades 1–4.

Zoom: A Mixed-Up Fairy Tale—http://pbskids.org/zoom/activities/playhouse/amixedupfairytale.html (accessed March 23, 2009).

Watch These Versions

The Frog Prince finds his way into modern television, whether in the Capital One and Cheerios commercials or in references to him in *Shrek 2*, when it is learned that King Harold was the Frog Prince! Show versions of the story so students have the same experience with the story.

Frog. BWE Video, 1987. 60 minutes.

> Arlo, who loves all reptiles, finds Gus, a frog who talks. Follow Arlo and Gus on a humorous journey to find a beautiful woman to change Gus into a prince.

The Frog Prince. Henson Associates, 1994. 54 min.

> The Muppets, including Kermit's nephew, Robin, tell a slightly different version.

Frogs. Public Media Video, 1991. 116 min.

> This movie is a sequel to *Frog*. Gus, now a lounge singer instead of a frog prince, returns to ask Gus for help in battling a wicked witch.

The Tale of the Frog Prince. Platypus Productions, 1982. 55 min.

> Frog says he needs a kiss from a princess to become human again.

Other Frog Characters

The Prince isn't the only fascinating "frig," as Miss Piggy would call Kermit. Frogs' amazing jumping ability and long, sticky tongues make them fun to watch. Their eyesight and hearing are well developed. They are sensitive, as evidenced by the loss of frogs worldwide in recent years because of habitat loss, climate change, and pollution. The night is not the same in many places without the resounding "ribbits," surpassing in magnitude what one might think possible for such small creatures. The sound gives meaning to laryngitis sufferers' horse words, "I have a frog in my throat." Frogs begin life in water among thousands of egg "brothers and sisters" and develop from tadpoles to full grown amphibians. Their ability to hibernate and the metamorphosis that occurs in their life cycle add to the variety from which fiction writers may draw ideas.

Children have learned to read using the *Frog and Toad* series by author and illustrator Arnold Lobel (1933–1987). These books were among the first chapter books written for beginning readers. Frog and Toad have complex adventures and relationships. Toad needs the support of Frog, and he gets it. Each adventure defines what friendship can be.

Days with Frog and Toad. New York: Harper & Row, 1979. 64p.

> Frog and Toad enjoy spending their days together, but realize that they enjoy spending some time alone as well.

Frog and Toad All Year. New York: Harper & Row, 1976. 64p.

Frog and Toad share adventures throughout the seasons of the year.

Frog and Toad Are Friends. New York: Harper & Row, 1970. 64p.

Five stories about Frog and Toad and their friendship. (Caldecott Honor Book, 1971.) This is available as a videocassette from SVE & Churchill Media (1985, 17 min.), narrated by Lobel.

Frog and Toad Together. New York: Harper & Row, 1972. 64p.

More adventures with Frog and Toad. (Newbery Honor Book, 1973.) It is available as a videocassette from Golden Book Video (1987, 30 min.). *Frog and Toad Together* plush toys are available from Crocodile Creek.

John M. Langstaff (1920–2005) achieved fame as a concert baritone, influential music educator, author, and cultural activist. His work with children included the BBC TV show for children, *Making Music, and Children Explore Books,* shown on NBC, and in 1955 he was head of music education at the Potomac School, Virginia, and Shady Hill School, Cambridge. Of his twenty-five books, probably the most well known is the Caldecott Award–winning *Frog Went a-Courting,* illustrated by Feodor Rojankovsky (New York: Scholastic, 1955. 32p. ISBN 10: 0590333011; ISBN 13: 978-0590333016). This book lends itself to singing along while learning more about Froggie. Follow such a sing-along with the many other versions of the folk song by such artists as Dominic Catalano, Chris Conover, Marjorie Priceman, or Wendy Watson.

Jim Henson introduced one of the most beloved frogs in 1955 on a show called *Sam and Friends.* He became most famous for his role on *Sesame Street,* his relationship with Miss Piggy and others in the cast, and his ability to get all the characters to work together. He was in numerous Muppet movies, including *The Frog Prince* in 1972. No one seemed to notice that he was made out of a thrown out green coat or that his eyes were made of ping pong balls. Kermit gives new meaning to "being green." He has a star on the Hollywood Walk of Fame. His movies, books, and toys are ubiquitous. Although his creator and friend, Jim Henson, died in 1990, Kermit continues to make appearances.

Another character who continues to be popular long after his author's demise is Beatrix Potter's Mr. Jeremy Fisher. He appeared in *The Tale of Mr. Jeremy Fisher* in 1906. Mr. Fisher is elegant but capable of getting out of the most terrible mishaps.

Jonathan London is another author who has created a whole series based on frogs, along with illustrator Frank Remkiewicz. Froggy is a fun-loving, sweet frog who gets into quite interesting situations. Somehow Froggy's Mom seems to always be one step ahead of the game, and she keeps him learning how to do things like swim without too many trials and tribulations. In *Froggy's Halloween,* his treat bag rips, and he ends up at home with no treats. Mom is able to give him a whole bowl of chocolate-covered fly treats when he gets home. None of the neighbors like these treats! The Froggy books are published by Viking Press. Titles include *Froggy Bakes a Cake* (2000); *Froggy Eats Out* (2001); *Froggy Gets Dressed* (1992); *Froggy Goes to Bed* (2002); *Froggy Goes to School* (1996); *Froggy Learns to Swim* (1995); *Froggy Goes to the Doctor* (2002); *Froggy Plays in the Band* (2002); *Froggy Plays Soccer* (1999); *Froggy's Baby Sister* (2003); *Froggy's Best Christmas* (2000); *Froggy's Day with Dad* (2006); *Froggy's First Kiss* (1998); *Froggy's Halloween* (1999); *Froggy's Sleepover* (2007); and *Let's Go Froggy* (1994)

Long Leaping Frog Reads!

These titles will entice those children who become enamored with frogs.

Burgess, Thornton W. *The Adventures of Grandfather Frog*. Illustrated by Harrison Cady. New York: Dover, 1920. 87p. ISBN 10: 0486274004; ISBN 13: 978-0486274003.

Grandfather Frog has all kinds of fun adventures when he decides to leave his familiar home and venture out into the world. (This is an example of a title now available free through many sources, including http://www.gutenberg.org/etext/14375 and http://manybooks.net/titles/burgesst14371437514375.html; both accessed March 23, 2009.) Grades 2–5.

Chang, Heidi. *Elaine and the Flying Frog*. New York: Random House, 1988. 62p. ISBN10: 0679908706; ISBN 13: 978-0679908708.

After Elaine moves she feels lonely and left out, until she meets Mary Lewis. Mary Lewis wishes frogs could fly, and Elaine's dad helps make that wish come true by helping the girls make a beautiful frog kite. Grades 2–5.

Rockwell, Anne. *Big Boss*. New York: Aladdin Paperbacks, 1987. 64p. ISBN 10: 0689808836; ISBN 13: 978-0689808838.

A frog tries to prove to a tiger that he is the big boss of the forest and that he eats tigers instead of the other way around. Grades 2–4.

Roy, Ron, and Victoria Chess. *The Great Frog Swap*. New York: Pantheon Books, 1981. 48p. ISBN 10: 0394844327; ISBN 13: 978-0394844329.

Frog trades abound as all the children in this book try to win a frog contest. Grades 2–4.

Sadler, Marilyn. *Alistair Underwater*. Illustrated by Roger Bollen. New York: Simon & Schuster Books for Young Readers, 1988. 43p. ISBN 10: 0241122317; ISBN 13: 978-0241122310.

Alistair builds a submarine and journeys underwater to a pond where there are frog people. Join Alistair as he saves the frog people from the Gooze. Grades 2–4.

Short Hop Frog Reads!

Brooks, Alan. *Frogs Jump: A Counting Book*. Illustrated by Steven Kellogg. New York: Scholastic Press, 1996. 40p. ISBN 10: 0590455281; ISBN 13: 978-0590455282.

Count up to twelve and back down again with the help of some fun frogs and a lot of other animals. Grades K–1.

Campbell, Wayne. *What a Catastrophe*. Illustrated by Eileen Christelow. New York: Bradbury Press, 1986. 32p. ISBN 10: 0027164209; ISBN 13: 978-0027164206.

A boy brings a frog home, and it escapes onto the family breakfast table. You can choose the ending you like best from four different choices. Grades K–1.

Foster, Kelli C., and Gina C. Erickson. *Frog Knows Best*. Illustrated by Keri Gifford. New York: Barron's Educational Series, 1992. 24p. ISBN 10: 0812048555; ISBN 13: 978-0812048551.

In this easy-to-read book, Frog gives advice to his friend's Hog and Dog. They don't listen but then wish that they had when Frog turns out to be right. Grades K–2.

Gregorich, Barbara. *Jog, Frog, Jog.* Illustrated by Rex Schneider. Grand Haven, Mich.: School Zone Publishing, 1992. 16p. ISBN 10: 0887434045; ISBN 13: 978-0887434044.

> Jogging never goes out of style in this very easy-to-read book about a frog who sticks to the jog. Grades K–1.

Joyce, William. *Bentley and Egg.* New York: HarperCollins, 1992. 32p. ISBN 10: 0060203854; ISBN 13: 978-0060203856.

> Bentley Hopperton is left in charge of his best friend's egg and has quite an adventure keeping it safe. Grades K–2.

Kalan, Robert. *Jump, Frog, Jump!* Illustrated by Bryan Barton. New York: Greenwillow Books, 1995. 30p. ISBN 10: 068813954X; ISBN 13: 978-0688139544.

> A frog tries to catch a fly without getting caught himself. (A sound recording is available from Live Oak Media, 1996.)

Kilborne, Sarah S. *Peach and Blue.* Illustrated by Steve Johnson and Lou Fancher. New York: Knopf, 1994. 34p. ISBN 10: 0679839291; ISBN 13: 978-0679839293.

> A frog named Blue befriends a peach and learns to see his world through new eyes while helping her see it. Grades K–2.

Kulling, Monica. *Waiting for Amos.* Illustrated by Vicky Lowe. New York: Bradbury Press, 1992. 32p. ISBN 10: 0027512452; ISBN 13: 978-0027512458.

> Homer waits for his friend Amos the turtle all day while other animals try to get him to do other things. They bet him Amos won't show up. What a surprise when the rock Homer is sleeping on wakes up and turns out to be his turtle friend! Grades K–2.

MacLachlan, Patricia. *Moon, Stars, Frogs, and Friends.* Illustrated by Tomie de Paola. New York: Pantheon Books, 1980. 32p. ISBN 10: 0394841387; ISBN 13: 978-0394841380.

> Randall the frog meets an enchanted prince, and they become friends. Grades K–2.

Manushkin, Fran. *Peeping and Sleeping.* Illustrated by Jennifer Plecas. New York: Clarion Books, 1994. 31p. ISBN 10: 0395643392; ISBN 13: 978-0395643396.

> Barry and his father find a surprise when they go on a walk to explore some peeing sounds they hear down by the pond. Grades K–2.

Mayer, Mercer. *Frog Goes to Dinner.* New York: Dial Press, 1974. 32p. ISBN 10: 0803728840; ISBN 13: 978-0803728844.

> This wordless book follows a frog as he escapes a boy's pocket and ruins a family's dinner at a fancy restaurant. (Don't miss the videocassette from BFA Films and Video, 1985. 12 min.) Grades K–2.

Priceman, Marjorie. *Friend or Frog.* Boston: Houghton Mifflin, 1989. 32p. ISBN 10: 039544523X; ISBN 13: 978-0395445235.

> Join Kate as she tries to find her frog friend a home. Grades K–1.

Primavera, Elise. *The Three Dots.* New York: Putnam, 1993. 32p. ISBN-10: 0399224297; ISBN 13: 978-0399224294.

> A frog, a moose, and a duck are all born with dots. They meet and form a band. They become wildly famous and are fast friends, until suddenly the moose becomes much more popular than the other animals. Will they be friends ever again? Grades K–3.

Schertle, Alice. *Little Frog's Song.* Illustrated by Leonard Everett Fisher. New York: HarperCollins, 1992. 32p. ISBN 10: 0060200596; ISBN 13: 978-0060200596.

> A storm washes a little frog away from his pond, and he needs people to befriend him. Grades K–2.

Schindel, John. *I'll Meet You Halfway.* Illustrated by James Watts. New York: Margaret K. McElderry Books, 1993. 32p. ISBN 10: 0689505647; ISBN 13: 978-0689505645.

> Titus Turtle and Fuller Frog meet halfway between their homes for a visit. The gifts they bring each other change quite a bit on the journey, but are enjoyed nonetheless. Grades K–3.

Stevenson, James. *The Pattaconk Brook.* New York: Greenwillow Books, 1993. 30p. ISBN 10: 0688119549; ISBN 13: 978-0688119546.

> Sidney the frog tries to write down all the songs of Pattaconk Brook and then decides to ride the brook down to the ocean to hear the ocean sounds. Grades K–3.

Stieg, William. *Gorky Rises.* New York: Farrar, Straus & Giroux, 1980. 32p. ISBN 10: 0374327521; ISBN 13: 978-0374327521.

> A frog awakens in the air holding a magic potion he created. Grades 1–3.

Thaler, Mike. *In the Middle of the Puddle.* Illustrated by Bruce Degen. New York: Harper & Row, 1988. 32p. ISBN 10: 006026053X; ISBN 13: 978-0060260538.

> Frog and Turtle watch as their puddle grows into a lake and then an ocean, until the sun comes out and turns the lake back into the friends' familiar puddle. Grades K–2.

Velthuijs, Max. *Frog and the Stranger.* New York: Tambourine Books, 1993. 26p. ISBN 10: 1842704664; ISBN 13: 978-1842704660.

> When Rat moves in, all the other animals are rude because Rat is different from them, but Frog befriends him and enjoys his company long before the other animals come around. Many other adventures happen to Frog in *Frog in Winter* (1992), *Frog Is a Hero* (2000), *Frog Is Frog* (2000), and *Frog and the Wide World* (2000). (The Dutch author is a recipient of the Hans Christian Andersen Award for illustration, the Dutch Silver Pencil Award, and the German Bestlist Award. This is an excellent example for introducing translations. Some editions are bilingual, in Albanian, Chinese, or other languages.) Grades K–3.

Walsh, Ellen Stoll. *Hop Jump.* San Diego: Harcourt Brace Jovanovich, 1993. 32p. ISBN 10: 0613066863; ISBN 13: 978-0613066860.

> A frog that is bored with hopping and jumping discovers dancing. Grades K–2.

Weisner, David. *Tuesday.* New York: Clarion Books, 1991. 32p. ISBN 10: 0395551137; ISBN 13: 978-0395551134.

> Frogs rise out of their pond on lily pads and float through a sleeping town. (This book won the Caldecott Medal Book, 1992.)

Wilson, Karma. *A Frog in the Bog.* Illustrated by Joan Rankin. New York: Margaret K. McElderry Books, 2003. 32p. ISBN 10: 1416927271; ISBN 13: 978-1416927273.

> Frog's belly grows bigger with each snack he eats. This counting book is similar to "I Know an Old Lady Who Swallowed a Fly."

Published Frog Paper Dolls

Frog paper dolls are not easy to find in antique shops. One of the few early examples is *Froggie Went a Courting*, produced by DeJournette Manufacturing Company between 1942 and 1962. It includes a petite mouse and a jocular frog with a special courting outfit. Dover currently offers a jaunty figure in the following format:

Petach, Heidi. *Frog Sticker Paper Doll*. Mineola, N.Y.: Dover, 1992. 4p. ISBN 10: 0486272524; ISBN 13: 978-0486272528.

    These color male and female sticker costumes are pressure sensitive and reusable, with one doll and thirty-two stickers. There are other outfits and accessories, such as royal wear, snorkeling, and cold weather gear.

A bit of paper doll fun can be found on the Internet at *Rib-Bit* (http://www.billybear4kids.com/paperdoll/froggy.html; accessed March 23, 2009).

Lesson Plan:
Ribbit! Ribbit!

Library Media Skills Objective:
The student will read or listen to a story and retell it with beginning, middle, and end.

Curriculum (subject areas) Objectives:
The activity may be included in a reading/language arts unit.

Grade Level: K–3

Resources:

Frog books

Paper doll handouts

Crayons, markers, and scissors

Materials for storytelling session (fabric or paper)

Instructional Roles:
The teacher or library media specialist may introduce the lesson and monitor student progress. Introduction of materials requires about 30 minutes. Student reading and creation of paper dolls takes an hour or more depending on the length of the books selected. At a follow-up session, the discussion of how to remember events in a story may take about 30 minutes. Practice in retelling the story takes several 10-minute sessions alone or with a friend. The time needed for final story retelling sessions will vary, and they may be performed over a period of a week or two.

Activity and Procedures for Completion:
Begin the frog retelling session by modeling retelling of a story. Retell the story of the Frog Prince and then show titles in which the story is found. Sing a version of "Froggie Went a Courting" and talk about story songs as retellings. Finally, read the story from a book. Talk about the differences between retelling a story and reading the story from a book as the author wrote it.

Explain that students will have their own chance to retell frog stories that they have read using their paper doll characters. Share some of the available titles and allow time for book selection. Distribute the frog paper dolls and suggest which costumes might be used for characters in books available to the students.

At a follow-up session, explain one method of retelling a story. Begin with the "Five Finger Approach," in which the little finger is the beginning and the thumb is the end. The three fingers in between are for the main events. Often there are several events before getting to the end, so use the knuckle on each finger. Dissect a story and talk about what comes first, second, and so forth. What does it take for the story to progress to the very end? Model the approach with a frog story. Other methods are available for helping students figure out what the main events in the story are. Provide time for students to think about their stories, identify the main events, and practice telling their own versions. Also explain that a good story isn't just about getting to the end. Talk about the words students want to use, the sound of their voices, and building suspense.

Students will have a chance to retell the stories or books they have chosen. They must complete their paper dolls and select the appropriate outfits. On the day of the retelling, make several green cut-outs in the shape of lily pads. These should be large enough for two or three children to sit on or around. They can be as elaborate or simple as desired. Play some "ribbit" night sounds as students come in. They should bring their outfitted frogs and sit cross-legged on or around the lily pads. One at a time, the paper dolls may begin the retelling of the stories from which they came. Caution students that they will be listening until it is their turn to retell a story.

Evaluation:

Each student will use his or her paper doll to retell a selected story with correct beginning, middle, and end. The event in the middle will include at least two or three of the event highlights. The teacher may consider the age of the student in terms of use of language, voice expression, and feeling used in the retellings.

Follow-Up:

Students may develop more elaborate costumes using mixed media to add pizzazz to their storytelling sessions. Videotape the events and the stories being retold. Put the retellings on the school Web site for book promotions.

Paper Dolls:
Frogs

Instructions: Color and cut out these frog paper dolls, then find a book to go with the clothes or make up your own story.

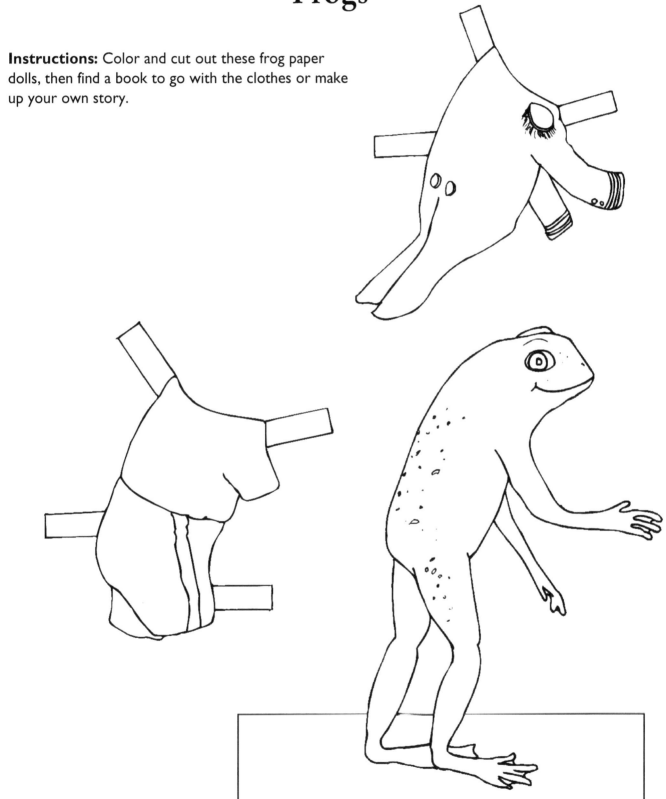

Chapter 7

The Big Ones: Giants around the World

Long ago the world was full of extraordinary creatures known as giants. Who were these giants? Where did they come from? What did they look like? Answers to such giant questions may be found in legends, myths, and other documents from ancient history.

Early artists, sculptors, and writers attempted to preserve their ideas and interpretations of giants through their works. Many stories about giants were passed down through the telling and retelling of myths and legends. Did they really exist? Did early artists and writers s-t-r-e-t-c-h out or exaggerate details to make their works more interesting?

Who Were These Giants? Supernatural vs. Earthbound

Research indicates that giants generally fall into two main categories. First are the supernatural giants of ancient times, which existed during the period between Earth's creation and the great Flood mentioned in the Bible and Babylonian texts. In the Bible, Genesis 1:4 says, "[T]here were giants in the earth in those days." Perhaps Goliath, who was killed by David with a stone from a sling, is the best known. Goliath stood about nine feet, three inches tall, and seemed to have superhuman strength. Hindus record the Daityas, a race of giants who fought the gods. Among these were Bali, Hiranyakashipu, and Hiranyaksha. In Norse mythology, humanity was created from the flesh of a giant, Ymir.

Supernatural giants played a major part in the myths and stories surrounding the creation of Earth. Giants are thought to have existed long before the gods and humans came along. Ancient Greeks and Romans believed their ancestors were huge beings with great power and strength. With the appearance of gods, giants and gods struggled in battles. In Greek legends, giants represented natural elements such as earth, air, and water. The gods felt the giants threatened their authority. The giants were envious of the power of the gods. The giants usually received the worst battle blows. When a giant was slain by a mighty god, the god would create heaven and earth from that giant's body.

The second category, Earthbound giants, ranged in height between ten and forty feet. The smaller ones were referred to as baby giants. Early humans respected giants for their size. Rock and hillside carvings that can still be seen today, as well as ancient giant statues, reflect this early awe of the giant. With the appearance of Christianity, the giant became an outcast. He was hated and feared because he was different. People began to connect giants with the devil and then began thinking of them as evil beings.

What Did Giants Look Like?

Giants seem to have had long arms that reached just below their knees. They had protruding, pot-bellied stomachs and chests covered with dense hair that helped them to survive in various climates. It is thought that the heavy body weight of giants was responsible for their slouching posture. Perhaps their knotted clubs were used not as weapons, but rather as a type of walking stick.

The mouths of giants were very large, and they were able to eat enormous quantities of food. It is said that many valleys and mountain gorges around the world were formed by the weight of giants trampling about while the earth's crust was still soft.

Where Did Giants Live? A Giant World Tour

Giants appear in the mythology of countries all over the world. A "Giant World Tour" grabs students' imagination and begs them to compare how various cultures have viewed size.

Giants in Europe

England and the British Isles

de la Mare, Walter. *Molly Whuppie.* Illustrated by Errol Le Cain. New York: Farrar, Straus & Giroux, 1983. 32p. ISBN 10: 0571119425; ISBN 13: 978-0571119424.

> "But as she drew out the purse from under the pillow, a gold piece dropped out of it and clanked on to the floor, and at the sound of it the giant awoke. Then Molly ran, and the giant ran, and they both ran."

Molly Whuppie is the youngest daughter of a woodcutter. Lost in a forest one day, she and her sisters come upon a giant's house. She manages to rescue her sisters from the giant's clutches. But she makes three return visits to steal precious items from the giant's home. If he catches her, she is sure to be eaten!

Other versions may be found in:

Jacobs, John. *English Fairy Tales.* Illustrated by John D. Batten. New York: Everyman's Library, 1993. Pages 125–130. ISBN 10: 0679428097; ISBN 13: 978-0679428091.

Philip, Neil. *Celtic Fairy Tales.* New York: Viking, 1999. Pages 86–91. ISBN 10: 0670883875; ISBN 13: 978-0670883875.

Shelby, Ann. *The Adventures of Molly Whuppie and Other Appalachian Folktales.* Chapel Hill: University of North Carolina Press, 2007. 96p. ISBN 10: 0807831638; ISBN 13: 978-0807831632.

Tatar, Maria. *The Annotated Classic Fairy Tales*. New York: W. W. Norton, 2002. Pages 201–205. ISBN 10: 0393051633; ISBN 13: 978-0393051636. (Teacher reference).

Yolen, Jane. *Favorite Folktales from Around the World*. New York: Pantheon, 1986. Pages 228–230. ISBN 10: 0394543823; ISBN 13: 978-0394543826.

Greece

Parin D'Aulaire, Ingri, and Edgar Parin D'Aulaire. *D'Aulaires Book of Greek Myths.* New York: Delacorte, 1992. 192p. ISBN 10: 0440406943; ISBN 13: 978-0440406945.

"When Gaea gave birth, Uranus was not proud. Their new children were also very huge, but each had only one glowing eye set in the middle of his forehead. They were the three Cyclopes and they were named Lightning, Thunder, and Thunderbolt" (p. 12).

Clearly the giants began life with the problem of a father who didn't like their looks. Events did not go well, and a conflict with the Olympian gods called the Gigantomachy had to be resolved by the hero Hercules. The results of the conflict became the explanations for earthquakes and volcanic eruptions. The stories are fun to read aloud. Most of the stories about the Titans can be found in collections of Greek myths.

Following are examples in which the Cyclopes appear.

Aliki. *The Gods and Goddesses of Olympus.* New York: HarperCollins, 1994. 48p. ISBN 10: 0060235306; ISBN 13: 978-0060235307.

Brazouski, Antoinette, and Mary J. Klatt. *Children's Books on Ancient Greek and Roman Mythology: An Annotated Bibliography*. Westport, Conn.: Greenwood Press, 1993. 208p. ISBN-10: 0313289735; ISBN 13: 978-0313289736. (Teacher reference).

Evslin, Bernard. *The Cyclopes.* New York: Chelsea House, 1987. 96p. ISBN 10: 1555462367; ISBN 13: 978-1555462369.

Hoena, B. A. *Cyclopes*. Mankato, Minn.: Capstone, 2004. 32p. ISBN 10: 0736824979; ISBN 13: 978-0736824972.

Hutton, Warwick. *Odysseus and the Cyclops.* New York: Margaret K. McElderry Books, 1995. 32p. ISBN 10: 0689800363; ISBN 13: 978-0689800368.

Nardo, Don. *Cyclops.* San Diego: KidHaven Press, 2004. 48p. ISBN 10: 0737726156; ISBN 13: 978-0737726152.

Osborne, Mary Pope. *Tales from the Odyssey: The One-Eyed Giant—Book #1*. Illustrated by Troy Howell. New York: 2003. 112p. ISBN 10: 0786809280; ISBN 13: 978-0786809288.

Richardson, I. M. *Odysseus and the Cyclops.* Mahwah, N.J.: Troll Associates, 1984. 32p. ISBN 10: 0816700087; ISBN 13: 978-0816700080. (Sound recording available).

Iceland

Helgadóttir, Gudrún. *Flumbra: An Icelandic Folktale.* Illustrated by Brian Pilkington and Idunn. Minneapolis, Minn.: Carolrhoda Books, 1986. 32p. ISBN 10: 0876142439; ISBN 13: 978-0876142431.

"Flumbra gave birth to eight sons. They were big and unbelievably ugly, very much like their father."

Flumbra is a giantess, but not very bright. She falls head over heels in love with a very lazy giant. When she sets out with her young family to visit her great big, ugly giant husband, her troubles begin.

Find stories about giants in these titles.

Bedell, J. M. *Hildur, Queen of the Elves: and Other Icelandic Legends*. Northampton, Mass.: Interlink Books, 2007. 267p. ISB 10: 1566566339; ISBN 13: 978-1566566339.

Colum, Padraic. *The Children of Odin*. New York: Simon & Schuster, 1984. 271p. ISBN-10: 0027228908; ISBN 13: 978-0027228908. (Available in digital audio format).

Limke, Jeff. *Thor and Loki: In the Land of Giants: A Norse Myth*. Illustrated by Ron Randall. New York: Graphic Universe, 2006. 48p. ISBN 10: 0822530872; ISBN13: 978-0822530879. (Graphic novel).

Ireland

DePaola, Tomie. *Fin M'Coul: The Giant of Knockmany Hill*. New York: Holiday House, 1981. 32p. ISBN 10: 082340384X; ISBN 13: 978-0823403844.

"Every giant in Ireland had been given a good beating by Cucullin. Every giant, that is, except Fin M'Coul."

Cucullin was the strongest giant in Ireland. He had beaten every giant except Fin M'Coul, and was determined to beat Fin, too. Fin's wife, Oonagh, was very clever and decided the time had come for her to help her husband confront Cucullin. Read what happens to Cucullin when he comes knocking at the M'Couls' door!

Following are some other versions.

Byrd, Robert. *Finn MacCoul and His Fearless Wife: A Giant of a Tale from Ireland*. New York: Dutton Children's Books, 1999. 40p. ISBN 10: 0525459715; ISBN 13: 978-0525459712.

Campbell, John Gregorson. *The Fians; or, Stories, Poems, & Traditions of Fionn and His Warrior Band: Collected entirely from Oral Sources*. Boston, Mass.: Adamant Media Corporation, 2005. 340p. ISBN 10: 1402178271; ISBN 13: 978-1402178276. (Teacher reference).

Evslin, Bernard. *The Green Hero: Early Adventures of Finn McCool*. Illustrated by Barbara Bascove. New York: Four Winds Press, 1975. 181p. ISBN 10: 0590071211; ISBN 13: 978-0590071215

Evslin, Bernard. *Pig's Ploughman*. New York: Chelsea House, 1990. 100p. ISBN 10: 1555462561; ISBN 13: 978-1555462567

Gleeson, Brian. *Finn McCoul*. Illustrated by Peter de Sève. New York: Simon & Schuster, 1995. 34 p. ISBN 10: 0887082718; ISBN 13: 978-0887082719. (An audio recording accompanies the book. A videotape is also available.)

Kerven, Rosalind. *Enchanted Kingdoms*. Lincolnwood, Ill.: NTC, 1997. 48p. ISBN 10: 0714121053; ISBN 13: 978-0714121055.

Llywelyn, Morgan. *Finn Mac Cool*. New York: T. Doherty Associates, 1995. 531p. ISBN 10: 0312854765; ISBN 13: 978-0312854768. (Teacher reference).

Osborne, Mary Pope, and Troy Howell. *Favorite Medieval Tales*. New York: Scholastic, 1998. Pages 1–7. ISBN 10: 0590600427; ISBN 13: 978-0590600422.

Souhami, Jessica. *Mrs. McCool and the Giant Cuhillin: An Irish Tale*. New York: Henry Holt, 2002. 28p. ISBN: 9780711218222.

Sutcliff, Rosemary. *The High Deeds of Finn Mac Cool*. Illustrated by Michael Charlton. New York: Dutton, 1967. 189p. ISBN 10: 0370010884; ISBN 13: 978-0370010885.

Zaczek, Iain. *Irish Legends*. New York: Barnes & Noble, 1998. 128p. ISBN 10: 0809228092; ISBN 13: 978-0809228096. (Teacher reference).
Videos include:

Finn McCoul. Westport, Conn.: Rabbit Ears, 1992. 25 min.

Irish Legends. West Long Branch, N.J.: Kultur, 1999. 52 min.

Italy

DePaola, Tomie. *The Mysterious Giant of Barletta*. New York: Harcourt Brace Jovanovich, 1984. ISBN 10: 0833517937; ISBN 13: 978-0833517937. (An audio recording is available.)
"No one knew where it had come from or when. The mysterious giant—for this is what the people called the statue."

The giant statue had always stood in front of a church in Barletta, Italy. One day the town was in a terrible panic. An army of a thousand men was destroying all the towns along the southern coast of Italy. Now this army was heading straight for Barletta. Will the mysterious stone giant come to the aid of his town?

Norway

"The Giant with No Heart in His Body." In *The Barefoot Book of Giants, Ghosts and Goblins*, by John Matthews. Illustrated by Giovanni Manna. Cambridge, Mass.: Barefoot Books, 1999. 80p. ISBN 10: 1902283279; ISBN 13: 978-1902283272.
"No sooner had Ashpattle hidden himself than the giant came home. He sniffed the air. "There's a terrible smell of human flesh in here," he bellowed."

Asphattle was the youngest of seven royal sons. One day his six brothers set out to find themselves princess brides. Many weeks passed, and they did not return. When Asphattle sets out to look for his brothers, he learns that a giant has turned them all to stone. Can the young prince confront the giant to get his brothers back again?

Other stories about giants from Norway may be found in the following sources.

Cole, Joanna. *Best Loved Folktales of the World*. New York: Anchor, 1983. 816p. ISBN 10: 0385189494; ISBN 13: 978-0385189491.

D'Aulaire, Ingri, and Edgar Parin. *Norse Gods and Giants*. Garden City, N.Y.: Doubleday, 1967. 154p. ISBN 10: 159017125X; ISBN 13: 978-1590171257.

The Giant without a Heart in His Body. http://oaks.nvg.org/ntales37.html#gihea (accessed March 23, 2009).

The Giant's Mountain. http://oaks.nvg.org/ntales22.html#gimo (accessed March 23, 2009).

"How Loki Outwitted the Giant." In *Tales of the Norse Gods,* by Barbara Picard. Illustrated by Rosamund Fowler. New York: Oxford University Press, 2001. ISBN 10: 0192751166; ISBN 13: 978-0192751164. pp113-118.

King Olaf and the Giant. http://www.pitt.edu/~dash/mbuilder.html#olaf (accessed March 23, 2009).

Giants in Africa

South Africa

Seeger, Pete. *Abiyoyo: Based on a South African Lullaby and Folk Story.* Illustrated by Michael Hays. New York: Simon & Schuster, 1994. 48p. ISBN 10: 0689718101; ISBN 13: 9780689718106.
　　"There was Abiyoyo! He had long fingernails 'cause he never cut 'em. He had slobbery teeth 'cause he didn't brush 'em, stinking feet 'cause he didn't wash 'em, matted hair 'cause he didn't comb it."

　　The people of the town had finally had enough. A young boy who played the ukulele was too noisy. The boy's father was a magician and performed mischief with his magic. The townsfolk forced the father and son to leave. One day the ground began to shake. A terrible giant named Abiyoyo was coming toward town. It was said he could eat people up! Everyone in the town was terrified, but the boy and his father were not.

West Africa

"A-Man-Among-Men." In *The Barefoot Book of Giants, Ghosts and Goblins,* by John Matthews. Illustrated by Giovanni Manna. Cambridge, Mass.: Barefoot Books, 1999. 80p. ISBN 10: 1902283279; ISBN 13: 978-1902283272.
　　" 'Why are you running?' asked the huge fella, whose name was Giant of the Forest."

　　'A-Man-Among-Men is after me,' cried the boaster."

　　'Never heard of him," said the Giant of the Forest. 'Sit and wait here awhile'."

　　There was once a foolish man who thought of himself as brave and superior to everyone else. Upon learning there was A-Man-Among-Men who was very strong, he was determined to confront him. While hiding to wait for him, the foolish man soon saw that A-Man-Among-Men was so big that his shadow was at least a mile long. He had a voice that sounded like a tornado. Will the boastful man confront the giant? A giant battle is soon to occur.

Giants in Asia

China

Yep, Laurence. *The City of Dragons.* Illustrated by Jean and Mou-Sien Tseng. New York: Scholastic Inc., 1995. 32p. ISBN 10: 0590478656; ISBN 13: 978-0590478656.
　　" 'Where are we going?' the boy asked as the giant splashed unconcernedly into the surf.

　　" 'The city of dragons,' the chief giant said as a wave washed over him and he disappeared from sight."

A boy with a face so sad that nobody wants to look at him runs away with a caravan of giants. The giants must travel to the city of dragons. They hope the boy will be useful when they meet the dragons. What adventures are in store for the sorrowful boy in the city of dragons? Read and find out!

Chinese legend and mythology collections contain other stories about giants, especially Pan Ku, the giant creator of the earth.

Birch, Cyril. *Tales from China*. Illustrated by Rosamund Fowler. New York: Oxford, 2001. 208p. ISBN 10: 1417654945; ISBN 13: 978-1417654949.

Carpenter, Frances. *Tales of a Chinese Grandmother*. Illustrated by Malthe Hasseiriis. Tuttle, 2001. 280p. ISBN 10: 0804834091; ISBN 13: 978-0804834094.

Werner, T. C. *Myths and Legends of China*. Mineola, N.Y.: Dover, 1994. 496p. ISBN 10: 0486280926; ISBN 13: 978-0486280929.

Japan

"Three Strong Women." In *Diane Goode's Book of Giants and Little People*. New York: Dutton Children's Books, 1997. 48p. ISBN 10: 0525456600; ISBN 13: 978-0525456605.
"Forever-Mountain raised his foot. He brought it down. There was a sound like thunder, the earth shook, and the other wrestler bounced into the air and out of the ring, as gracefully as a soap bubble."

Long ago in Japan, a famous giant wrestler was on his way to wrestle before the Emperor. He came upon a young girl with powerful strength. She led the wrestler back to her home, where her mother and grandmother agreed on a plan for the wrestler. They would make the wrestler into what they thought a strong man should be. The wrestler is in for the workout of his life!

North American Giants

Canada and United States: Alaska

Sloat, Teri. *The Hungry Giant of the Tundra*. Illustrated by Robert Sloat. New York: Dutton Children's Books, 1993. 32p. ISBN 10: 0525451269; ISBN 13: 978-0525451266.
" 'I smell little children warm in the sun. I'll eat them all, one by one.' 'I found little children warm in the sun. I'll start my dinner with the smallest one.' "

A*ka*gua*gan*kak! The giant came across the tundra looking for his evening meal. When he spotted several children playing outside a village, he ran after them and caught them. He tied them up in his trouser bag and hung them from a tree. Only a chickadee and crane will be able to help them. This Yupik tale instructs children on how to deal with their environment in Alaska.

United States: Virgin Islands

Gershator, Phillis. *Tukama Tootles the Flute*. Illustrated by Synthia Saint James. New York: Orchard, 1994. 32p. ISBN 10: 0531068110; ISBN 13: 978-0531068113.
"Tukama climbed up on the giant's chest and tootled and sang,

'Tanto, tanto tango/Bombwiti, bombwiti,/Guavaberry, mango,/Bimbala, bango.' "

Tukama, a wild boy, is captured by a two-headed giant. He is held prisoner by the giant's wife. Can a little flute save the boy from becoming the giant's next meal?

United States: Hawaii

Cabcabin Moran, Edna. *The Sleeping Giant: A Tale from Kaua'i*. Ewa Beach, Hawai'i: Beachhouse Publishing, 2006. 32p. ISBN 10: 1933067209; ISBN 13: 978-1933067209.
"Taking a closer look, the fisherman saw ears streaming from the fishes eyes, forming a small puddle in his canoe."

A fisherman catches a magical fish. He takes the catch home, and he and the villagers are surprised as the fish grows and grows. His scales fall off, and he becomes a hungry giant. As he devours all the poi, the villagers become concerned. Finally a young girl is able to tame the giant.

United States: General

Mason, Jane B. *Paul Bunyan and Other Tall Tales*. New York: Scholastic, 2002. 107p. ISBN 10: 0439291542; ISBN 13: 978-0439291545.
"He stood more than fifty feet tall. And his feet were the size of school buses. Paul's dark eyes wee as big as serving platters, his nose like a giant leg of lamb. His bristly black beard (which some swear he was born with) was so long and so thick that he used a dozen ten-foot pine boughs just to comb it in the morning." pg 5-6.

Paul Bunyan was a lumberjack, a logging man who never had an equal. According to American legends, he was the biggest and best at anything. He was said to have practically "built" the United States single-handed. He formed the Mississippi River or the Rocky Mountains. Students may not believe everything about Paul Bunyan, but they're sure to love reading about America's best-loved giant hero!

There are so many versions of Paul Bunyan's story that it is difficult to choose one. These are found in school library media centers across the United States. James Stevens is noted for one of the earliest publications. Check out versions by copyright to see how the retelling and illustration of the story have changed over time.

Anderson, J. I. *I Can Read about Paul Bunyan*. Illustrated by Joel Snyder. Mahwah, N.J.: Troll Associates, 1977. ISBN 10: 0893750417; ISBN 13: 978-0893750411. (A sound recording is available.)

Balcziak, Bill. *Paul Bunyan*. Illustrated by Patrick Girouard. Minneapolis, Minn.: Compass Point Books, 2003. 32p. ISBN 10: 0756504597; ISBN 13: 978-0756504595.

Becker, Sandra. *Paul Bunyan*. Mankato, Minn.: Weigl, 2003. 24p. ISBN 10: 1590360761; ISBN 13: 978-1590360767.

Blair, Eric. *Paul Bunyan*. Illustrated by Micah Chambers-Goldberg. Minneapolis, Minn.: Picture Window Books, 2005. 32p. ISBN 10: 1404809767; ISBN 13: 978-1404809765.

Blassingame, Wyatt. *John Henry and Paul Bunyan Play Baseball*. Illustrated by Herman B. Vestal. Champaign, Ill.: Garrard Publishing, 1974. 39p. ISBN 10: 0811640272; ISBN 13: 978-0811640275.

Blassingame, Wyatt. *Paul Bunyan Fights the Monster Plants*. Illustrated by Herman B. Vestral. Champaign, Ill.: Garrard Publishing, 1969. 40p. ISBN 10: 0811640396; ISBN 13: 978-0811640398.

De Leeuw, Adèle. *Paul Bunyan Finds a Wife*. Illustrated by Ted Schroeder. Champaign, Ill.: Garrard Publishing, 1969. 30p. ISBN 10: 0811640132.

DeLeeuw, Adele Louise. *Paul Bunyan and His Blue Ox.* Illustrated by Ted Schroeder. Champaign, Ill.: Garrard Publishing, 1968. 36p. ISBN 10: 0811640078; ISBN 13: 978-0811640077.

Dolan, Ellen M. *Paul Bunyan.* St. Louis, Mo.: Milliken Publishing, 1987. 30p. ISBN 10: 0883355817; ISBN 13: 978-0883355817.

Dolbier, Maurice. *Paul Bunyan.* Illustrated by Leonard Everett Fisher. New York: Random House, 1959. 54p. ISBN 10: 0394901592; ISBN 13: 978-0394901596.

Emberley, Barbara. *The Story of Paul Bunyan.* Illustrated by Ed Emberley. Northampton, Mass.: Half Moon Books, 1963. 32p. ISBN 10: 0138507848; ISBN 13: 978-0138507848.

Felton, Harold W. *Legends of Paul Bunyan.* Illustrated by Richard Bennett. New York: A. A. Knopf, 1944. 377p. ISBN 10: 0394913183; ISBN 13: 978-0394913186.

Feuerlicht, Roberta Strauss. *The Legends of Paul Bunyan.* Illustrated by Kurt Werth. New York: Collier Books, 1966. 128p. ISBN 10: 0027345106; ISBN 13: 978-0027345100.

Gleeson, Brian. *Paul Bunyan.* Illustrated by Rick Meyerowitz. Saxonville, Mass.: Rabbit Ears Books, 1990. 40p. ISBN 10: 088708303X; ISBN 13: 978-0887083037.

Gleiter, Jan, and Kathleen Thompson. *Paul Bunyan and Babe the Blue Ox.* Illustrated by Yoshi Miyake. New York: Torstar Books, 1985. 32p. ISBN 10: 0811483525; ISBN 13: 978-0811483520.

Gregg, Andy. *Paul Bunyan and the Winter of the Blue Snow: A Tall Tale.* Illustrated by Carolyn R. Stich. Spring Lake, Mich.: River Road Publications, 2000. 56p. ISBN 10: 093868258X; ISBN 13: 978-0938682585.

Jensen, Patricia. *Paul Bunyan and His Blue Ox.* Illustrated by Jean Pidgeon. Mahwah, N.J.: Troll Associates, 1994. 32p. ISBN 10: 0816731624; ISBN 13: 978-0816731626. (Sound and video recordings are available.)

Johnston, Marianne. *Paul Bunyan.* New York: Rosen Publishing Group's PowerKids Press, 2000. 24p. ISBN 10: 082395580X; ISBN 13: 978-0823955800.

Kellogg, Steven. *Paul Bunyan: A Tall Tale Retold.* New York: Mulberry Paperback Book, 1984. 32p. ISBN 10: 0688038492; ISBN 13: 978-0688038496.

Krensky, Stephen. *Paul Bunyan.* Illustrated by Craig Orback. Minneapolis, Minn.: Millbrook Press, 2007. 48p. ISBN 10: 157505888X; ISBN 13: 978-1575058887.

Kumin, Maxine. *Paul Bunyan.* Illustrated by Dirk Gringhuis. New York: Putnam 1966. 32p. ISBN 10: 0399605061; ISBN 13: 978-0399605062.

Langhead, W. B. *The Marvelous Exploits of Paul Bunyan.* Rockville, Md.: Wildside Press, 2004. 104p. (Available as e-book/Kindle edition).

Lyman, Nanci A. *Paul Bunyan.* Illustrated by Bert Dodson. Mahwah, N.J.: Troll Associates, 1977. 48p. ISBN 10: 0893753092; ISBN 13: 978-0893753092.

McCormick, Dell J. *Paul Bunyan Swings His Axe.* Caldwell, Idaho: Caxton Printers, Ltd., 1936. 111p. ISBN 10: 0870040936; ISBN 13: 978-0870040931.

McCormick, Dell J. *Tall Timber Tales: More Paul Bunyan Stories*. Illustrated by Lorna Livesley. Caldwell, Idaho: Caxton Printers, 1939. 155p. ISBN 10: 0870044486 (pb.); ISBN 13: 978-0870044489 (pb.).

Ottolenghi, Carol. *Paul Bunyan*. Illustrated by Steve Haefele. Columbus, Ohio: McGraw-Hill Children's Publishing, 2004. 32p. ISBN 10: 061390012X; ISBN 13: 978-0613900126.

Rogers, D. Laurence. *Paul Bunyan: How a Terrible Timber Feller Became a Legend*. Bay City, Mich.: Historical Press, 1993. 192p. ISBN 10: 0963536907; ISBN 13: 978-0963536907. (Teacher reference).

Rounds, Glen. *The Morning the Sun Refused to Rise: An Original Paul Bunyan Tale*. New York: Holiday House, 1984. 48p. ISBN 10: 0823405141; ISBN 13: 978-0823405145.

Rounds, Glen. *Ol' Paul, the Mighty Logger: Being a True Account of the Seemingly Incredible Exploits and Inventions of the Great Paul Bunyan*. New York: Holiday House, 1949. 93p. ISBN 10: 082340269X; ISBN 13: 978-0823402694.

Sabin, Louis. *Paul Bunyan*. Illustrated by Dick Smolinski. Mahwah, N.J.: Troll Associates, 1980. 26p. ISBN10: 0816702543; ISBN 13: 978-0816702541.

Shapiro, Irwin. *Paul Bunyan Tricks a Dragon*. Illustrated by Raymond Burns. Champaign, Ill., Garrard Publishing, 1975. 48p. ISBN 10: 0811640426; ISBN 13: 978-0811640428.

Shephard, Esther. *Paul Bunyan*. Illustrated by Rockwell Kent. New York: Harcourt Brace Jovanovich, 1941. 256p. ISBN 10: 0152058575; ISBN 13: 978-0152058579.

Stevens, James. *Paul Bunyan*. New York: Fredonia Books, 2001. 264p. ISBN 10: 1589631625 (pb.); ISBN 13: 978-1589631625 (pb.). (Originally published in 1925 by Knopf). Stevens's song "The Frozen Logger" has been recorded by many performers.

Turney, Ida Virginia. *Paul Bunyan, the Work Giant*. Illustrated by Norma Madge Lyon and Harold L. Price. Binfords and Mort, 1941. 80p. ISBN 10: 0832301639 (pb.); ISBN 13: 978-0832301636 (pb.).

Whiting, Jim. *Paul Bunyan*. Hockessin, Del.: Mitchell Lane Publishers, 2007. 32p. ISBN 10: 1584155744; ISBN 13: 978-1584155744.

Internet

Legends of Paul Bunyan—http://www.paulbunyanscenicbyway.org/tales/Paul,%20the%20True%20Story.shtm (accessed March 23, 2009).

Audio Recordings

The New Adventures of Paul Bunyan: The Ironwood Contest. Castaic, Calif.: Carousel Classics, 1993.

Paul Bunyan in Story and Song. Read by Ed Begley. Sung by Oscar Brand. New York: Caedmon, 1969.

Rip Roarin' Paul Bunyan Tales. Bradford, NH : Odds Bodkin, Inc., 1994.

Video Recordings

American Legends Volume 2: John Henry, Paul Bunyan, and the Saga of Windwagon Smith. Elk Grove Village, Ill.: Disney Educational Productions, 2005.

Paul Bunyan. Wynnewood, Pa.: Schlessinger Media, 2006.

Paul Bunyan: A Tall Tale. Lincoln, Neb.: GPN Educational Media, 2004.

Belief in Giants

Those who believed in giants long ago used to think that certain things in the natural world were caused by the actions of giants. For example:

- Thunder is the sound of a giant laughing.

- Lakes are a giant's footprints filled with water.

- Sand dunes and great boulders show where a giant emptied the sand and gravel out of his shoes.

- Earthquakes happen when a giant sneezes so hard the earth shakes.

Understanding of the concepts large and small plays out in most cultures in the form of giants and little people. This also includes giant or miniature objects. Giants are malevolent in many cases, but are less so when authors want to soften the fear, as in more modern children's literature.

Perhaps one of the more malevolent well-known giants is found in the Jack and the Beanstalk stories. Variations of the story can be found in many places, including America's own Appalachian tales. Again, comparisons are easily made when sharing more than one version.

The following traditional versions may be compared for illustration and adaptation. In this version, simple Jack sells the family cow for beans. His mother throws out the beans, which grow into a beanstalk reaching into the clouds. Jack climbs the stalk, finds the giant, and steals a hen, a harp, and gold treasure. In the end, Jack kills the giant and triumphs. Many of these versions rely on the Joseph Jacobs version of the English tale.

Bell, Anthea. *Jack and the Beanstalk: An English Fairy Tale*. Illustrated by Aljoscha Blau. New York: North-South Books, 2000. 32p. ISBN 10:0735813752; ISBN 13: 9780735813755. Grades K–4.

Beneduce, Ann Keay. *Jack and the Beanstalk*. Illustrated by Gennady Spirin. New York: Philomel, 1999. 32p. ISBN 10: 0399231188; ISBN 13: 978-0399231186. Grades K–4.

Berman, Craig. *Jack and the Beanstalk*. Morris Plains, N.J.: Unicorn Publishing House, 1993. 36p. ISBN 10: 0881012939; ISBN 13: 978-0881012934. Grades K–3.

Biro, Val. *Jack and the Beanstalk*. New York: Oxford University Press, 1996. 32p. ISBN 10: 0192723049 (pb.); ISBN 13: 978-0192723048 (pb.). Grades K–3.

Bofill, Francesc. *Jack and the Beanstalk = Juan Y Los Frijoles Magicos*. Illustrated by Arnal Ballester. New York: Chronicle Books, 1998. 32p. ISBN 10: 0811818438; ISBN 13: 978-0811818438. Grades 2–4.

Cauley, Lorinda Bryan. *Jack and the Beanstalk*. New York: Putnam, 1983. 32p. ISBN 10: 0399209018; ISBN 13: 978-0399209017. Grades K–4.

Daynes, Katie. *Jack and the Beanstalk*. Illustrated by Paddy Mounter. Tulsa, Okla.: EDC Publishing, 2006. 48p. ISBN 10: 0794512380; ISBN 13: 978-0794512385. Grades K–3.

De Regniers, Beatrice Schenk. *Jack and the Beanstalk: Retold in Verse for Boys & Girls to Read Themselves.* Illustrated by Anne Wilsdorf. New York: Atheneum, 1985. 46p. ISBN 10: 0689311745; ISBN 13: 978-0689311741. Grades K–6.

Dolan, Ellen M. *Jack and the Beanstalk.* St. Louis, Mo.: Milliken, 1987. 30p. ISBN 10: 0883355833 (pb.); ISBN 13: 978-0883355831 (pb.). Grades K–3.

Edens, Cooper. *Jack & the Beanstalk.* San Marcos, Calif.: Green Tiger Press, 1990. 45p. ISBN 10: 088138139X; ISBN 13: 978-0881381399. Grades K–4.

Faulkner, Matt. *Jack and the Beanstalk.* New York: Scholastic, 1965. 32p. ISBN 10: 0590401645; ISBN 13: 978-0590401647 (pb.). (An audiocassette is available with the book.). Grads K-3.

Galdone, Paul. *Jack and the Beanstalk.* New York: Clarion, 1979. 32p. ISBN 10: 0395288010; ISBN 13: 978-0395288016. Grades K–3.

Garner, Alan. *Jack and the Beanstalk.* Illustrated by Julek Heller. New York: Doubleday Books for Young Readers, 1992. 32p. ISBN 10: 0385306938; ISBN 13: 978-0385306935. Grades 1–4.

Greenway, Jennifer. *Jack and the Beanstalk.* Illustrated by Richard Bernal. Kansas City: Andrews and McMeel, 1993. 32p. ISBN 10: 0836249038; ISBN 13: 978-0836249033. Grades K–3.

Hillert, Margaret. *The Magic Beans.* Illustrated by Mel Pekarsky. Chicago: Norwood House Press, 2006. 30p. ISBN 10: 1599530252; ISBN 13: 978-1599530253. Grades K–2.

Howe, John. *Jack and the Beanstalk.* Boston: Little, Brown, 1989. 32p. ISBN 10: 0316375799; ISBN 13: 978-0316375795. Grades K–2.

Kellogg, Steven. *Jack and the Beanstalk.* New York: Mulberry, 1991. 48p. ISBN 10: 0688102506; ISBN 13: 978-0688102500. Grades K–3.

Kincaid, Lucy. *Jack and the Beanstalk.* Illustrated by Eric Kincaid. Windermere, Fla.: Rourke Corp., 1983. 32p. ISBN 10: 0865921768; ISBN 13: 978-0865921764. Grades K–3.

McKay, Sindy. *Jack and the Beanstalk.* Illustrated by Lydia Halverson. Redwood City, Calif.: Treasure Bay, 1998. 44p. ISBN 10: 1891327003; ISBN 13: 978-1891327001. Grades K–3.

Metaxas, Eric. *Jack and the Beanstalk.* Illustrated by Edward Sorel. Edina, Minn.: Abdo Publishing, 2005. 32p. ISBN 10: 0887081886; ISBN 13: 978-0887081880. (Audiotape and videotape versions are available.). Grades K–4.

Moore, Maggie. *Jack and the Beanstalk.* Illustrated by Steve Cox. Minneapolis, Minn.: Picture Window Books, 2002. 31p. ISBN 10: 140480059X; ISBN 13: 978-1404800595. Grades K–2.

Murphy, Chuck. *Jack and the Beanstalk.* New York: Little Simon, 1998. 14p. ISBN 10: 0689823134; ISBN 13: 978-0689823138. (Pop-up version). Grades K–3.

Nesbit, E. *Jack and the Beanstalk.* Illustrated by Matt Tavares. Cambridge, Mass.: Candlewick Press, 2006. 48p. ISBN 10: 0763621242; ISBN 13: 978-0763621247. (Original version published in 1902). Grades K–3.

Ottolenghi, Carol. *Jack and the Beanstalk.* Illustrated by Guy Porfirio. Columbus, Ohio: School Specialty Children's Publishing, 2002. 32p. ISBN 10: 1577683773; ISBN 13: 978-1577683773. Grades K–2.

Patience, John. *Jack and the Beanstalk.* Ashland, Ohio: Landoll, 1993. 32p. ISBN 0710504640. Grades K–3.

Pearson, Susan. *Jack and the Beanstalk.* Illustrated by James Warhola. New York: Simon & Schuster Books for Young Readers, 1989. 40p. ISBN 10: 0671671960; ISBN 13: 978-0671671969. Grades K–3.

Many authors and adapters opt to make changes in the traditional retelling of this story. The differences may be in the characters, the setting, or a twist in the plot. Such changes are appealing to older listeners and readers who already know the story. They offer a surprise. Here are some examples of these changed versions.

Birdseye, Tom. *Look Out Jack! The Giant Is Back!* Illustrated by Will Hillenbrand. New York: Holiday House, 2003. 32p. ISBN 10: 082341776X; ISBN 13: 978-0823417766.
   Mr. G., brother of the dead giant, is after Jack, who moves to North Carolina with his mother. Grades K–3.

Compton, Kenn, and Joanne Compton. *Jack the Giant Chaser: An Appalachian Tale.* New York: Holiday House, 1993. 32p. ISBN 10: 0823409988; ISBN 13: 978-0823409983.
   Jack is quick witted and nimble in the Appalachian Mountain setting. Grades K–3.

DeSpain, Pleasant. *Strongheart Jack and the Beanstalk.* Illustrated by Joe Shlichta. Little Rock, Ark.: August House, 1995. 32p. ISBN 10: 0874834147; ISBN 13: 978-0874834147.
   Jack has his father's sword and help from lovely Elinor and his cat, Octavia, to overcome the giant. Grades 2–5.

Grawowsky, Alvin. *Giants Have Feelings, Too/Jack and the Beanstalk (Another Point of View).* Illustrated by Henry Buerchkholtz. New York: Steck-Vaughn, 1995. 48p. ISBN 10: 0811466361; ISBN 13: 978-0811466363.
   First the traditional story is told, then the giant's point of view is given, with various illustrations. Grades K–4.

Haley, Gail E. *Jack and the Bean Tree.* New York: Crown, 1986. 48p. ISBN 10: 0517557177; ISBN 13: 978-0517557174.
   A boy climbs to the top of a giant bean tree and outsmarts a giant to make a fortune for himself and his mother, in Appalachian style. Grades 1–4.

Harris, Jim. *Jack and the Giant: A Story Full of Beans.* Flagstaff, Ariz.: Northland/Rising Moon, 1997. 32p. ISBN 10: 0873586808; ISBN 13: 978-0873586801.
   Jack, a cowpoke, lives on a dude ranch with his mother, Annie Okey-Kokey. A giant has stolen their cattle, and Jack must sell the last cow—for beans. Grades 1–5.

Hindley, Judy. *Zoom on a Broom! Six Fun-Filled Stories.* Illustrated by Toni Goffe. New York: Kingfisher Books, 1992. 60p. ISBN 10: 1856978265; ISBN 13: 978-1856978262.
   Tom, a clever trickster, manages to outwit a giant thief and win the hand of a princess. Grades 1–4.

Johnson, Janet P. *Lucky Jack and the Giant: An African-American Legend.* Illustrated by Charles Reasoner. Mahwah, N.J.: Troll, 1998. 32p. ISBN 10: 0816743487; ISBN 13: 978-0816743483.
   Lucky Jack sets out to the home of the evil giant, Long Beard, who has a daughter, Julie. (An audiocassette version is available.) Grades K–4.

Johnson, Paul Brett. *Jack Outwits the Giants*. New York: M. K. McElderry Books, 2002. 32p. ISBN 10: 0689839022; ISBN 13: 978-0689839023.

Jack is trapped by a two-headed giant, but he proves he knows the Appalachian ways. Grades K–4.

Lorenz, Albert. *Jack and the Beanstalk: How a Small Fellow Solved a Big Problem*. New York: H. N. Abrams, 2002. 40p. ISBN-10: 0810911604; ISBN-13: 978-0810911604.

Not only does the author retell the story, but he ghoulishly offers pages on which one must search for Jack, solve problems, and find a recipe for "100 Ways to Cook Boys." Grades 2–5.

Muldrow, Diane. *Jacky and the Giant*. Illustrated by Vince Andriani. New York: Scholastic, 1999. 24p. ISBN 10: 0590688103; ISBN 13: 978-0590688109.

Jacky is a young girl, and the setting is an urban area.. Grades K–2.

Osborne, Mary Pope. *Kate and the Beanstalk*. Illustrated by Giselle Potter. New York: Atheneum Books for Young Readers, 2000. 40p. ISBN 10: 0689825501; ISBN 13: 978-0689825507.

Kate is not a simpleton, nor is she is afraid of the giant! Grades K–4.

Palmer, Judd. *The Giant Killer, Number 5: Preposterous Fables for Unusual Children*. Calgary, Alb.: Bayeux Arts, Inc., 2004. 144p. ISBN 10: 1896209475; ISBN 13: 978-1896209470.

Only one giant remains for Jack, but the hero is old, and times have changed. Grades 4–6.

Paulson, Tim. *Jack and the Beanstalk and the Beanstalk Incident*. Illustrated by Mark Corcoran. New York: Birch Lane Press, 1990. 13p. ISBN 10: 1559720484; ISBN 13: 978-1559720489.

Read one way, and one finds the traditional story. Turn the book upside down, and the giant's version appears. Grades 1–4.

Ransom, Candice. *Giant in the Garden: Time Spies, Book 3* (Time Spies). Renton, Wash.: Mirrorstone, 2007. 128p. ISBN 10: 0786940743; ISBN 13: 978-0786940745.

Alex, Mattie, and Sophie find a gigantic vine in their backyard and set out to climb it. Grades 2–5.

Schorsch, Kit. *Jack and the Beanstalk*. Illustrated by Kitty Diamantis. New York: Checkerboard Press, 1989. 24p. ISBN 10: 002898241X; ISBN 13: 978-0028982410.

Retells the story from the rebus formation. Grades K–3.

Stanley, Diane. *The Giant and the Beanstalk*. New York: HarperCollins, 2004. 32p. ISBN 10: 0060000104; ISBN 13: 978-0060000103.

In this mixed-up version, the giant Otto is a sweet, gentle guy who keeps a pet hen. He was very distressed when knave Jack was caught stealing his pet. The adventure begins when Otto follows Jack down the beanstalk. Grades 1–3.

Swope, Sam. *Jack and the Seven Deadly Giants*. Illustrated by Carll Cneut. New York: Farrar, Straus & Giroux, 2004. 112p. ISBN 10: 0374336709; ISBN 13: 978-0374336707.

Instead of one giant, Jack has taken on all the problems of "gianthood." Grades 4–6.

Walker, Richard. *Jack and the Beanstalk*. Illustrated by Niamh Sharkey. Cambridge, Mass.: Barefoot Books, 1999. 32p. ISBN 10: 1902283139; ISBN 13: 978-1902283135. (A version with a CD is available.)

The story is recognizable, but the giant's famous "fee, fi, fos" are different. Outer space figures into the ending. Grades K–3.

Wells, Rosemary. *Jack and the Beanstalk*. Illustrated by Norman Messenger. New York: Dorling Kindersley, 1997. 32p. ISBN 10: 0789411709; ISBN 13: 978-0789411709.

> The author changes the giant's famous refrain, and he no longer has a wife, but a cook. Grades 1–5.

Video Recordings

Jack and the giant have appeared in many audio and video presentations of the books listed. The plot has also been used by Abbot and Costello in a spoof, *Jack in the Beanstalk* (Good Times Video, 2001, 84 min.). Shelley Duvall and Jean Stapleton appeared in a 1983 Fairy Tale Theatre version, *Jack and the Beanstalk* (Starmaker II, 2004, 53 min.). Although not the original story, such spoofs are fun for those who know the actual story.

> *Jack and the Beanstalk—The Real Story*. Lions Gate, 2002. 184 min. Grades 3–6.

> *Mickey and the Beanstalk*. Walt Disney, 1995. 73 min. Grades K–5.

Giants in Modern Tales

There are many fairy tales and modern fantastical stories in which giants appear. Sometimes the giants are very dim-witted, greedy, and fond of human flesh. However, not all giants are evil. In some fairy tales and fantasy works, giants are kind beings who are friends to children, as in Roald Dahl's *BFG (Big Friendly Giant)*. Fantasy writers seem to gravitate to giants. John Bunyan envisioned Despair as a giant in *Pilgrim's Progress* (1678). Jonathan Swift included the Brobdingnagians in *Gulliver's Travels* (1726). Aslan brings life to good giant Rumblebuffin in *Lion, the Witch and the Wardrobe*. In the Harry Potter series, Grawp is a full-fledged giant. Giants abound in the Spiderwick Chronicles. These titles and others have been popular reading and have been transformed into movies and other media.

No discussion of giants would be complete without mentioning ogres, large hideous creatures with large heads, huge bellies, and strong bodies. Perrault's Puss and Boots outwitted a terrible ogre and managed to secure wealth for his master. Anyone watching the movie *Time Bandits* knows that the boys were found on a ship by an ogre and his wife. Tamora Pierce writes about ogres and giants in her fantasy series set in the Tortall universe. One of the most endearing ogres is Shrek. The green protagonist is reluctant and would rather be left alone in his swamp, but he is called to be a hero. These characters lend themselves to imaginary play with paper dolls.

Examples of modern giant and ogre characters may be found in these books.

Andreasen, Dan. *The Giant of Seville: A "Tall" Tale Based on a True Story*. New York: Abrams Books for Young Readers, 2007. 32p. ISBN 10: 081090988X; ISBN 13: 978-0810909885.

> Captain Martin Van Buren searches for a place to settle. It is a problem because he is almost eight feet tall. Grades 2–5.

Beaty, Andrea. *When Giants Come to Play*. Illustrated by Kevin Hawkes. New York: Abrams Books for Young Readers, 2006. 32p. ISBN 10: 0810957590; ISBN 13: 978-0810957596.

> Anna and her two giant friends play hide-and-seek, gather flowers, and play catch. Grades K–1.

Blade, Adam. *Cypher the Mountain Giant*. New York: Scholastic Inc., 2007. 80p. ISBN 10: 0439922259; ISBN 13: 978-0439922258.

> The one-eyed giant comes under a wicked spell and must be rescued before he destroys more towns. Grades 2–4.

Bottoms, Bud. *Davey and The GOM*. Lompoc, Calif.: Summerland Publishing, 2008. 46p. ISBN 10: 0979544416; ISBN 13: 978-0979544415.

> Davy works to overcome an oil monster. Grades 1–4.

Carle, Eric. *Watch Out! A Giant!* New York: Simon, 1978. 32p. ISBN 10: 0689849648; ISBN 13: 978-0689849640.

> Follow two children as they escape a giant through tunnels and secret places. Grades K–2.

Choldenko, Gennifer. *How to Make Friends with a Giant*. Illustrated by Amy Walrod. New York: Putnam Juvenile, 2006. 32p. ISBN 10: 0399237798; ISBN 13: 978-0399237799.

> Jake, the smallest kid in class, befriends the new kid, Jacomo, the largest kid ever. Grades K–2.

Dahl, Roald. *The BFG*. Illustrated by Quentin Blake. New York: Farrar, Straus & Giroux, 1982. 221p. ISBN 10: 0374304696; ISBN 13: 978-0374304690.

> Sophie is kidsnatched from her orphanage by a BFG (Big Friendly Giant), who spends his life blowing happy dreams to children. Sophie and the BFG together plot to save the world from nine other man-gobbling giants. (The unabridged audiotape read by Natasha Richardson is available from HarperChildrensAudio, 2002. An audio download is available from http://www.audible.com/adbl/entry/offers/productPromo2.jsp?BV_UseBVCookie=Yes&productID=BK_HARP_001 207 (accessed March 23, 2009). The DVD is available through A&E Home Video, 2006. 88 min. The videocassette is available from Just For Kids Home Video, 95 min.) Grades 3–6.

Della-Sera, Robert. *Giant Behind the House*. Bel Air, Calif,: Tandem Library, 2001. 120p. ISBN 10: 0613987780; ISBN 13: 978-0613987783.

> During a voyage across a continent, a boy and a dying giant find friendship.

Donaldson, Julia. *The Spiffiest Giant in Town*. Illustrated by Axel Scheffler. New York: Dial, 2003. 32p. ISBN 10: 0803728484; ISBN 13: 978-0803728486.

> Giant George gets a new outfit, but proceeds to give items away until he is beltless, with his pants falling down and people snickering. He must find his old clothes and friends. Grades K–2.

Dunbar, Joyce. *The Sand Children*. Illustrated by Mark Edwards. New York: Crocodile Books, 1999. 32p. ISBN 10: 1566563097; ISBN 13: 978-1566563093.

> A father and young son build a sand giant who comes to life. Grades K–2.

Farley, Jacqui. *Giant Hiccups*. Illustrated by Pamela Venus. Milwaukee, Wis.: Gareth Stevens, 1998. 32p. ISBN 10: 0836820908; ISBN 13: 978-0836820904.

> Giant Ayesha gets the hiccups, and the villagers try many remedies to help her get rid of them. Grades K–3.

Feldman, Eve. *A Giant Surprise*. Illustrated by Istvan Banyai. Austin, Tex.: Raintree, 1989. 32p. ISBN 10: 0817235272; ISBN 13: 978-0817235277.

> A young girl has a very large surprise guest. Grades K–1.

Fienberg, Anna and Barbara. *Tashi and the Giants*. Illustrated by Kim Gamble. Crows Nest, New South Wales: Allen & Unwin, 2007. 64p. ISBN 10: 1741149665; ISBN 13: 978-1741149661.

> Tashi encounters a dragon, a giant, and a bandit's wife with bravado. Grades 2–4.

Fox, Mem. *Where the Giant Sleeps*. Illustrated by Vladimir Radunsky. San Diego: Harcourt Children's Books, 2007. 32p. ISBN 10: 0152057854; ISBN 13: 978-0152057855.

> As a child sleeps, the reader sees fairies in a giant's hair, witches, and more. Grades K–2.

Loredo, Elizabeth. *Giant Steps*. Illustrated by Barry Root. New York: Putnam, 2004. 32p. ISBN 10: 0399234918; ISBN 13: 978-0399234910.

> Five giants are bored, so they play a game of giant steps, in which one counts while the others run. Grades K–4.

Morpurgo, Michael. *Gentle Giant*. Illustrated by Michael Foreman. New York: HarperCollins, 2004. 32p. ISBN 10: 0007110642; ISBN 13: 978-0007110643.

> Villagers ridicule the giant "Beastman," until he comes to the rescue and saves a young woman and a polluted lake. Grades K–3.

Pelley, Kathleen T. *The Giant King*. Washington, D.C.: Child & Family Press, 2003. 32p. ISBN 10: 0878688803; ISBN 13: 978-0878688807.

> Rabbie, a woodcarver, encourages the village to feed and clothe a giant, who in turn behaves with the kindness shown him. Grades K–2.

Ruzzier, Sergio. *The Little Giant*. New York: Laura Geringer, 2004. 32p. ISBN 10: 0060529512; ISBN 13: 978-0060529512.

> Angelino is a giant who is too small, and Osvaldo is a dwarf who is too big. They become friends and manage to help when the giants and dwarfs go to war. Grades K–3.

Scheidl, Gerda Marie. *The Crystal Ball*. Illustrated by Nathalie Duroussy. New York: North-South Books, 1993. 32p. ISBN 10: 1558581987; ISBN 13: 9781558581982.

> After unsuccessful attempts to get rid of a fierce giant, a princess and a glassblower try an act of kindness that brings about peace between the people of a kingdom and the giant. Grades K–3.

Steig, William. *Shrek!* New York: Farrar, Straus & Giroux, 1993. 32p. ISBN 10: 0374368775; ISBN 13: 978-0374368777.

> People flee when Shrek comes around because of his size and ugly appearance. A witch prophesizes that he will marry a princess who is more ugly than he is, and off he goes to find out how this can be. (The book was the basis for the films *Shrek* [2001]; *Shrek 2* [2004], and *Shrek the Third* [2007]. There are sound tracks and video games as well as toys and movie spin-off books.)

Strong, Jeremy. *Giant Jim and the Hurricane*. New York: Penguin, 1999. 32p. ISBN 10: 0754063321; ISBN 13: 978-0754063322.

> The villagers ask Jim to leave because his size is a problem, but he proves himself in a hurricane. (An audiocassette is available.) Grades K–2.

Swift, Jonathan. *Gulliver's Travels*. Illustrated by Willy Pogeny and David Small. New York: Morrow, 1983. 96p. ISBN 10: 0688020445; ISBN 13: 978-0688020446.

> Look for other versions of the story of this classic.

Thurber, James. *The Great Quillow*. Illustrated by Steven Kellogg. San Diego: Harcourt Brace Jovanovich, 1994. 54p. ISBN 10: 0152325441; ISBN 13: 978-0152325442.

> Quillow, a tiny toy maker, defeats a ferocious giant named Hunder and saves his town from destruction. Grades K–5.

Umansky, Kaye. *The Romantic Giant*. Illustrated by Doffy Weir. New York: Penguin, 1999. 32p. ISBN 10: 0241134501; ISBN 13: 978-0241134504.
Heavy Hetty the Wrestler helps Waldo, a giant, in his quest for the love of beautiful Princess Clarissa. Grades K-3.

Wilde, Oscar. *The Selfish Giant*. Illustrated by Lisbeth Zwerger. New York: Simon & Schuster, 1991. 28p. ISBN 10: 0907234305; ISBN 13: 978-0907234302.
A once selfish giant welcomes the children to his previously forbidden garden and later is rewarded by an unusual little child. There are many other versions, such as those done by illustrators: Michael Foreman and Freire Wright (Metheun, 1978. 32p. ISBN 10: 0458934208; ISBN 13: 978-0458934201); S. Saelig Gallagher (New York: Putnam, 1995. 32p. ISBN 10: 0399224483; ISBN 13: 978-0399224485); and Fabian Negrin (New York: Knopf, 2000. 32p. ISBN 10: 037580319X; ISBN 13: 978-0375803192.)

Willey, Margaret. *Clever Beatrice*. Illustrated by Heather M. Solomon. New York: Simon & Schuster, 2001. 32p. ISBN 10: 0689832540; ISBN 13: 978-0689832543.
Little Beatrice makes a wager with a giant. Grades K–3.

Know Your Giants

Stories in collections allow the reader to become familiar with a wide range of giants. Reading such short stories sparks the imagination and helps develop a long list of giant characters. These collections will prove helpful in developing such a list.

Baxter, Nicola. *Giants, Ogres and Trolls*. Illustrated by Ken Morton. Enderby, UK: Armadillo, 2001. 79 p. ISBN 10: 1900465329; ISBN 13: 978-1900465328. Grades 1–4.

Hamilton, John. *Ogres and Giants*. Edina, Minn.: ABDO & Daughters, 2004. ISBN 10: 1591977142; ISBN 13: 978-1591977148. Grades 2–5.

Hayes, Barbara. *The Enchanted World of—Giants and Ogres*. Illustrated by Geoffrey Campion. Vero Beach, Fla.: Rourke Enterprises, 1986. 24p. ISBN 10: 0865923167; ISBN 13: 978-0865923164. Grades 2–5.

Hayes, Sarah. *Gruesome Giants*. Illustrated by Chris Riddell. New York: Derrydale Books; distributed by Crown, 1985. 34p. ISBN 10: 0517615460; ISBN 13: 978-0517615461. Grades 1–4.

Hoke, Helen. *Giants! Giants! Giants! From Many Lands and Many Times*. Illustrated by Stephen Lavis. New York: Franklin Watts, 1980. 157p. ISBN 10: 0531041727; ISBN 13: 978-0531041727. Grades 3–6.

Larkin, David. *Giants*. Illustrated by Julek Heller, Carolyn Scrace, and Juan Wijngaard. New York: H. N. Abrams, 1979. 191p. ISBN 10: 0810909553. Grades 6–8.

Mayes, Walter M. *Walter the Giant Storyteller's Giant Book of Giant Stories*. Illustrated by Kevin O'Malley. New York: Walker Books for Young Readers, 2005. 48p. ISBN-10: 0802789749; ISBN 13: 978-0802789747. Grades 3–5.

Mayne, William. *William Mayne's Book of Giants; Stories*. Illustrated by Raymond Briggs. New York: Dutton, 1969. 215p. ISBN 10: 0525428100; ISBN 13: 978-0525428107. Grades 2–5.

Odor, Ruth Shannon. *Learning About Giants.* New York: Children's Press, 1981. 46p. ISBN 10: 0516065343; ISBN 13: 978-0516065342. Grades 1–4.

Olliver, Jane. *A Treasury of Giant and Monster Stories.* Illustrated by Annabel Spenceley. New York: Kingfisher Books, 1992. 156p. ISBN 10: 0862729750; ISBN 13: 978-0862729752. Grades 2–6.

Stoutenburg, Adrien. *Fee, Fi, Fo, Fum; Friendly and Funny Giants.* Illustrated by Rocco Negri. New York: Viking Press, 1969. 126p. ISBN 10: 0670311286; ISBN 13: 978-0670311286. Grades 2–5.

Walker, Paul Robert. *Giants! Stories from Around the World.* Illustrated by James Bernardin. San Diego: Harcourt Brace, 1995. 73p. ISBN 10: 0152008837; ISBN 13: 978-0152008833. Grades 3–6.

Waters, Fiona. *Giant Tales.* Illustrated by Amanda Hall. London: Chrysalis Books, 2003. 96p. ISBN 10: 1843650177; ISBN 13: 978-1843650171. Grades 2–5.

Wood, Audrey. *Rude Giants.* San Diego: Voyager Books/Harcourt Brace, 1993. 32p. ISBN 10: 0152694129; ISBN 13: 978-0152694128

Published Giant Paper Dolls

Giants themselves do not figure prominently in paper dolls from the past, although there are a few examples of Bible figures (David and Goliath), Paul Bunyan, and Jack's giant. In the 1970s, an Excello ad featured a standup Paul Bunyan and Ox Babe.

Today there are a few dolls available, including the following:

Dolls from Storyland. Gallery Graphics. Order from http://www.paperdollreview.com/catalog/index.php?main_page=index&cPath=17 (accessed March 23, 2009).
Seven dolls and twenty-three outfits, including Jack and the Beanstalk.

"Storybook Characters." *Paper Doll Studio* no. 84 (Winter 2006). Order from http://www.paperdollreview.com/catalog/index.php?main_page=index&cPath=16&zenid=tq5ftiihvmkenpm11qhgg8kav6 (accessed March 23, 2009).
The issue includes paper dolls for Oscar Wilde's *The Selfish Giant.*

Many sources include instructions for making a giant-sized paper doll of oneself.

"Elisabeth's Doppelganger." In *Artful Paper Dolls: New Ways to Play with a Traditional Form,* by Terry Taylor, 28–31. Ashville, N.C.: Lark Books, 2006.
This book provides a detailed set of instructions for making a paper doll of oneself.

Lesson Plan:
A Giant above Giants!

Library Media Skills Objective:

The student will select poetry, folktales, and modern stories about giants and prepare a description that includes a paper doll representation.

Curriculum (Subject Areas) Objectives:

The activity may be incorporated into a language arts unit and creative arts lessons. In language arts, the focus may include themes of good versus evil and the concept of size (relationship of large and small). In art, students may learn how to enlarge. The activity may also be used by guidance personnel to talk about characteristics that are valued and what makes people "giants."

Grade Level: 3–6

Resources:

> Books about giants
>
> Butcher-block paper
>
> Pencils, paper, poster paint
>
> Scissors
>
> Paper doll handout

Instructional Roles:

The teacher and library media specialist may collaborate to introduce the lesson and choose books. The teacher may instruct students in the writing and art portions of the lesson. The introduction may take 45–60 minutes. The time needed for students to read on their own will vary with the selections. Artwork and enlargement will take 1 to 2 hours depending on the level of complexity of the dolls and clothes. After reading, students will need at least an hour for composition and corrections. Wall preparation and presentation requires at least 1 hour.

Activity and Procedures for Completion:

Before the unit and lessons begin, prepare a large bulletin board with a map. Use arrows or string to connect the cut-out paper dolls and lists of books to specific countries or areas.

Introduce the lessons and activities with several readings of "giant" poetry to a class. Poems such as the following work well:

"I Am an Ant and a Gi-ant," by P Brewster. In *The Poetry Break: An Annotated Anthology with Ideas for Introducing Children to Poetry,* by Caroline Feller Bauer. New York: H. W. Wilson, 1994.

"Five Giants," by J. Prelutsky. In *Monday's Troll,* by Jack Prelutsky. New York: Greenwillow, 1996.

Select a story such as Elizabeth Loredo's *Giant Steps* and play the following game. Introduce some of the giants and begin a list on a board or chart paper that can be added to and displayed during the activities. As a finale, ask students to help in the reading and retelling of Beatrice Schenk de Regniers' *Jack and the Beanstalk: Retold in Verse for Boys & Girls to Read Themselves*. This may be done in several ways. If more than one copy of the book is available, divide students into small groups. Allow them four or five minutes to read over assigned portions. Then the entire book may be shared, with groups taking turns reading the verses together in turn as directed. If only one copy of the book is available, project the verses on a screen and divide the students into groups. Point to each group and have them read selected verses aloud together.

Students are ready for the assignment. They will be making paper dolls of a giant and then making paper dolls of themselves as giants larger than the giants. Discuss how size is relative. Sometimes individuals can be giants with or without increasing in physical size. Students will read about a selected giant and then think about how they might be a "giant" to the character they select. Provide time for students to look for books about giants. At this point, a review of searching the library media catalog may be appropriate. If poetry indexes and folktale indexes are available, instruct students in their use and suggest that they might want to consider looking for a story about a giant in collections. On the bulletin board, with the students' help identify some of the giants around the world. Post the list of giants and add to it as the sessions go on.

Students should have time to select books and read on their own. Follow up the reading by providing the paper doll handouts so that students may begin to color and prepare their book giants.

In an art session, students will make their own paper dolls of themselves. They will trace themselves on butcher-block paper with a partner's help, then paint and cut out the doll. The doll may be dressed, or the students may make separate outfits for themselves, again by tracing part of the doll they have made. Students may paint the outfits and use other items for decoration such as fabric, glitter, buttons, feathers, and media objects. The art teacher may discuss and share other ideas for decorating the dolls and their clothes.

Students will display the giant paper dolls of themselves holding the paper doll of a giant about whom they have read. These paper dolls may be mounted on the wall of a long corridor and named "Wall or Hall of the Giants." Each student must write one or more paragraphs that answer the following questions:

Who is the giant (complete with bibliographic citations)?

What was special about the giant? (What did the character do?)

Why do you consider yourself a giant to this character?

Invite the principal or other individuals for a "giant" presentation of the giants. Students may talk about their readings and what struck them about the characteristics of their giant paper doll.

Evaluation:

Each student will select poetry, folktales, or a modern story about giants and prepare a description and a paper doll representation of the character in the story. The level of competence exhibited in the paragraphs and the paper dolls will depend on student abilities and teacher expectations.

Follow-Up:

Another option is to sponsor a human paper doll parade or exhibit, for which students make paper doll outfits, complete with tabs, to wear as they hold their completed dolls and discuss the characters.

Paper Dolls:
Giants

Instructions: Dress your own favorite giant!

Paul Bunyan

Asian giant

African giant

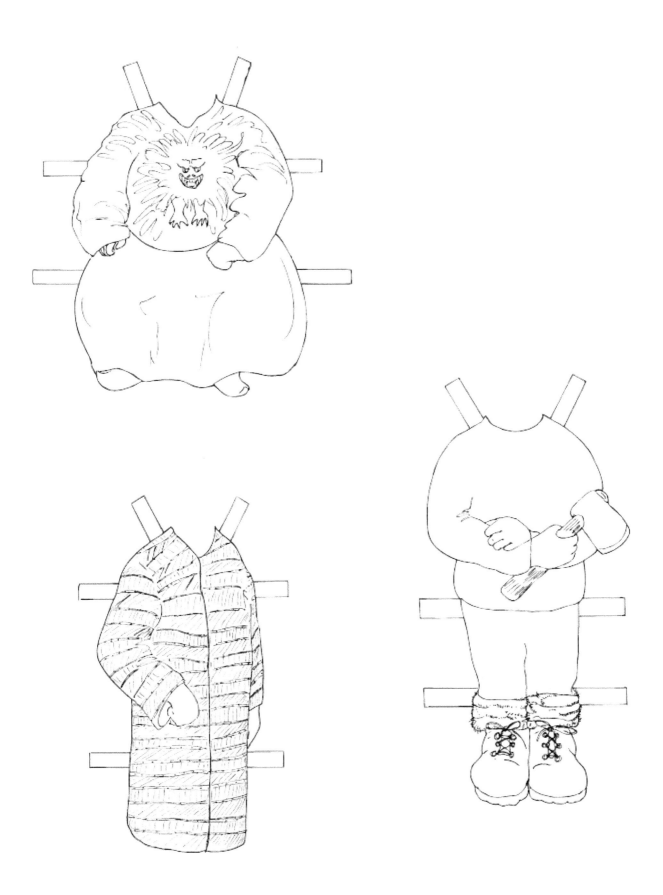

Chapter 8

Judgment of Paris

Imagine a wonderful party that you are not invited to. That is what happened to Eris, the goddess of discord. She had caused so much trouble on Olympus that she was not allowed there anymore. Eris found out that she had not been invited to the wedding of Thetis, a sea goddess, and a king named Peleus. She was angry and decided to get even. She tossed a golden apple onto a table at the feast. The words on the apple said, "For the fairest." All the goddesses at the feast tried to claim the prize. At last there were three goddesses left. Hera, Athena, and Aphrodite called Zeus to make a decision. He knew that he could not win, no matter whom he chose. The other two would be angry with him. Zeus asked Paris, a shepherd, to make the decision.

Each goddess tried to convince Paris to choose her. Hera promised him power and wealth. Athena promised him wisdom and greatness in war. Aphrodite promised him the most beautiful woman in the world.

These events prepared the way for the Trojan War and the journeys thereafter. More on the full story can be found in the following sources.

Books

Claybourne, Anna. *The Adventures of Ulysses*. Illustrated by Jeff Anderson. London: Usborne, 1998. 112p. ISBN 10: 0881109711; ISBN 13: 978-0881109719. Grades 3–7.

Claybourne, Anna, and Kamini Khanduri. *Greek Myths: Ulysses and the Trojan War*. Illustrated by Jeff Anderson. London: Usborne, 1999. 159p. ISBN 10: 079450535X; ISBN 13: 978-0794505356. Grades 3–7.

Colum, Padraic. *The Trojan War and the Adventures of Odysseus*. Illustrated by Barry Moser. New York: Morrow, 1997. 192p. ISBN 10: 0688145884; ISBN 13: 978-0688145880. Grades 4–8.

Colum, Padraic. *The Children's Homer*. Illustrated by Willy Pogany. New York: Macmillan, 1946. 245p. ISBN 10: 0808572857; ISBN 13: 978-0808572855. Grades 4–8.

Connolly, Peter. *The Legend of Odysseus*. New York: Oxford University Press, 1986. 80p. ISBN 10: 0199171432; ISBN 13: 978-0199171439. Grades 4–7.

Coolidge, Olivia E. *The Trojan War*. Boston: Houghton Mifflin, 1952. 256p. ISBN 10: 0618154272; ISBN 13: 978-0618154272. (See "The Golden Apple" on pages 3–10.) Grades 4–7.

Cooper, Gilly Cameron. *The Trojan Horse*. Milwaukee, Wis.: World Almanac Library, 2007. 48p. ISBN 10: 0836881508; ISBN 13: 978-0836881509. Grades 3–6.

Edmondson, Elizabeth. *The Trojan War*. Illustrated by Harry Clow. New York: Maxwell Macmillan International, 1992. 32p. ISBN 10: 075020625X; ISBN 13: 978-0750206259. Grades 2–5.

Fontes, Justine, and Ron Fontes. *The Trojan Horse: The Fall of Troy: A Greek Myth*. Illustrated by Gordon Purcell and Barbara Schulz. Minneapolis, Minn.: Graphic Universe, 2007. 48p. ISBN 10: 082256484X; ISBN 13: 978-0822564843. Grades 4–7.

Gates, Doris. *A Fair Wind for Troy*. Illustrated by Charles Mikolaycak. New York: Viking Press, 1984. 84p. ISBN 10: 0670305057; ISBN13: 978-0670305056. Grades 3–6.

Hovey, Kate. *Voices of the Trojan War*. Illustrated by Leonid Gore. New York: Margaret K. McElderry Books, 2004. 128p. ISBN 10: 0689857683; ISBN 13: 978-0689857683. Grades 5–9.

Hutton, Warwick. *The Trojan Horse*. New York: Margaret K. McElderry Books, 1992. 32p. ISBN 10: 0689505426; ISBN 13: 978-0689505423. Grades 3–6.

Khanduri, Kamini. *Tales of the Trojan War*. Illustrated by Jeff Anderson. London: Usborne, 1998. 160p. ISBN 10: 0794503233; ISBN 13: 978-0794503239. Grades 3–6.

Lister, Robin. *The Odyssey*. Illustrated by Alan Baker. New York: Kingfisher, 1987. 96p. ISBN 10: 0862722853; ISBN 13: 978-0862722852. Grades 4–7.

Little, Emily. *The Trojan Horse: How the Greeks Won the War*. Illustrated by Michael Eagle. New York: Random House, 1988. 48p. ISBN 10: 0394996747; ISBN 13: 978-0394996745. Grades 2–5.

Lorenz, Albert. *The Trojan Horse*. Illustrated by Joy Schleh. New York: Abrams Books for Young Readers, 2006. 40p. ISBN 10: 0810959860; ISBN 13: 978-0810959866. Grades 3–6.

Lupton, Hugh, and Daniel Morden. *The Adventures of Odysseus*. Illustrated by Christina Balit. Cambridge, Mass.: Barefoot Books, 2006. 96p. ISBN 10: 1841488003; ISBN 13: 978-1841488004. (Audio CD available). Grades 3–7.

McCarty, Nick. *The Iliad*. Illustrated by Victor G. Ambrus. Boston: Kingfisher, 2004. 96p. ISBN 10: 0753453304; ISBN 13: 978-0753453308. Grades 4–8.

McCaughrean, Geraldine. *The Odyssey*. Illustrated by Victor G. Ambrus. New York: Oxford University Press, 1993. 94p. ISBN 10: 1562884336; ISBN 13: 978-1562884338. Grades 4–7.

Mitchell, Adrian. *The Odyssey*. Illustrated by Stuart Robertson. New York: Dorling Kindersley, 2000. 64p. ISBN 10: 0789454556; ISBN 13: 978-0789454553. Grades 3–7.

Osborne, Mary Pope. *The Final Battle, Book 6*. Illustrated by Troy Howell. New York: Hyperion Paperbacks for Children, 2004. 112p. ISBN 10: 078680775X; ISBN 13: 978-0786807758. Grades 3–6.

Osborne, Mary Pope. *Return to Ithaca, Book 5*. Illustrated by Troy Howell. New York: Hyperion Paperbacks for Children, 2004. 112p. ISBN 10: 0786807741; ISBN 13: 978-0786807741. Grades 3–6.

Picard, Barbara Leonie. *The Iliad of Homer*. Illustrated by Joan Kiddell-Monroe. New York: Oxford University Press, 1991. 224p. SBN 10: 0192741470 (pb.); ISBN 13: 978-0192741479 (pb.). Grades 5–8.

Picard, Barbara Leonie. *The Odyssey of Homer*. Illustrated by Joan Kiddell-Monroe. New York: Oxford University Press, 1952. 288p. ISBN 10: 0192750755 (pb.); ISBN 13: 978-0192750754 (pb.). Grades 5–8.

Reeves, James. *The Voyage of Odysseus: Homer's Odyssey*. Illustrated by Eric Fraser. New York: Bedrick/Blackie, 1992. 192p. ISBN 10: 0872260925; ISBN 13: 978-0872260924. Grades 5–8.

Strachan, Ian. *The Iliad*. Illustrated by Victor Ambrus. New York: Kingfisher, 1997. 95p. ISBN 10: 0753451077; ISBN 13: 978-0753451076. Grades 4–7.

Sutcliff, Rosemary. *Black Ships before Troy: The Story of the Iliad*. Illustrated by Alan Lee. New York: Delacorte, 1993. 128p. ISBN 10: 0385310692; ISBN 13: 978-0385310697. (See "Golden Apple" on pages 6–13 for the full story.) Grades 5–8.

Sutcliff, Rosemary. *The Wanderings of Odysseus: The Story of the Odyssey*. New York: Laurel-Leaf, 1995. 144p. ISBN 10: 0553494821 (pb.); ISBN 13: 978-0553494822 (pb.). Grades 5–8.

Tyler, Deborah. *The Greeks and Troy*. New York: Dillon Press, 1993. 32p. ISBN 10: 0875185371; ISBN 13: 978-0875185378. Grades 3–6.

Williams, Marcia. *The Iliad and the Odyssey*. Cambridge, Mass.: Candlewick Press, 1996. 32p. ISBN 10: 0763600539; ISBN 13: 978-0763600532. Grades 2–5.

Yolen, Jane, and Robert J. Harris. *Odysseus in the Serpent Maze*. New York: HarperCollins, 2001. 256p. ISBN 10: 0060287349; ISBN 13: 978-0060287344. Grades 3–7.

Audio Recordings

Colum, Padraic. *The Children's Homer*. Ashland, OR: Blackstone Audiobooks, 1999.

Osborne, Mary Pope. *Tales from the Odyssey. Volume 1*. New York: HarperChildren's Audio, 2002.

Osborne, Mary Pope. *Tales from the Odyssey. Volume 2*. New York: Harper Children's Audio, 2003.

Video Recordings

The Iliad. Great Neck, N.Y.: Best Film & Video, 1986.

Internet

Amazon Research Network—http://www.myrine.at/ (accessed March 24, 2009).

Bulfinch's Mythology—http://www.bulfinch.org/ (accessed March 24, 2009).

Bulfinch's Mythology: The Age of Fable or Stories of Gods and Heroes—http://www.online-literature.com/bulfinch/mythology_fable/ (accessed March 24, 2009).

Classical Myth: The Ancient Sources—http://web.uvic.ca/grs/department_files/classical_myth/index.html (accessed March 24, 2009).

Encyclopedia Mythica—http://www.pantheon.org/ (accessed March 24, 2009).

Gods, Heroes, and Myth: Greek and Roman: Myths & Legends—http://www.gods-heros-myth. com/grmyths.html (accessed March 24, 2009).

Greek Mythology: From the Iliad to the Fall of the Last Tyrant—http://www.messagenet.com/ myths/ (accessed March 24, 2009).

Greek Mythology Today and the Myth of the Month—http://mythman.com/ (accessed March 24, 2009).

Images of the Trojan War Myth—http://www.temple.edu/classics/troyimages.html (accessed March 24, 2009).

Introduction to Greek Mythology—http://www.geocities.com/Athens/Acropolis/5065/ greek1.htm (accessed March 24, 2009).

The Minneapolis Institute of Arts: World Myths & Legends in Art—http://www. artsmia.org/world-myths/ (accessed March 24, 2009).

Mythography: Exploring Greek, Roman, and Celtic Myth and Art!—http://www.loggia.com/ myth/myth.html (accessed March 24, 2009).

Mythology Guide—http://www.online-mythology.com/ (accessed March 24, 2009).

Mythweb—http://www.mythweb.com/ (accessed March 24, 2009).

Olympian Gods—http://geocities.com/Athens/Parthenon/6542/or%5Fgods.html (accessed March 24, 2009).

Pegasus' Paradise—http://library.thinkquest.org/4553/ (accessed March 24, 2009).

Perseus Digital Library—http://www.perseus.tufts.edu (accessed March 24, 2009).

Temple University: Directory: Classical Mythology—http://www.temple.edu/classics/ mythdirectory.html (accessed March 24, 2009).

Topical Index of Gods and Goddesses—http://www.windows.umich.edu/mythology/ gods_n_goddesses.html (accessed March 24, 2009).

Winged Sandals. http://www.wingedsandals.com/ (accessed March 24, 2009).

Who Were the Players?

Paris was the son of King Priam and Hecuba. When his mother dreamed that he would bring ruin to the city, she and her husband sent the child to Mount Ida to be left to die. A shepherd found the baby and raised him. Paris grew up strong and handsome. Eventually he found out who his parents were. He took part in the Trojan War.

Hera was the wife of Zeus and queen of the gods on Olympus. She was the goddess of marriage, women, and birth. Hera's symbols were the cow, pomegranate, and peacock.

Athena was the goddess of war, wisdom, handicrafts, and agriculture. She was born fully armed from the forehead of Zeus. She was his favorite child and was allowed to use his breastplate and thunderbolts. Her symbols were the owl and olive tree.

Aphrodite was the goddess of love, who it was said was born from the foam of the sea. She was the wife of the smith-god Hephaestus, who was both ugly and lame, and mother of Eros. Her symbols were the myrtle tree, dove, swan, and dolphin.

From the decision of Paris about the goddesses came the seeds of a major war.

Each god and goddess and his or her many stories can provide the impetus for imagining scenes with characters in various costumes. Each brings the possibility of outfitting a paper doll.

Aliki. *The Gods and Goddesses of Olympus*. New York: HarperCollins, 1994. 48p. ISBN 10: 0060235306; ISBN 13: 978-0060235307.

> In part one, stories tell of the gods who created the universe; part two provides profiles of the gods and goddesses. Grades 3–6.

Amery, Heather. *Greek Myths for Young Children*. Illustrated by Linda Edwards. Tulsa, Okla.: EDC Publishing, 1999. 128p. ISBN 10: 0746037252; ISBN 13: 978-0746037256.

> This gentler retelling may fit the needs for read-aloud of younger children. Grades 1–5.

Ardagh, Philip. *Ancient Greek Myths & Legends*. Illustrated by Virginia Gray. Parsippany, N.J.: Dillon Press, 1999. 48p. ISBN 10: 038239996X; ISBN 13: 978-0382399961.

> The highlights focus on major stories, with background explanations. Grades 2–6.

D'Aulaire, Ingri, and Edgar Parin. *D'Aulaire's Book of Greek Myths*. Doubleday, 1962. 192p. ISBN 10: 0385015836; ISBN 13: 978-0385015837.

> See the story of the golden apple on pages 178–181. Grades 2–5.

Fisher, Leonard Everett. *The Olympians: Great Gods and Goddesses of Ancient Greece*. New York: Holiday House, 1984. 32p. ISBN 10: 0823405222; ISBN 13: 978-0823405220.

> Short biographies reveal symbols and basic information about the major Greek gods and goddesses. Grades 2–6.

Gibson, Michael. *Gods, Men and Monsters from the Greek Myths*. Illustrated by Giovanni Caselli. New York: Schocken Books, 1977. 160p. ISBN 10: 0856540277; ISBN 13: 978-0856540271.

> Basic collection includes stories of the gods and goddesses of ancient Greece. Grades 5–8.

Green, Roger Lancelyn. *Tales of the Greek Heroes*. Illustrated by Betty Middleton-Sandford. New York: Puffin, 1974. 208p. ISBN 10: 0140301194 (pb.); ISBN 13: 978-0140301199 (pb.).

> This readable version includes the origin of the Greek pantheon, the adventures of Perseus, the seven labors of Heracles, and the voyage of Jason and the Argonauts. (An audio CD and a download are available.) Grades 4–7.

Lines, Kathleen. *The Faber Book of Greek Legends*. Illustrated by Faith Jaques. Boston: Faber and Faber, 2001. 268p. ISBN 10: 0571098304; ISBN 13: 978-0571098309.

> Twenty-five stories about the gods and goddesses, include some of the less well-known stories. Grades 5–7.

Low, Alice. *The Simon and Schuster Book of Greek Gods and Heroes*. Illustrated by Arvis Stewart. New York: Simon & Schuster, 1985. 192p. ISBN 10: 0027613909; ISBN 13: 978-0027613902.

Includes more than forty stories of the Greek pantheon, from the origins of the earth to the wanderings of Odysseus. Grades 4–8.

Martell, Hazel. *Myths and Civilization of the Ancient Greeks*. Illustrated by Francesca D'Ottavi and Ivan Stalio. New York: Peter Bedrick Books, 1998. 48p. ISBN 10: 0872262839; ISBN 13: 978-0872262836.
   Each myth is followed by one or two overview pages of pictures and factual explanations about clothing, jewelry, or material goods related to the story. Grades 4–8.

Masters, Anthony. *Greek Myths and Legends*. Illustrated by Andrew Skilleter. New York: P. Bedrick Books, 2000. 48p. ISBN 10: 0872266095; ISBN 13: 978-0872266094.
   Five stories feature Greek gods and heroes with superhuman strength. Grades 2–5.

McCaughrean, Geraldine. *Greek Gods and Goddesses*. Illustrated by Emma Chichester Clark. New York: Margaret K. McElderry Books, 1998. 112p. ISBN 10: 0689820844; ISBN 13: 978-0689820847.
   A retelling of how Paris judged who was the fairest goddess of all and fourteen other tales make up this collection. Grades 3–6.

McCaughrean, Geraldine. *Greek Myths*. Illustrated by Emma Chichester Clark. New York: Margaret K. McElderry Books, 1993. 96p. ISBN 10: 0689505833; ISBN 13: 978-0689505836.
   Whether the interest is in curious Pandora, musical Apollo, or incredible hulk Hercules, the reader will find the familiar in this volume. Grades 4–6.

Mitton, Jacqueline, and Christina Balit. *Once Upon a Starry Night: A Book of Constellation Stories*. Washington, D.C.: National Geographic, 2003. 32p. ISBN 10: 0792263324; ISBN 13: 978-0792263326.
   Ten stories about the constellations are condensed into a few short paragraphs to accompany the explanation of each constellation. Grades K–3.

Orgel, Doris. *My Mother's Daughter: Four Greek Goddesses Speak*. Illustrated by Peter Malone. Brookfield, Conn.: A Neal Porter Book Roaring Brook Press, 2003. 128p. ISBN 10: 0761316930; ISBN 13: 978-0761316930.
   Leto, Artemis, Demeter, and Persephone tell their stories. Grades 6–8.

Vinge, Joan D. *The Random House Book of Greek Myths*. Illustrated by Oren Sherman. New York: Random House, 1999. 160p. ISBN 10: 0679823778; ISBN 13: 978-0679823773.
   A comprehensive look at the Greek gods and goddesses from the beginning. Grades 2–7.

Williams, Marcia. *Greek Myths for Young Children*. Cambridge, Mass.: Candlewick Press, 1992. 40p. ISBN 10: 1564021157; ISBN 13: 978-1564021151.
   Pandora, Arion, Orpheus, Heracles, Daedalus, Perseus, Theseus, and Arachne are shown as cartoonlike figures. Grades 1–5.

Gods, Goddesses, and Other Heroes and Villains

Many gods and goddesses as well as special human beings can be found among the stories that will interest children. Story and art become intertwined. The illustrations in the books may serve as inspiration for costumes. The portrayal is certain to warrant comparison to early Greek works of art. Here are titles specific to certain characters.

Aphrodite or Venus

Gates, Doris. *Two Queens of Heaven: Aphrodite, Demeter*. Illustrated by Trina Schart Hyman. New York: Viking, 1974. 94p. ISBN 10: 0670736805; ISBN 13: 978-0670736805. Grades 7–9.

Loewen, Nancy. *Venus*. New York: RiverFront Books, 1999. 48p. ISBN 10: 0736800506; ISBN 13: 978-0736800501. Grades 4–7.

Apollo

Barber, Antonia. *Apollo & Daphne: Masterpieces of Greek Mythology*. Illustrated with Paintings from the Great Art Museums of the World. Los Angeles: J. Paul Getty Museum, 1998. 46p. ISBN 10: 0892365048; ISBN 13: 978-0892365043. Grades 5–8.

Gates, Doris. *The Golden God, Apollo*. Illustrated by Constantinos CoConis. New York: Viking, 1973. 110p. ISBN 10: 0670344125; ISBN 13: 978-0670344123. Grades 5–7.

Arachne

Espeland, Pamela. *The Story of Arachne*. Illustrated by Susan Kennedy. Minneapolis, Minn.: Carolrhoda Books, 1980. 32p. ISBN 10: 0876141300; ISBN 13: 978-0876141304. Grades 2–5.

Hovey, Kate. *Arachne Speaks*. Illustrated by Blair Drawson. New York: M. K. McElderry Books, 2000. 48p. ISBN 10: 0689829019; ISBN 13: 978-0689829017. Grades 3–6.

Simons, Jamie, and Scott Simons. *Why Spiders Spin: A Story of Arachne*. Illustrated by Anthony Acardo. Englewood Cliffs, N.J.: Silver Burdett, 1991. 32p. ISBN 10: 0671691244; ISBN 13: 978-0671691240. Grades 2–5.

Atalanta

Bass, L. G. *Atalanta: The Wild Girl*. Illustrated by Peter Bollinger. New York: Scholastic, 1997. 32p. ISBN 10: 0590845527 (pb.); ISBN 13: 978-0590845526 (pb.). Grades 4–7.

Climo, Shirley. *Atalanta's Race: A Greek Myth*. Illustrated by Alexander Koshkin. New York: Clarion Books, 1995. 40p. ISBN 10: 0395673224; ISBN 13: 978-0395673225. Grades 2–5.

Martin, Claire. *The Race of the Golden Apples*. Illustrated by Leo Dillon and Diane Dillon. New York: Dial Books for Young Readers, 1991. 32p. ISBN 10: 0803702485; ISBN 13: 978-0803702486. Grades 2–4.

Yolen, Jane, and Robert J. Harris. *Atalanta and the Arcadian Beast*. New York: HarperCollins, 2003. 224p. ISBN 10: 006029454X; ISBN 13: 978-0060294540. Grades 4–6.

Athena or Minerva

Gates, Doris. *The Warrior Goddess: Athena*. Illustrated by Don Bolognese. New York: Puffin Books, 1972. 121p. ISBN 10: 0670749966; ISBN 13: 978-0670749966. Grades 4–7.

Hoena, B. A. *Athena*. Mankato, Minn.: Capstone Press, 2003. 24p. ISBN 10: 0736834532; ISBN 13: 978-0736834537. Grades 2–5.

Loewen, Nancy. *Athena*. New York: RiverFront Books, 1999. 48p. ISBN 10: 0736800484; ISBN 13: 978-0736800488. Grades 4–7.

Osborne, Mary Pope. *The Gray-eyed Goddess, Book 4*. Illustrated by Troy Howell. New York: Hyperion Paperbacks for Children, 2003. 128p. ISBN 10: 0786807733; ISBN 13: 978-0786807734. Grades 5–7.

Woff, Richard. *Bright-eyed Athena: Stories from Ancient Greece*. Los Angeles: J. Paul Getty Museum, 1999. 48p. ISBN 10: 0892365587; ISBN 13: 978-0892365586. Grades 4–7.

Cyclops

Evslin, Bernard. *The Cyclopes*. New York: Chelsea House Publishers, 1987. 96p. ISBN 10: 1555462367; ISBN 13: 978-1555462369. Grades 5–7.

Fisher, Leonard Everett. *Cyclops*. New York: Holiday House, 1991. 32p. ISBN 10: 0823408914; ISBN 13: 978-0823408917. Grades 4–6.

Hutton, Warwick. *Odysseus and the Cyclops*. New York: Margaret K. McElderry Books, 1995. 32p. ISBN 10: 0689800363; ISBN 13: 978-0689800368. Grades 3–6.

Nardo, Don. *Cyclops*. Detroit: KidHaven Press, Thomson/Gale, 2005. 48p. ISBN 10: 0737726156; ISBN 13: 978-0737726152. Grades 4–6.

Osborne, Mary Pope. *The One-eyed Giant, Book 1*. Illustrated by Troy Howell. New York: Hyperion Paperbacks for Children, 2002. 112p. ISBN 10: 0786807709; ISBN 13: 978-0786807703. Grades 4–7.

Demeter or Ceres

Birrer, Cynthia, and William Birrer. *Song to Demeter*. New York: Lothrop, Lee & Shepard Books, 1987. 32p. ISBN 10: 0688040403; ISBN 13: 978-0688040406. Grades 1–3.

Fontes, Justine, and Ron Fontes. *Demeter & Persephone: Spring Held Hostage: A Greek Myth*. Illustrated by Steve Kurth and Barbara Schulz. Minneapolis, Minn.: Graphic Universe, 2007. 48p. ISBN 10: 0822565706; ISBN 13: 978-0822565703. Grades 4–7.

Richardson, I. M. *Demeter and Persephone, the Seasons of Time*. Illustrated by Robert Baxter. Mahwah, N.J.: Troll Associates, 1983. 31p. ISBN 10: 0893758639; ISBN 13: 978-0893758639. Grades 2–4.

Hades or Pluto

McMullan, Kate. *Have a Hot Time, Hades!* Illustrated by David La Fleur. New York: Volo/Hyperion, 2002. 160p. ISBN 10: 0786808578; ISBN 13: 978-0786808571. Grades 4–7.

Riordan, Rick. *The Lightning Thief*. Waterville, Me.: Thorndike Press, 2006. 384p. ISBN 10: 064172344X; ISBN 13: 978-0786856299. (The fictionalized tale is available on audiocassette and audio download). Grades 6–9.

Hercules

Burleigh, Robert. *Hercules.* Illustrated by Raul Colón. San Diego: Harcourt Brace, 1999. 32p. ISBN 10: 0152016678; ISBN 13: 978-0152016678. Grades 3–6.

Cerasini, Marc A. *The Twelve Labors of Hercules.* Illustrated by Isidre Mones. New York: Random House, 1997. 48p. ISBN 10: 0679983937; ISBN 13: 978-0679983934. Grades 2–4.

Charbonnet, Gabrielle. *Disney's Hercules: I Made Herc a Hero by Phil.* New York: Disney Press, 1997. 57p. ISBN 10: 0786841958; ISBN 13: 978-0786841950. (From the animated film). Grades 2–4.

Conklin, Thomas. *The Adventures of Hercules.* New York: Random House, 1996. 123p. ISBN 10: 0679882634; ISBN 13: 978-0679882633. Grades 4–6.

Harris, John. *Strong Stuff: Herakles and His Labors.* Illustrated by Gary Baseman. Los Angeles: J. Paul Getty Museum, 2005. 32p. ISBN 10: 0892367849; ISBN 13: 978-0892367849. Grades 2–5.

Lasky, Kathryn. *Hercules: The Man, the Myth, the Hero.* Illustrated by Mark Hess. New York: Hyperion Books for Children, 1997. 32p. ISBN 10: 0786803290; ISBN 13: 978-0786803293. Grades 4–6.

Loewen, Nancy. *Hercules.* New York: RiverFront Books, 1999. 48p. ISBN 10: 0736800492; ISBN 13: 978-0736800495. Grades 4–7.

Marsoli, Lisa Ann. *Hercules: Classic Storybook.* Illustrated by Judith Holmes Clarke, Denise Shimabukuro, Scott Tilley, and Atelier Philippe Harchy. New York: Mouse Works, 1997. 126p. ISBN 10: 0762402318; ISBN 13: 978-0762402311. (From the animated Disney film). Grades 4–7.

McCaughrean, Geraldine. *Hercules.* Chicago: Cricket Books, 2003. 152p. ISBN 10: 0812627377; ISBN 13: 978-0812627374. Grades 5–8.

Moore, Robin. *Hercules: Hero of the Night Sky.* Illustrated by Alexa Rutherford. New York: Aladdin Paperbacks, 1997. 80p. ISBN 10: 0613021622; ISBN 13: 978-0613021623. Grades 2–5.

Moroz, Georges. *Hercules: The Twelve Labors of a Legendary Hero.* New York: Bantam Doubleday Dell Books for Young Readers, 1998, c1997. 96p. ISBN 10: 0440415217 (pb.); ISBN-13: 978-0440415213 (pb.). Grades 4–7.

Riordan, James. *The Twelve Labors of Hercules.* Illustrated by Christina Balit. Brookfield, Conn.: Millbrook Press, 1997. 64p. ISBN 10: 0761303154; ISBN 13: 978-0761303152. Grades 4–6.

Storrie, Paul D. *Hercules: The Twelve Labors, a Greek Myth.* Illustrated by Steve Kurth and Barbara Schulz. Minneapolis, Minn.: Graphic Universe, 2007. 48p. ISBN 10: 0822564858; ISBN 13: 978-0822564850. (Graphic novel). Grades 4–7.

Hippolyta

Yolen, Jane, and Robert J. Harris. *Hippolyta and the Curse of the Amazons.* New York: HarperCollins, 2002. 248p. ISBN 10: 0060287365; ISBN 13: 978-0060287368. Grades 5–7.

Jason

Brooks, Felicity. *Jason and the Argonauts*. Illustrated by Graham Humphreys. Tulsa, Okla.: EDC, 1997. 160p. ISBN 10: 0746051999 (pb.); ISBN 13: 978-0746051993 (pb.). Grades 3–6.

Colum, Padraic. *The Golden Fleece and the Heroes Who Lived Before Achilles*. Illustrated by Willy Pogany. New York: Aladdin, 1921. 320p. ISBN 10: 0689868847; ISBN 13: 978-0689868849 (pb.). (Newbery Honor 1922). Grades 5–8.

Fisher, Leonard Everett. *Jason and the Golden Fleece*. New York: Holiday House, 1990. 32p. ISBN 10: 0823407942; ISBN 13: 978-0823407941. Grades 3–6.

Herdling, Glenn. *Greek Mythology: Jason and the Golden Fleece*. New York: PowerKids Press, 2007. 24p. ISBN 10: 1404223398; ISBN 13: 978-1404223394. Grades 2–4.

Mosley, Francis. *Jason and the Golden Fleece*. London: Andre Deutsch, 1989. 32p. ISBN 10: 0233983252; ISBN 13: 978-0233983257. Grades 3–6.

Naden, Corinne J. *Jason and the Golden Fleece*. Illustrated by Robert Baxter. Mahwah, N.J.: Troll Associates, 1981. 32p. ISBN 10: 0893753602; ISBN 13: 978-0893753603. (Audio recording available). Grades 3–6.

Osborne, Will, and Mary Pope. *Jason and the Argonauts*. Illustrated by Steve Sullivan. New York: Scholastic, 1988. 84p. ISBN 10: 0590411527 (pb.); ISBN 13: 978-0590411523 (pb.). Grades 4–6.

Riordan, James. *Jason and the Golden Fleece*. Illustrated by Jason Cockcroft. London: Frances Lincoln/Publishers Group West, 2003. 64p. ISBN 10: 0711220816; ISBN 13: 978-0711220812. Grades 4–7.

Yolen, Jane, and Robert J. Harris. *Jason and the Gorgon's Blood*. New York: HarperCollins, 2004. 256p. ISBN 10: 0060294523; ISBN 13: 978-0060294526. Grades 4–6.

Zarampouka, Sofia. *Jason and the Golden Fleece: The Most Adventurous and Exciting Expedition of All the Ages*. Los Angeles: J. Paul Getty Museum, 2004. 56p. ISBN 10: 0892367563; ISBN 13: 978-0892367566. Grades 5–8.

Medusa

Evslin, Bernard. *Medusa*. New York: Chelsea House Publishers, 1987. 81p. ISBN 10: 1555462383; ISBN 13: 978-1555462383. Grades 3–6.

Lattimore, Deborah Nourse. *Medusa*. New York: HarperCollins, 2000. 32p. ISBN 10: 0060279044; ISBN 13: 978-006027904. Grades 2–5.

Naden, Corinne J. *Perseus and Medusa*. Illustrated by Robert Baxter. Mahwah, N.J.: Troll Associates, 1981. 32p. ISBN 10: 0893753629; ISBN 13: 9780893753627. Grades 2–5.

Nardo, Don, and Bradley Steffens. *Medusa*. Detroit: KidHaven Press, Thomson/Gale, 2005. 48p. ISBN 10: 0737726172; ISBN 13: 978-0737726176. Grades 4–7.

Osborne, Will, and Mary Pope. *The Deadly Power of Medusa.* Illustrated by Steve Sullivan. New York: Demco Media, 1992. 92p. ISBN 10: 0606018093; ISBN 13: 978-0606018098. Grades 4–7.

Spinner, Stephanie. *Snake Hair: The Story of Medusa.* Illustrated by Susan Swan. New York: Grosset & Dunlap, 1999. 48p. ISBN 10: 0448419815; ISBN 13: 978-0448419817. Grades 2–5.

Midas

Banks, Lynne Reid. *The Adventures of King Midas.* Illustrated by Joseph A. Smith. New York: HarperCollins, 1992. 158p. ISBN 10: 0688108946; ISBN 13: 978-0688108946. Grades 3–5.

Craft, Charlotte. *King Midas and the Golden Touch.* Illustrated by K. Y. Craft. New York: Morrow Junior Books, 1999. 32p. ISBN 10: 0688131654; ISBN 13: 978-0688131654. Grades 1–4.

Demi. *King Midas: The Golden Touch.* New York: Margaret K. McElderry, 2002. 48p. ISBN 10: 0689832974; ISBN 13: 978-0689832970. Grades K–4.

Espeland, Pamela. *The Story of King Midas.* Illustrated by George Overlie. Minneapolis, Minn.: Carolrhoda Books, 1980. 32p. ISBN 10: 0876141297; ISBN 13: 978-0876141298. Grades 3–6.

Hewitt, Kathryn. *King Midas and the Golden Touch.* San Diego.: Harcourt Children's Books, 1987. 32p. ISBN 10: 0152428003. ISBN 13: 978-0152428006. Grades 1–4.

McKissack, Pat, and Frederick McKissack. *King Midas and His Gold.* Illustrated by Tom Dunnington. Chicago: Children's Press, 1986. 32p. ISBN 10: 0516039849; ISBN 13: 978-0516039848. Grades 1–4.

Metaxas, Eric. *King Midas and the Golden Touch.* Illustrated by Rodica Prato. Saxonville, Mass.: Picture Book Studio Ltd., 1992. 40p. ISBN 10: 1599613093; ISBN 13: 978-1599613093. (Audio- and videocassettes available). Grades K–4.

Newby, Robert. *King Midas: With Selected Sentences in American Sign Language.* Illustrated by Dawn Majewski. Washington, D.C.: Kendall Green Publications, Gallaudet University Press, 1990. 52p. ISBN 10: 0930323750; ISBN 13: 978-0930323752. Grades 1–6.

Stewig, John W. *King Midas: A Golden Tale.* Illustrated by Omar Rayyan. New York: Holiday House, 1999. 32p. ISBN 10: 082341423X; ISBN 13: 978-0823414239. Grades 1–5.

Storr, Catherine. *King Midas.* Illustrated by Mike Codd. Milwaukee, Wis.: Raintree Children's Books, 1985. 48p. ISBN 10: 0811471489; ISBN 13: 978-0811471480. Grades K–4.

Pandora

Burleigh, Robert. *Pandora.* Illustrated by Raul Colon. New York: Silver Whistle, 2002. 32p. ISBN 10: 0152021787; ISBN 13: 978-0152021788. Grades 3–5.

Marzollo, Jean. *Pandora's Box: A Greek Myth.* New York: Little, Brown, 2006. 32p. ISBN 10: 0316741337; ISBN 13: 978-0316741330. Grades 2–4.

Osborne, Mary Pope. *Pandora's Box.* Illustrated by Lisa Amoroso. New York: Scholastic, 1987. 32p. ISBN 10: 0590407678 (pb.); ISBN 13: 978-0590407670 (pb.). Grades 2–4.

Theseus and the Minotaur

Byrd, Robert. *The Hero and the Minotaur: The Fantastic Adventures of Theseus*. New York: Dutton Children's Books, 2005. 40p. ISBN 10: 0525473912; ISBN 13: 978-0525473916. Grades 3–6.

Evslin, Bernard. *The Minotaur*. New York: Chelsea House Publishers, 1987. 85p. ISBN 10: 1555462375; ISBN 13: 978-1555462376. Grades 6–9.

Fisher, Leonard Everett. *Theseus and the Minotaur*. New York: Holiday House, 1988. 32p. ISBN 10: 0823407039; ISBN 13: 978-0823407033. Grades 2–5.

Hutton, Warwick. *Theseus and the Minotaur*. New York: Margaret K. McElderry Books, 1989. 32p. ISBN 10: 068950473X; ISBN 13: 978-0689504730. Grades 2–5.

McCaughrean, Geraldine. *Theseus and the Minotaur*. New York: Orchard, 1998. 48p. ISBN 10: 1860395295 (pb.); ISBN 13: 978-1860395291 (pb.). Grades 4–7.

McMullen, Kate. *Stop That Bull, Theseus!—Book #5*. Illustrated by David Lafleur. New York: Hyperion, 2003. 160p. ISBN 10: 0786808616; ISBN 13: 978-0786808618. Grades 3–6.

Spinner, Stephanie. *Monster in the Maze: The Story of the Minotaur*. Illustrated by Susan Swan. New York: Grosset & Dunlap, 2000. 48p. ISBN 10: 0606202684; ISBN 13: 978-0606202688. Grades 4–6.

Storr, Catherine. *Theseus and the Minotaur*. Illustrated by Ivan Lapper. Raintree Steck-Vaughn Publishers, 1992. 32p. ISBN 10: 0416536506; ISBN 13: 978-0416536508. Grades 3–6.

Welvaert, Scott R. *Theseus and the Minotaur*. Mankato, Minn.: Capstone Press, 2004. 24p. ISBN 10: 0736847138; ISBN 13: 978-0736847131. Grades 2–4.

Zeus

Gates, Doris. *Lord of the Sky, Zeus*. Illustrated by Robert Handville. New York: Viking, 1972. 126p. ISBN-10: 0670440515; ISBN-13: 978-0670440511. Grades 6–8.

Loewen, Nancy. *Zeus*. Mankato, Minn.: Capstone Books, 1999. 48p. ISBN 10: 0736800514; ISBN 13: 978-0736800518. Grades 4–6.

Video Recordings

Defying the Gods. Wynnewood, Pa.: Schlessinger Media, 2004.

The Gods of Olympus. Wynnewood, Pa.: Schlessinger Media, 2004.

Jason and the Argonauts. Burbank, Calif.: Columbia TriStar Home Video, 1963.

Jim Henson's the Storyteller: Greek Myths. Culver City, Calif.: Jim Henson Home Entertainment, 1999.

Who's Who in Greek and Roman Mythology. Huntsville, Tex.: Educational Video Network, 2001.

Published Greek Mythology Paper Dolls

Several options are available for those who wish to purchase Greek mythological paper dolls or to download them from the Web. These sources should prove helpful

OPDAG. *Paper Doll Studio Issue 88. Mythology Paper Dolls.* http://www.paperdollreview.com/catalog/index.php?main_page=product_info&cPath=16&products_id=304 (accessed March 24, 2009).

Also available from Paperdoll Review, PO Box 14, Kingfield, ME 04947, 207-265-2500, 800-290-2928.

Paper Dali: Free Historic Paper Dolls—Ancient Greece. http://www.paperdali.com/dalis.html (accessed March 24, 2009).

Two simple dolls and three costumes may be downloaded.

Tierney, Tom. *Ancient Greek Costumes: Paper Dolls.* Mineola, N.Y.: Dover Publications, 1998. 8p. ISBN 10: 0486405745; ISBN 13: 978-0486405742.

Male and female dolls may be dressed in sixteen costumes from the archaic (ca. 750–500 BC), classical (ca. 500–336 BC), and Hellenistic (336–146 BC) periods.

Lesson Plan:
Copy What You See

Library Media Skills Objective:

The student will read about a mythological figure and find and use a book, other medium, or the Internet to locate artwork related to that character and create a paper doll and costume from that image.

Curriculum (Subject Areas) Objectives:

This lesson may be used in art, social studies, or history. Several concepts may be developed. The focus will vary depending on whether the students look more at the history of the time from which the costumes come or at the costumes themselves. The art teacher may focus on the works of art themselves; the language arts teacher may want to highlight the stories.

Grade Level: 2–5

Resources:

Books in the collection

Internet

- *Classical Myth: The Ancient Sources*—http://web.uvic.ca/grs/department_files/classical_myth/index.html (accessed March 24, 2009). See the images of Aphrodite, Athene, and Hera.

- *List Greek Mythology Images.*—http://www.mlahanas.de/Greeks/Mythology/ListGreek MythologyImages.html (accessed March 24, 2009).

- Melanie Ann Apel, *Art and Religion in Ancient Greece* (New York: PowerKids Press, 2004. 24p. ISBN 10: 0823967700; ISBN 13: 978-0823967704).

Teacher references

- Suzanne Barchers, *From Atalanta to Zeus: Readers Theatre from Greek Mythology* (Littleton, Colo.: Teacher Idea Press, 2001. 203p. ISBN-10: 1563088150; ISBN 13: 978-1563088155).

- Antoinette Brazouski and Mary J. Klatt, *Children's Books on Ancient Greek and Roman Mythology: An Annotated Bibliography* (Westport, Conn.: Greenwood Press, 1993. 208p. ISBN 10: 0313289735; ISBN 13: 978-0313289736).

- Iris Brooke, *Costume in Greek Classic Drama* (Mineola, N.Y.: Dover Publications, 2003. 128p. ISBN 10: 0486429830; ISBN 13: 978-0486429830).

- Thomas Hope, *Costumes of the Greeks and Romans* (Mineola, N.Y.: Dover Publications, 1962. 300p. ISBN 10: 0486200213; ISBN 13: 978-0486200217).

- Mary Noble, *Ancient Greek Designs* (Dover Pictorial Archive Series) (Mineola, N.Y.: Dover Publications, 2000. 48p. ISBN-10: 0486412288; ISBN 13: 978-0486412283).
- Marianne Saccardi, *Art in Story: Teaching Art History to Elementary School Children* (North Haven, Conn.: Linnet, 1997. ISBN 10-0-208-02431-X). Chapter 4 (pp. 30–39) provides other suggestions for art lessons.

Instructional Roles:

The teacher or library media specialist may tell a story and assign the work, which will take about 45 minutes. The library media specialist provides samples and a list of possible sources; this will take 30 minutes. The teacher shows students how to trace and make outfits from the pictures; this takes 15 minutes. Most of the time will be taken up by students reading their books and creating their figures. Students' display and discussion should require about an hour.

Activity and Procedures for Completion:

Begin with the story of the Golden Apple. For fun, paint a plastic apple to introduce the story and to leave as a reminder and display after the storytelling. Share the books that include the story as well as other mythology books. This is a good time to discuss the difference between collections of stories and stories that focus on one individual or event. Knowledge of the tables of contents and indexes of these books is important. Compare the tables of contents and indexes to search engines and Web pages.

Follow up by providing students with copies of the paper dolls of Paris and the three goddesses. Ask students to consider how artists know how to draw and illustrate the dolls and books or make films about ancient Greeks. Much of what we know is from the art (mosaics, paintings, pottery, jewelry, and sculpture) that they left behind. Share pictures or copies of some of the stories of the Judgment of Paris. For this example, include those that are clothed.

Amphora

- *Amphora by Antimenes Painter (c. 530 BCE): Judgement of Paris*—http://www.wisc.edu/arth/ah301/15-laterbf/13.image.html (accessed March 24, 2009).
- http://www.goddess-athena.org/Museum/Paintings/Paris/Judgment_of_Paris_Antimenes_painter_f.htm (more views) (accessed March 24, 2009).
- http://www.perseus.tufts.edu/cgi-bin/imbrow?type=sor&query=a.value%20%3D%20%27W%26uuml%3Brzburg%20L%20186%27 (accessed March 24, 2009).
- *Black-Figure Neck Amphora. Unknown. Greek, Euboea, about 570–560 B.C.*—http://www.getty.edu/art/gettyguide/artObjectDetails?artobj=13765&handle=li (accessed March 24, 2009).
- *Witt Painter. Judgement of Paris. Attic black-figure amphora, 560/50 BC*—http://www.mlahanas.de/Greeks/Mythology/JudgementOfParisLouvreF31.html (accessed March 24, 2009).

Mosaics

- *Judgment of Paris Mosaic. Antrim House*—http://www.sacred-destinations.com/turkey/antioch-mosaic-photos/judgement-of-paris.jpg.html (accessed March 24, 2009).
- http://www.theoi.com/Gallery/Z4.1B.html (accessed March 24, 2009).

Statues

- *Statue of Paris. British Museum*—http://www.geh.org/fm/stm/htmlsrc/m199607250014_ful.html#topofimage (accessed (accessed March 24, 2009).).

Compare the art from the Greek period with more modern works with the same subjects, such as paintings of Helen of Troy:

Helen of Troy, by Evelyn de Morgan (1898)

Helen of Troy, by Dante Gabriel Rossetti (1863)

Helen on the Ramparts of Troy, by Gustave Moreau (1885)

Helen of Troy, by Frederic Leighton

Helen, by Franz von Stuck (1925)

Students will complete several tasks. First they will make their paper dolls and retell the story. Allow time for students to begin coloring, painting, and cutting out the dolls. The second part of the task is to select a book about a specific god, goddess, or hero. The student will locate artwork that shows the god or goddess and prepare a costume representing that story and god or goddess. The paper doll figures on the handouts may be used for this task.

Suggest and model a search strategy for finding books and artwork. Suggest search terms. For example, students might use the books on Greek mythology to find images of the god or goddess they selected. for the images, they might search the Internet or other art books. (Explain that many of the figures in the artworks will not be clothed, and that for this exercise they are not useful. Students might go to Internet sites that focus on Greek mythology and search for the selected god or goddess. They will be searching for art that comes from the ancient Greeks, not more modern examples. The time periods—for example the archaic (ca. 750–500 BC), classical (ca. 500–336 BC), and Hellenistic (336–146 BC)—may be provided.

When students have selected their figures, found their books or stories, and located and printed out copies of the works of art, they are ready for the third task, preparing the costumes. The following Internet site is helpful in the initial search for images: *List Greek Mythology Images* (http://www.mlahanas.de/Greeks/Mythology/ListGreekMythologyImages.html; accessed March 24, 2009).

Students will be doing what many or most artists do. They will research the ancient images. The students will use the male or female figure for their selected story. Show students how to gently trace around the figure. A second option is to make a small dotted line with pencil around the figure. The student will observe the features in the picture and draw the clothes using the traced lines as a guide, to make sure the new costume will fit on the figure. After the costume has been drawn, they should be sure to put tabs on it so the clothes may be attached to the figure. Students may want to use colors; not all clothing was white. The new costume should be colored, cut out, and placed on the figure.

The students are ready to display their work. The display may consist of a printout of the work of art, information about the god or goddess represented, a short paragraph summarizing the story, and the cut-out figure dressed in the newly created costume.

Evaluation:

Each student will select and read about a mythological figure. He or she will find and use a book, other medium, or the Internet to locate artwork related to that figure. Based on the artwork, the student will create a costume for a paper doll figure of the mythological character.

Follow-Up:

Display artworks and place them in a time frame. Discuss where some of the works are and provide time to view them.

Encourage more research on the clothing of the Greeks (colors, accessories, fabrics, sewing and weaving, and fashion).

Select a modern-day illustrator from the listed books and research that person. Find out how the illustrator located information to accurately portray the figures he or she drew.

Set up a Greek fashion salon based on museums' works.

Paper Dolls: Greek Mythology

Whom do you think Paris picked?

Instructions: Re-create your version of the story with these paper action figures.

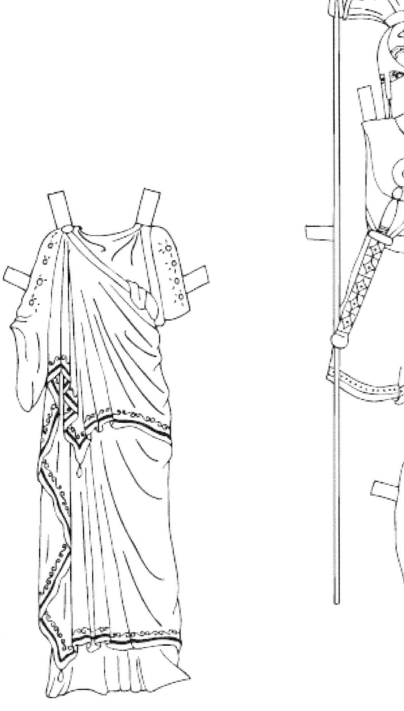

Chapter 9

Guiding Us Along: Characters as Guides

Trail Guides.
Tour Guides.
Museum Guides . . . and more.
Teachers guide their classes on field trips.
Dogs can be guides.
Libraries and books have guides!

Guide characters in fiction stories help people learn new things. Fiction guide characters are teachers, nature guides, grandparents, children, birds, dogs, and even magic carpets! All have something in common. In general, guides lead, direct, or advise. In the most intense form, guides are models. In simpler forms, guides can be live beings who direct, or even pamphlets and words that provide direction.

Who Is Crinkleroot?

Crinkleroot is a fictional character who guides readers on journeys through the natural world. He teaches about mammals, birds, trees, and fish. He also guides readers through animal habitats. He makes the world an interesting place for those willing to read and follow the path. All one needs to do is grab a beautifully illustrated book and begin one of Crinkleroot's guided world tours of nature.

Readers will find adventure in the writing and illustration of Jim Arnosky, the recipient of the Key Lifetime Achievement Award for Excellence in Science Books from the Science Book and Film review publication of the America Association for the Advancement of Science (AAAS) and Subaru in 2005. Visit him at his Web site and learn about him and nature. He adds animals to color from his list of the 100 animals every kid should know. He has written more than 100 books, and they are listed at the site. Share in his many visits to animal sites, at http://www.jimarnosky.com/ (accessed April 7, 2008). A favorite character from his books is the guide, Crinkleroot, who was introduced in the book *I Was Born in a Tree and Raised by Bees* (New York: Simon & Schuster, 1977. 46p.). Since that time Crinkleroot has served as a guide in many other beautifully illustrated volumes.

Crinkleroot's Book of Animal Tracking. New York: Bradbury Press, 1989. 48p. ISBN 10: 0027058514; ISBN 13: 978-0027058512.
>   Crinkleroot explains how to find and understand animal tracks. Grades 3–5.

Crinkleroot's Guide to Knowing Animal Habitats. New York: Simon and Schuster, 1997. 32p. ISBN 10: 0689805837; ISBN 13: 978-0689805837.
>   Crinkleroot explores animal habitats. This book would be useful for making a diorama of a favorite animal habitat. Grades K–3.

Crinkleroot's Guide to Knowing the Birds. New York: Bradbury Press, 1991. 32p. ISBN 10: 0027058573; ISBN 13: 978-0027058574.
>   Crinkleroot introduces readers to bird observation basics in the woods. Grades 1–4

Crinkleroot's Guide to Knowing Butterflies and Moths. New York: Bradbury, 1996. 32p.ISBN-10: 068980587X; ISBN-13: 978-0689805875.
>   Crinkleroot and Sassafras, his snake, tell about butterfly life cycles and moths while on day and night walks. Grades K–4.

Crinkleroot's Guide to Knowing the Trees. New York: Bradbury, 1992. 32p. ISBN 10: 0027058557; ISBN 13: 978-0027058550.
>   Crinkleroot shows readers how to identify trees using the bark and leaves, how to distinguish hardwoods from soft woods, and even how trees get their shapes. Grades K–4.

Crinkleroot's Guide to Walking in Wild Places. New York: Bradbury Press, 1990. 32p. ISBN 10: 0689717539; ISBN 13: 978-0689717536.
>   Crinkleroot suggests what children will see when they take a hike. This is a perfect book to read before hiking, because it covers not only how to make observations, but how to dress properly, clean up and leave no traces of litter, and even avoid ticks and poisonous plants. Grades 2–5.

Crinkleroot's Nature Almanac. New York: Simon & Schuster Books for Young Readers, 1998. 64p. ISBN 10: 0689805349; ISBN 13: 978-0689805349.
>   Crinkleroot follows animals and plants through the four seasons and describes what happens to them. Grades 1–5.

Crinkleroot's 25 Birds Every Child Should Know. New York: Bradbury Press, 1994. 32p. ISBN 10: 002705859X; ISBN 13: 978-0027058598.
>   Crinkleroot describes the birds and includes pictures of twenty-five common shorebirds, land birds, and water birds he thinks children should know about. Grades K–4.

Crinkleroot's 25 Fish Every Child Should Know. New York: Bradbury Press, 1993. 32p. ISBN 10: 0027058441; ISBN 13: 978-0027058444.
>   Crinkleroot explains a little about fish and then provides pictures of twelve freshwater and thirteen saltwater varieties. Did you know them all? Grades K–4.

Crinkleroot's 25 Mammals Every Child Should Know. New York: Bradbury Press, 1994. ISBN 10: 002705845X; ISBN 13: 978-0027058451.

Crinkleroot explains a little about mammals and then provides pictures of twenty-five common mammals, including the dog, beaver, and elephant. Grades 1–4.

Crinkleroot's 25 More Animals Every Child Should Know. New York: Bradbury Press, 1994. 32p. ISBN 10: 0027058468; ISBN 13: 978-0027058468.

Crinkleroot shows children vivid pictures of twenty-five common animals and encourages readers to name creatures such as the frog, starfish, and grasshopper.

Crinkleroot's Visit to Crinkle Cove. New York: Simon & Schuster Books for Young Readers, 1998. 32p. ISBN 10: 0689816022; ISBN 13: 978-0689816024.

Visit Crinkle Cove and help Crinkleroot find his pet snake, while discovering other fun things about Crinkle Cove.

A complete set of the Crinkleroot books is available on CD from Jim Arnosky, PO Box 25, South Ryegate, VT 05069:

Disc 1, Volume 1

1. *Crinkleroot's 25 Birds Every Child Should Know*
2. *Crinkleroot's 25 Mammals Every Child Should Know*
3. *Crinkleroot's Book of Animal Tracking*
4. *I Was Born in a Tree and Raised by Bees*
5. *Crinkleroot's Guide to Knowing Animal Habitats*
6. *Crinkleroot's Guide to Knowing the Trees*

Disc 2, Volume 2

1. *Crinkleroot's 25 Fish Every Child Should Know*
2. *Crinkleroot's 25 More Animals Every Child Should Know*
3. *Crinkleroot's Guide to Knowing Butterflies & Moths*
4. *Crinkleroot's Guide to Walking in Wild Places*
5. *Crinkleroot's Guide to Knowing the Birds*

Who Is Ms. Frizzle, and What Is Her Magic School Bus?

Ms. Frizzle, a fictional teacher and guide character, leads her class on fantastic, magical field trips. The class bus, which is magical, can change its size and shape and even fly if the need arises. Ms. Frizzle has a trusty helper, a lizard named, appropriately enough, Liz. Ms. Frizzle relies on Liz to help with the field trips. They make sure everything goes as it should. The Magic School Bus and Ms. Frizzle have been featured in books, videos, computer games, and even a TV show. Joanna Cole and Bruce Degen collaborate on the books. Joanna Cole researches the information before synthesizing, writing, and making a book dummy that includes ideas for sketches, the text, speech bubbles, and student reports. The dummy is reviewed by a science expert for accuracy and then given to illustrator Bruce Degen for art. Their books have been transformed into sound and video/DVD recordings, games, toys, and hardcover and paperback editions. Here are some of the books:

The Magic School Bus at the Waterworks. New York: Scholastic, 1986. 39p. ISBN 10: 0590403613; ISBN 13: 978-0590403610.

Ms. Frizzle guides the class, dressed in scuba gear, on an inside look at what happens in a water purification system, from mountain stream to the faucet. Grades 2–5.

The Magic School Bus Explores the Senses. New York: Scholastic, 1999. 56p.ISBN-10: 0590446975; ISBN 13: 978-0590446976.

Only Ms. Frizzle can drive the bus that takes her class on a trip through the senses, literally! They go into a policeman's eye and a dog's nose, among other body parts. Grades 2–5.

The Magic School Bus in the Arctic: A Book About Heat. Scholastic, 1998. 32p. ISBN 10: 0590187244; ISBN 13: 978-0590187244.

The magic school bus takes the children and Ms. Frizzle to the Arctic to learn about how heat and insulation work. Grades 1–5.

The Magic School Bus in the Time of the Dinosaurs. New York: Scholastic, 1994. 48p. ISBN 10: 0590446886; ISBN 13: 978-0590446884.

When the class is disappointed not to see a Maiasaura nesting ground at an archaeological dig, the magic school bus becomes a time machine, roaming the earth with the dinosaurs in the Late Triassic period, the Late Jurassic period, the Late Cretaceous period, and the Cretaceous period. Grades 2–5.

The Magic School Bus Inside a Beehive. New York: Scholastic, 1996. 47p. ISBN 10: 0590446843; ISBN 13: 978-0590446846.

The school bus turns into a beehive, and the class dresses in bee suits, antennae, and wings to collect nectar and visit inside the hive. Grades 1–4.

The Magic School Bus Inside a Hurricane. New York: Scholastic, 1995. 48p. ISBN 10: 059044686X; ISBN 13: 978-0590446860.

It's easy to imagine the whirling winds as the class learns all about hurricanes from Ms. Frizzle in the school bus, which has been transformed into a weather plane. Grades 1–5.

The Magic School Bus Inside the Earth. New York: Scholastic, 1987. 48p. ISBN 10: 0590407597; ISBN 13: 978-0590407595.

Ms. Frizzle's class and her magic bus descend toward the center of the earth, collecting rock samples in each stratum. Grades 2–5.

The Magic School Bus Inside the Human Body. New York: Scholastic, 1989. 48p. ISBN 10: 0590414267; ISBN 13: 978-0590414265.

Arnold swallows the Magic School Bus, the class, and Ms. Frizzle as she takes them through the human body and finally out the nose, when Arnold sneezes. Grades 1–4.

Magic School Bus Lost in the Snow. New York: Cartwheel Books/Scholastic, 2004. 32p. ISBN 10: 0439569907; ISBN 13: 978-0439569903.

In this easy reader, the bus becomes a sleigh as the class careens through a snowstorm. Grades K–2.

The Magic School Bus: Lost in the Solar System. New York: Scholastic, 1990. 48p. ISBN 10: 0590414283; ISBN 13: 978-0590442732.

The planetarium is closed, so Ms Frizzle must improvise and take the class into space on the magic school bus, where they fly past the Moon, Venus, Mars, and other planets. Grades 1–5.

The Magic School Bus on the Ocean Floor. New York: Scholastic, 1992. 48p. ISBN 10: 0590414305; ISBN 13: 978-0590414302.

> Ms. Frizzle guides her class on a school bus field trip of the ocean, in which the bus morphs into a submarine, a submersible, a glass-bottom boat, and a surfboard, as they observe geologic strata and plant and animals at the various depths. Grades 2–5.

The Magic School Bus Ups and Downs: A Book About Floating and Sinking. New York: Scholastic, 1997. 32p. ISBN 10: 0590921584 (pb.); ISBN 13: 978-0590921589 (pb.).

> Ms. Frizzle's class takes a field trip to a lake, looking for a monster, and learns all about floating and sinking. Grades 1–5.

The television program featuring the Magic School Bus continued the escapades of Ms. Frizzle and her class. New episodes were based on Joanna Cole's and Bruce Degen's work. A complete listing of the fifty-two programs can be found at http://www.scholastic.com/MagicSchoolBus/tv/tv.htm (accessed March 24, 2009). Parent and teacher guides are also available at the Web site. Several authors, such as Linda Beech, Anne Capeci, Kristin Earhart, Kirsten Hall, Gail Herman, Nancy Krulik, Eva Moore, Judith Bauer Stamper, and Nancy White, and illustrators such as Ted Enik, Carolyn Bracken, Lindy Burnett, Steve Haefele, Hope Gangloff, and John Speirs, have adapted spin-off titles.

For more information about the authors, books, games, videos, and other spin-offs, visit http://www.scholastic.com/magicschoolbus/ (accessed March 24, 2009).

Teachers as Guides

Teachers guide their classes on trips every day. Through books and other educational materials, teachers take children to places they and their brains might not otherwise get to go. Sometimes teachers guide children on field trips to real places. Field trips are special, because they bring to life the learning children do in the classroom. There are many books about adventures that fictional teachers have taken. Some of the field trips are ones that children might really take, whereas others are trips back in time, just like Ms. Frizzle's.

Anderson, Scoular. *A Puzzling Day in the Land of the Pharaohs*. Cambridge, Mass.: Candlewick Press, 1996. 32p. ISBN 10: 1564028771; ISBN 13: 978-1564028778.

> Join the Nile Street School kids as their teacher guides them while they explore the land of the pharaohs. Grades 3–6.

Brorstrom, Gay Bishop. *A Class Trip to Miss Hallberg's Butterfly Garden*. Illustrated by Kathy Goetzel. Sebastopol, Calif.: Pipevine Press, 2000. 32p. ISBN 10: 0967683904; ISBN 13: 978-0967683904.

> The children of Oak Grove elementary walk to see Miss Hallberg and her assistant and are guided through the natural world to learn more about nature and butterflies. Grades K–2.

Burkett, Kathy. *Out of This World! Ethan Flask and Professor von Offel Take on Space Science*. (Mad Science Series). New York: Scholastic, 2001. 112p. ISBN 10: 0439417708; ISBN 13: 978-0439417709.

> The teacher and children of Einstein Elementary will be led by a mad scientist to study space science. Grades 3–6.

Butterworth, Nick, and Mick Inkpen. *The School Trip*. New York: Delacorte Press, 1990. 28p. ISBN 10: 0385302428; ISBN 13: 978-0385302425.

    Mrs. Jefferson guides her class on a trip to a museum and manages for all to have a good time in spite of a child who is late joining them and one who is nauseated. Grades K–2.

Clayton, Elaine. *Ella's Trip to the Museum*. Crown, 1996. 32p. ISBN 10: 0517700808; ISBN 13: 978-0517700808.

    Mrs. Jasper, Ella's teacher, seems oblivious to many of the class antics as she nervously guides her class on a tour of a museum, where Ella discovers all sorts of wonderful things about the paintings and statues. Grades K–3.

Dadey, Debbie, and Marcia Thornton Jones. *Mrs. Jeepers on Vampire Island*. Illustrated by John Steven Gurney. New York: Scholastic, 2001. 118p. ISBN 10: 0613504763; ISBN 13: 978-0613504768.

    Teacher Mrs. Jeepers isn't worried when her class is shipwrecked on a strange island while on a three-day field trip. Other titles in the *Adventures of the Bailey School Kids Series*, such as *Mrs. Jeepers Batty Vacation* or *Mrs. Jeepers' Monster Class Trip*, may also be of interest. Grades 2–5.

Daniels, Teri. *Math Man*. Illustrated by Tim Bush. New York: Orchard Books, 2001. 32p. ISBN 10: 0439293081; ISBN13: 978-0439293082.

    Mrs. Gourd receives help and a bit of lively fun from stock boy Garth when she takes her class on a field trip to the supermarket to see how math is important in daily life. Grades 1–4.

Figley, Marty Rhodes. *The Schoolchildren's Blizzard*. Illustrated by Shelly O. Haas. Minneapolis, Minn.: Carolrhoda Books, 2004. 48p. ISBN 10: 1575056194; ISBN 13: 978-1575056197.

    This story is based on a true incident. Minnie Freeman tied her sixteen children together and led them to safety during the deadly blizzard of January 12, 1888, in Nebraska, when the roof of the school blew off. Grades 2–4.

Finchler, Judy. *Miss Malarkey's Field Trip*. Illustrations by Kevin O'Malley. New York: Walker, 2004. 32p. ISBN 10: 080278917X; ISBN 13: 978-0802789174.

    In the fifth book about Miss Marlarkey, she is off to the Science Center with very unruly children, who give her a headache and much concern as they misbehave. Grades K–4.

Gabler, Mirko. *Brakus. Krakus . . .: Or the Incredible Adventure of Mr. Skola's Tourist Club*. New York: Henry Holt, 1993. 32p. ISBN 10: 0805019634; ISBN 13: 978-0805019636.

    Mr. Skola takes the tourist club to visit the mysterious castle of Kost. He guides them on a wonderful adventure, full of magic and interesting escapades. Grades 1–4.

Giff, Patricia Reilly. *Next Stop, New York City!* (The Polk Street Kids on Tour). Bantam Doubleday Dell Books for Young Readers, 1997. 128p. ISBN 10: 0613021886; ISBN 13: 978-0613021883.

    When Ms. Rooney and her class go to New York City on a field trip, Emily helps Ms. Rooney guide the class through New York City, even though she knows very little about the city. Book 9 in the <u>Polk Street Kids Series</u> includes a guide to New York City written by the Polk Street kids. Other books in the series that might be of interest are *Let's Go, Philadelphia!* and *Look Out, Washington, D.C.!* Grades 2–5.

Guest, Elissa Haden. *Iris and Walter and the Field Trip*. Illustrated by Christine Davenier. Orlando, Fla.: Harcourt, 2005. 44p. ISBN 10: 0152050140; ISBN 13: 978-0152050146.

    When Iris and Walter become lost on a field trip to the aquarium, Miss Cherry calmly helps the class retrace their steps until they find their lost classmates. Grades 1–3.

Hahn, Mary Downing. *Janey and the Famous Author*. Illustrated by Timothy Bush. New York: Clarion, 2005. 48p. ISBN 10: 0618354085; ISBN 13: 978-0618354085.

    Janey's favorite author, Lily May Appleton, the writer of the *Bob the Dog Detective series*, becomes the guide when Janey is separated from her class at the book festival. Grades 2–5.

Kenah, Katharine. *The Best Seat in Second Grade*. Illustrated by Abby Carter. New York: HarperCollins, 2005. 48p. ISBN 10: 0060007346; ISBN 13: 978-0060007348.

    Mr. Hopper gives an appropriate punishment to Sam when he takes the class hamster, George, to the science museum on a field trip. Grades 1–4.

Kline, Suzy. *Song Lee and the Leech Man*. Illustrated by Frank Remkiewicz. New York: Viking, 1995. 64p. ISBN 10: 067085848X; ISBN 13: 978-0670858484.

    When Miss Mackle takes her class on a field trip to a pond, Song Lee tries to resolve the rift between Harry and Sidney. Miss Mackle is featured in many other titles about Horrible Harry and his classmates, such as *Horrible Harry Goes to Sea* and *Song Lee and the I Hate You Notes*. (A sound recording is available from Recorded Books.) Grades 2–5.

Korman, Justine. *The Grumpy Bunny's Field Trip*. Illustrated by Lucinda McQueen. Mahwah, N.J.: WhistleStop, 1998. 32p. ISBN 10: 0613116062; ISBN 13: 978-0613116060.

    Reluctant Hopper must take ten little bunnies to the museum on a field trip. Grades K–1.

Krulik, Nancy E. *No Bones about It*. Illustrated by John [Krulik] and Wendy [Krulik]. New York: Grosset & Dunlap, 2004. 80p. ISBN 10: 0448433583; ISBN 13: 978-0448433585.

    Mr. Weir is a mean old tour guide at the natural history museum, who disappears and must be replaced by young Katie. Grades 2–5.

Park, Barbara. *Junie B. Jones Has a Peep in Her Pocket*. Illustrated by Denise Brunkus. New York: Random House, 2000. 80p. ISBN 10: 0375900403; ISBN 13: 978-0375900402.

    It takes fast talking by parents, the teacher, and the farmer to help Junie get over her fear of ponies and go on the farm field trip. (Sound recording is available). Grades K–4.

Slate, Joseph. *Miss Bindergarten Takes a Field Trip with Kindergarten*. Illustrated by Ashley Wolff. New York: Dutton, 2001. 32p. ISBN 10: 0525467106; ISBN 13: 978-0525467106.

    The canine teacher takes her class to the bakery, library, fire station, post office, and park while teaching shapes, alphabet, and other concepts. Other Miss Bindergarten books also show the teacher's crazy leadership abilities. Grades K–1.

Willner-Pardo, Gina. *Spider Storch's Fumbled Field Trip*. Illustrated by Nick Sharratt. New York: Albert Whitman, 1998. 68p. ISBN 10: 080757581X; ISBN 13: 978-0807575819.

    Ms. Schmidt takes Spider's class on a field trip to the Institute of Life Sciences and must send Spider back to the bus. Grades 2–4.

Yorke, Malcolm. *Molly the Mad Basher*. Illustrated by Margaret Chamberlain. New York: Dorling Kindersley, 1994. 32p. ISBN 10: 1564584593; ISBN 13: 978-1564584595.

    Miss Molly Cuddle takes her class to the shopping mall, and the students find out a secret about her. Grades K–3.

Ziefert, Harriet. *Trip Day*. Boston: Little, Brown, 1987. 63p. ISBN 10: 0316987654; ISBN 13: 978-0316987653.

    Mr. Rose takes his class on a trip to the pond for much exploration. Grades 1–4.

Zindel, Paul. *Fifth Grade Safari*. New York: Skylark Book, 1993. 129p. ISBN 10: 0553480855; ISBN 13: 978-0553480856.

    Mrs. Wilmont guides her class on a trip to the zoo. She wants them to learn to respect all creatures, but they also end up dealing with tricks played by other students. Part of the <u>Wacky Fact Bunch</u> series. Grades 4–7.

Grandparents as Guides

Grandparents often have the pleasure of having relationships with children that are unlike those the parents have. Many grandparents are retired and have time to attend to the needs of children. They also have the experience and, usually, less responsibility. Trips with grandparents can bring new understanding for the young. Often they have unexpected results.

Besson, Luc. *Arthur and the Forbidden City*. New York: HarperTrophy, 2005. 192p. ISBN 10: 0060596260; ISBN 13: 978-0060596262.

    Arthur searches for his missing grandfather in Africa and has shrunk to about one inch in size. Grades 4–6.

Blackstone, Stella. *Grandma Went to Market*. Boston: Houghton Mifflin, 1996. 32p. ISBN 10: 0395740452; ISBN 13: 978-0395740453.

    From Istanbul to Mexico, follow Grandma around the world as she buys different numbers of things from various places. Grades K–2.

George, Jean Craighead, and John George Craighead. *Dipper of Copper Creek*. Illustrated by Jean Craighead George. New York: Dutton Children's Books, 1996. 228p. ISBN 10: 0525287248; ISBN 13: 978-0525287247.

    A young boy stays with his grandfather in the Colorado Rockies and begins to gain independence as he watches a bird at a waterfall grow up. Grades 4–7.

Rylant, Cynthia. *Henry and Mudge and the Great Grandpas*. Illustrated by Suçie Stevenson. New York: Simon & Schuster, 2005. 40p. ISBN 10: 0689811705; ISBN 13: 978-0689811708.

    Henry and his family visit Great-Grandpa Bill at his retirement home and find all the grandpas hiking, swimming, relaxing in the sun, and having a great time. Grades 2–4.

Spinelli, Eileen. *Something to Tell the Grandcows*. Illustrated by Bill Slavin. Grand Rapids, Mich.: Eerdmans Books for Young Readers, 2004. 32p. ISBN 10: 080285236X; ISBN 13: 978-0802852366.

    Cow Emmadine signs up for Admiral Richard E. Byrd's expedition to the South Pole along with two other cows and ends up having an adventure that she will tell her grandkids. (The story is based on facts from the Byrd trip.) Grades K–5.

Stanley, Diane. *Roughing It on the Oregon Trail*. Illustrated by Holly Berry. New York: HarperCollins, 2000. 48p. ISBN-10: 0060270659; ISBN-13: 978-0060270650.

    Elizabeth and Lenny's Grandmother puts on her magic hat and guides them on a trip back in time to the Oregon Trail in 1843.

Winthrop, Elizabeth. *Dancing Granny*. Illustrated by Sal Murdocca. New York: Marshall Cavendish, 2003. 32p. ISBN 10: 0761451412; ISBN 13: 978-0761451419.

    When Granny takes her granddaughter to the zoo after hours, the visit turns into a riotous dancing party. Grades K–3.

Guides in Many Situations

Wagon train scouts and safari leaders are among the more intriguing guides. The fear of the unknown and the anticipation of danger romanticize these jobs, which were difficult and took a great toll on the individuals involved. Some may remember *Wagon Train*, the television series that ran from 1957 to 1965 and featured Ward Bond as the leader of the wagon train and Robert Horton as his scout. Each week the popular show dealt with an event that an 1870s "wagon train" might have encountered while making its way across the American West. Others may remember the young Clint Eastwood as a ramrod in the television series *Rawhide*, which aired on CBS from 1959 to 1966. The scout, Pete Nolan, had to make sure the cattle drive made it. Nobel Prize winner Ernest Hemingway wrote about his safari in East Africa in 1933 in *Green Hills of Africa*.

Other titles in which the adventure includes the journey and a guide will appeal to many young adventurers.

Anderson, Scoular. *MacPelican's American Adventure*. Cambridge, Mass.: Candlewick Press, 1998. 32p. ISBN 10: 0763604437; ISBN 13: 978-0763604431.

> Join the MacPelicans from Scotland as they guide the reader on a journey across many states and territories to get to the Grand Louisiana Exhibition in 1898, in game book format. Grades 2–5.

Brode, Robyn. *Safari Guide! Scouting for Wildlife in Africa*. Photographed by Todd Wayne and illustrated by Paul Hayes. Hauppauge, N.Y.: Barron's, 2002. 32p. ISBN 10: 0764121529; ISBN 13: 978-0764121524.

> A young girl accompanies her uncle on a safari through one of Africa's game parks. Part of a nonfiction series. Grades 1–5.

Czernecki, Stefan. *Zorah's Magic Carpet*. New York: Hyperion Books for Children, 1995. 32p. ISBN 10: 078680081X; ISBN 13: 978-0786800810.

> Zorah sets a sheep free, and in return the sheep provides her with wool for a magic carpet. The magic carpet takes her from Morocco to other places and inspires her to weave more rugs to sell. Grades K–3.

Gerrard, Roy. *Wagons West!* New York: Farrar, Straus & Giroux, 1996. 32p. ISBN 10: 0374482101; ISBN 13: 978-0374482107.

> Buckskin Dan guides a wagon train west to Oregon in this rhyming book in which an Arapaho child is rescued, cattle bandits are rousted, and rivers are forded. Grades 1–5.

Nunes, Susan. *To Find the Way*. Illustrated by Cissy Gray, Honolulu: University of Hawaii Press, 1992. 48p. ISBN 10: 0824813766; ISBN 13: 978-0824813765.

> Teva's grandfather, Vahi-roa, uses his knowledge of the stars to guide the Tahitian people on a voyage to Hawaii. Grades 5–8.

Published Guide Paper Dolls

Paper dolls have reflected scouting and, indirectly, guides through camping paper dolls and outfits. Among after-school and extracurricular activities, scouting and campfire activities rank high in popularity with children as well as their parents. Leaders are important as models in Boy Scouts, Cub Scouts, Girl Scouts, Campfire Boys, Campfire Girls, and other such clubs. Leaders perform the same roles as teachers and mentors for children in many subject areas, including camping and outdoor exploration. Such leadership has lasting effects on the children involved. Steven Spielberg was an Eagle Scout, and his father was a Life Scout. Perhaps this explains the scouts in the movie *Indiana Jones and the Last Crusade*. The opening shows a young Indiana with his scout troop, trying to take a gold cross from grave robbers. It is easy to understand that this type of adventure would be reflected in paper dolls.

Girl Scouts appear in paper dolls in many places. The DeJournette Manufacturing Company published a number of Brownie and Girl Scout paper dolls beginning in 1948 and throughout the early 1950s. Sets include dolls and outfits such as uniforms. Other sets by various publishing companies have appeared since then. The change in uniforms is a fashion study in itself.

Camping has also appeared in several forms. Although guides are not shown directly, the outfits are similar to what would be worn in situations where guides might be involved. The *Paper Doll Family and Their Trailer*, published in 1938 by Merrill Publishing Company, featured a family of four ready for the outdoors with their new car and trailer. Togetherness in walking and the outdoors was featured in *We're a Family* (Whitman, 1954). In this set, everyone is dressed alike: skirts for women and vests and hiking boots for men. In 1963, "Betsy McCall Goes Camping" appeared in *McCall's* magazine. Barbie has made her appearance camping in several publications. In 1973, Whitman published *Barbie Country Camper and Paper Dolls*, a cut-out that featured a camper to fold up and many outdoor outfits. *Barbie and P.J.: A Camping Adventure Coloring Book with Paper Dolls* followed in 1974, and *Barbie and Skipper: Campsite at Lucky Lake* was issued in 1977.

Guide Paper Dolls in Print

Degenhardt, Mary, and Judith Kirsch. *Girl Scout Collectors' Guide: A History of Uniforms, Insignia, Publications, And Memorabilia*. Lubbock: Texas Tech University Press, 2005. 586p. ISBN 10: 0896725464; ISBN 13: 978-0896725461. (This is not a paper doll book, but serves as a very useful reference.)

Hunt, Kathryn McMurtry. *Helping Hands: A Paper Doll History of the Girl Scout Uniform, Volume Three*. Illustrated by Lynette C. Ross. Lubbock: Texas Tech University Press, 2004. 28p. ISBN 10: 0896725219; ISBN 13: 978-0896725218.

Hunt, Kathryn McMurtry. *On My Honor: A Paper Doll History of the Girl Scout Uniform, Volume One*. Illustrated by Lynette C. Ross. Lubbock: Texas Tech University Press, 1994. 28p. ISBN 10: 089672333X

Hunt, Kathryn McMurtry. *Whene'er You Make a Promise: A Paper Doll History of the Girl Scout Uniform, Volume Two*. Illustrated by Lynette C. Ross. Lubbock: Texas Tech University Press, 1996. 32p. ISBN 10: 0896723615; ISBN 13: 978-0896723610.

Young, Sheila. *Polly Pratt Paper Dolls*. Mineola, N. Y.: Dover Publications, 1993. 32p. ISBN 10: 0486273741; ISBN 13: 978-0486273747. (Includes camping or safari outfit).

Guide Paper Dolls on the Internet

These free, reproducible dolls and outfits allow for some creativity in coloring. Children can use their imagination in cutting and playing.

Billy Bear—http://www.billybear4kids.com/worksheets/start-paperdolls.html (accessed March 24, 2009). Scroll down to find several Brownie, Girl Scout, Cub Scout, and Boy Scout paper dolls.

Brownie Paper Doll Craft—http://www.dltk-kids.com/scouts/mbrowniedoll.htm (accessed March 24, 2009).

Bunny Blue Northern Guide—http://ca.geocities.com/nunavut_guide/paper_dolls.htm (accessed March 24, 2009).

Dora the Explorer—http://100megsfree4.com/gogators4/DoraExplorer.html (accessed April 27, 2008).

Girl Guide Paper Dolls—http://www.dltk-kids.com/scouts/dolls.htm (accessed March 24, 2009).

Lena (Safari Costume)—http://users.cybercity.dk/~ccc29141/Card-w-9.htm (accessed March 24, 2009).

Making Friends Paper Dolls—http://www.makingfriends.com/friends/f_scouts.htm (accessed March 24, 2009).

Navy Scouts Paper Doll—http://www.paperdollreview.com/catalog/index.php?main_page=product_info&products_id=189 (accessed March 24, 2009).

Outdoor Friends—http://www.makingfriends.com/friends/f+outdoor.htm and http://www.makingfriends.com/friends/f_scouts.htm (accessed March 24, 2009).

Texas Department of Health Services. Dress Jessica—http://www.dshs.state.tx.us/kids/doll/ (accessed March 24, 2009).

Lesson Plan: Outfitting a Paper Doll Guide

Library Media Skills Objective:

The student will select and read a book related to a given theme.

The student will scan newspapers, catalogs, shopping guides, and Web pages for specific information.

Curriculum (Subject Areas) Objectives:

The activity may be part of a reading and language arts thematic unit as well as a consumer math unit on pricing and budgeting.

Grade Level: 2–6

Resources:

Books about guides

Newspapers, catalogs, and old magazines

Paper doll handouts

Scissors, crayons, markers, and pencils

Instructional Roles:

The teacher or library media specialist may complete this activity. The introduction to the topic of guides will take approximately 30 minutes. Students will take at least 30 minutes to select a book from a list of guide-themed books, read the materials, and begin to think about the paper dolls they wish to create. A second group meeting, in which guides are discussed, assignments explained, and strategies for finding information for pricing are developed, will take 30–45 minutes depending on how extensive the shopping is to be. Students will need time to read their books, locate the prices, and design the collages. This will take at least 2 to 3 hours, depending on the book selected.

Activity and Procedures for Completion:

Be creative and dress as a particular kind of guide. For example, wear a backpack and sturdy shoes and carry a walking stick for Crinkleroots. Students may guess why you are dressed with the props and begin a conversation about guides. Share excerpts from videos and introduce many of the various kinds of guides in short booktalk blurbs. Provide a list of books and media that the library media center owns. Discuss what guides do and the meaning of the word *guide*. Show students the dictionary definitions of the word guide and brainstorm the many meanings. How many guides have students known or used? (People, museum guides, explorers, scouts, as well as guide words!) Discuss the difficulty of being a guide as well as the pleasures that the role may entail.

Explain that students will have a chance to explore this concept further as they consider various kinds of guides. Begin with guides that many students may have some familiarity with, such as grandparents. Share a story about a grandparent guide. Hand out paper dolls for students to complete. Students will select books about guides and begin thinking about what it takes to be the particular kind of guide they select. They may complete the grandparent paper dolls at this point.

At a second session, discuss what students have learned from their reading. Talk about both the material items needed and the knowledge and personality required. Use a model such as a grandparent taking children on a simple hiking trip. List the knowledge needed and the items the grandparent might take along, such as a backpack, water, etc. How might the grandparent dress? What would he or she need to know? How much would such an adventure cost? Make a list of items on chart paper. Share newspaper clippings and paste them next to the listed item. Distribute newspapers with ads, catalogs, and any hiking guides that include what to take on such a trip. One group may look on the Internet at bookmarked sites for information. Students may locate prices, and this information may be added to the chart. Outline some strategies for students to find prices of the items they think their guides will need. When all the items have been listed and priced, add up the costs.

Students will use the model to begin the assignment. Each student should select a book and a specific guide. Students will identify and list what their guides need in terms of clothing, equipment, and personal attributes and knowledge. These list wills form the basis of the search for the prices of the items in ads, catalogs, and Internet shopping sites. If appropriate, students may also watch television programs that discuss costs of outdoor items. The concept of comparison shopping may be introduced. The students will find the prices and total them for outfitting the guide. When the lists are complete, the students will each outfit one of the paper dolls. (If students have selected a person such as a grandparent or scoutmaster, they may paste the face from a scanned photograph of this person on their dolls.) The doll is to be dressed with the items on the list. A collage of all the items should be made on a standard sized backdrop sheet. It should include pictures of the items, a list of the attributes, and a total of the costs (for example, backpack $20, water bottle $1, etc.—experience priceless!). The collage should also the title of the book read or the medium viewed. Students will dress their paper dolls and display them with their backdrops. You may want to include time for students to introduce their creations.

Evaluation:

Each student will select and read a book related to guides. Each will select a kind of guide; identify what it takes to be this type of guide; and scan newspapers, catalogs, shopping guides, and Web pages for specific information about the costs of being such a guide. The student will use the information to prepare a dressed paper doll guide and a collage backdrop that highlights what he or she has learned about the cost of being that type of guide.

Follow-Up:

Students may share the lists with their guides.

Students may share information with a local outfitting store or a travel agent.

Students may "outfit" a scout or safari guide and identify the cost of that outfit a hundred years ago.

Paper Dolls: Guides

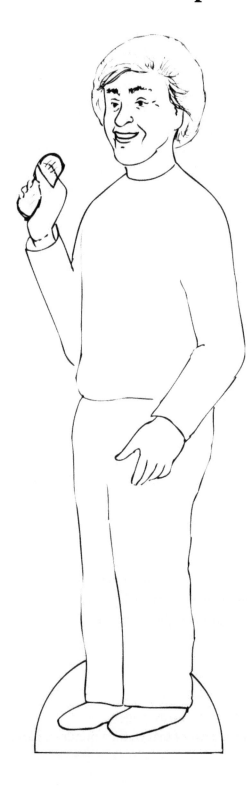

Instructions: Color the figures and costumes on these three pages, then cut them out. Dress them as your favorite guides. If you like, take a picture of a guide in your own life, such as one of your grandparents, and paste that person's face on one of the figures.

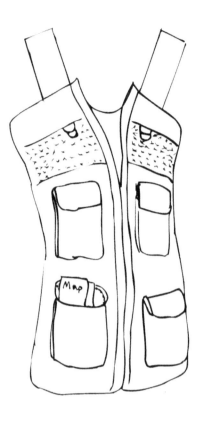

From *Paper Action Figures of the Imagination: Clip, Color and Create* by Paula K. Montgomery.
Santa Barbara, CA: Libraries Unlimited. Copyright © 2009.

149

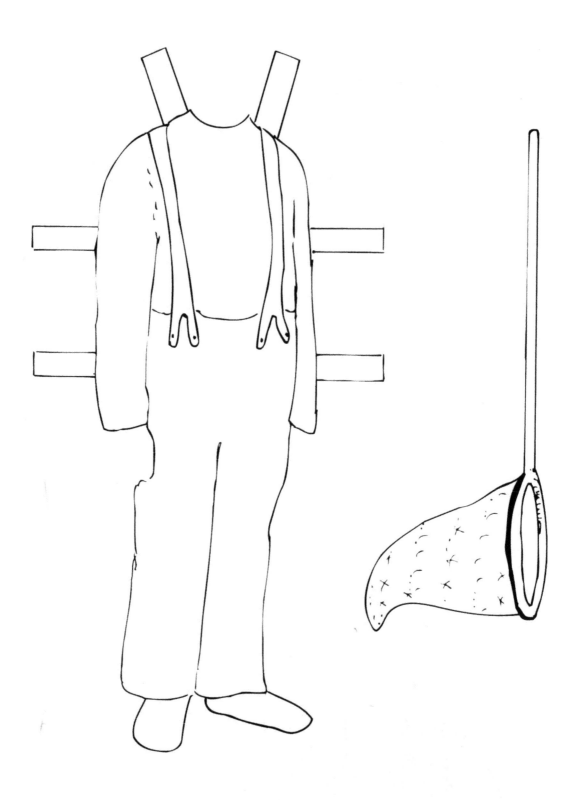

Chapter 10

Check Out Some RRRRoarin' Good Reads!

Aesop, Shel Silverstein, Walt Disney, and C. S. Lewis all have at least one thing in common. Here's a clue:

He's known for courage, strength and might.
You'll see him in the stars at night.
He once was thankful to a mouse.
The wide savannah is his house.
Have you guessed this character, or are you still tryin'
To figure out that it's a lion.

Baum, Frank L. *The Wizard of Oz*. Illustrated by Lisbeth Zwerger. New York: North-South Books, 1996. 103p. ISBN 10: 1558586385; ISBN 13: 978-1558586383

Ingoglia, Gina. *Disney's The Lion King*. Illustrated by Marshall Toomey and Michael Humphries. New York : Disney Press, 1996. 93p. ISBN 10: 156282628X; ISBN 13: 978-1562826284.

Lewis, C. S. *The Complete Chronicles of Narnia*. Illustrated by Pauline Baynes. New York: HarperTrophy, 1994. 528p. ISBN 10: 0060281375; ISBN 13: 978-0060281373. (Titles include *The Magician's Nephew*, *The Lion, the Witch, and the Wardrobe*, *The Horse and His Boy*, *Prince Caspian*, *The Voyage of the Dawn Treader*, *The Silver Chair*, and *The Last Battle*.)

Pfister, Marcus. *How Leo Learned to Be King*. Translated by J. Alison James. New York: North-South Books, 1998. 32p. ISBN 10: 1558589139; ISBN 13: 978-1558589131.

Silverstein, Shel. *Uncle Shelby's Story of Lafcadio, the Lion Who Shot Back*. New York: Harper & Row, 1963. 112p. ISBN 10: 0060256753; ISBN 13: 978-0060256753.

Wang, Mary Lewis. *The Lion and the Mouse: An Aesop Tale Retold*. Illustrated by Tom Dunnington. New York: Children's Press, 1986. 31p. ISBN 10: 0516039814; ISBN 13: 9780516039817.

These authors and creators have told stories in which lions are main characters. For a "quick" self-evaluation on lions in fiction, draw a line from the name of the lion to the name of the author. Next draw a line from the author's name to the correct title in which the lion character appeared.

LIONS	AUTHORS	TITLES
Aslan	Marcus Pfister	__?__: The Lion Who Shot Back
Lafcadio	Walt Disney Productions	The Lion, the Witch and the Wardrobe
Cowardly Lion	Aesop	The Lion King
Grateful lion	Frank L. Baum	How __?__ Learned to Be King
Simba	Shel Silverstien	The Wizard of Oz
"Lazy" lion	C. S. Lewis	The Lion and the Mouse

Answers to Quiz

LIONS	AUTHORS	Titles
Aslan	C. S. Lewis	The Lion, the Witch and the Wardrobe
Lafcadio	Shel Silverstein	Lafcadio: The Lion Who Shot Back
Cowardly Lion	Frank L. Baum	The Wizard of Oz
Grateful Lion	Aesop	The Lion and the Mouse
Simba	Walt Disney	The Lion King
"Lazy" Lion	Marcus Pfister	How Lazy Lion Learned to Be King

Aslan, in his wisdom and majesty, captures our imagination when we think of lions. C. S. Lewis manages to transcend all animals, and we see Aslan as a splendid being. Simba and his humility and Aesop's grateful lion provide lessons about what greatness is. The Lazy Lion exhibits the opposite of greatness, and Lafcadio provides us with laughter. We laugh at the lion who pleads for his life as we see the opposite point of view when he eats the hunter. The anthropomorphism of these lions makes the characters memorable and touches on basic lessons to be learned in our lives.

Lions have been symbols of royalty, ferocity, and power, as well as dauntless courage. Anthropomorphism is a common feature of children's literature. The animal character takes on human characteristics. When authors anthropomorphize the noble lion, the lion symbolism becomes the motivation for the literary characters. In some cases it is the lack of characteristics that becomes a major part of the plot. The lion who is lacking in courage, as in the *Wizard of Oz*; the lion who is less than a king; the beast who can no longer roar ferociously—all make their way into the literature. It is always a mystery how illustrators decide whether or not to clothe the characters. In the case of lions, few pictures in fiction titles include lion characters that wear clothing. This is in stark contrast to bears in fiction, who seem to be dressed quite often! The following titles have clothed lion characters in their illustrations. These may be useful for making lion paper doll figures.

Brierley, Louise. *King Lion and His Cooks*. New York: Holt, Rinehart & Winston, 1981. 32p. ISBN 10: 0862640083; ISBN 13: 978-0862640088.
> King Lion has a cook for all the weekdays, but is on his own for the weekends. Grades K–3.

Durkee, Sarah. *The Lucky Duck*. Illustrated by David Prebenna. New York: Golden Books Publishing, 2000. 48p. ISBN 10:0307165027.
> Lionel the Lion tries to help Lucky the Duck become fiercer. Grades 1–4.

Freeman, Don. *Dandelion*. New York: The Viking Press, 1964. 48p.
> Dandelion dresses for a party, but isn't allowed in because he isn't recognized. (Audio and video recordings are available.) Grades K–4.

Hefter, Richard. *Lion Is Down in the Dumps*. New York: Holt, Rinehart & Winston, 1977. 32p. ISBN 10: 0030214416; ISBN 13: 978-0030214417.
> Lion wants to have his roller skates and lend them, too. Grades 1–3.

Hurd, Edith Thacher. *Johnny Lion's Rubber Boots*. Illustrated by Clement Hurd. New York: HarperCollins, 2000. 32p. ISBN 10: 0060293381; ISBN 13: 978-0060293383.
> Johnny is stuck inside because of the rain and is rescued when his father brings home a pair of boots. Grades K–3.

Rogers, Paul. *Forget-me-not*. Illustrated by Celia Berridge. New York: Viking Penguin, 1984. 32p. ISBN 10: 0722658702; ISBN 13: 978-0722658703.
> While on a trip to see his friend, a lion loses all of his possessions. Grades K–3.

Zelinsky, Paul O. *The Lion and the Stoat; Based in Part on Natural History by Pliny the Elder*. New York: Greenwillow Books, 1984. 40p. ISBN 10: 0688025625; ISBN 13: 978-0688025625.
> A lion and a stoat are artistic competitors. Grades 1–5.

For those who are not interested in whether or not their lion characters are clothed, these titles will serve the imagination just as well.

Andreae, Giles. *The Lion Who Wanted to Love*. Illustrated by] David Wojtowycz. Waukesha, Wis.: Little Tiger Press, 1998. 32p. ISBN 10: 1888444258; ISBN 13: 978-1888444254.

> Leo doesn't want to kill anyone and is banished from the pride. He helps other animals, who in turn eventually help him. Grades K–2.

Anholt, Catherine, and Laurence Anholt. *A Kiss Like This*. New York: Barrons, 1997. 32p. ISBN 10: 0764150685; ISBN 13: 978-0764150685.

> A sleepy, little lion cub enjoys kisses from all different animals, but only his Mama's kisses are just right. Grades K–2.

Brady, Jennifer. *Jambi and the Lions*. Kansas City, Mo.: Landmark Editions, 1992. 32p. ISBN 10: 0933849419; ISBN 13: 978-0933849419.

> Kenyan Jambi searches for the pride of lions that poachers have taken and puts himself at risk. Grades K–4.

Brenner, Barbara, and William H. Hooks. *Lion and Lamb*. Illustrated by Bruce Degen. New York: Bantam, 1990. 48p. ISBN 10: 0553058290; ISBN 13: 978-0553058291.

> Lamb can see that Lion is really a gentle creature. Grades 1–4.

Brenner, Barbara, and William H. Hooks. *Lion and Lamb Step Out*. Illustrated by Bruce Degen. Milwaukee, Wis.: Gareth Stevens, 1990. 48p. ISBN 10: 0553058606; ISBN 13: 978-0553058604.

> Lion and Lamb go off on a hike and to the circus. Grades 1–4.

Brenner, Barbara, and William H. Hooks. *Ups and Downs with Lion and Lamb*. Illustrated by Bruce Degen. New York: Gareth Stevens, 1999. 48p. ISBN 10: 0836817834; ISBN 13: 978-0836817836.

> Lion's family is going to move, and this brings a threat to Lion and Lamb's friendship. Grades 1–4.

Campbell, Eric. *The Place of Lions*. San Diego: Harcourt Brace Jovanovich, 1990. 185p. ISBN 10: 0152624082; ISBN 13: 978-0152624088.

> When their plane crashes, Chris must help his injured father and the pilot by setting out for help. He encounters a pride of lions and an aging male lion, who become involved in his search. Grades 4–8.

Collins, David R. *Leo's Amazing Paws and Jaws*. Illustrated by Jim Theodore. Cleveland, Ohio: Modern Curriculum Press, 1987. 32p. ISBN 10: 0813656826; ISBN 13: 978-0813656823.

> The young cub grows daily and learns how to survive in Central Africa. Grades 1–4.

Cottringer, Anne. *Ella and the Naughty Lion*. Illustrated by Russell Ayto. Boston: Houghton Mifflin, 1996. 32p. ISBN 10: 0434971790; ISBN 13: 978-0434971794.

> A naughty lion strangely appears when Ella's mother brings home the new baby. Grades K–2.

Daugherty, James Henry. *Andy and the Lion*. New York: Viking Press, 1939. 72p. ISBN 10: 0670124338; ISBN 13: 978-0670124336.

> Andy meets a lion on his way to school and befriends him by removing a thorn from his paw, in this classic retelling of "Androcles and the Lion." (Sound and video recordings and a download are available.) Grades K–5.

Davies, Andrew, and Diana Davies. *Poonam's Pets*. Illustrated by Paul Dowling. New York: Viking, 1990. 32p. ISBN 10: 0670833215; ISBN 13: 978-0670833214.

    Poonam is a shy little girl who surprises her class on Pet Day with six performing lions. Grades K–2.

Davis, Douglas F. *The Lion's Tail*. Illustrated by Ronald Himler. New York: Atheneum, 1980. 32p. ISBN 10: 0689501536; ISBN 13: 978-0689501531.

    Both the Masai tribe and the lions want the cattle, so how will the battle go? Grades K–4.

Demarest, Chris L. *Clemens' Kingdom*. New York: Lothrop, Lee & Shepard Books, 1983. 32p. ISBN 10: 068801657X; ISBN 13: 978-0688016579. T

    The stone lion on the steps of the public library is bored and goes inside to see what he can find. Grades K–2.

DeSaix, Frank. *Hilary and the Lions*. Illustrated by Debbi Durland DeSaix. New York: Farrar, Straus & Giroux, 1996. 32p. ISBN 10: 0374332371; ISBN 13: 978-0374332372.

    When Hilary becomes separated from her parents in New York City, she wanders to and falls asleep at the feet of the public library lions, who come to life and take her on a magic ride. Grades K–2.

Dickinson, Peter. *The Iron Lion*. Illustrated by Pauline Baynes. New York: Bedrick/Blackie, 1983. 32p. ISBN 10: 0911745181; ISBN 13: 978-0911745184.

    If a suitor will bring the princess a lion (dead or alive), she will marry him. Grades 1–4.

Du Bois, William Pène. *Lion*. New York: Puffin, 1956. ISBN: 0670429503; ISBN 13: 9780670429509.

    An artist keeps adding parts until he has a lion. Grades K–3.

Färber, Werner. *The Night Lion*. Illustrated by Barbara Mossmann. Boston: Houghton Mifflin, 1991. 24p. ISBN 10: 0434950297; ISBN 13: 978-0434950294.

    Laura's favorite toy, Lion, promises to take care of her as she tries to fall asleep. Grades K–2.

Fatio, Louise. *The Happy Lion*. Illustrated by Roger Duvoisin. New York : Whittlesey House, 1954. 32p. ISBN 10: 0375827595; ISBN 13: 978-0375827594.

    When the zookeeper forgets to close the gate, the happy Lion goes off to visit all the lovely people who stopped to see him at the zoo. Grades K–3.

Fatio, Louise. *The Happy Lion Roars*. Illustrated by Roger Duvoisin. New York: Whittlesey House, 1957. 40p. ISBN 10: 0375838872; ISBN 13: 978-0375838873.

    Happy Lion wants a friend of his own. Grades K–3.

Fatio, Louise. *The Happy Lioness*. Illustrated by Roger Duvoisin. New York: McGraw-Hill, c1980. 32p. ISBN 10: 0070200696; ISBN 13: 978-0070200692.

    Happy Lion is in the hospital and Happy Lioness gets help from friends. Grades K–2. Other Happy Lion titles include:

    The Happy Lion in Africa. Illustrated by Roger Duvoisin. New York: McGraw, 1955. 32p. ISBN 10: 0070200432; ISBN 13: 978-0070200432.

    The Happy Lion's Quest. Illustrated by Roger Duvoisin. New York: Whittlesey House 1961. 32p. ISBN 10: 0370007255; ISBN 13: 978-0370007250.

    The Happy Lion's Treasure. Illustrated by Roger Duvoisin. New York: McGraw-Hill, 1970. 32p. ISBN 10: 0070200645; ISBN 13: 978-0070200647.

The Happy Lion's Vacation. Illustrated by Roger Duvoisin. New York: McGraw Hill, 1967. 32p. ISBN 10: 0070200629; ISBN 13: 978-0070200623

Fields, Julia. *The Green Lion of Zion Street.* Illustrated by Jerry Pinkney. New York : Maxwell Macmillan International, 1993. 32p. ISBN 10: 0689716931; ISBN 13: 978-0689716935.
   A lion statue guarding the bridge seems to bring fear to children in the fog. Grades 1–4.

Frascino, Edward. *My Cousin the King.* Englewood Cliffs, N.J.: Prentice-Hall, 1985. 32p. ISBN 10: 0136084230; ISBN 13: 978-0136084235.
   A cat learns the lion is related to him and arranges a circus lion's escape, only to find out what a carnivorous beast the lion is! Grades K–3.

Frost, Erica. *Mr. Lion Goes to Lunch.* Illustrated by Len Epstein. Mahwah, N.J.: Troll Associates, 1986. 48p. ISBN 10: 0816706387; ISBN 13: 978-0816706389.
   Mr. Lion's lunch is disturbed when animals around him make too much noise. Grades K–3.

Greaves, Margaret. *Sarah's Lion.* Illustrated by Honey de Lacey. Hauppauge, N.Y.: Barron's, 1992. 32p. ISBN 10: 0812062795; ISBN 13: 978-0812062793.
   When the queen does not allow Princess Sarah to leave the palace, a lion appears, and Sarah eventually goes off with it. Grades K–3.

Hadith, Mwenye. *Lazy Lion.* Illustrated by Adrienne Kennaway. Boston: Little, Brown, 1990. 32p. ISBN 10: 0340512652; ISBN 13: 978-0340512654.
   Lion is too lazy to build his own house and so must roam the plains when the rains come. Grades K–3.

Hawkins, Mark. *A Lion under Her Bed.* Illustrated by Jean Vallario. New York: Holt, Rinehart & Winston, 1978. 32p. ISBN 10: 0030403812; ISBN 13: 978-0030403811.
   Her parents think Molly is pretending when she tells them there is a lion under her bed. Grades K–2.

Herman, Gail. *The Lion and the Mouse.* Illustrated by Lisa McCue. New York: Random House, 1998. 32p. ISBN 10: 0613117859; ISBN 13: 978-0613117852
   An adventuresome mouse proves that even small creatures are capable of great deeds, when he rescues the King of the Jungle. Grades K–3.

Hurd, Edith Thacher. *Johnny Lion's Bad Day.* Illustrated by Clement Hurd. New York: Harper & Row, 1970. 64p. ISBN 10: 0060293357; ISBN 13: 978-0060293352.
   Johnny is home in bed sick with medicine that gives him bad dreams, until his parents help him with a soothing song in their bed. Grades 1–4.

Hurd, Edith Thacher. *Johnny Lion's Book.* Illustrated by Clement Hurd. New York: HarperCollins, 1965. 64p. ISBN 10: 0060293330; ISBN 13: 978-0060293338.
   Johnny stays home and reads a book while his parents go out hunting. Grades 1–3.

Jackson, Kathryn. *Tawny Scrawny Lion.* Illustrated by Gustaf Tenggren. Racine, Wis.: Western, 1980. 24p. ISBN 10: 0307021688; ISBN 13: 978-0307021687.
   Ten little bunnies teach a lion to eat carrots, so he won't eat them. Grades K–3.

Jarrett, Clare. *Catherine and the Lion*. Minneapolis, Minn.: Carolrhoda Books, 1997. 28p. ISBN 10: 1575050358; ISBN 13: 978-1575050355.

    Catherine gets an imaginary lion friend soon after the birth of her baby sister. Grades K–1.

Kleven, Elisa. *The Lion and the Little Red Bird*. New York: Dutton Children's Books, 1992. 32p. ISBN 10: 0140558098; ISBN 13: 978-0140558098.

    Little Bird can't understand why Lion's tail changes color every day, until he invites her into his cave. Grades K–3.

Krensky, Stephen. *The lion Upstairs*. Illustrated by Leigh Grant. New York: Atheneum, 1983. 32p. ISBN 10: 0689309694; ISBN 13: 978-0689309694.

    Sam goes on a safari in his own living room and brings home a lion. Grades K–3.

Lee, Dennis. *Lizzy's Lion*. Illustrated by Marie-Louise Gay. Toronto: Stoddart, 1984. 32p. ISBN 10: 0773700781; ISBN 13: 978-0773700789.

    Lizzy gets over her fears with a guardian lion in her closet. Grades K–2.

MacDonald, Suse. *Nanta's Lion: A Search-and-find Adventure*. New York: Morrow, 1995. 32p. ISBN 10: 0688131255; ISBN 13: 978-0688131258. 32p.

    Nanta sets out to find the lion that is terrorizing her village. She never sees the lion, but the reader will. Grades 1–4.

McKean, Thomas. *Hooray for Grandma Jo!* Illustrated by Chris Demarest. New York: Crown, 1994. 32p. ISBN 10: 0517578425; ISBN 13: 978-0517578421.

    Grandma Jo loses her glasses in a pot of stew and is unable to read the letter saying her grandson Lloyd can't come to visit or the newspaper article about an escaped lion. The frivolity begins when she picks up a lion at the train station! Grades 1–4.

McPhail, David M. *Snow Lion*. New York: Parents, 1982. 48p. ISBN 10: 0819310980; ISBN 13: 978-0819310989.

    A lion is tired of the hot jungle and visits the mountains to play in the snow. Grades K–2.

Moers, Hermann. *Evie to the Rescue!* Illustrated by Gusti. New York: North-South Books, 1997. 24p. ISBN 10: 1558587934; ISBN 13: 978-1558587939.

    Evie convinces a lion to set out for a warmer clime than the zoo offers. Grades K–2.

Moers, Hermann. *Hugo the Baby Lion*. Illustrated by Józef Wilkon. New York: North-South Books, 1986. 24p. ISBN 10: 0831796219; ISBN 13: 978-0831796211.

    Hugo is off for his first hunt with his mother. Grades K–3.

Moers, Hermann. *Hugo's Baby Brother*. Illustrated by Jozef Wilkon. North-South Books, 1992. 24p. ISBN 10: 1558581375; ISBN 13: 9781558581371.

    Hugo learns to adjust to a baby brother. Grades K–2.

Mollel, Tololwa M. *Dume's Roar*. Illustrated by Kathy Blankley Roman. Buffalo, N.Y.: Stoddart Kids, 1998. 32p. ISBN 10: 0773730036; ISBN 13: 978-0773730038.

    At first the animals are going to elect Kobe the tortoise as king, but Dume the Lion roars and gets their attention. It becomes exhausting serving the new king, but the threat of hunters brings them around. Grades 1–4.

Montenegro, Laura Nyman. *Sweet Tooth*. Boston: Houghton Mifflin, 1995. 32p. ISBN 10: 0395680786; ISBN 13: 978-0395680780.

> A lion's sweet tooth causes him to be sold from the circus. Grades 2–5.

Morpurgo, Michael. *The Butterfly Lion*. New York: Viking, 1997. 90p. ISBN 10: 0670874612; ISBN 13: 978-0670874613.

> Bertie rescues an orphaned white lion from the African veld, but is separated from him when he goes off to boarding school. Grades 3–6.

Ness, Evaline. *Fierce the Lion*. New York: Holiday House, 1980. 32p. ISBN 10: 0823404129; ISBN 13: 9780823404124.

> Fierce the Lion is dissatisfied with his job in the circus and sets out to find a new job. Grades K–3.

Newberry, Clare Turlay. *Herbert the Lion*. New York: Smithmark Publishing, 1998. ISBN 10: 0765190575; ISBN 13: 978-0765190574.

> Originally published in 1931 and a Caldecott Honor book, this volume tells about a young girl whose mother brings home a real lion cub. Grades K–3.

Ngumy, James. *The Boy Who Rode a Lion*. Illustrated by Shirley Tourett. New York: Chelsea, 1992. 32p. ISBN 10: 0613877403; ISBN 13: 978-0613877404.

> A young boy gets away from a lion by climbing a tree, but falls onto the lion's back and can't get off. Grades K–3.

Peet, Bill. *Eli*. Boston: Houghton Mifflin, 1978. 38p. ISBN 10: 0808535714; ISBN 13: 978-0808535713.

> A proud but decrepit lion learns a lesson about friendship from he vultures he despises. Grades K–4.

Peet, Bill. *Randy's Dandy Lions*. Boston: Houghton Mifflin, 1964. 48p. ISBN 10: 0395274982; ISBN 13: 978-0395274989.

> When a cruel lion tamer is hired to make five cowardly lions perform, things do not go as hoped, and the whole circus suffers from the mistreatment of the animals. Grades K–4.

Pitcher, Caroline. *The Time of the Lion*. Illustrated by Jackie Morris. Hillsboro, Ore.: Beyond Words Publishing, 1998. 32p. ISBN 10: 1885223838; ISBN 13: 978-1885223838.

> Young Joseph plays with a lion cub but fears that traders will want to take the lion away. Grades K–3.

Supraner, Robyn. *Mystery at the Zoo*. Illustrated by Bert Dodson. Mahwah, N.J.: Troll Associates, 1979. 48p. ISBN 10: 0893750913; ISBN 13: 9780893750916.

> When his favorite lion escapes from the zoo, Michael takes it upon himself to find him. Grades 1–4.

Vaughan, Marcia K. *Riddle by the River*. Illustrated by Reynold Ruffins. Englewood Cliffs, N.J.: Silver Burdett, 1995. 32p. ISBN 10: 0382246039; ISBN 13: 978-0382246036.

> Only Monkey seems able to trick Lion in his riddles, asked by the river. Grades K–3.

Waber, Bernard. *A Lion Named Shirley Williamson*. Boston: Houghton Mifflin, 1996. 40p. ISBN 10: 0395809797; ISBN 13: 978-0395809792.

> When Shirley Williamson the lion gets an unusual amount of attention from zookeeper Seymour, the other zoo lions grow jealous. Grades K–3.

Wilhelm, Hans. *The Big Boasting Battle*. New York: Scholastic, 1995. 32p. ISBN 10: 0590222112; ISBN 13: 978-0590222112.

   Lion Horace and snake Sylvester argue over who is better. Grades K–2.

Wolf, Gita. *The Very Hungry Lion: A Folktale*. Illustrated by Indrapramit Roy. New York: Annick Press, 1996. 24p. ISBN 10: 1550374613; ISBN 13: 978-1550374612.

   Singam Lion is hungry, but he's too lazy to hunt for his food, so he makes his way to a village, making bumbling efforts to find food all the way. Grades K–4.

Lion characters have made their way into the movies and videos/DVDs. (This list does not include favorites such as *Born Free*, *To Walk with Lions*, or *Clarence the Cross-Eyed Lion*.) Fictional lion movie stars have become immortalized in plush toys and games related to them. In some cases, the movies came first, followed by the books.

The Chronicles of Narnia: The Lion, the Witch, and he Wardrobe. Walt Disney, 2006. 125 min.

The Chronicles of Narnia: Prince Caspian. Walt Disney, 2008. 149 min.

The Lion King. Walt Disney Home Video; distributed by Buena Vista Home Video, 1995. 88 min. VHS.

The Lion King II: Simba's Pride. Walt Disney Home Video/Buena Vista Home Video, 1998. 75 min. Videotape. (Software is available for *Disney's The Lion King II: Simba's Pride*. Disney Interactive, 1998.)

The Lion, the Witch and the Wardrobe. Wonderworks Family Movies/Public Media Production, 1988. 174 min. (This movie is part one of a three-part series that has been aired on PBS stations.)

The Wizard of Oz. Metro-Goldwyn/Turner, 1996. 106 min.

   One of the main characters is the cowardly lion, played by actor Bert Lahr.

Published Lion Paper Dolls

Lions are sparse in the paper doll world. A few can be found in circus-style products. "Animal Land Leo" appeared in an early *Children's Playmate Magazine*. A more current offering, a lion wearing a plush bathrobe and shower cap, casual wear, and royal togs, is the Dover reusable sticker paper dolls:

Beylon, Cathy. *Lion Sticker Paper Dolls*. Mineola, N.Y.: Dover, 1995. 4p. ISBN 10: 0486284239; ISBN 13: 978-0486284231.

Narnia paper dolls are available. The children with Aslan are found in a bound cut-out version:

Collier, Mary. *The Narnia Paper Dolls: The Lion, the Witch and the Wardrobe Collection*. New York: HarperCollins Children's Books, 1998. 24p. ISBN 10: 0694010782; ISBN 13: 978-0694010783.

On the Internet is a six-page download of the four Pevensie children, with outfits to color and a map of Narnia. Scroll down and click on the link to download "Games" (http://www.narniaresources.com/pdfdownloads/; accessed March 24, 2009).

   Three of the Narnia figures can also be found and dressed at *The Lion's Call: Aravis Paper Doll* (http://www.thelionscall.com/activities/aravis_paper_doll.cfm; accessed March 24, 2009).

Lesson Plan:
The Beast Roars On

Library Media Skills Objective:

The student will select and read a story with a lion character.

The student will summarize a story about a fictional lion and identify the main attributes of the character and his or her motives in a story.

Curriculum (Subject Areas) Objectives:

This activity may be completed in reading/language arts as part of a study of grammar. The students will recognize grammar and point of view in a story. The students will differentiate among first, second, and third person in a story.

Grade Level: 2–5

Resources:

Books with lion characters

Paper doll handouts

Art supplies, including paper, scissors, and crayons or paints

Audio equipment (tape recorders, computer software and microphones, etc.)

Instructional Roles:

The library media specialist can supply books and an introduction. The classroom teacher may also introduce books and instruct in grammar and point of view. The lesson will require 1 hour for introduction and instruction, with time for follow-up as appropriate. Student writing and work will take about 2 hours, depending on the level of the students and expectations for the story and paper dolls.

Activity and Procedures for Completion:

Pull and display books about lions. In an introduction, highlight selected stories that represent first and third person narrative. It should be noted, and students may discuss, how this changes or makes a story different. Read examples of material in the third person and discuss point of view in stories. Eric Campbell's *The Place of Lions*, in which a young boy, Chris, and his father are in a plane crash in Africa, features alternating points of view. Chris must go search for help and comes upon a pride of lions. The lions become part of the search, especially an aging male lion. The book alternates between the voice of Chris and that of the lion.

The teacher may plan instruction or review of grammatical persons and personal pronouns. For example: "The personal pronouns I (singular) and we (plural) are in the first person. The personal you is in the second person, both the singular and plural. He, she, it, and they are in the third person." The teacher may select a short story about a lion character in which the writing is in the third person. After reading it aloud, it may be paraphrased in the first person from the lion's point of view.

For this exercise, students will be given the lion paper dolls to color and cut out. They must select a book about a lion character and determine the point of view of the story. If the story is written in the first person, the student must retell the story in the third person. If the story is in the third person, it must be changed and retold in the first person. Students may practice retelling their stories before putting them on paper or recording them on audiotape. There may be two options. One options is an audio version, in which students tape the retelling, and a second options is a written retelling of the tale.

A lion paper doll should be made to accompany the audio or written retelling. The students may make clothes such as a simple bandana as an outfit. The lion paper dolls may be introduced to the class and shared. Written versions of the retelling may be displayed for others to view on their own.

Evaluation:

Each student will select and read a book about a lion character. The student will summarize a story about a fictional lion and identify the main attributes of the character and his or her motives in a story, either in writing or on audio. The written or audio version will be in the first or third person, varying from the original story. A lion paper doll will be completed to accompany the story.

Follow-Up:

Students may put their audio and text versions of the story, along with pictures of the paper doll lions, on a library Web site as reading motivation.

Paper Dolls: Lions

Instructions: Color the lion characters and their clothes and cut them out. Dress each as one of the lion characters you like best.

From *Paper Action Figures of the Imagination: Clip, Color and Create* by Paula K. Montgomery.
Santa Barbara, CA: Libraries Unlimited. Copyright © 2009.

Chapter 11

Books with Mice Are Twice as Nice!

Why have so many authors chosen to write stories about such tiny creatures as mice? One look at the face of a mouse might give you a hint. Bright eyes, comical ears, buckteeth, a curious nose, and frisky whiskers are sure to make you smile. For many years, readers have enjoyed stories, cartoons, and movies about mice. Walt Disney introduced the most famous mouse ever, Mickey! People all over the world love Mickey Mouse and his girlfriend, Minnie. Cartoon lovers have watched Jerry and little Tuffy drive Tom crazy in *Tom and Jerry*. Speedy Gonzales has given Sylvester a run for his money. Mighty Mouse has captured the imagination of youngsters for several generations. Pinky and the Brain are determined to take over the world. In movies, there have been Mrs. Frisby, Stuart Little, and Basil, the Great Mouse Detective. In adult fiction, there have been more serious mice. The tearjerker *Flowers for Algernon* invokes sadness when, at the end, Charlie asks in a letter to a friend that flowers be put on mouse Algernon's grave, perhaps for what both have lost. Poet Robert Burns wrote "To a Mouse" in 1785 when he overturned a mouse's nest while he was plowing.

> *"But Mousie, thou are no thy-lane,*
> *In proving foresight may be vain:*
> *The best laid schemes o' Mice an' Men,*
> *Gang aft agley,*
> *An' lea'e us nought but grief an' pain,*
> *For promis'd joy!"*

Real mice are mammals. Some live in fields, but others, like the house mouse, scurry inside walls and attics. They like to eat many of the same foods people eat. They also like to snuggle with their babies and stay warm. Do mice think and feel the same way people do? When a writer gives human feelings and thoughts to an animal, he or she is using a writing or *literary* tool called *personification*, a very common technique in children's books about the rodent. Mice are so tiny that they can squeeze into small spaces and get into big trouble. That's when the fun begins!

Authors and Mouse Characters

What would it be like to be a mouse? Let your imagination wander! Let's say you decide to write about a girl mouse. Would she live in a snug old farmhouse under the kitchen floorboards, where cookie crumbs might fall? Would she live in a field where she could make a cozy underground nest with flowery furniture? Does she bathe in a seashell? Does she wear earrings?

What would she use to keep her babies warm? Could she use lint from a clothes dryer? Would she use a cereal box she's shredded with her own little teeth? Will she encounter danger getting her treasures back to her nest? What if her best friend was a chipmunk?

Imagine a boy mouse. Does he like to dart around a flower garden and take naps in an old sneaker? Does he snore? Is there a calico cat waiting to pounce on him at any moment?

How would he escape if a mean old lady ran after him with a broom? What if he were *really* hungry and smelled a delicious piece of cheddar cheese sitting atop a treacherous mousetrap? Might he invent a mouse-sized fishing pole to get it?

Many authors go through the same imaginative process. If the mouse character is shy, brave, or jolly or has any other human characteristic, that is personification. Go a step further! Many authors illustrate their own stories. Will the mouse character be chubby? Will he have giant ears? Will she wear a coat or a dress? Artwork brings characters to life for readers.

Mice Characters and the Authors Who Love Them

Beverly Cleary

Author Beverly Cleary used to be a children's librarian. While her son lay ill in a hotel bed, she imagined a hotel mouse named Ralph. In *The Mouse and the Motorcycle*, Ralph meets a boy with a toy motorcycle, and his little whiskers go wild! Using half a ping pong ball as a helmet, he rides into trouble all over the hotel! Will Ralph be sucked up by the maid's monstrous vacuum cleaner?

Brian Jacques

Brian Jacques likes to write stories about good versus evil. His heroes and heroines are brave, loyal mice. The villains are weasels, snakes, rats, foxes, and ferrets. In the Redwall fantasy series, you can meet the characters living in Redwall Abbey. *Redwall, Mossflower, Martin the Warrior*, and many other books relate gigantic deeds of tiny warriors.

E. B. White

Writer E. B. White (the initials stand for Elwyn Brooks) imagined a small mouselike fellow in *Stuart Little*. Stuart is as smart as a whip, but his tiny stature is a big problem. From getting rolled up inside a window shade to zipping around in a car with a five-drop gas tank, Stuart is a riot! *Stuart Little* was Mr. White's first book for children. In another book, *Charlotte's Web*, he personified a pig and a spider.

Kevin Henkes

Bespectacled Kevin Henkes lives in Wisconsin, where any mouse might like to spend his vacation. Why? The people of Wisconsin produce lots of cheese! In *Chrysanthemum*, a girl mouse is teased about her "perfect" name, until her teacher does the *unexpected*. In *Owen*, a little mouse refuses to give up his favorite blanket. Can nosy Mrs. Tweezers help his parents trick Owen into giving up his dirty friend?

Dav Pilkey

Author Dav Pilkey (Dav is a nickname for Dave!) used his own pet mice when he wrote and photo-illustrated *Kat Kong* and *Dogzilla*. His mice were kept in line by his cat, Blueberry. Mr. Pilkey had a hard time behaving when he was in grade school. His teachers yelled at him for drawing pictures in class. When he started college, a teacher with a good sense of humor encouraged him to write children's books. The rest is history!

Mouse Mania!

Once students have nibbled a bit on mouse character books, they may find others appealing. A bibliography of mice books allows them to rate materials and to learn more about authors and illustrators who appeal to their own preferences.

How Many of These Mouse Books Have You Nibbled?

Check out these titles. If you have read

> 1–5, you're just squeaking by!

> 6–10, your whiskers are showing!

> 11–15, you're the Mousiest!

> 16 and up, EEEEK! You are a real Mouse-iac!

Something special to read for: How many mouse books can you find in which the author and illustrator are the same person?

Ada, Alma Flor. *Friend Frog*. Illustrated by Lori Lohstoeter. New York: Scholastic Inc., 2000. 32p. ISBN 10: 0152015221; ISBN 13: 978-0152015220.
> Field Mouse feels inadequate beside Frog and feels that they can never be friends, because she has nothing to offer. Grades K–2.

Alborough, Jez. *Watch Out! Big Bro's Coming!* Cambridge, Mass.: Candlewick Press, 1997. 32p. ISBN 10: 0763601306; ISBN 13: 978-0763601300.
> Everyone is afraid of Big Bro coming, until mouse looks out to confirm that *his* Big Bro is coming. Big Bro turns out to be mouse's brother. Grades K–3.

Allen, Laura Jean. *Rollo and Tweedy and the Case of the Missing Cheese*. New York: Harper & Row, 1983. 48p. ISBN 10: 0060200979; ISBN 13: 978-0060200978.

> Two clever mice go to Paris to follow clues related to missing cheese. Grades K–2.

Allen, Laura Jean. *Rollo and Tweedy and the Ghost at Dougal Castle*. New York: HarperCollins, 1992. 64p. ISBN 10: 0060201061; ISBN 13: 978-0060201067.

> The mouse detectives fly to Scotland to find a ghost who is looking for the lord's treasure. Grades K–2.

Allen, Laura Jean. *Where Is Freddy?* New York: Harper & Row, 1986. 64p. ISBN 10: 0060200995; ISBN 13: 978-0060200992.

> Detectives Tweedy and Rollo must find Freddy, Mrs. Twombly's missing grandson. Grades K–2.

Althea. *Jeremy Mouse and Cat*. Windermere, Fla.: Rourke Enterprises, 1981. 24p. ISBN 10: 0865925623; ISBN 13: 978-0865925625.

> Mouse's practical joke on cat is almost a disaster. Grades K–2.

Aragon, Jane Chelsea. *The Major and the Mousehole Mice*. Illustrated by John O'Brien. New York: Simon & Schuster Books for Young Readers, 1990. 32p. ISBN 10: 0671688537; ISBN 13: 978-0671688530.

> When a major and his wife move into a mouse-infested house, the major wants to get rid of the mice, but things don't quite turn out the way he plans. Grades K–4.

Archambault, John, and Bill Martin Jr. *A Beautiful Feast for a Big King Cat*. Illustrated by Bruce Degen. New York: HarperTrophy, 1994. 32p. ISBN 10: 0060229039; ISBN 13: 978-0060229030.

> Mouse is a big tease with cat, and it almost does him in. Grades K–3.

Arnosky, Jim. *Mouse Writing*. San Diego: Harcourt Brace Jovanovich, 1983. 48p. ISBN 10: 0152560289; ISBN 13: 978-0152560287.

> Two little mice trace the letters of the alphabet in cursive while ice-skating. Grades K–2.

Asch, Frank. *Here Comes the Cat!* Illustrated by Vladimir Vasilevich Vagin . New York: Scholastic Inc., 1989. 32p. ISBN 10: 0590418599; ISBN 13: 978-0590418591.

> The mice know that the cat is coming, but things don't turn out the way one might expect. Grades K–3.

Asch, Frank Asch. *Mrs. Marlowe's Mice*. Illustrated by Devin Ash. Toronto: Kids Can Press, 2007. 32p. ISBN 10: 1554530229; ISBN 13: 978-1554530229.

> Cat, Mrs. Marlowe, works at the Purrington Street Library and is secretly harboring mice. Is she fattening them up with good cheese to eat them, or is she just a soft-hearted mouse sympathizer?

Asch, Frank. *Pearl's Pirates*. New York: Delacorte, 1987. 167p. ISBN 10: 0385295464; ISBN 13: 978-0385295468.

> Mice Pearl and Wilburn are left when their owner jay is in the hospital after an accident, so they end up in a crate on a ship to France. Grades 2–5.

Asch, Frank. *Pearl's Promise*. New York: Delacorte, 1984. 152p. ISBN 10: 0385293259; ISBN 13: 978-0385293259.

> Pearl helps save her brother from a python in a pet store. Grades 2–5.

Avi. *Poppy*. Illustrated by Brian Floca. New York: Orchard Books, 1995. 160p. ISBN 10: 0531094839; ISBN 13: 978-0531094839.

> Poppy is inspired to go against the tyranny of the owl who watches over them in the farmhouse in order to find a new home for the family. Grades 3–6.

Avi. *Poppy and Rye*. New York: HarperTrophy, 1999. 208p. ISBN 10: 0380797178; ISBN 13: 978-0380797172.

> As Poppy faces the death of her fiancé, Ragweed, who was killed by the owl, she travels to tell Ragweed's parents the news and meets Rye, Ragweed's dreamy brother. Grades 3–6.

Avi. *Poppy's Return*. New York: HarperCollins, 2005. 240p. ISBN 10: 0060000120; ISBN 13: 978-0060000127.

> Poppy returns to Gray House with her rebellious son Junior to visit her sister, Lilly. Grades 3–6.

Avi. *Ragweed*. Illustrated by Brian Floca. New York: HarperTrophy/HarperCollins, 1999. 192p. ISBN 10: 0380976900; ISBN 13: 978-0380976904.

> A brave mouse, Ragweed, goes off to the city and becomes excited by the city life in Amperville and involved in a revolt against the cat gang F.E.A.R. Grades 3–6.

Aylesworth, Jim. *The Completed Hickory Dickory Dock*. Illustrated by Eileen Christelow. New York: Aladdin Books, 1994. 32p. ISBN 10: 0689316062; ISBN 13: 978-0689316067.

> Each strike on the hour of the clock finds the rambunctious mouse doing something different. Grades K–1.

Aylesworth, Jim. *Two Terrible Frights*. Illustrated by Eileen Christelow. New York: Atheneum, 1987. 28p. ISBN 10: 0689313276; ISBN 13: 978-0689313271.

> The young girl upstairs and the little mouse downstairs are getting ready for bed and meet in the kitchen for a bit of a fright. Grades K–1.

Baehr, Patricia Goehner. *Mouse in the House*. Illustrated by Laura Lydecker. New York: Holiday House, 1994. 32p. ISBN 10: 0823411028; ISBN 13: 978-0823411023.

> Mrs. Teapot tries to get rid of a pesky mouse by getting other pets, but that just makes her life worse. Grades L-2.

Baker, Alan. *Mouse's Christmas*. Brookfield, Conn.: Cooper Beach Books, 1996. 24p. ISBN 10: 0761305033; ISBN 13: 978-1856135290.

> Mouse goes out to visit his forest friends, but they are all too busy, so he goes home to a surprise. Grades K–2.

Baker, Alan. *Mouse's Halloween*. Brookfield, Conn.: Millbrook Press, 1997. 32p. ISBN 10: 0761306285; ISBN 13: 978-0761306283.

> Mouse sees monsters in place of his friends on Halloween. Grades K–2.

Baker, Alan. *Two Tiny Mice*. New York: Dial Books for Young Readers, 1991. 32p. ISBN 10: 0803709730; ISBN 13: 978-0803709737.

> Two little field mice give a view of their world. Grades K–3.

Baker, Keith. *Hickory Dickory Dock*. New York: Harcourt, 2007. 32p. ISBN 10: 0152058184; ISBN 13: 978-0152058180.

> Follow each hour of the day as mousey runs up and down the clock. Grades K–2.

Balet, Jan B. *Ladismouse; or, The Advantages of Higher Education*. New York: H. Z. Walck, 1971. 22p. ISBN 10: 0809811804; ISBN 13: 978-0809811809.

    A father mouse knows what to do when his children see a blue-striped cat. Grades K–2.

Balian, Lorna. *Mother's Mother's Day*. Nashville, Tenn.: Abingdon, 1982. 32p. ISBN 10: 1932065393; ISBN 13: 978-1932065398.

    When Hazel goes to visit her mother on Mother's Day, she finds that mother has gone to visit her own mother for the day. Grades K–2.

Barbaresi, Nina. *Firemouse*. New York: Crown, 1987. 40p. ISBN 10: 0375822941; ISBN 13: 978-0375822940.

    Mack moves into a firehouse because his own house is destroyed and starts a mouse fire brigade with seven other mice. Grades K–2.

Barber, Antonia. *Satchelmouse and the Dinosaurs*. Illustrated by Claudio Muñoz. New York: Barron's, 1987. 32p. ISBN 10: 0812058720; ISBN 13: 978-0812058727.

    Satchelmouse is able to blow his magic horn to go to the time of dinosaurs so that he can finish a school project. Grades K–3.

Barklem, Jill. *Autumn Story*. New York: Philomel Books, 1980. 32p. SBN 10: 0689830548; ISBN 13: 978-0689830549.

    Lord Woodmouse's daughter is supposed to help with the harvest but got lost daydreaming. Grades K–4.

    Other Brambly Hedge books by the author in which the mice characters' stories are told include:

Baby Mice of Brambly Hedge. New York: Picture Lions, 1999. 64p. ISBN 10: 0001983261; ISBN 13: 978-0001983267.

The Four Seasons of Brambly Hedge. New York: Philomel, 1988. 144p. ISBN 10: 0001840266; ISBN 13: 978-0001840263.

The High Hills. New York: Atheneum, 1999. 32p. ISBN 10: 0689830548; ISBN 13: 978-0689830549.

Outings for the Mice of Brambly Hedge. New York: Picture Lions, 1999. 64p. ISBN 10: 000198327X; ISBN 13: 978-0001983274.

Poppy's Babies. New York: Philomel Books, 1995. 32p. ISBN 10: 0689831722; ISBN 13: 978-0689831720.

Sea Story. New York: Philomel Books, 1991. 32p. ISBN 10: 0001845632; ISBN 13: 978-0001845633.

The Secret Staircase. New York : Atheneum Books for Young Readers, 1983. 32p. ISBN 10: 0689830904; ISBN 13: 978-0689830907.

Spring Story. New York : W. Collins Publishers, 1980. ISBN 10: 0689830599; ISBN 13: 978-0689830594.

Summer Story. New York: Philomel Books, 1980. 32p. ISBN 10: 0689830599; ISBN 13: 978-0689830594

Wilfred to the Rescue. New York: Atheneum, 2006. 32p. ISBN 10: 141690901X; ISBN 13: 978-1416909019

Winter Story. New York: Philomel Books, 1980. 32p. ISBN 10: 0689830572; ISBN 13: 978-0689830570.

Barnes, Peter W., and Cheryl Shaw Barnes. *Alexander, the Old Town Mouse*. Alexandria, Va.: Vacation Spot Publishing, 1994. 32p. ISBN 10: 0963768816; ISBN 13: 978-0963768810.

Alexander can be found in many historic sites in Alexandria, Virginia, and he ends up at a ball. Grades K–3.

Barnes, Peter W., and Cheryl Shaw Barnes. *Cornelius Vandermouse: The Pride of Newport*. Illustrated by Susan Arciero. Alexandria, Va.: Rosebud Books, 1997. 32p. ISBN 10: 0963768859; ISBN 13: 978-0963768858.

Cornelius is a grand mouse who searches Newport grand houses looking for a good luck charm. Grades K–3.

Barnes, Peter W., and Cheryl Shaw Barnes. *House Mouse, Senate Mouse*. Alexandria, Va.: VSP Books, 1996. 32p. ISBN 10: 0963768840; ISBN 13: 978-0963768841.

This is a spoof on the legislative process in which mice who are trying to get laws accomplished. Grades 3–6.

Barnes, Peter W., and Cheryl Shaw Barnes. *Marshall, the Courthouse Mouse: A Tail of the U.S. Supreme Court*. Alexandria, VA : VSP Books, 1998. 32p. ISBN 10: 0963768867; ISBN 13: 978-0963768865.

The Mouse Supreme Court rules on whether the Mouse Congress can decree that a different kind of cheese must be eaten on each day of the week. Grades 4–6.

Barnes, Peter W., and Cheryl Shaw Barnes. *Woodrow, the White House Mouse*. Alexandria, Va.: Vacation Spot Publishing, 1995. 32p. ISBN 10: 0963768891; ISBN 13: 978-0963768896.

The United Mice of America elect President Woodrow G. Washingtail, who goes to the White House with his family. Grades 3–6.

Bastin, Marjolein. *A Little Dog for Vera*. New York: Stewart, Tabori, & Chang, 1991. 26p.

Little Mouse, Vera's rag dog, comes to life and is the reason cousin Bianca is invited to come stay. Grades 1–4.

Other titles about Vera include:

Games with Vera. New York: Barron's, 1988. 26p. ISBN 10: 0812060865; ISBN 13: 978-0812060867.

My Name Is Vera. New York: Barron's, 1985. 26p. ISBN 10: 0812056906; ISBN 13: 978-0812056907.

Vera and Her Friends. New York: Barron's, 1985. 26p. ISBN 10: 0812056892; ISBN 13: 978-0812056891.

Vera Dresses Up. New York: Barron's, 1985. 26p. ISBN 10: 0812056914; ISBN 13: 978-0812056914.

Vera the Mouse. New York: Barron's, 1986. 26p. ISBN 10: 0812073916; ISBN 13: 978-0812073911. (An animated movie is available.)

Vera in the Garden. New York: Barron's, 1988. 26p. ISBN 10: 081206089X; ISBN 13: 978-0812060898.

Vera in the Kitchen. New York: Barron's, 1985. 26p. ISBN 10: 0812060873; ISBN 13: 978-0812060874

Vera in the Washtub. New York: Barron's, 1988. 26p. ISBN 10: 0812060881; ISBN 13: 978-0812060881.

Vera's Special Hobbies. New York: Barron's, 1985. 26p. ISBN 10: 0812056922; ISBN 13: 978-0812056921

Belpré, Pura. *Perez and Martina: A Puerto Rican Folktale*. Illustrated by Carlos Sanchez. New York: Viking, 1932, 1960. 64p. ISBN 10: 0670841668; ISBN 13: 978-0670841660.
Mouse Perez convinces Martina to wed him. Grades 2–5.

Benjamin, A. H. *It Could Have Been Worse*. Illustrated by Tim Warnes. Waukesha, Wis.: Little Tiger Press, 1998. 28p. ISBN 10: 1584310154; ISBN 13: 978-1584310150.
A little mouse tries to find his way home from the city but keeps running into misadventures. Grades K–3.

Berson, Harold. *A Moose Is Not a Mouse*. New York: Crown, 1975. 32p. ISBN 10: 0517559463; ISBN 13: 978-0517559468.
A picture of a moose leads Mouse to think that he will grow up to be bigger than the cat he fears. Grades K–3.

Bianchi, John. *The Toad Sleeps Over*. Kingston, Ont.: Bungalo Books, 1995. 24p. ISBN 10: 0921285418; ISBN 13: 978-0921285410.
It is a learning experience for memo Mouse when his friend Toad sleeps over. Grades K–2.

Bluth, Brad. *Siegfried's Silent Night*. Illustrated by Toby Bluth. Milwaukee, Wis.: Ideals Publishing, 1983. 32p. ISBN 10: 082498059X; ISBN 13: 9780824980597.
A rat evicts the Muse family on Christmas eve. Grades K–2.

Boegehold, Betty Virginia Doyle. *Pippa Mouse; Six Read-aloud/Read-alone Stories*. Illustrated by Cyndy Szekeres. New York, Knopf, 1973. 62p. ISBN 10: 0394926714; ISBN 13: 978-0394926711.
Little Pippa Mouse gets into mischief with her family in everyday activities like cleaning house. Grades K–2.

Other titles that feature Pippa include:

Here's Pippa! Twelve Stories for Reading Aloud or Reading Alone. Illustrated by Cyndy Szekeres. Nw York: Knopf, 1989. 115p. ISBN 10: 0394827023; ISBN 13: 978-0394827025.

Here's Pippa Again! Six Read-aloud/Read-alone Stories. Illustrated by Cyndy Szekeres. New York: Knopf, 1975. 55p. ISBN 10: 0394930908; ISBN 13: 978-0394930909.

Hurray for Pippa! Four Read-Aloud/Read-Alone Stories. Illustrated by Cyndy Szekeres. New York: Dell, 1980. 55p. ISBN 10: 0394940679; ISBN 13: 978-0394940670.

Pippa Mouse's House. Illustrated by Julie Durrell. New York: Random House, 1998. 24p. ISBN 10: 0679891919; ISBN 13: 978-0679891918.

Pippa Pops Out! Illustrated by Cyndy Szekeres. New York: Knopf, 1979. 32p. ISBN 10: 0440468655; ISBN 13: 978-0440468653.

Bogacki, Tomasz. *Cat and Mouse*. New York: Farrar, Straus & Giroux, 1996. 32p. ISBN 10: 0374312257; ISBN 13: 978-0374312251.

    A curious cat and mouse do not pay attention to the prejudices of their mothers and play together. Grades K–2.

Bogacki, Tomasz. *Cat and Mouse in the Night*. New York: 32p. ISBN 10: 0374311900; ISBN 13: 978-0374311902.

    Cat and Mouse stay out late into the night and become afraid of the dark. Grades K–2.

Bogacki, Tomasz. *Cat and Mouse in the Rain*. New York: Farrar, Straus & Giroux, 1997. 32p. ISBN 10: 0374311897; ISBN 13: 978-0374311896.

    Warned not to go out in the rain, cat and mouse find out how to play together in the drizzle together anyway. Grades K–2.

Bogacki, Tomasz. *Cat and Mouse in the Snow*. New York: Farrar, Straus & Giroux, 1999. 32p. ISBN 10: 0374311927; ISBN 13: 978-0374311926.

    Instead of green meadows, cat and mouse find fields covered in snow, with opportunities to meet new friends. Grades K–2.

Bond, Felicia. *The Halloween Play*. New York: HarperCollins, 1983. 32p. ISBN 10: 0060544430; ISBN 13: 978-0060544430.

    Roger Mouse is ready behind the curtain for his part in the Halloween play, but he has a bit of stage fright. Grades K–2.

Bond, Michael. *Here Comes Thursday!* London: Harrap, 1966. 128p. ISBN 10: 0245586881; ISBN 13: 978-0245586880.

    When a mouse arrived in a bag attached to a balloon, the Peck church mouse family adopted him as their twentieth child and named him Thursday. Grades 3–6.

Other books about Thursday include:

    Thursday Ahoy! Illustrated by Leslie Wood. New York: Lothrop, Lee & Shepard, 1970. 134p. ISBN 10: 0245598251; ISBN 13: 978-0245598258. Grades 3–6.

    Thursday in Paris. London: Puffin, 1974. 119p. ISBN-10: 0140307303; ISBN 13: 978-0140307306. Grades 3–6.

    Thursday Rides Again. New York: Lothrop, Lee & Shepard, 1968. 128p. ISBN: 1854799428 (pb.); ISBN-13: 9781854799425 (pb.).

Boynton, Sandra. *If at First . . .* Boston: Little, Brown, 1980. 32p. ISBN-10: 0316104876d; ISBN 13: 978-0316104876.

    A mouse tries and tries to move an elephant up the hill. Grades K–2.

Brady, Irene. *A Mouse Named Mus*. Boston: Houghton Mifflin, 1972. 93p. ISBN 10: 0395131510; ISBN 13: 978-0395131510.

    It is life and death for a little mouse who escapes to the house. Grades 2–5.

Brady, Susan Horvath. *Find My Blanket*. New York: Lippincott, 1988. 32p. ISBN 10: 039732247X; ISBN 13: 978-0397322473.

    Sam Mouse wants attention before bedtime, so he hides his blanket and gets his brothers and sisters to help him find it. Grades K–2.

Brandenberg, Franz. *It's Not My Fault*. Illustrated by Aliki. New York: Greenwillow Books, 1980. 63p. ISBN 10: 0688802354; ISBN 13: 978-0688802356.

> It isn't a good day for the Fieldmouse children, until they gather around for soup. Grades K–3.

Brandenberg, Franz. *Nice New Neighbors*. Illustrated by Aliki. New York: Mulberry, 1991. 32p. ISBN 10: 0590300709; ISBN 13: 978-0590300704.

> When no one wants to play with the Fieldmouse children, they must be creative. Grades K–3.

Brandenberg, Franz. *Six New Students*. Illustrated by Aliki. New York: Greenwillow Books, 1978. 56p. ISBN 10: 0688801242; ISBN 13: 978-0688801243.

> The six Fieldmouse children learn that school is more fun than they thought. Grades K–3.

Brandenberg, Franz. *What Can You Make of It?* Illustrated by Aliki. New York: Greenwillow Books, c1977. 56p. ISBN 10: 0688800831; ISBN 13: 978-0688800833.

> The Fieldmouse family must find a creative solution for their trash. Grades K–3.

Brenner, Barbara. *Mr. Tall and Mr. Small*. Illustrated by Mike Shenon. New York: H. Holt, 1994. 32p. ISBN 10: 0805027572; ISBN 13: 978-0805027570.

> A giraffe and a mouse argue over who is better, until a fire threatens both of them. Grades K–2.

Brown, Palmer. *Cheerful: A Picture-story*. New York: Harper & Row, 1957. 58p. ISBN 10: 0060208953; ISBN 13: 978-0060208950.

> A little mouse wishes to see the countryside his mother sang about. Grades K–4.

Brown, Palmer. *Hickory*. New York: Harper & Row, 1978. 42p. ISBN 10: 0060208872; ISBN 13: 978-0060208875.

> An indoor mouse finds happiness by going out into the world. Grades 2–4.

Brown, Ruth. *A Dark, Dark Tale: Story and Pictures*. New York: Dial Press, 1981. 32p. ISBN 10: 0862640016; ISBN 13: 978-0862640019.

> A black cat ventures into a dark house and finds another resident. Grades K–3.

Browne, Eileen. *No Problem*. Illustrated by David Parkins. Cambridge, Mass.: Candlewick Press, 1993. 40p. ISBN 10: 0744522056; ISBN 13: 978-0744522051.

> Mouse receives a construction kit and her friends try to help her build other vehicles, but she finally gets it right. Grades K–4.

Buchanan, Lou. *Danger Mouse: The Wizard of Odd*. Illustrated by Joe Ewers. Boston: Little, Brown, 1986. 32p. ISBN 10: 0316757241; ISBN 13: 978-0316757249.

> Dangermouse and Penfold meet a tin man, a scarecrow, a cowardly lion, and the villain who has switched around all the colors in the world. (DVDs of the ten Danger Mouse series stories are available.) Grades K–4.

Bullock, Kathleen. *A Surprise for Mitzi Mouse*. New York: Simon & Schuster Books for Young Readers, 1989. 32p. ISBN 10: 0671673319; ISBN 13: 978-0671673314.

> Mitzi is happy until a new baby sister arrives. (The story is available online at http://www.candlelightstories.com/Stories/MitziMouse.htm; accessed March 24, 2009.) Grades K–2.

Bunting, Eve. *The Mother's Day Mice.* Illustrated by Jan Brett. New York: Ticknor & Fields, 1986. 32p. ISBN 10: 0899193870; ISBN 13: 978-0899193878.

Three mouse brothers go out looking for something special for their mother. Grades K–2.

Burningham, John. *Trubloff, the Mouse who Wanted to Play the Balalaika.* New York: Crown, 1994. 32p. ISBN 10: 0224608347; SBN 13: 978-0224608343.

It is the dream of Trubloff to become the greatest balalaika player in the world. Grades K–3.

Butler, M. Christina. *Stanley in the Dark.* Illustrated by Meg Rutherford. New York: Barron's, 1990. 28p. ISBN 10: 0812061586; ISBN 13: 978-0812061581.

Stanley has a wild night when he mistakes the moon for cheese. (An audiocassette is available.) Grades K–2.

Butler, Stephen. *The Mouse and the Apple.* New York: Tambourine Books, 1994. 32p. ISBN 10: 0688128106; ISBN 13: 9781845072117.

Mouse waits patiently for the apple, while the other animals try different strategies to make if fall. Grades K–2.

Cameron, John. *If Mice Could Fly.* New York: Atheneum, 1979. 30p. ISBN 10: 0689307314; ISBN 13: 978-0689307317.

No matter what, mice want to get the upper hand with cats. Grades K–2.

Carey, Mary. *Mrs. Brisby's Important Package.* Illustrated by A. O. Williams. New York: Golden Press, 1982. 24p. ISBN 10: 0307118851; ISBN 13: 978-0307118851.

When Mrs. Brisby tries to befriend a crow, she endures a great deal of stress and is put in danger. Grades K–2.

Carlstrom, Nancy White. *I'm Not Moving, Mama!* Illustrated by Thor Wickstrom. New York: Macmillan, 1990. 32p. ISBN 10: 0027172864; ISBN 13: 978-0027172867.

It is moving day, and little mouse does not want to move, for a great many reasons. Grades K–2.

Cartlidge, Michelle. *A Mouse's Diary.* New York: Lothrop, Lee & Shepard Books, 1981. 32p. ISBN 10: 0525451951; ISBN 13: 978-0525451952.

Like any little girl, Mouse writes in her diary about ballet class and the other things that fill her day. Grades 1–4.

Cartlidge, Michelle. *Pippin and Pod.* New York: Pantheon Books, 1978. 32p. ISBN 10: 0394938453; ISBN 13: 978-0394938455.

Two little mice run off while their mother is shopping; everything is fun until they realize they are lost. Grades K–2.

Castle, Caroline, and Peter Weevers. *Herbert Binns and the Flying Tricycle.* New York: Dial, 1987. 32p. ISBN 10: 0803700415; ISBN 13: 978-0803700413.

Tiny but brilliant mouse Herbert invents a flying tricycle, and his enemies steal the starting pin. Grades K–3.

Chica. *Celestine Decorates Her House.* Windermere, Fla.: Silver Burdett, 1981. 32p. ISBN 10: 0865930260; ISBN 13: 978-0865930261.

Celestine is trapped in the attic when a cupboard falls on her. Other titles are *Celestine Goes to Market, Celestine High in the Sky, Celestine in the Snow,* and *Celestine, the School Teacher.* Grades K–3.

Chorao, Kay. *Cathedral Mouse*. New York: Dutton, 1988. 32p. ISBN 10: 0525444009; ISBN 13: 978-0525444008.

Mouse escapes a pet store and runs to the Cathedral, where he overcomes his fears of the strange statues and finds a home. Grades K–3.

Christian, Peggy. *The Bookstore Mouse*. Illustrated by Gary A. Lippincott. San Diego: Jane Yolen Books/Harcourt Brace, 1995. 144p. ISBN 10: 0152002030; ISBN 13: 978-0152002039.

Cervantes is a mouse who eats books and subsequently the words lead him to new adventures. Grades 3–6.

Cleary, Beverly. *The Mouse and the Motorcycle*. Illustrated by Louis Darling. New York: HarperTrophy, 1965. 208p. ISBN 10: 0688216986; ISBN 13: 978-0688216986.

Ralph the mouse has always wanted his very own motorcycle. He soon gets his wish when young Keith and his family move into the hotel with his toy motorcycle. (Audio and animated versions are available.) Grades 3–6.

Cleary, Beverly. *Ralph S. Mouse*. Illustrated by Paul O. Zelinsky. New York: Morrow Junior Books, 1982. 160p. ISBN 10: 0688014526; ISBN 13: 978-0688014520.

Ralph has problems because his motorcycle is getting worn and his relatives are messing up the hotel lobby where they live. (Audio and animated versions are available.) Grades 3–6.

Cleary, Beverly. *Runaway Ralph*. Illustrated by Tracy Dockray. New York: Avon, 1970. 224p. ISBN 10: 068821701X; ISBN 13: 978-0688217013.

Ralph wants freedom, so he leaves the hotel on his motorcycle and arrives at Happy Acres Camp, where he meets a boy named Garf. (Audio and animated versions are available.) Grades 3–6.

Clifford, Sandy. *The Roquefort Gang*. New York: Bantam, 1981. 79p. ISBN 10: 0395295211; ISBN 13: 978-0395295212.

A brave trio help rescue mice being held in a prison. Grades 2–4.

Coombs, Patricia. *Mouse Café*. New York: Lothrop, Lee & Shepard Co., 1972. 46p. ISBN 10: 0688413803; ISBN 13: 978-0688413804.

A hardworking little mouse meets her prince charming. Grades K–2.

Corbett, W. J. *Pentecost and the Chosen One*. New York: Delacorte Press, 1987. 237p. ISBN 10: 0385295499; ISBN 13: 978-0385295499.

A prophetic badger foretells a great adventure in which little mouse Pentecost will go to the old city and overthrow a tyrant, with the help of another mouse called the Chosen mouse. Grades 3–7.

Corbett, W. J. *The Song of Pentecost*. Illustrated by Martin Ursell. New York: Dutton, 1982. 215p. ISBN 10: 0525440518; ISBN 13: 978-0525440512.

Pentecost leads a group of mice to help Sanke get his inheritance and to find a new home in Lickey Hills. Grades 3–7.

Corbett, W. J. *Pentecost Of Lickey Top*. New York: Methuen, 1987. 224p. ISBN 10: 041602372X; ISBN 13: 978-0416023725.

Pentecost shows his heroism by saving his family from the eviction that Owl is threatening them with. Grades 3–7.

Craig, Helen. *Charlie and Tyler at the Seashore*. Cambridge, Mass.: Candlewick Press, 1995. 32p. ISBN 10: 156402573X; ISBN 13: 978-1564025739.

Two adventurous mice go to the seaside and have an exciting boat ride, run from a seagull, and get lost in a toy theater. Grades K–2.

Cressey, James. *Max the Mouse*. Illustrated by Tamasin Cole. Englewood Cliffs, N. J.: Prentice-Hall, 1977. 32p. ISBN 10: 0135662990; ISBN 13: 978-0135662991.

A very large mouse arrives and interrupts the peace of a little mouse family. Grades K–2.

Crimi, Carolyn. *Tessa's Tip-tapping Toes*. New York: Scholastic Inc., 2002. 32p. ISBN 10: 0439317681; ISBN 13: 978-0439317689.

A toe-tapping mouse and warbling cat get together to make music. Grades K–2.

Crust, Linda and John Brindle. *Melvin's Cold Feet*. Illustrated by John Brindle. Milwaukee, Wis.: Gareth Stevens Children's Books, 1991. 32p. ISBN 10: 0356167453; ISBN 13: 978-0356167459.

A spider helps a little mouse who has cold feet. Grades K–2.

Cunningham, Julia. *A Mouse Called Junction*. Illustrated by Michael Hague. New York: Pantheon Books, 1980. 32p. ISBN 10: 0394941128; ISBN 13: 978-0394941127.

Junction is the last of his family and wants to seek more than his present life holds for him. Grades K–2.

Currey, Anna. *Tickling Tigers*. Hauppauge, N.Y.: Barron's Educational Series, 1996. 32p. ISBN 10: 0812065948; ISBN 13: 978-0812065947.

Little mouse Hannibal brags that he can tickle a tiger with a blade of grass. Grades K–2.

Cushman, Doug. *Uncle Foster's Hat Tree*. New York: Puffin, 1988. 48p. ISBN 10: 0525444106; ISBN 13: 978-0525444107.

Uncle Foster tells Merle stories about the hats on his hat tree. Grades 1–3.

Daly, Niki. *Vim, the Rag Mouse*. New York: Atheneum, 1979. 32p. ISBN 10: 0689501412; ISBN 13: 978-0689501418.

A toy mouse would like to have an adventure than he can share with the other toys. Grades K–2.

Damon, Laura. *Secret Valentine*. Illustrated by Anne Kennedy. Mahwah, N. J.: Troll Associates, 1988. 32p. ISBN 10: 0816711011; ISBN 13: 978-0816711017.

Molly Mouse has a secret admirer, and she would like to know who it is. Grades K–2.

De Regniers, Beatrice Schenk. *How Joe the Bear and Sam the Mouse Got Together*. Illustrated by Bernice Myers. New York: Lothrop, Lee & Shepard Books, 1990. 32p. ISBN 10: 0688090796; ISBN 13: 978-0688090791.

Bear and Mouse would like to be friends, but they can't agree on anything. Grades K–2.

Delacre, Lulu. *Nathan and Nicholas Alexander*. New York: Scholastic Inc., 1986. 32p. ISBN 10: 0590415735; ISBN 13: 978-0590415736.

Mouse Nicholas Alexander finds a home in Nathan the elephant's toy box, and they must learn how to share. Grades K–2.

Delacre, Lulu. *Nathan's Balloon Adventure*. New York: Scholastic, 1991. 32p. ISBN 10: 0590449761; ISBN 13: 978-0590449762.

   At first Henri is unhappy that elephant Nathan goes on the balloon ride, but when Nathan helps inflate the balloon, all is forgiven. Grades K–2.

Delaney, Ned. *Two Strikes, Four Eyes*. Boston: Houghton Mifflin, 1976. 32p. ISBN 10: 0395247446; ISBN 13: 978-0395247440.

   Toby is ashamed to wear his glasses, but really needs them to play baseball well. Grades K–2.

Demarest, Chris L. *Kitman and Willy at Sea*. New York: Simon & Schuster Books for Young Readers, 1991. 32p. ISBN 10: 0671798499; ISBN 13: 978-0671798499.

   Cat and mouse pals make a boat and set out for adventure. They end up trying to figure out how to save captured animals. Grades K–2.

Demarest, Chris L. *The Lunatic Adventure of Kitman and Willy*. New York: Simon & Schuster Books for Young Readers, 1988. 32p. ISBN 10: 0671656953; ISBN 13: 978-0671656959.

   The cat and mouse friends venture into space. Grades K–2.

Dennard, Deborah. *Travis and the Better Mousetrap*. Illustrated by Theresa Burns. New York: Cobblehill Books/Dutton, 1996. 32p. ISBN 10: 0525651780; ISBN 13: 978-0525651789.

   Travis builds a trap to catch a mouse, but ends up with a very large mouse and new problems. Grades K–2.

Derby, Sally. *The Mouse who Owned the Sun*. Illustrated by Friso Henstra. New York: Maxwell Macmillan International, 1993. 32p. ISBN 10: 0027669653; ISBN 13: 978-0027669657.

   Mouse thinks he controls the rising of the sun. Grades K–2.

Di Fiori, Lawrence. *Muffin Mouse's New House*. Racine, Wis.: Western Publishing, 1991. ISBN 10: 0307660281; ISBN 13: 978-0307660282.

   When Muffin Mouse looses her home in a storm, she finds a perfect place, with Frankie Frog's help. Grades K–2.

Dionetti, Michelle. *Mice to the Rescue!* Illustrated by Carol Newsom. Mahwah, N.J.: Troll Associates, 1995. 95p. ISBN 10: 0816737126; ISBN 13: 978-0816737123.

   When a human has evil plans about the fabric store, the mice band together to protect the store. Grades K–3.

Drury, Roger W. *The Champion of Merrimack County*. Illustrated by Fritz Wegner. Boston: Little, Brown, 1976. 198p. ISBN 10: 0316193496; ISBN 13: 978-0316193498.

   The Berryfield family finds a bike-riding mouse in their bathtub. Grades 3–6.

Dubanevich, Arlene. *Tom's Tail*. New York: Puffin Books, 1992. 32p. ISBN 10: 0670830216; ISBN 13: 978-0670830213.

   Old Tom is tired after keeping the mice out of the house and only comes back to life when mice come out to jump on his tail. Grades K–2.

Duke, Kate. *Aunt Isabel Tells a Good One*. New York: Penguin Books, 1992. 32p. ISBN 10: 0525448357; ISBN 13: 978-0525448358.

   Little Penelope helps her aunt weave a story about Lady Nell and a Prince. Grades K–2.

Dunbar, Joyce. *Ten Little Mice.* Illustrated by Maria Majewska. San Diego: Harcourt Brace, 1990. 26p. ISBN 10: 015200601X; ISBN 13: 978-0152006013.
> Ten little mice count backwards as they frolic. Grades K–1.

Dungan, Riana. *A Tale of Ten Town Mice.* Windermere, Fla.: R. Rourke Publishing, 1982. 32p. ISBN 10: 0865921229; ISBN 13: 978-0865921221.
> When the mouse family moves to the forest, they are not quite prepared for the mishaps that occur. Grades K–2.

Elzbieta. *Brave Babette and Sly Tom.* New York: Dial Books for Young Readers, 1989. 32p. ISBN 10: 0571154271; ISBN 13: 978-0571154272.
> Babette is left alone when her mother escapes the cat by catching a flyaway balloon. She is adopted by a crow and always wonders why she does not look like her crow mother. Grades K–2.

Emberley, Michael. *Ruby.* Boston: Little, Brown, 1990. 26p. ISBN 10: 0316888591; ISBN 13: 978-0316888592.
> Ruby goes on her way to deliver pies to her sick grandmother. She is warned not to talk to strangers and especially never to trust a cat, but she forgets when a smooth-talking cat helps her after a slimy reptile steals her goodies. Grades K–3.

Emberley, Michael. *Ruby and the Sniffs.* Boston: Little, Brown, 2004. 32p. ISBN 10: 0316236640; ISBN 13: 978-0316236645.
> Ruby hides from her babysitter at the house of three pigs who are not home. Grades K–3.

Engel, Diana. *Eleanor, Arthur, and Claire.* New York: Macmillan, 1992. 32p. ISBN 10: 0027334627; ISBN 13: 978-0027334623.
> Claire spends summers with her grandparents until her grandpa Arthur dies. Grades K–3.

Engel, Diana. *Gino Badino.* New York: Morrow Junior Books, 1991. 32p. ISBN 10: 068809502X; ISBN 13: 978-0688095024.
> Ginos saves his family pasta business when he invents pasta mice. Grades K–3.

Erkel, Cynthia Rogers. *The Farmhouse Mouse.* Illustrated by Michael Erkel. New York: Putnam, 1994. 32p. ISBN 10: 0399224440; ISBN 13: 978-0399224447.
> A little mouse enjoys the warmth of the farmhouse. The farmer and his wife are convinced that there is more than one mouse.

Ezra, Mark. *The Sleepy Dormouse.* Illustrated by Gavin Rowe. New York: Crocodile Books, 1994. 32p. ISBN 10: 1566561922; ISBN 13: 978-1566561921.
> A weasel captures the sleepy little mouse and takes him home to fatten him up. Grades K–2.

Fearnley, Jan. *Martha in the Middle.* Cambridge, Mass.: Candlewick Press, 2008. 40p. ISBN 10: 0763638005; ISBN 13: 978-0763638009.
> Martha is always caught in the middle between siblings and wants to run away. Grades K–3.

Finklea, Michael. *The Worldwide Adventures of Winston and Churchill. Book One, Europe.* Illustrated by Wesley Ortiz. Atlanta, Ga.: Ozark Publishing, 1998. 44p. ISBN 10: 1567634060; ISBN 13: 978-1567634068.
> Two mice cousins visit relatives in five different countries in Europe. Grades K–4.

Flack, Marjorie. *Walter, the Lazy Mouse.* Illustrated by Cyndy Szekeres. Garden City, N.Y.: Doubleday, 1963. 96p. ISBN 10: 0385027729; ISBN 13: 978-0385027724.

    Walter is so lazy that he never gets up for school, and his family forgets about him and moves out, leaving him behind. Grades 2–4.

Fleming, Denise. *Lunch.* New York: H. Holt, 1995. 32p. ISBN 10: 0805016368; ISBN 13: 978-0805016369.

    A very hungry mouse nibbles and crunches his way through a colorful vegetarian feast. Grades K–1.

Freeman, Don. *Norman the Doorman.* New York: Puffin Books, 1959. 32p.

    Norman views the art treasures as he manages the mouse hole door at the museum. (Audio and video versions are available.) Grades K–3.

Freeman, Lydia, and Don Freeman. *Pet of the Met.* New York: Viking/Puffin 1953. 72p. ISBN 10: 0670061786; ISBN 13: 978-0670061785.

    Maestro Petrini, the page-turner for the Prompter at the Metropolitan Opera House, gets carried away by Mozart's *Magic Flute* and joins the performers onstage. Grades K–4.

French, Vivian. *Christmas Mouse.* Illustrated by Chris Fisher. Cambridge, Mass.: Candlewick Press, 1997. 32p. ISBN 10: 0744572126; ISBN 13: 978-0744572124.

    Little Mouse had a cold at Christmas, and it makes him less than jolly. Grades K–1.

Freschet, Berniece. *Bear Mouse.* Illustrated by Donald Carrick. New York: Scribner, 1973. 32p. ISBN 10: 0684133202; ISBN 13: 978-0684133201.

    Mother Mouse has a struggle feeding and caring for her family during the cold winter. Grades K–2.

Freschet, Berniece. *Bernard and the Catnip Caper.* New York: Scribner's, 1981. 40p. ISBN 10: 0684171570; ISBN 13: 978-0684171579.

    Bernard receives a ransom note when a shy little mouse is catnapped. Grades 1–4.

Freschet, Berniece. *Bernard of Scotland Yard.* Illustrated by Gina Feschet. New York: Scribner, 1978. 48p. ISBN 10: 0684159317; ISBN 13: 978-0684159317.

    A Boston mouse helps catch thieves who have taken a cache of jewels. Grades 1–4.

Freschet, Berniece. *Bernard Sees the World.* New York: Scribner, 1976. 48p. ISBN 10: 0684146711; ISBN 13: 978-0684146713.

    Bernard Mouse sees the world from the vantage point of the moon. Grades 1–4.

Gackenbach, Dick. *The Perfect Mouse.* New York: Macmillan, 1984. 32p. ISBN 10: 0027367606; ISBN 13: 978-0027367607.

    Mother and Father Mouse set out to find the perfect husband for their perfect daughter. Grades K–4.

Gaffney, Timothy R. *Wee and the Wright Brothers.* Illustrated by Bernadette Pons. New York: H. Holt, 2004. 40p. ISBN 10: 0805071725; ISBN 13: 978-0805071726.

    Wee and his mouse family live in the Wright brothers' bike shop and he tags along to Kitty Hawk when the brothers test their plane in 1903. Grades 1–4.

Gag, Wanda. *Snippy and Snappy.* New York: Smithmark, 1998. 48p. ISBN 10: 0816642451; ISBN 13: 978-0816642458.

    Two little mice wander away and must be rescued by their father. Grades K–3.

Garland, Michael. *How Many Mice?* New York: Dutton, 2008. 32p. ISBN 10: 0525478337; ISBN 13: 978-0525478331.

Ten hungry mice go out on a food collecting expedition. Grades K–2.

Geraghty, Paul. *Look Out, Patrick!* New York: Macmillan, 1990. 28p. ISBN 10: 0027358224; ISBN 13: 978-0027358223.

As Patrick the Mouse goes out for a summer stroll, he is oblivious to his near encounters with danger. Grades K–2.

Gibbons, Gail. *The Magnificent Morris Mouse Clubhouse.* New York: Franklin Watts, 1981. 32p.

Morris has a problem with his tail getting in the way, until he starts to build a clubhouse. Grades K–2.

Ginsburg, Mirra. *Four Brave Sailors.* Illustrated by Nancy Tafuri. New York: Greenwillow Books, 1987. 24p. ISBN 10: 0688065147; ISBN 13: 978-0688065140.

Four brave mice sail into what appears to be a little boy's dream.

Godden, Rumer. *Mouse House.* Illustrated by Adrienne Adams. New York: Viking Press, 1957. 64p. ISBN 10: 0670491470; ISBN 13: 978-0670491476.

Baby mouse Bonnie looks for a place of her own where she will have room. Grades K–4.

Godden, Rumer. *The Mousewife.* Illustrated by Heidi Holder. New York: Viking, 1982. 31p. ISBN 10: 0670491802; ISBN 13: 978-0670491803.

A little mouse thinks she would like more from life than caring for her family. Grades K–3.

Goodall, John S. *Creepy Castle.* New York: Margaret K. McElderry Books, 1998. 32p. ISBN 10: 0689822057; ISBN 13: 978-0689822056.

A brave mouse and his fair lady do not know they are being followed into a deserted castle. Grades K–3.

Goodall, John S. *Naughty Nancy.* New York: Margaret K. McElderry Books, 1999. 32p. ISBN 10: 068-9823584; ISBN 13: 978-0689823589.

Nancy is supposed to be the flower girl at her sister's wedding, but she causes mischief at every step of the ceremony. Grades K–3.

Goodall, John S. *Naughty Nancy Goes to School.* New York: Atheneum, 1985. 32p. ISBN 10: 0689825633; ISBN 13: 978-0689825637.

Nancy can't seem to help herself when she teases a boy, climbs to the schoolhouse roof, and knocks the teacher down. Grades K–3.

Goodall, John. *Shrewbettina's Birthday.* New York: Atheneum, 1998. 32p. ISBN 10: 0689822065; ISBN 13: 978-0689822063.

After Shrewbettina's purse has been recovered from a purse snatcher, a birthday party is thrown for her. Grades K–3.

Goodman, Joan E. *Hillary Squeak's Dreadful Dragon.* Racine, Wis.: Western Publishing, 1987. 24p. ISBN 10: 0307609065; ISBN 13: 978-0307609069.

Hilary walks through the woods and imagines all kinds of dangers. Grades K–2.

Gorbachev, Valeri. *Arnie the Brave*. New York: Grosset, 1997. 22p. ISBN 10: 0613045181; ISBN 13: 978-0613045186.

    Arnie wants to go to sea but is afraid of sharks and other sea dangers. Grades K–2.

Grambling, Lois G. *Elephant and Mouse Get Ready for Christmas*. Illustrated by Deborah Maze. New York: Barron's, 1990. 32p. ISBN 10: 0812061853; ISBN 13: 978-0812061857.

    When elephant and mouse hang their stockings and elephant switches so that mouse will not get fewer presents, Santa fixes everything. Grades K–2.

Gregory, Valiska. *Babysitting for Benjamin*. Illustrated by Lynn Munsinger. Boston: Little, Brown, 1993. 32p. ISBN 10: 0316327859; ISBN 13: 978-0316327855.

    Frances and Ralph, an elderly mouse couple, aren't as ready for Benjamin as they think. Grades K–3.

Gurney, Nancy and Eric Gurney. *The King, the Mice and the Cheese*. New York: Beginner Books, 1965. 63p. ISBN 10: 0394800397; ISBN 13: 978-0394800394.

    The king tries to keep mice from eating his favorite food. Grades K–3.

Harris, Leon A. *The Great Diamond Robbery*. Illustrated by Joseph Schindelman. New York: Atheneum, 1985. 38p. ISBN 10: 0689311885; ISBN 13: 978-0689311888.

    French mouse Maurice settles in Neiman Marcus department store, where he witnesses a jewelry robbery. Grades K–3.

Henkes, Kevin. *Chester's Way*. New York: Mulberry Books, 1988. 32p. ISBN 10: 0688076076; ISBN 13: 978-0688076078.

    Lily must prove herself before Chester and Wilson will accept her. (Audio and video versions are available.) Grades K–3.

Henkes, Kevin. *Chrysanthemum*. New York: Greenwillow, 1991. 32p. ISBN 10: 0061119741; ISBN 13: 978-0061119743.

    On the first day of school, Chrysantheum begins to feel that her name is not so perfect when children make fun of it. (Audio and video versions are available.) Grades K–3.

Henkes, Kevin. *Julius, the Baby of the World*. New York: Mulberry Books, 1995. 32p. ISBN 10: 0688089437; ISBN 13: 978-0688089436.

    Lilly is very unhappy about Julius, the new baby, until a cousin says something against him. (An audio recording is available.) Grades K–3.

Henkes, Kevin. *Julius's Candy Corn*. New York: HarperFestival, 2003. 24p. ISBN 10: 0060537892; ISBN 13: 978-0060537890.

    Julius begins to count the candy corns on the Halloween cake and ends up eating them. Grades K–2.

Henkes, Kevin. *Lilly's Big Day*. New York: Greenwillow Books, 2006. 32p. ISBN 10: 0060742364; ISBN 13: 978-0060742362.

    Lilly wants to be the flower girl in Mr. Slinger's wedding. (An audio version is available.) Grades K–3.

Henkes, Kevin. *Lilly's Chocolate Heart*. New York: Greenwillow, 2004. 24p. ISBN 10: 0060560665; ISBN 13: 978-0060560669.

    Lilly tries to find the perfect hiding place for her last chocolate heart. Grades K–2.

Henkes, Kevin. *Lilly's Purple Plastic Purse*. New York: Greenwillow, 1996. 32p. ISBN 10: 0688128971; ISBN 13: 978-0688128975.

> Lilly is upset when her favorite teacher, Mr. Slinger, confiscates her purple purse, so she decides to get even. (An audio version is available.) Grades K–3.

Henkes, Kevin. *Owen*. New York: Greenwillow Books, 1993. 32p. ISBN 10: 0439686180; ISBN 13: 978-0688114497.

> Owen calls his baby blanket Fuzzy, and he doesn't want to give it up. (Caldecott Honor Book). Grades K–3.

Henkes, Kevin. *Sheila Rae, the Brave*. New York: Scholastic, 1987. 32p. ISBN 10: 0688071554; ISBN 13: 978-0688071554.

> Sheila decides to take a different way home and gets lost. (An audio recording is available.) Grades K–3.

Henkes, Kevin. *Sheila Rae's Peppermint Stick*. New York: Greenwillow, 1993. 24p. ISBN 10: 0060294515; ISBN 13: 978-0060294519.

> Louise wants a lick of Sheila Rae's peppermint stick. Grades K–2.

Henkes, Kevin. *A Weekend with Wendell*. New York: Puffin, 1987. 32p. ISBN 10: 0688140246; ISBN 13: 978-0688140243.

> Sophie and her parents can't wait for Wendell's visit to be over because he is such a trouble maker. (An audio recording is available.) Grades K–3.

Henkes, Kevin. *Wemberly Worried*. New York: Harper Collins, 2000. 32p. ISBN 10: 0688170277; ISBN 13: 978-0688170271.

> Wemberly is a little mouse who worries about everything. (An audio version is available.) Grades K–2.

Hillman, Priscilla. *The Merry-mouse Schoolhouse*. Garden City, N.Y.: Doubleday, 1982. 32p. ISBN 10: 0385171064; ISBN 13: 978-0385171069.

> The three Nibble children get ready for school. Grades K–2.

Hoban, Lillian. *It's Really Christmas*. New York: Greenwillow Books, 1982. 39p. ISBN 10: 0688008305; ISBN 13: 978-0688008307.

> Mouse wants to see Christmas because he was born in the summer among the Christmas decorations.

Hoban, Russell. *Charlie Meadows*. Illustrated by Martin Baynton. New York: Holt, Rinehart & Winston, 1984. 24p.

> Charlie Meadows is dancing in the moonlight and is almost eaten by an owl. Grades K–2.

Hoban, Russell. *Mouse and His Child*. Illustrated by David Small. New York: HarperCollins, 1967. 256p. ISBN 10: 0439098262; ISBN 13: 978-0439098267.

> Two wind-up tin mice (father and son) joined at the hands begin a quest to become self-winding. Grades 4–7.

Hoeye, Michael. *Time Stops for No Mouse: A Hermux Tantamoq Adventure.* New York: Speak, 1999. 277p. ISBN 10: 0670913065; ISBN 13: 978-0670913060.

    Mouse watchmaker Hermux Tantamoq encounters Ms. Linka Perflinger when she brings her watch to be fixed and begins an adventure filled with intrigue, spies, and villains. (Audio versions are available.) Grades 5–8.

    Other books in the series include:

    No Time Like Show Time: A Hermux Tantamoq Adventure. New York: Putnam, 2004. 288p. ISBN 10: 0399238808; ISBN 13: 978-0399238802

    The Sands of Time: A New Hermux Tantamoq Adventure. New York: Speak, 2003. 288p. ISBN 10: 0399238794; ISBN 13: 978-0399238796.

    Time to Smell the Roses: A Hermux Tantamoq Adventure. New York: Putnam, 2007. 288p. ISBN 10: 0399244905; ISBN 13: 978-0399244902.

Hoff, Syd. *Baseball Mouse.* New York: Putnam, 1969. 48p. ISBN 10: 0399600434; ISBN 13: 978-0399600432.

    Bernard, an infield mouse, wants to help the losing team. Grades K–3.

Hoff, Syd. *Mrs. Brice's Mice.* New York: HarperCollins, 1988. 32p. ISBN 10: 0064441458; ISBN 13: 978-0064441452.

    Mrs. Brice has twenty-five mice, and all but one of them do everything together. Grades K–2.

Holabird, Katharine. *Angelina Ballerina.* Illustrated by Helen Craig. New York: Clarkson Potter, 1983. 32p. ISBN 10: 0670060267; ISBN 13: 978-0670060269.

    Little Angelina mouse wants more than anything to be a great ballerina. (Video recordings are available. See the Web site for more information about the television program and books: http://www.angelinaballerina.com/usa/home.html; accessed on March 24, 2009.) Grades K–3.

    Other books in the series are *Angelina and the Princess, Angelina's Christmas, Angelina at the Fair, Angelina on Stage, Angelina and Alice, Angelina's Birthday Surprise, Angelina's Baby Sister, Angelina Ice Skates, Angelina's Halloween, Angelina and the Butterfly, Angelina's Birthday, Angelina's Ballet Class, Angelina and Henry, Angelina Loves, Angelina and the Rag Doll, Angelina Ballerina's Invitation to the Ballet, Angelina, Star of the Show, Angelina's Silver Locket, Angelina at the Palace,* and *A Dance of Friendship.* Grades K–2.

Holl, Adelaide. *Minnikin, Midgie, and Moppet: A Mouse Story.* Illustrated by Priscilla Hillman. New York: Golden Press, 1977. 48p. ISBN 10: 0307123626; ISBN 13: 978-0307123626.

    Three little mice say farewell to their mother and go out to seek their fortune. Grades K–4.

Holl, Adelaide. *Sylvester, the Mouse with the Musical Ear.* Illustrated by N. M. Bodecker. New York: Golden Press, 1973. 32p. ISBN 10: 0307202046; ISBN 13: 978-0307202048.

    A little mouse finds a home in a music shop after his home in the meadow is mowed down. Grades K–3.

Holm, Jennifer L., and Matthew Holm. *Babymouse.* New York: Random House, 2007. 91p. ISBN 10: 0375832297; ISBN 13: 978-0375832291.

    In this graphic novel, Babymouse is a sassy little mouse. Grades 4–6.

Homer, Winslow. *The Eventful History of Three Blind Mice.* New York: Oxford University Press, 1996. 32p. ISBN 10: 0195105583; ISBN 13: 978-0195105582.

Originally published in 1858, this story tells of three little mice, Frisky, Graysey, and Longtail, who were seldom very naughty, but they couldn't resist Mrs. Grumpy's mince pies and slabs of cheese. Grades 3–6.

Hoppe, Matthias. *Mouse and Elephant.* Illustrated by Jan Lenica. Boston: Little, Brown, 1990. 24p. ISBN 10: 0316372846; ISBN 13: 978-0316372848.

Mouse Nicole has everything but a friend, so she sets out to find one. Grades K–2.

Howe, James. *Horace and Morris but Mostly Dolores.* Illustrated by Amy Walrod. New York: Atheneum Books for Young Readers, 1999. 32p. ISBN 10: 068931874X; ISBN 13: 978-0689318740.

Horace and Morris join a boys' club, so Dolores joins a girls' club, but they miss playing together. (An audio version is available.) Grades K–3.

Hurd, Edith Thacher. *Come and Have Fun.* Illustrated by Clement Hurd. New York: Harper & Row, 1962. 32p. ISBN 10: 0437960285; ISBN 13: 978-0437960283.

Cat seems to love chasing mouse. Grades K–2.

Hurd, Thacher. *Blackberry Ramble.* New York: HarperTrophy/HarperCollins, 1989. 32p. ISBN 10: 0517573490; ISBN 13: 978-0517573495.

The mouse family spring cleans while baby mouse explores. Grades K–1.

Hurd, Thacher. *Little Mouse's Big Valentine.* New York: HarperCollins, 1990. 32p. ISBN 10: 0060261927; ISBN 13: 978-0060261924.

Little Mouse must find someone who wants his enormous valentine. Grades K–2.

Hurd, Thacher. *The Pea Patch Jig.* New York: HarperTrophy, 1995. 32p. ISBN 10: 051756307X; ISBN 13: 978-0517563076.

Farmer Clem doesn't know that he shares his home with the tiny Mouse family, so when baby mouse wanders away and falls asleep in a head of lettuce that the farmer gathers for his salad fixings, adventure follows. Grades K–2.

Hurd, Thacher. *Santa Mouse and the Ratdeer.* New York: Scholastic Inc., 1998. 40p. ISBN 10: 0060276940; ISBN 13: 978-0060276942.

Santa Mouse is having a bad day, from missing clothes and grumpy ratdeer to a crashed sleigh, but Rosie Mouse has hot chocolate and cookies. Grades K–3.

Hurd, Thacher. *Tomato Soup.* New York: Crown, 1992. ISBN 10: 0517582376; ISBN 13: 978-0517582374.

Baby Mouse has a cold and doesn't want a shot from the doctor, so she sneaks out of bed and hides in Farmer Clem's package of seeds, which the farmer is about to plant. Grades K–3.

Ivimey, John W. *The Complete Story of the Three Blind Mice.* Illustrated by Paul Galdone. New York: Clarion Books, 1987. 32p. ISBN 10: 0899194818; ISBN 13: 978-0899194813.

The mice escape the cat but are caught by the farmer's wife. (Following are two other versions of the same story.) Grades K–4.

Ivimey, John W. *The Complete Story of the Three Blind Mice.* Illustrated by Victoria Chess. New York: Joy Street Books, 1990. 32p. ISBN 10: 0899194818; ISBN 13: 9780899194813. Grades K-4.

Ivimey, John W. *Three Blind Mice: The Classic Nursery Rhyme*. Illustrated by Lorinda Bryan Cauley. New York: Putnam, 1991. 32p. ISBN 10: 0399217754; ISBN 13: 978-0399217753.

Iwamura, Kazuo. *The 14 Forest Mice and the Harvest Moon Watch*. Milwaukee, Wis.: Gareth Stevens, 1991. 32p. ISBN 10: 0836812689; ISBN 13: 978-0836812688.

    Mouse family climbs a tree to view the moon. Grades K–2.

Jacques, Brian. *The Bellmaker*. Illustrated by Allan Curless. New York: Philomel, 1994. 336p. ISBN 10: 0399228055; ISBN 13: 978-0399228056.

    Joseph the Bellmaker is worried about his daughter Mariel and journeys to find her, where she is held by evil Foxwolf Nagru. Grades 3–7.

Jacques, Brian. *The Great Redwall Feast*. Illustrated by Christopher Denise. New York: Puffin, 1996. 64p. ISBN 10: 0399227075; ISBN 13: 978-0399227073.

    The animals prepare to honor the abbot of the abbey of Redwall. Grades 2–5.

Jacques, Brian. *The Legend of Luke*. Illustrated by Fangorn. New York: Philomel Books, 1999. 374p. ISBN 10: 039923490X; ISBN 13: 978-0399234903.

    Martin the Warrior sets out to find his birthplace and learns about his real father, Luke the Warrior Chieftain. Grades 3–7.

Jacques, Brian. *Mariel of Redwall*. Illustrated by Gary Chalk. New York: Ace Books, 1991. 387p. ISBN 10: 0399221441; ISBN 13: 978-0399221446.

    Mariel fights pirate rat Gabool the Wild and is victorious in a sea battle. Grades 3–7.

Jacques, Brian. *Martin the Warrior*. New York: Philomel, 1993. 376p. ISBN 10: 0399226702; ISBN 13: 978-0399226700.

    Martin is captured by the stoat Badrang, and he vows to free himself and destroy the evil villain. Grades 3–7.

Jacques, Brian. *Mattimeo*. Illustrated by Gary Chalk. New York: Avon Books, 1990. 446p. ISBN 10: 039921741X; ISBN 13: 978-0399217418.

    Son of Matthias, Mattimeo finally takes up the sword and becomes one of the fighters who battle Slagar the fox and his attempt to take Redwall. (An audio recording is available.). Grades 3–7.

Jacques, Brian. *Mossflower*. New York: Philomel, 1988. 431p. ISBN 10: 0399215492; ISBN 13: 978-0399215490.

    Martin the Warrior must find the ruler of Mossflower to help in the battle against the wildcat who has come to power. Grades 3–7.

Jacques, Brian. *Redwall*. Illustrated by Gary Chalk. New York: Philomel, 1986. 351p. ISBN 10: 0399214240; ISBN 13: 978-0399214240.

    Evil rat Cluny has come to Redwall and taken over, so young mouse Matthias finds the sword of Martin the Warrior in order to rid Redwall of the rats. (Audio and video recordings are available.) Grades 3–7.

Jarvis, Robin. *The Crystal Prison*. San Francisco: SeaStar Books, 2001. 234p. ISBN 10: 0750004878; ISBN 13: 978-0750004879.

    Audrey journeys with a rat to the country, where she witnesses the return of evil rat supernatural events. Grades 4–8.

Jarvis, Robin. *The Dark Portal*. San Francisco: SeaStar Books, 2000. 241p. ISBN 10: 1587170213; ISBN 13: 978-1587170218.

    In a frightening and daring rescue mission, the mice venture into the sewers where the rats devour mice. (An audio recording is available.) Grades 4–8.

Jarvis, Robin. *The Final Reckoning*. San Francisco: Chronicle Books, 2003. 298p. ISBN 10: 1587171929; ISBN 13: 978-1587171925.

    The Deptford Mice must battle the rats, who have become too powerful. Grades 4–8.

Jensen, Patricia. *Little Mouse's Rescue*. Illustrated by Malgorzata Dzierzawska. Pleasantville, N.Y.: Reader's Digest Kids, 1993. 32p. ISBN 10: 0895775816; ISBN 13: 978-0895775818.

    A silly little mouse ventures into a farmhouse to stuff herself, even though two cats live there. Grades K–3.

Jeram, Anita. *Contrary Mary*. Cambridge, Mass.: Candlewick, 1995. 32p. ISBN 10: 1564026442; ISBN 13: 978-1564026446.

    Mary is determined to do the opposite of everything, until her mother does the same. Grades K–2.

Jeram, Anita. *Daisy Dare*. Cambridge, Mass.: Candlewick Press, 1995. 24p. ISBN 10: 1564026450; ISBN 13: 978-1564026453.

    Daisy is hesitant to take the bell off the cat, even though she usually accepts dares. Grades K–2.

Johnson, Pamela. *A Mouse's Tale*. San Diego: Harcourt Brace Jovanovich, 1991. 32p. ISBN 10: 0152560327; ISBN 13: 978-0152560324.

    A little mouse who wants to see the sea builds her own boat from what she finds. Grades K–2.

Joly, Fanny, and and Brigitte Boucher. *Marceau Bonappétit*. Illustrated by Agnès Mathieu. Minneapolis, Minn.: Carolrhoda Books, 1989. 31p. ISBN 10: 0876143699; ISBN 13: 978-0876143698.

    While a little mouse's parents are away, he visits five friends and learns different ways of eating. Grades K–2.

Keller, Holly. *The New Boy*. New York: Greenwillow Books, 1991. 24p. ISBN 10: 0688098274; ISBN 13: 978-0688098278.

    First Milton Mouse is too bad, and then he becomes too good. Grades K–2.

Kellogg, Steven. *The Island of the Skog; Story*. New York: Dial Press, 1973. 32p. ISBN 10: 0803738420; ISBN 13: 978-0803738423.

    Jenny and her friends sail from the city to an island and discover the inhabitant, the Skog. Grades K–3.

Kerr, Phyllis Forbes. *I Tricked You!* New York: Simon & Schuster Books for Young Readers, 1990. 32p. ISBN 10: 0671694081; ISBN 13: 978-0671694081.

    The other mice don't like Morris's silly tricks. Grades K–2.

King-Smith, Dick. *Magnus Powermouse*. Illustrated by Mary Rayner. New York: Harper & Row, 1982. 120p. ISBN 10: 0060232315; ISBN 13: 978-0060232313.

    Magnus won't stop growing and is caught by the rat catcher. Grades 2–5.

King-Smith, Dick. *Martin's Mice*. Illustrated by Jez Alborough. New York: Crown, 1988. 122p. ISBN 10: 0517571137; ISBN 13: 978-0517571132.
　　Martin keeps a family of mice in the barn as pets. Grades 2–4.

King-Smith, Dick. *A Mouse Called Wolf*. Illustrated by Jon Goodell. New York: A. A. Knopf, 1997. 98p. ISBN 10: 0517709732; ISBN 13: 978-0517709733.
　　A musical mouse shares his gift with a concert pianist. Grades 2–4.

King-Smith, Dick. *The School Mouse*. Illustrated by Cynthia Fisher. New York: Hyperion Books for Children, 1995. 123p. ISBN 10: 0786800364; ISBN 13: 978-0786800360.
　　Little Flora saves her family when a crisis comes up. Grades 2–4.

King-Smith, Dick. *Three Terrible Trins*. Illustrated by Mark Teague. New York: Crown, 1994. 128p. ISBN 10: 0517598280; ISBN 13: 978-0517598283.
　　Three mice buck the class system and befriend a mouse from a lower class. (An audio recording is available.) Grades 2–4.

Kingsley, Emily Perl. *An American Tail: The Storybook*. Illustrated by David Kirschner. New York: Grosset & Dunlap, 1986. 64p. ISBN 10: 0091727049; ISBN 13: 978-0091727048.
　　Flevel Mousekewitz is an immigrant mouse who comes to New York City. Grades 2–4.

Kirby, Mansfield. *The Secret of Thut-Mouse III: Or Basil Beaudesert's Revenge*. Illustrated by Mance Post. New York: Farrar, Straus & Giroux, 1985. 63p. ISBN 10: 0374366772; ISBN 13: 978-0374366773.
　　Pa-Ti-Paw, a Siamese cat, comes to the museum, and this creates problems for mouse scholar Basil Beaudesert and his nephew, Danny. Grades 2–4.

Koller, Jackie French. *Fish Fry Tonight*. Illustrated by Catharine O'Neill. New York: Crown Publishers, 1992. 32p. ISBN 10: 0517578158; ISBN 13: 978-0517578155.
　　A little mouse catches a fish and brings it home to feed his friends. Grades K–2.

Kraus, Robert. *Another Mouse to Feed*. Illustrated by Jose Aruego and Ariane Dewey. New York: Prentice-Hall Books for Young Readers, 1980. 32p. ISBN 10: 0671665227; ISBN 13: 978-0671665227.
　　Little mice decide to help their parents when they are tired. Grades K–2.

Kraus, Robert. *Big Squeak, Little Squeak*. Illustrated by Kevin O'Malley. New York: Orchard, 1996. 32p. ISBN 10: 053109474X; ISBN 13: 978-0531094747.
　　Mr. Kit Kat runs a cheese store, and two little mice can't resist going in, putting themselves in great danger. Grades K–2.

Kraus, Robert. *Come Out and Play, Little Mouse*. Illustrated by Jose Aruego and Ariane Dewey. New York: Mulberry Books, 1987. 32p. ISBN 10: 068805837X; ISBN 13: 978-0688058371.
　　Little mouse helps his parents during the week, but gets to play on the weekend. Grades K–2.

Kraus, Robert. *Dr. Mouse, Bungle Jungle Doctor*. Racine, Wis.: Western Publishing , 1992. 32p. ISBN 10: 0307695506; ISBN 13: 978-0307695505.
　　Dr. Mouse treats patients throughout the day. Grades K–2.

Kraus, Robert. *The Hoodwinking of Mrs. Elmo*. New York: Delacorte Press, 1987. 109p. ISBN 10: 0385295774; ISBN 13: 978-0385295772.
　　A cousin wants to cheat Mrs. Elmo, but a mouse couple protect her. Grades K–2.

Kraus, Robert. *Mrs. Elmo of Elephant House*. New York: Delacorte Press, 1986. 89p. ISBN 10: 0385294441; ISBN 13: 978-0385294447.

    A little mouse couple come to work for an elephant, Mrs. Elmo. Grades K–2.

Kraus, Robert. *Where Are You Going, Little Mouse?* Illustrated by Jose Aruego and Ariane Dewey. New York: Greenwillow Books, 1986. 34p. ISBN 10: 0688042945; ISBN 13: 978-0688042943.

    A little mouse runs away, but he finds that he misses his family when it gets dark. Grades K–2.

Kraus, Robert. *Whose Mouse Are You?* Illustrated by Jose Aruego. New York: Aladdin Books, 1970. 32p. ISBN 10: 0689840527; ISBN 13: 978-0689840524.

    A little mouse has to figure out how to get his family back together. Grades K–2.

Krensky, Stephen. *The Three Blind Mice Mystery.* Illustrated by Lynn Munsinger. New York: Yearling First Choice Chapter Book, 1995. 46p. ISBN 10: 0385321317; ISBN 13: 978-0385321310.

    Simple Simon tries to solve nursery rhyme mysteries. Grades K–2.

Kroll, Steven. *The Biggest Pumpkin Ever.* Illustrated by Jeni Bassett. New York: Scholastic, 1984. 32p. ISBN 10: 0439929466; ISBN 13: 978-0439929462.

    Two little mice are secretly helping a pumpkin grow. Grades K–2.

Kumin, Maxine, and Anne Sexton. *Joey and the Birthday Present.* Illustrated by Evaline Ness. New York: McGraw-Hill, 1971. 40p. ISBN 10: 0070356351; ISBN 13: 978-0070356351.

    A caged mouse and a field mouse become friends. Grades K–2.

Kwitz, Mary DeBall. *The Bell Tolls at Mousehaven Manor.* Illustrated by Stella Ormai. New York: Scholastic, 1991. 125p. ISBN 10: 0590438417; ISBN 13: 978-0590438414.

    Count Von Flittermouse kidnaps Violet Mae Mouse. Grades 2–5.

Kyte, Dennis. *Zackary Raffles.* New York: Doubleday, 1989. 30p. ISBN 10: 0385246528; ISBN 13: 978-0385246521.

    Zachary is able to overcome his fears when the moon illuminates the night. Grades K–2.

Lawson, Robert. *Ben and Me: A New and Astonishing Life of Benjamin Franklin as Written by His Good Mouse Amos Lately Discovered.* New York: Dell, 1939. 113p. ISBN 10: 0316517321; ISBN 13: 978-0316517324.

    Amos makes his home in Ben Franklin's old fur hat and gives Ben advice. (An audio recording is available.) Grades 3–6.

Leigh, Oretta. *Aloysius Sebastian Mozart Mouse.* Illustrated by Lulu Delacre. New York: J. Messner, 1984. 24p. ISBN 10: 0671477919; ISBN 13: 978-0671477912.

    A little mouse wants to play an organ with ten thousand pipes. Grades K–3.

Lewison, Wendy Cheyette. *Shy Vi.* Illustrated by Stephen John Smith. New York: Simon & Schuster, 1993. 28p. ISBN 10: 0671769685; ISBN 13: 978-0671769680.

    Shy Vi speaks much too softly, so her parents do everything they can to help her overcome her shyness. Grads K-2.

Lionni, Leo. *Alexander and the Wind-up Mouse.* New York: A. A. Knopf, 1969. 32p. ISBN 10: 0394809149; ISBN 13: 978-0394809144.

    Alexander wants to be a toy mouse like his friend Willy. (Caldecott Honor Book). Grades K–2.

Lionni, Leo. *A Busy Year*. New York: A. A. Knopf, 1992. 32p. ISBN 10: 0679924647; ISBN 13: 978-0679924647.

> Mouse twins take care of a tree and watch it grow. (An audio recording is available.) Grades K–2.

Lionni, Leo. *Frederick*. New York: Dragonfly, 1967. 32p. ISBN 10: 0394810406; ISBN 13: 978-0394810409.

> A poetic mouse stores up something valuable for the winter. (Audio and video versions are available.) (Caldecott Honor Book). Grades K–2.

Lionni, Leo. *Geraldine, the Music Mouse*. New York: Pantheon Books, 1979. 31p. ISBN-10: 0394942388; ISBN 13: 978-0394942384.

> Geraldine nibbles a piece of cheese into the shape of a mouse playing a flute, with a special benefit. Grades K–3.

Lionni, Leo. *The Greentail Mouse*. New York: Pantheon Books, 1973. 32p. ISBN 10: 0394926781; ISBN 13: 978-0394926780.

> The mice become involved in their Mardi Gras masquerade and forget why they are doing it. Grades K–3.

Lionni, Leo. *Matthew's Dream*. New York: A. A. Knopf, 1991. 32p. ISBN 10: 0679810757; ISBN 13: 978-0679810759.

> When Matthew visits an art museum, he is inspired to become a painter. Grades K–3.

Lionni, Leo. *Mouse Days: A Book of Seasons*. New York: Pantheon Books, 1981. 32p. ISBN 10: 039484548X; ISBN 13: 978-0394845487.

> Mice activities are seen throughout the year. Grades K–2.

Lionni, Leo. *Nicolas, Where Have You Been?* New York: A. A. Knopf, 1987. 32p. ISBN 10: 0375844503; ISBN 13: 978-0375844508.

> Not all birds are the enemies that Nicolas thought they were. Grades K–2.

Lionni, Leo. *Tillie and the Wall*. New York: Dragonfly/Knopf, 1989. 32p. ISBN 10: 0394921550; ISBN 13: 978-0394921556.

> Tillie wants to find out what is on the other side of the wall. Grades K–2.

Lobel, Arnold. *Martha, the Movie Mouse*. New York: Harper & Row, 1966. 32p. ISBN 10: 0060239700; ISBN 13: 978-0060239701.

> If it wasn't for the movie theater, Martha would not have found a friend and happiness. Grades K–3.

Lobel, Arnold. *Mouse Soup*. New York: Harper & Row, 1983. 63p. ISBN 10: 0060239670; ISBN 13: 978-0060239671.

> Mouse needs ingredients from several stories to make mouse soup. Grades K–3.

Lobel, Arnold. *Mouse Tales*. New York: Harper & Row, 1987. 61p. ISBN 10: 0060239417; ISBN 13: 978-0060239411.

> Papa tells seven mouse stories, one for each of his mouse sons. Grades K–2.

Low, Joseph. *The Christmas Grump*. New York: Atheneum, 1977. 32p. ISBN 10: 0689500920; ISBN 13: 978-0689500923.

> Mouse is very unhappy that there are never any presents under the tree for him. Grades K–3.

Lundell, Margo. *The Wee Mouse Who Was Afraid of the Dark*. Illustrated by Lucinda McQueen. New York: Grosset & Dunlap, 1990. 32p. ISBN 10: 044840060X; ISBN 13: 978-0448400600.
>Mother and Father try different ways to help Wee Mouse overcome her fear of the dark. Grades K–2.

Majewski, Joe. *A Friend for Oscar Mouse*. Illustrated by Maria Majewska. New York: Dial Books for Young Readers, 1988. 28p. ISBN 10: 0803703481; ISBN 13: 978-0803703483.
>When Oscar goes to the country, his friend shows him the positives and negatives of life. Grades K–3.

Manson, Christopher. *Here Begins the Tale of the Marvellous Blue Mouse*. New York: H. Holt, 1992. 28p. ISBN 10: 0805016228; ISBN 13: 978-0805016222.
>Emperor Charlemagne's adviser has help from a mouse to expose an evildoer. Grades K–4.

Martin, Bill. *A Beasty Story*. Illustrated by Steven Kellogg. San Diego: Harcourt, 1999. 40p. ISBN 10: 015201683X; ISBN 13: 978-0152016838.
>Mice proceed through a dark woods to a house with dark red stairs and a surprise waiting for them. Grades K–3.

Martin, Jacqueline Briggs. *Bizzy Bones and the Lost Quilt*. Illustrated by Stella Ormai. New York: Lothrop, Lee & Shepard, 1988. 36p. ISBN 10: 0688074073; ISBN 13: 978-0688074074.
>Uncle Ezra and the mice try to make Bizzy a quilt so he can go to sleep. Grades K–3.

Martin, Jacqueline Briggs. *Bizzy Bones and Uncle Ezra*. Illustrated by Stella Ormai. New York: Lothrop, Lee & Shepard Books, 1984. 32p. ISBN 10: 0688037828; ISBN 13: 978-0688037826.
>Uncle Ezra convinces Bizzy that his show home will not blow away. Grades K–3.

Martin, Melanie. *Morris, the Millionaire Mouse*. Illustrated by G. Brian Karas. Mahwah, N.J.: Troll Associates, 1989. 47p. ISBN 10: 0816713391; ISBN 13: 978-0816713394.
>When Morris wins a raffle, he quits his job and buys all he ever wanted. Grades K–4.

McBratney, Sam. *The Dark at the Top of the Stairs*. Illustrated by Ivan Bates. Cambridge, Mass.: Candlewick Press, 1996. 32p. ISBN 10: 156402640X; ISBN 13: 978-1564026408.
>An older mouse agrees to show three little mice the monster at the top of the stairs. Grades K–3.

McCully, Emily Arnold. *The Christmas Gift*. New York: HarperTrophy, 1988. 32p. ISBN 10: 0060242116; ISBN 13: 978-0060242114.
>Little Mouse's Christmas gift is broken, and grandpa opens his toy train to comfort him. Grades K–2.

McCully, Emily Arnold. *First Snow*. New York: Harper & Row, 1985. 32p. ISBN 10: 0066238528; ISBN 13: 978-0066238524.
>A shy little mouse finds joy in sledding in the first snow. Grades K–2.

McCully, Emily Arnold. *Monk Camps Out*. New York: Arthur A. Levine Books, 2000. 32p. ISBN 10: 0439099765; ISBN 13: 978-0439099769.
>Monk wants to camp out alone in the backyard, but his parents aren't so sure. Grades K–2.

McCully, Emily Arnold. *Mouse Practice*. New York: Arthur A. Levine Books/Scholastic Press, 1999. 32p. ISBN 10: 0590682202; ISBN 13: 978-0590682206.
> Mouse learns that practice is the key to success in everything. Grades K–3.

McCully, Emily Arnold. *New Baby*. New York: Harper & Row, 1988. 31p. ISBN 10: 0060241306; ISBN 13: 978-0060241308.
> Little mouse is excited about the arrival of a new baby. Grades K–2.

McDonald, Megan. *Tundra Mouse: A Storyknife Book*. Illustrated by S. D. Schindler. New York: Orchard Books, 1997. 32p. ISBN 10: 0531300471; ISBN 13: 978-0531300473.
> Two little mice make a nest out of Christmas tinsel. Grades K–2.

McMullan, Kate. *Pearl and Wagner: Two Good Friends*. Illustrated by R. W. Alley. New York: Dial Books for Young Readers, 2003. 48p. ISBN 10: 0803725744; ISBN 13: 978-0803725744.
> Pearl and Wagner must work together to complete their science robot project. Grades K–3.

Mendoza, George. *Henri Mouse*. Illustrated by Joelle Boucher. New York: Viking Kestrel, 1985. 32p. ISBN 10: 0670366897; ISBN 13: 978-0670366897.
> Everything Henri paints disappears and is transferred to his canvas. Grades K–3.

Milgrim, David. *See Pip Point*. New York: Atheneum Books for Young Readers, 2003. 32p. ISBN 10: 0689851162; ISBN 13: 978-0689851162.
> Pip the Mouse floats off with a robot's balloon. Grades K–2.

Miller, Edna. *Mousekin Takes a Trip*. Englewood Cliffs, N.J.: Prentice-Hall, 1976. 32p. ISBN 10: 013-6043631; ISBN 13: 978-0136043638.
> Mousekin climbs into a house with wheels and takes an unexpected trip to the desert. Grades K–4.
>
> Other Mousekin books are *Mousekin's Christmas Eve*; *Mousekin's Easter Basket*; *Mousekin's Family*; *Mousekin's Frosty Friend: Story and Pictures*; *Mousekin's Golden House*; *Mousekin's Lost Woodland*; *Mousekin's Mystery*; *Mousekin's Woodland Birthday*; *Mousekin's Woodland Sleepers*; and *Mousekin's Thanksgiving*.

Moore, Lilian. *Don't Be Afraid, Amanda*. Illustrated by Kathleen Garry McCord. New York: Atheneum, 1992. 57p. ISBN 10: 0689317255; ISBN 13: 978-0689317255.
> Amanda overcomes her fears and comes to visit Adam in the country. Grades 1–4.

Moore, Lilian. *I'll Meet You at the Cucumbers*. Illustrated by Sharon Wooding. New York: Bantam, 1988. 63p. ISBN 10: 0689312431; ISBN 13: 978-0689312434.
> When Adam and Julius go to the city, Adam is upset when his friend wants to stay. Grades K–3.

Moreton, Daniel. *Martí and the Mango*. New York: Workman Publishing, 1993. 32p. ISBN 10: 1556702647; ISBN 13: 978-1556702648.
> Martí learns to distinguish a mango from other fruit. Grades K–3.

Morris, Ann. *Eleanora Mousie Catches a Cold*. Illustrated by Ruth Young. New York: Macmillan, 1987. 24p. ISBN 10: 0027675009; ISBN 13: 978-0027675009.
> Eleanora learns what is necessary for curing a cold. Grades K–2.

Noll, Sally. *Watch Where You Go*. New York: Greenwillow Books, 1990. 32p. ISBN 10: 0688084982; ISBN 13: 978-0688084981.
    A little gray mouse travels though what he thinks is a forest. Grades K–2.

Numeroff, Laura Joffe. *If You Give a Mouse a Cookie*. Illustrated by Felicia Bond. New York: Scholastic, 1985. 32p. ISBN 10: 0060245867; ISBN 13: 978-0060245863.
    Numerous requests from a mouse for a cookie take a young boy through the day. (An audio version is available.) Grades K–3.

Numeroff, Laura Joffe. *If You Take a Mouse to School*. Illustrated by Felicia Bond. New York: Laura Geringer Books, 2002. 32p. ISBN 10: 0060283289; ISBN 13: 978-0060283285.
    A boy and his mouse make their way through the day at school. (An audio recording is available.) Grades K–2.

Oakley, Graham. *The Church Mice Adrift*. New York: Atheneum, 1976. 36p. ISBN 10: 0689305621; ISBN 13: 978-0689305627.
    Church mice us their heads to get rid of rats who have taken over the church. Grades K–4.

Oakley, Graham. *The Church Mice and the Moon*. London: Macmillan, 1974. 36p. ISBN 10: 0689304374; ISBN 13: 978-0689304378.
    Two church mice are kidnapped for training as astronauts. Grades K–4.

Oakley, Graham. *The Church Mice and the Ring*. New York: Atheneum, 1992. 36p. ISBN 10: 0689317905; ISBN 13: 978-0689317903.
    The church mice make plans to find a home for Percy, a stray dog. Grades K–4.

Oakley, Graham. *The Church Mice at Bay*. New York: Atheneum, 1978. 36p. ISBN 10: 0689306296; ISBN 13: 978-0689306297.
    The church mice and the cat make plans to get rid of the substitute vicar. Grades K–4.

Oakley, Graham. *The Church Mice at Christmas*. New York: Atheneum, 1980. 38p. ISBN 10: 0689307977; ISBN 13: 978-0689307973.
    The church mice plan a party, with disastrous results. Grades K–4.

Oakley, Graham. *The Church Mice in Action*. New York: Atheneum, 1982. 36p. ISBN 10: 0333336356; ISBN 13: 978-0333336359.
    The church mice enter Sampson the cat in a show to help win money to fix the church roof. Grades K–4.

Oakley, Graham. *The Church Mice Spread Their Wings*. New York: Atheneum, 1975. 36p. ISBN 10: 068930496X; ISBN 13: 978-0689304965.
    The church mice go on an outing, with Sampson the church cat as their bodyguard. Grades K–4.

Oakley, Graham. *The Church Mouse*. New York: Atheneum, 1972. 36p. ISBN 10: 0689300581; ISBN 13: 978-0689300585.
    A lonely mouse and a cat make plans to get all of the town mice to move into the church. Grades K–4.

Oakley, Graham. *The Diary of a Church Mouse.* New York: Atheneum, 1987. 32p. ISBN-10: 0333474872; ISBN 13: 978-0333474877.

    Humphrey the Schoolmouse decides to keep a diary and tell about the daily happenings of the church mice. Grades 2–5.

O'Brien, Robert C. *Mrs. Frisby and the Rats of NIMH.* Illustrated by Zena Bernstein. New York: Atheneum, 1972. 240p. ISBN 10: 0689206518; ISBN 13: 978-0689206511.

    When Mrs. Frisby, a widowed mouse with four kids, must move, but little Timothy has pneumonia, she meets the rats of NIMH, who help her. (Audio and video versions are available.) (Newbery Medal Book). Grades 4–7.

Ormondroyd, Edward. *Broderick.* Illustrated by John Larrecq. Boston: Houghton Mifflin, 1969. 32p. ISBN 10: 0590759493; ISBN 13: 978-0686865803.

    Broderick practices on a tongue depressor to become the best world surfing mouse. Grades K–3.

Ostheeren, Ingrid. *Jonathan Mouse.* Illustrated by Agnès Mathieu. New York: North-South Books, 1997. 25p. ISBN 10: 1558580646; ISBN 13: 978-1558580640.

    A spell causes Jonathan to turn the color of everything he eats. Grades K–2.

    Other titles about Jonathan are *Jonathan Mouse and the Baby Bird, Jonathan Mouse and the Magic Box,* and *Jonathan Mouse at the Circus.*

Packard, Mary. *Sleep-over Mouse.* Illustrated by Kathy Wilburn. Chicago: Childrens Press, 1994. 32p. ISBN 10: 0516246380; ISBN 13: 978-0516246383.

    Squeak loves sleepovers. Grades K–1.

Palazzo-Craig, Janet. *Max and Maggie in Autumn.* Illustrated by Paul Meisel. Mahwah, N.J.: WhistleStop/Troll Associates, 1994. 32p. ISBN 10: 0816733481; ISBN 13: 978-0816733484.

    Max and Maggie play in the leaves and look for the largest pumpkins. Grades K–1.

Palazzo-Craig, Janet. *Max and Maggie in Winter.* Illustrated by Paul Meisel. Mahwah, N.J.: Troll Associates, 1995. 32p. ISBN 10: 0816733546; ISBN 13: 978-0816733545.

    Max and Maggie ski and make snowmen. Grades K–1.

Palazzo-Craig, Janet. *Valentine's Day Mess.* Illustrated by Deborah Morse. Mahwah, N.J.: Troll Associates, 1994. 32p. ISBN 10: 081673254X; ISBN 13: 978-0816732548.

    Jen and Ken wreck their valentine greetings for each other. Grades K–1.

Paré, Roger. *On the Go.* Illustrated by Roger Pare. Toronto: Annick Press, 1995. 22p. ISBN 10: 0613783948; ISBN 13: 978-0613783941.

    Two little mice travel via different modes all over the country. Grades K–2.

Parry, Marian. *I Am a Big Help.* New York: Greenwillow Books, 1980. 32p. ISBN 10: 068884250X; ISBN 13: 978-0688842505.

    A little mouse helps water plants, dry the dishes, and play with the baby. Grades K–1.

Partridge, Jenny. *Colonel Grunt.* New York: Holt, Rinehart & Winston, 1980. 28p. ISBN 10: 0437661717; ISBN 13: 978-0437661715.

    An elderly mouse makes tea when the butler and cook are off for the day. Grades K–2.

Partridge, Jenny. *Peterkin Pollensnuff*. New York: Holt, Rinehart & Winston, 1980. 28p. ISBN 10: 003-0615089; ISBN 13: 978-0030615085.

    A wood mouse who delivers newspapers gets a flat tire, and a dragonfly helps him deliver his papers. Grades K–2.

Pellowski, Michael. *The Big Surprise*. Illustrated by Diane Paterson. Mahwah, N. J.: Troll Associates, 1986. 46p. ISBN 10: 0816705763; ISBN 13: 978-0816705764.

    Forgetful Freda has tied a string around her finger to help her remember something, but what is it? Grades K–3.

Peppé, Rodney. *The Kettleship Pirates*. New York: Lothrop, Lee & Shepard Books, 1983. 32p. ISBN 10: 0722658370; ISBN 13: 978-0722658376.

    Pip mouse sets out in a kettle that has been converted into a pirate ship. Grades K–2.

Peppé, Rodney. *The Mice and the Clockwork Bus*. New York: Lothrop, Lee & Shepard Books, 1986. 32p. ISBN 10: 0670810983; ISBN 13: 978-0670810987.

    Mice family builds their own clockwork bus. Grades K–2.

Peppé, Rodney. *The Mice and the Flying Basket*. New York: Lothrop, Lee & Shepard Books, 1985. 32p. ISBN 10: 068804252X; ISBN 13: 978-0688042523.

    Mice make a plane out of a basket. Grades K–2.

Peppé, Rodney. *The Mice on the Moon*. New York: Doubleday Book for Young Readers, 1993. 32p. ISBN 10: 0385308396; ISBN 13: 978-0385308397.

    The mice family make a spaceship out of an egg cartoon. Grades K–2.

Pilkey, Dav. *Dogzilla: Starring Flash, Rabies, Dwayne, and Introducing Leia as the Monster*. San Diego: Harcourt Brace Jovanovich, 1993. 32p. ISBN 10: 0152239448; ISBN 13: 978-0152239442.

    Big Cheese's troops are scattered by a gigantic dog. Grades 1–4.

Pilkey, Dav. *Kat Kong*. New York: Scholastic, 1993. 32p. ISBN 10: 0152049517; ISBN 13: 978-0152049515.

    The inhabitants of Mousopolis are plagued by Kat Kong. Grades 1–5.

Pilkey, Dav. *Ricky Ricotta's Giant Robot, An Adventure Novel*. Illustrated by Martin Ontiveros. New York: Scholastic, 2000. 111p. ISBN 10: 0590307193; ISBN 13: 978-0590307192.

    Ricky saves a robot from his creator and in turn receives help from the robot. Grades 2–5.

    Other titles in the series are *Ricky Ricotta's Mighty Robot vs. the Mutant Mosquitoes from Mercury, Ricky Ricotta's Mighty Robot vs. the Voodoo Vultures from Venus, Ricky Ricotta's Mighty Robot vs. the Mecha Monkeys from Mars, Ricky Ricotta's Mighty Robot vs. the Jurassic Jackrabbits from Jupiter,* and *Ricky Ricotta's Mighty Robot vs. the Stupid Stinkbugs from Saturn.*

Pinkney, Jane. *The Mice of Nibbling Village*. New York: Dutton, 1986. 32p. ISBN 10: 0517028964; ISBN 13: 978-0517028964.

    A mouse village goes about it daily chores. Grades K–2.

Pochocki, Ethel. *The Attic Mice*. Illustrated by David Catrow. New York: Dell, 1990. 113p. ISBN 10: 0805012982; ISBN 13: 978-0805012989.

    A mouse family finds a human kitchen a godsend for their Christmas holiday celebrations. Grades K–3.

Popov, Nikolai. *Why?* New York: North-South Books, 1996. 40p. ISBN 10: 1558585346; ISBN 13: 978-1558585348.

A frog is attacked by a mouse and his umbrella. Grades K–2.

Potter, Beatrix. *The Tale of Johnny Town Mouse.* New York: F. Warne, 1918. 48p. ISBN 10: 072320604X; ISBN 13: 978-0723206040.

Johnny Town-Mouse and Timmy Willy country mouse decide that they love their own homes best. (Audio and video versions are available. See also http://wiredforbooks.org/kids/Town-Mouse/Jt00.htm; accessed March 24, 2009.) Grades K–3.

Potter, Beatrix. *The Tailor of Gloucester.* New York: F. Warne, 1983. 59p. ISBN 10: 0723247722; ISBN 13: 978-0723247722.

Mice help a Gloucester tailor sew a coat for the mayor. (Audio and video versions are available.) Grades K–2.

Potter, Beatrix. *The Tale of Mrs. Tittlemouse.* New York: F. Warne, 1910. 64p. ISBN 10: 0723247803; ISBN 13: 978-0723247807.

Mrs. Tittlemouse must get rid of some messy guests. (Audio and video versions are available. See also http://etext.virginia.edu/toc/modeng/public/PotMrsT.html; accessed March 24, 2009.) Grades K–3.

Potter, Beatrix. *The Tale of Two Bad Mice.* New York: F. Warne, 1987. 64p. ISBN 10: 0723234647; ISBN 13: 978-0723234647.

Two bad little mice take things from the dollhouse while the dolls are away. (Audio and video versions are available. See also http://wiredforbooks.org/kids/beatrix/bm0.htm; accessed March 24, 2009.) Grades K–3.

Preller, James. *Wake Me in Spring.* Illustrated by Jeffrey Scherer. New York: Scholastic Inc., 1994. 32p. ISBN 10: 0590475002; ISBN 13: 978-0590475006.

Bear is getting ready to hibernate for the winter, and mouse is sad. Grades K–2.

Pryor, Bonnie. *Louie and Dan Are Friends.* Illustrated by Elizabeth Miles. New York: Morrow Junior Books, 1997. 32p. ISBN 10: 0688085601; ISBN 13: 978-0688085605.

Two brothers are very different but manage to be friends anyway. Grades K–2.

Pryor, Bonnie. *The Porcupine Mouse.* Illustrated by Mary Jane Begin. New York: Morrow Junior Books, 1988. 32p. ISBN 10: 1587171856; ISBN 13: 978-1587171857.

Two mouse brothers are having problems because a cat has threatened to catch one of them. Grades K–2.

Quackenbush, Robert M. *Chuck Lends a Paw.* New York: Clarion Books, 1986. 33p. ISBN 10: 0899193633; ISBN 13: 978-0899193632.

Chuck helps Maxine move a chest of drawers. Grades K–2.

Quackenbush, Robert M. *Mouse Feathers.* New York: Clarion Books, 1988. 30p. ISBN 10: 0517029774; ISBN 13: 978-0517029770.

Two little mice come down with a case of mouse feathers because of a pillow fight. Grades K–2.

Quackenbush, Robert M. *No Mouse for Me!* New York: Franklin Watts, 1981. 32p. ISBN 10: 0531043037; ISBN 13: 978-0531043035.
    A pet mouse can ruin a house. Grades K–2.

Rand, Gloria. *Willie Takes a Hike.* Illustrated by Ted Rand. San Diego: Harcourt Brace, 1996. 32p. ISBN 10: 0152002723; ISBN 13: 978-0152002725.
    Willie disobeys the rules when he goes on a hike alone and gets lost. Grades K–2.

Roche, P. K. *Good-bye Arnold!* New York: Dial Press, 1979. 32p. ISBN 10: 0803730322; ISBN 13: 978-0803730328.
    Webster Mouse's brother goes away for a week, so he has his parents all to himself. Grades K–2.

Roche, P. K. *Webster and Arnold Go Camping.* New York: Viking Kestrel, 1988. 32p. ISBN 10: 067081993X; ISBN 13: 978-0670819935.
    Two mouse brothers go camping in their own backyard. Grades K–2.

Roth, Susan L. *My Love for You.* New York: Dial Books for Young Readers, 1996. 32p. ISBN 10: 080-3727968; ISBN 13: 978-0803727960.
    Little brown mouse and big white mouse show their love for each other throughout the year. Grades K–2.

Ryder, Joanne. *Under the Moon.* Illustrated by Cheryl Harness. New York: Random House, 1989. 26p. ISBN-10: 0394819608; ISBN-13: 978-0394819600.
    Mama Mouse teaches baby mouse how to recognize home from sounds, sights, and smells. Grades K–1.

Sampson, Pamela. *The Incredible Invention of Alexander Woodmouse.* Chicago: Rand McNally, 1982. 58p. ISBN 10: 0528824120; ISBN 13: 978-0528824128.
    Professor Woodmouse's apprentice becomes very inventive himself. Grades K–4.

Sathre, Vivian. *Three Kind Mice.* Illustrated by Rodger Wilson. San Diego: Harcourt Brace, 1997. 32p. ISBN 10: 0152012664; ISBN 13: 978-0152012663.
    Three mice bake a birthday cake and make quite a few mistakes. Grades K–2.

Scarry, Richard. *Richard Scarry's Christmas Mice.* Racine, Wis.: Western Publishing, 1992. 24p. ISBN 10: 0756777526; ISBN 13: 978-0756777524.
    Two little mice awaken on Christmas morning and find the presents left for everyone else, but wonder if there is something for them. Grades K–3.

Schoenherr, Ian. *Pip and Squeak.* New York: Greenwillow, 2007. 32p. 32p. ISBN 10: 0060872535; ISBN 13: 978-0060872533.
    Pip and Squeak are invited to a birthday party, but they forget the present, so they must make do with gifts found while walking through the snow. Grades K–2.

Schories, Pat. *Mouse Around.* New York: Farrar, 1993. 33p. ISBN 10: 0374350809; ISBN 13: 978-0374350802.
    A little mouse falls out of his safe nest into a plumber's pocket and has a long adventure, until he finally gets home. (A video recording is available.) Grades K–3.

Schwartz, Roslyn. *Rose and Dorothy*. New York: Orchard Books, 1991. 32p. ISBN 10: 0531059189; ISBN 13: 978-0531059180.

> Mouse and Elephant live very happily together. Grades K–2.

Selden, George. *The Cricket in Times Square*. Illustrated by Garth Williams. New York: Farrar, Straus & Giroux, 1960. 144p. ISBN 10: 0374316503; ISBN 13: 978-0374316501.

> A cricket is befriended by a mouse, a cat, and a boy when he comes to New York for the summer. (Audio and video versions are available.) (Newbery Honor Book). Grades 3–6.

Selden, George. *Harry Kitten and Tucker Mouse*. Illustrated by Garth Williams. New York: Farrar, Straus & Giroux, 1986. 81p. ISBN 10: 0374328609; ISBN 13: 978-0374328603 .

> A mouse and kitten each find adventure and their fortune in New York. Grades 2–5.

Selden, George. *Tucker's Countryside*. Illustrated by Garth Williams. New York: Dell, 1969. 167p. ISBN 10: 0374378541; ISBN 13: 978-0374378547.

> The city mouse and cat go to the Connecticut countryside to visit their friend, the cricket. Grades 3–6.

Sharmat, Marjorie Weinman. *Twitchell the Wishful*. Illustrated by Janet Stevens. New York: Holiday House, 1981. 40p. ISBN-10: 0823403793; ISBN 13: 978-0823403790.

> Twitchell becomes less envious when his friends give him everything he thought he ever wanted. Grades K–3.

Sharp, Margery. *Bernard into Battle: A Miss Bianca Story*. Illustrated by Leslie Morrill. Boston: Little, Brown, 1978. 57p. ISBN 10: 0316783269; ISBN 13: 978-0316783262.

> Bernard manages to repel the army of rats in the Ambassador's basement. Grades 2–5.

Sharp, Margery. *Bernard the Brave: A Miss Bianca Story*. Illustrated by Leslie Morrill. Boston: Little, Brown, 1977. 128p. ISBN 10: 0316782920; ISBN 13: 978-0316782920.

> Bernard tries to rescue an heiress who was kidnapped by her guardian. Grades 2–5.

Sharp, Margery. *Miss Bianca*. Illustrated by Garth Williams. Boston: Little, Brown, 1962. 152p. ISBN 10: 0316783102; ISBN 13: 978-0316783101.

> Miss Bianca is a clever white mouse who helps Bernard rescue a little girl being held captive. Grades 2–5.

Sharp, Margery. *Miss Bianca and the Bridesmaid*. Illustrated by Erik Blegvad. Boston: Little, Brown, 1972. 123p. ISBN: 0316782998; ISBN-13: 9780316782999.

> Miss Bianca and Bernard search for the bride's sister, who goes missing the day before the wedding. Grades 2–5.

Sharp, Margery. *Miss Bianca in the Antarctic*. Illustrated by Erik Blegvad. Boston: Little, Brown, 1971. 134p. ISBN 10: 0316782947; ISBN 13: 978-0316782944.

> Miss Bianca and Bernard are stranded in the Antarctic when they try to rescue a friend. Grades 2–5.

Sharp, Margery. *Miss Bianca in the Orient*. Boston: Little, Brown, 1970. 144p. ISBN 10: 0316783196; ISBN 13: 978-0316783194.

> Miss Bianca is president of the Mouse Prisoners' Aid Society and works to save a court page's life. Grades 2–5.

Sharp, Margery. *Miss Bianca in the Salt Mines*. Illustrated by Garth Williams. Boston: Little, Brown, 1966. 148p. ISBN 10: 0316783110; ISBN 13: 978-0316783118.

   The rescuers must help a little girl who is stuck in a salt mine and waits on a duchess. Grades 2–5.

Sharp, Margery. *The Rescuers*. Illustrated by Garth Williams. Boston: Little, Brown, 1959. 149p. ISBN 10: 0316783145; ISBN 13: 978-0316783149.

   The Prisoners' Aid Society is at work to free a poet from the dungeon of the Black Castle. (Videos of the Walt Disney movies the *Rescuers* and *The Rescuers Down Under* are available.) Grades 2–6.

Sharp, Margery. *The Turret*. Illustrated by Garth Williams. Boston: Little, Brown, 1963. 138p. ISBN 10: 0316783188; ISBN 13: 978-0316783187.

   The mice must decide whether to help a horrible servant of the evil duchess who perhaps should be saved. Grades 2–5.

Siracusa, Catherine. *The Giant Zucchini*. New York: Hyperion Books for Children, 1993. 45p. ISBN 10: 1562822861; ISBN 13: 978-1562822866.

   Edgar Mouse and Robert Squirrel want to win at the fair, so they grow a huge zucchini that turns out to have magical powers. Grades K–3.

Slotboom, Wendy. *King Snake*. Illustrated by John Manders. Boston: Houghton Mifflin Co., 1997. 32p. ISBN 10: 0395746809; ISBN 13: 978-0395746806.

   Henry and Tinkerton use their wits to escape from the King Snake. Grades K–3.

Soto, Gary. *Chato's Kitchen*. Illustrated by Susan Guevara. New York : Putnam c1995. 32p. ISBN 10: 0399226583; ISBN 13: 978-0399226588.

   Five little mice are invited to dinner by Chato, a cool cat. (An audio recording is available.) Grades K–3.

Spinelli, Eileen. *Three Pebbles and a Song*. Illustrated by S. D. Schindler. New York: Dial Books for Young Readers, 2003. 32p. ISBN 10: 0803725280; ISBN 13: 978-0803725287.

   Little Mouse is supposed to be collecting food for the winter, but he is constantly distracted. Grades K–2.

Standiford, Natalie. *Dollhouse Mouse*. Illustrated by Denise Fleming. New York: Random House, 1989. 32p. ISBN 10: 0394999355; ISBN 13: 978-0394999357.

   Lucy lives in a dollhouse and decides to have an adventure outside the house. Grades K–2.

Stanley, Diane. *The Conversation Club*. New York: Simon & Schuster, 1990. 32p. ISBN 10: 0027867404; ISBN 13: 978-0027867404.

   Peter Fieldmouse is overwhelmed in the conversation club, so he starts a listening club. Grades K–3.

Steig, William. *Abel's Island*. New York: Farrar, Straus & Giroux, 1976. 128p. ISBN 10: 0374300100; ISBN 13: 978-0374300104.

   Abelard Hassam di Chirico Flint tries to rescue his wife's scarf but is swept away in a rainstorm and stranded on a river island for a year. (Audio and video recordings are available.) (Newbery Honor Book). Grades 3–6.

Steig, William. *Amos and Boris*. New York: Viking Penguin, 1971. 32p. ISBN 10: 0374302278; ISBN 13: 978-0374302788.

  Amos the Mouse and Boris the Whale have almost nothing in common, except that they save each other's lives. Grades K–3.

Steig, William. *Doctor De Soto*. New York: Scholastic, 1982. 30p. ISBN 10: 0374318034; ISBN 13: 978-0374318031.

  Doctor De Soto treats the toothaches of all kinds of animals, including a fox. (Audio and video versions are available.) (Newbery Honor Book). Grades K–4.

Steig, William. *Doctor De Soto Goes to Africa*. New York: HarperCollins Publishers, 1992. 30p.

  Dr. De Soto is called to Africa to help a desperate elephant with a toothache. (Audio and video versions are available.) Grades K–3.

Stern, Peter. *Max the Dragon*. New York: Crown, 1990. 32p. ISBN 10: 0517575876; ISBN 13: 978-0517575871.

  In this fractured fairy tale, Fragus, a tap-dancing mouse, tricks a dragon and helps the kingdom become peaceful again. Grade K-3.

Stevens, Janet, and Susan Stevens Crummel. *Shoe Town*. Illustrated by Janet Stevens. San Diego: Green Light Readers/Harcourt Brace, 1999. 32p. ISBN 10: 0152048820; ISBN 13: 978-0152048822.

  Mama Mouse wants to fill a shoe with water for a long bath, but friends keep showing up. Grades K–2.

Stevenson, James. *All Aboard!* New York: Greenwillow Books, 1995. 32p. ISBN 10: 0688124380; ISBN 13: 978-0688124380.

  Hubie gets on the wrong train and heads toward California instead of the New York World's Fair of 1939 with his parents and older brother. Grades K–3.

Stone, Bernard. *The Charge of the Mouse Brigade*. Illustrated by Tony Ross. New York: Pantheon Books, 1980. 32p. ISBN 10: 0905478657; ISBN 13: 978-0905478654.

  The mice of Mouseville form a brigade to get back their stolen cheese from the cats. Grades K–3.

Stone, Bernard. *Emergency Mouse*. Illustrated by Ralph Steadman. Englewood Cliffs, N. J.: Prentice-Hall, 1978. 32p. ISBN-10: 086592127X; ISBN 13: 978-0865921276.

  At night in a boy's hospital bedroom, mice operate their own hospital. Grades K–2.

Stone, Bernard. *Inspector Mouse*. Illustrated by Ralph Steadman. New York: Holt, Rinehart & Winston, 1980. 32p. ISBN 10: 0905478843; ISBN 13: 978-0905478845.

  A mouse detective discovers the culprits in a Limburger cheese theft. Grades K–3.

Stone, Bernard. *The Tale of Admiral Mouse*. Illustrated by Tony Ross. New York, N.Y.: Holt, Rinehart & Winston, 1981. 32p. ISBN 10: 0030612217; ISBN 13: 978-0030612213.

  English mice go to war with French mice to protect their cheese. 21p. Grades K–4.

Stone, Bernard. *Quasimodo Mouse*. Illustrated by Ralph Steadman. London: Trafalgar Square, 1984. 32p. ISBN 10: 0862640725; ISBN 13: 9780862640729.

  Quasimodo journeys into Southern France. Grades K–3.

Summers, Kate. *Milly and Tilly: The Story of a Town Mouse and a Country Mouse.* Illustrated by Maggie Kneen. New York: Dutton Children's Books, 1997. 32p. ISBN 10: 0525458018; ISBN 13: 978-0525458012.

> This modern retelling of Aesop's tale finds Milly the City Mouse inviting Tilly to stay. Grades K–3.

Szekeres, Cyndy. *A Busy Day.* Racine, Wis.: Western Publishing, 1989. 24p. ISBN 10: 0307619885; ISBN 13: 978-0307619884.

> Follow the mouse family through the day. Grades K–2.

Szekeres, Cyndy. *Cyndy Szekeres' Counting Book 1 to 10.* Racine Wis.: Western Publishing, 1984. 24p. ISBN 10: 0307621219; ISBN 13: 978-0307621214.

> Learn to count with ten little mice. Grades K–2.

Szekeres, Cyndy. *A Fine Mouse Band.* Racine, Wis.: Western Publishing, 1989. 24p. ISBN 10: 0307619990; ISBN 13: 978-0307619990.

> The mouse family has a fine time being musical together. Grades K–2.

Szekeres, Cyndy. *Ladybug, Ladybug, Where Are You?* Racine, Wis.: Western Publishing, 1991. 24p. ISBN 10: 0307123405; ISBN 13: 978-0307123404.

> Mice Sam and Emily capture insects while their mother and father gather seeds. Grades K–2.

Szekeres, Cyndy. *Moving Day.* Racine, Wis.: Western Publishing, 1989. 24p. ISBN 10: 0307619974; ISBN 13: 978-0307619976.

> The mouse family must find a new home when they are rained out. Grades K–2.

Szekeres, Cyndy. *The New Baby.* Racine, Wis.: Western Publishing, 1989. 24p. ISBN 10: 0307619982; ISBN 13: 978-0307619983.

> Mouse Elizabeth decides she is never coming out of her room, because she doesn't like to be a new big sister. Grades K–2.

Szekeres, Cyndy. *Toby's New Brother.* New York: Little Simon, 2000. 32p. ISBN 10: 0689826516; ISBN 13: 978-0689826511.

> Toby finds lots to do being a new big brother. (There are many other Toby books, including *Santa Toby's Busy Christmas*; *Toby Counts His Marbles*; *Toby: Do You Love Me?*; *Toby: I Can Do It*; *Toby's Alphabet Walk*; *Toby's Good Night*; *Toby's Holiday Hugs and Kisses*; *Toby's New Flying Lesson*; *Toby's Rainbow Clothes*; *Toby's Silly Faces*, and *Toby! Toby!*). Grades K–1.

Takao, Yuko. *A Winter Concert.* Brookfield, Conn.: Millbrook Press, 1995. 32p. ISBN 10: 0761304266; ISBN 13: 978-0761304265.

> When a mouse attends a concert, her black-and-white world is transformed into color by the music. Grades K–3.

Thayer, Jane. *The Mouse on the Fourteenth Floor.* Illustrated by Beatrice Darwin. New York: Morrow, 1977. 32p. ISBN 10: 0688320945; ISBN 13: 978-0688320942.

> A mouse runs from floor to floor in a large apartment building, trying to get out and go home to his farm. Grades K–3.

Tichenor, Tom. *Neat-O, the Supermarket Mouse.* Illustrated by Ray Cruz. Nashville, Tenn.: Abingdon, 1981. 32p. ISBN 10: 068727690X; ISBN 13: 978-0687276905.

> Little mouse wants to belong to a neighborhood gang, so he quits taking his daily bath. Grades K–2.

Titus, Eve. *Anatole*. Illustrated by Paul Galdone. New York: Knopf, 2006, c1956. 32p. ISBN 10: 0375839011; ISBN 13: 978-0375839016.

Anatole becomes a cheese taster at the Duvall cheese factory and helps the company make the best cheese in Paris. (A video recording is available.) Grades K–4.

Other titles about Anatole include:

Anatole and the Cat. Illustrated by Paul Galdone. New York: Bantam Books, 1990. 32p. ISBN 10: 037583902X; ISBN 13: 978-0375839023. Grades K–3.

Anatole and the Piano. Illustrated by Paul Galdone. New York: Bantam Books, 1966. 32p. ISBN 10: 0553348884; ISBN 13: 978-0553348880. Grades K–3.

Anatole and the Pied Piper. Illustrated by Paul Galdone. New York: McGraw-Hill, 1979. 32p. ISBN 10: 0070648972; ISBN 13: 978-0070648975. Grades K–3.

Anatole and the Poodle. Illustrated by Paul Galdone. New York: McGraw-Hill, 1965. 32p. ISBN 10: 0070648948; ISBN 13: 978-0070648944. Grades K–3.

Anatole and the Robot. Illustrated by Paul Galdone. New York: McGraw-Hill, 1960. 32p. ISBN 10: 0070649146; ISBN 13: 978-0070649149. Grades K–3.

Anatole and the Thirty Thieves. Illustrated by Paul Galdone. New York: Bantam Books, 1990, c1969. 32p. ISBN 10: 0553348892; ISBN 13: 978-0553348897. Grades K–3.

Anatole and the Toyshop. Illustrated by Paul Galdone. New York: Bantam Books, 1991. 36p. ISBN 10: 0070648859; ISBN 13: 978-0070648852. Grades K–3.

Anatole in Italy. Illustrated by Paul Galdone. New York: McGraw Hill, 1973. 32p. ISBN 10: 0070648964; ISBN 13: 978-0070648968. Grades K–3.

Anatole over Paris. Illustrated by Paul Galdone. New York: Bantam, 1991. 32p. ISBN 10: 0070650004; ISBN 13: 978-0070650008. Grades K–3.

Titus, Eve. *Basil of Baker Street*. Illustrated by Paul Galdone. New York: Archway, 1970, c1958. 112p. ISBN 10: 0671702874 (pb.); ISBN 13: 978-067170287 (pb.).

Basil, the Sherlock Holmes of the Mouse World, and his associate, Dr. Dawson, solve the kidnapping of the mouse twins Angela and Agatha. (A Walt Disney movie, *The Great Mouse Detective*, is available on videocassette and DVD.) Grades 3–6.

Other titles featuring Basil include:

Basil and the Lost Colony: A Basil of Baker Street Mystery. Illustrated by Paul Galdone. New York: Pocket, 1989. 111p. ISBN 10: 0671298801 (pb.); ISBN 13: 978-0671298807 (pb.). Grades 3–6.

Basil and the Pygmy Cats: A Basil of Baker Street Mystery. Illustrated by Paul Galdone. New York: Aladdin, 1989, 1971. 96p. ISBN 10: 0671641190 (pb.); ISBN 13: 978-0671641191 (pb.). Grades 3–6.

Basil in Mexico: A Basil of Baker Street Mystery. Illustrated by Paul Galdone. New York: Pocket, 1990, c1976. 115p. ISBN 10: 0671641174 (pb.); ISBN 13: 978-0671641177 (pb.). Grades 3–6.

Basil in the Wild West. Illustrated by Paul Galdone. New York: Aladdin, 1990, c1982. 95p. ISBN 10: 0671641182 (pb.); ISBN 13: 978-0671641184 (pb.). Grades 3–6.

Van Leeuwen, Jean. *The Great Christmas Kidnapping Caper*. Illustrated by Steven Kellogg. New York: Dial Press, 1975. 133p. ISBN 10: 0803754159; ISBN 13: 978-0803754157.

>   Merciless Marvin the Magnificent and his mouse gang think the Macy's Santa has been kidnapped. Grades 3–6.

Van Leeuwen, Jean. *The Great Rescue Operation*. Illustrated by Margot Apple. New York: Dell, 1982. 167p. ISBN-10: 068501455X; ISBN-13: 978-0685014554.

>   Merciless Marvin and Raymond set about finding a missing mouse friend. Grades 3–6.

Van Leeuwen, Jean. *The Great Summer Camp Catastrophe*. Illustrated by Diane de Groat. New York: Dial Books for Young Readers, 1992. 192p. ISBN 10: 0803711069; ISBN 13: 978-0803711068.

>   Marvin and his mouse friends are busy eating from a box of cookies in Macy's when they are unexpectedly bought with the box and sent to a summer camp in Vermont. Grades 3–6.

Vincent, Gabrielle. *Ernest and Celestine*. New York: Greenwillow, 1981. 25p. ISBN 10: 0688008550; ISBN 13: 978-0688008550.

>   Ernest the bear and Celestine the mouse lose her stuffed bird in the snow and must try to find it. (A film version is available.) Grades K–2.

>   Other titles about Ernest and Celestine include:

>   *Bravo, Ernest and Celestine!* New York: Greenwillow Books, 1982. 25p. ISBN 10: 0688008577; ISBN 13: 978-0688008574.

>   *Breakfast Time, Ernest and Celestine*. New York: Greenwillow Books, 1982. 18p. ISBN 10: 068-8045553; ISBN 13: 978-0688045555.

>   *Ernest and Celestine at the Circus*. New York: Greenwillow Books, 1989. 26p. ISBN 10: 068-8086845; ISBN 13: 978-0688086848.

>   *Ernest and Celestine's Patchwork Quilt*. New York: Greenwillow Books, 1982. 18p. ISBN 10: 068-804557X; ISBN 13: 978-0688045579.

>   *Ernest and Celestine's Picnic*. New York: Greenwillow, 1982. 26p. ISBN 10: 0688012507; ISBN 13: 978-0688012502.

>   *Feel Better, Ernest!* New York: Greenwillow Books, 1988. 26p. ISBN 10: 0688077250; ISBN 13: 978-0688077259.

>   *The Lost Toy*. London: East-West Publications, 1996. 40p. ISBN 10: 0856922064; ISBN 13: 978-0856922060.

>   *Merry Christmas, Ernest and Celestine*. New York: Mulberry, 1983. 34p. ISBN 10: 0688026060; ISBN 13: 978-0688026066.

>   *Smile, Ernest and Celestine*. New York: Greenwillow Books, 1982. 24p. ISBN 10: 0688012493; ISBN 13: 978-0688012496.

>   *Where Are You, Ernest and Celestine?* New York: Greenwillow Books, 1986. 26p. ISBN 10: 0688062342; ISBN 13: 978-0688062347.

Waber, Bernard. *Do You See a Mouse?* Boston: Houghton Mifflin, 1995. 32p. ISBN 10: 0395722926; ISBN 13: 978-0395722923.

> Simon the doorman does not see the mouse at the Park Snoot Hotel, but readers will! Grades K–2.

Waber, Bernard. *Mice on My Mind.* Boston: Houghton Mifflin, 1977. 48p. ISBN 10: 0395259355; ISBN 13: 978-0395259351.

> Poor Cat can't get mice off his mind. Grades K–2.

Waber, Bernard. *The Mouse That Snored.* Boston: Walter Lorraine Books/Houghton Mifflin, 2000. 32p. ISBN 10: 0395975182; ISBN 13: 978-0395975183.

> A man and his wife, a parrot, and a cat are surprised one night by a mouse who moves in and snores.

Waddell, Martin. *Mimi and the Dream House.* Illustrated by Leo Hartas. Cambridge, Mass.: Candlewick Press, 1998. 32p. ISBN 10: 0763605875; ISBN 13: 978-0763605872.

> Everyone has ideas about the mouse house, but Mimi wants it to be hers. Grades K–2.

Waddell, Martin. *Mimi's Christmas.* Illustrated by Leo Hartas. Cambridge, Mass.: Candlewick Press, 1997. 32p. ISBN 10: 0744548780; ISBN 13: 978-0763604134.

> Little Mimi wants something special for this family Christmas. Grades K–2.

Waddell, Martin. *Squeak-a-lot.* Illustrated by Virginia Miller. New York: Greenwillow Books, 1991. 32p. ISBN 10: 0688102441; ISBN 13: 978-0688102449.

> A lonely mouse sets out to find a playmate among the many animals around him and finally finds friends when he plays "squeak-a-lot" by himself. Grades K–2.

Wagener, Gerda. *A Mouse in the House!* Illustrated by Uli Waas. New York: North-South Books, 1995. 32p. ISBN 10: 1558585060; ISBN 13: 978-1558585065.

> Children try to catch the mouse that the cat brought into the house. Grades K–2.

Wagner, Karen. *Bravo, Mildred & Ed!* Illustrated by Janet Pedersen. New York: Walker, 2000. 32p. ISBN 10: 0802787347; ISBN 13: 978-0802787347.

> Because of scheduling conflicts for art and music, Mildred and Ed learn that they can do things separately; but being together is the most fun. Grades K–2.

Wagner, Karen. *A Friend Like Ed.* Illustrated by Janet Pedersen. New York: Walker, 1998. 32p. ISBN 10: 0802786626; ISBN 13: 978-0802786623.

> Ed's button collection is a bit "nerdy," but Mildred learns that he is a good friend. Grades K–2.

Wahl, Jan. *The Six Voyages of Pleasant Fieldmouse.* Illustrated by Tim Bowers. New York: Tor, 1994. 96p. ISBN 10: 0812524039; ISBN 13: 978-0812524031.

> Little Pleasant Fieldmouse wants to learn more about the world. Grades 2–4.

Waite, Judy. *Mouse, Look Out!* Illustrated by Norma Burgin. New York: Dutton Children's Books, 1998. 32p. ISBN 10: 1854304666; ISBN 13: 978-1854304667.

> Mouse barely escapes the claws of the cat. Grades K–2.

Walsh, Ellen Stoll. *Mouse Count.* San Diego: Voyager Books/Harcourt Brace, 1991. 32p. ISBN 10: 0152560238; ISBN 13: 978-0152560232.

> Ten mice outsmart a snake who thinks he has a delicious lunch. Grades K–2.

Walsh, Ellen Stoll. *Mouse Paint*. San Diego: Voyager Books/Harcourt Brace, 1989. 32p. ISBN 10: 0152560254; ISBN 13: 978-0152560256.
> Three white mice get into red, yellow, and blue paint cans, and the color begins! Grades K–2.

Waters, Tony. *The Sailor's Bride*. New York: Doubleday, 1991. 32p. ISBN 10: 0385414412; ISBN 13: 978-0385414418.
> Susanna the mouse marries Whitewhiskers despite warnings from her mother about the hazards of the sea. When Susanna learns that her love is lost at sea, she goes off to find him. Grades 1–3.

Watson, Clyde. *How Brown Mouse Kept Christmas*. Illustrated by Wendy Watson. New York: Farrar, Straus & Giroux, 1980. 32p. ISBN 10: 0374334943; ISBN 13: 978-0374334949.
> The mice party on Christmas Eve in front of a sleeping cat. Grades K–2.

Weigelt, Udo. *The Strongest Mouse in the World*. Illustrated by Nicolas d'Aujourd'hul. New York: North-South, 1998. 32p. ISBN 10: 1558588957; ISBN 13: 978-1558588950.
> Birthday girl Lizzie brags that she is the strongest person in the world and challenges Albert the bear, whom she beats, but . . . . Grades K–3.

Wells, Rosemary. *Noisy Nora*. New York: Dial Books for Young Readers, 1973. 32p. ISBN 10: 0670887226; ISBN 13: 978-0670887224.
> Nora is noisy because her mother and father pay attention to her older sister and younger brother. Grades K–2.

Wells, Rosemary. *Shy Charles*. New York: Dial Books for Young Readers, 1988. 32p. ISBN 10: 0670887293; ISBN 13: 978-0670887293.
> Charles's quietness and reserve worry his parents, until he needs to become active in an emergency. Grades K–2.

Wells, Rosemary. *Stanley and Rhoda*. New York: Dial, 1978. 40p. ISBN 10: 0803782497; ISBN 13: 978-0803782495.
> Stanley must learn to deal with his little sister. Grades 1–4.

Wenning, Elisabeth. *The Christmas Mouse*. Illustrated by Barbara Remington. New York: Holt, Rinehart & Winston, 1959. 48p. ISBN 10: 0030150663; ISBN 13: 978-0030150661.
> A little hungry mouse chews and eats the church organ bellows, which causes the priest and organist to scramble to write a song, "Silent Night, Holy Night." Grades 1–5.

Wheeler, Lisa. *One Dark Night*. Illustrated by Ivan Bates. San Diego: Harcourt, 2003. 32p. ISBN 10: 0152023186; ISBN 13: 978-0152023188.
> Mouse and Mole go out at night and become frightened about what they are afraid is waiting for them. Grades K–2.

White, E. B. *Stuart Little*. Illustrated by Garth Williams. New York: Harper & Row, 1945. 131p. ISBN 10: 0060263954; ISBN 13: 978-0060263959.
> The Little family have a new member in Stuart, who happens to be a mouse, and become involved in his adventures. (Audio formats are available. Four movies based on the book are also available.) Grades 2–5.

Whitney, Alexandra. *Mouse Surprise*. Kansas City, Mo.: Landmark Editions, 1997. 29p. ISBN 10: 0933849648; ISBN 13: 978-0933849648.

    Mice try hard not to wake the cat as they run around the kitchen creating a surprise. Grades K–2.

Wilbur, Richard. *Loudmouse*. Illustrated by Don Almquist. New York: Harcourt Brace Jovanovich, 1982. 32p. ISBN 10: 0152494944; ISBN 13: 978-0152494940. 30p.

    A mouse with a very loud mouth saves his family from a trap. Grades K–3.

Willard, Barbara. *The Pocket Mouse*. Illustrated by M. Harford-Cross. New York: J. MacRae Books, 1981. 32p. ISBN 10: 0744523648; ISBN 13: 978-0744523645.

    Colin finds a real mouse to replace the toy mouse he has in his pocket. Grades K–2.

Williamson, Roger. *The Cheesemaker Mice and the Giant*. Illustrated by Linda Birch. New York: Franklin Watts, 1983. 48p. ISBN 10: 0862031303; ISBN 13: 978-0862031305.

    Hubert and Mary find out the cheese they have been supplying to the giant is being used for a terrible purpose. Grades K–3.

Wood, Don, and Audrey Wood. *The Little Mouse, the Red Ripe Strawberry, and the Big Hungry Bear*. Illustrated by Don Wood. New York: Childs Play, 1992, 1984. 32p. ISBN 10: 0859531821; ISBN 13: 978-0859531825.

    Reader interaction is part of this story, in which the strawberry must be taken from the mouse. Grades K–2.

Willis, Jeanne. *Cottonball Colin*. Illustrated by Tony Ross: Grand Rapids, Mich.: Eerdmans Books for Young Readers, 2008. 24p. ISBN 10: 0802853315; ISBN 13: 978-0802853318.

    Colin is the smallest of ten children, and his mother worries about him constantly, so his grandmother steps in with an idea. Grades K–2.

Wooding, Sharon. *Arthur's Christmas Wish*. New York: Atheneum, 1986. 30p. ISBN 10: 0689312113; ISBN 13: 978-0689312113.

    Arthur's Christmas wish, given to him by his fairy godfather, must make someone else happy if he gets it. Grades K–3.

Woychuk, Denis. *Mimi & Gustav in Pirates!* Illustrated by Kim Howard. New York: Lothrop, Lee & Shepard Books, 1992. 32p. ISBN 10: 0688103367; ISBN 13: 978-0688103361.

    Mimi the hippo is captured by pirates, but Gustav the mouse is able to find a way to save her. Grades K–3.

Woychuk, Denis. *The Other Side of the Wall*. Illustrated by Kim Howard. New York: Lothrop, Lee & Shepard Books, 1991. 32p. ISBN 10: 0688098959; ISBN 13: 978-0688098957.

    Gustav, a mouse inventor, is separated by a wall from his love, Mimi, a hippo ballerina. Grades K–3.

Wright, Cliff. *Crumbs!* Nashville, Tenn.: Ideals Children's Books, 1990. 32p. ISBN 10: 0824984919; ISBN 13: 978-0824984915.

    Thomas dresses like a mouse and becomes one in order to raid his own birthday cake. Grades K–3.

Yamashita, Haruo. *Mice at the Beach*. Illustrated by Kazuo Iwamura. New York: Morrow, 1987. 36p. ISBN 10: 0688070639; ISBN-13: 9780688070632.

  Daddy Mouse is stranded while sleeping on the beach, and his seven children must figure out a way to save him. Grades K–3.

Yolen, Jane. *Beneath the Ghost Moon*. Illustrated by Laurel Molk. Boston : Little, Brown, 1993. 32p. ISBN 10: 061310496X; ISBN 13: 978-0613104968

  Little mice frolic on the night before Ghost Moon. Grades K–2.

Yolen, Jane. *Mice on Ice*. Illustrated by Lawrence Di Fiori. New York: E. P. Dutton, 1980. 71p. ISBN 10: 0525348727; ISBN 13: 978-0525348726.

  The skating star of the Mice Capades is kidnapped and must be rescued. Grades 2–4.

Yolen, Jane. *Mouse's Birthday*. Illustrated by Bruce Degen. New York: Putnam 1995. 32p. ISBN 10: 0399228454; ISBN 13: 978-0399228452.

  Everyone tries to squeeze into Mouse's house for his birthday, with catastrophic results.

York, Carol Beach. *Miss Know It All and the Good Day Mice: A Butterfield Square Story*. Illustrated by Victoria De Larrea. New York: Bantam Books, 1989. 98p. ISBN 10: 0553153730; ISBN 13: 978-0553153736.

  Mother and Father Mouse move their family to the cellar of the Good Day Orphanage, which is full of frightening children.

Young, Ed. *Seven Blind Mice*. New York: Philomel 1992. 48p. ISBN 10: 0399222618; ISBN 13: 978-0399222610.

  Seven mice of different colors encounter something strange each day of the week in this variation on an Indian folktale. Sound recordings are available.) (Caldecott Honor Book). Grades K–3.

Zelinsky, Paul O. *The Maid and the Mouse and the Odd-shaped House: A Story in Rhyme*. New York: Dutton/Putnam, 1981. 32p. ISBN 10: 0525450955; ISBN 13: 978-0525450955.

  As a maid and a mouse who live together make changes in their house, it begins to take the shape of a cat. Grades K–3.

Ziefert, Harriet. *A Car Trip for Mole and Mouse*. Illustrated by David Prebenna. New York: Puffin, 1994. 30p. ISBN 10: 0670838586. ISBN 13: 978-0670838585.

  Mouse and Mole take a ride to see the neighborhood.

Ziefert, Harriet. *A Clean House for Mole and Mouse*. Illustrated by David Prebenna. New York: Viking Penguin, 1988. 30p. ISBN 10: 0670820326; ISBN 13: 978-0670820320.

  Mole and Mouse clean their house and then stay outside, because they don't want to get it dirty again. Grades K–2.

Ziefert, Harriet. *A New House for Mole and Mouse*. Illustrated by David Prebenna. New York: Viking Penguin, 1987. 30p. ISBN 10: 0670817201; ISBN 13: 978-0670817207.

  Roommates Mouse and Mole enjoy learning everything about their new house. Grades K–2.

Published Mouse Paper Dolls

Mice paper dolls can be found on store shelves and on the Internet, ready to cut out. Here are some that are of interest:

Baird, Roberta. *Millie the Mouse.* http://robertabaird.com/fun.htm (accessed on March 24, 2009). Several outfits are downloadable.

Bracken, Carolyn. *Mouse Sticker Paper Doll.* Mineola, N.Y.: Dover, 1993. 4p. ISBN 10: 0486274365; ISBN 13: 978-0486274362.

Collins, Crystal. *Victorian Mouse Paper Dolls in Full Color.* Mineola, N.Y.: Dover, 1986. 32p. ISBN 10: 0486250458; ISBN 13: 978-0486250458.

Lesson Plan:
Two Mice Are Not the Same as One

Library Media Skills Objective:

The student will read two or more books with the same animal subject (mouse) or the same mouse characters and compare differences in the motivation and characteristics of two main mouse characters.

Curriculum (Subject Areas) Objectives:

The activity may be completed in reading/language arts during a study of motivation of characters.

Grade Level: 2–4

Resources:

Paper doll handout

Crayons, paints, and scissors

String or cord

Mice books

Curtain rods, curtain fabric, and backdrop fabric

Instructional Roles:

The library media specialist or classroom teacher may complete this activity. The introduction and discussion will take approximately a half hour. Student reading and the making of the paper dolls will take at least an hour; some of this will be done on the students' own time. The demonstration of the differences between the paper dolls will take an hour or more depending on the number of students and the discussions that follow.

Activity and Procedures for Completion:

Read aloud stories in which the main characters are markedly different in some way. For example, Aesop's Country Mouse and City Mouse are different in basics. Depending on the book selected, the characters may have other differences. Discuss the kinds of differences, such as the physical differences that one might see as well as those in action, personality, or ways of thinking.

There are many retellings of this story; here are a few:

City Mouse, Country Mouse and Two More Mouse Tales from Aesop. Retold and illustrated by John Wallner. New York: Scholastic, 1970. 30p.

Country Mouse and City Mouse. Retold by Patricia McKissack and Fredrick McKissack. Illustrated by Anne Sikorski. Chicago: Children's Press, 1986. 31p.

The Country Mouse and the City Mouse. Retold by Maxine P. Fisher. Illustrated by Jerry Smath. New York: Random House, 1994.

The Country Mouse and the City Mouse: A Retelling of Aesop's Fable. Retold by Eric Blair. Illustrated by Dianne Silverman. Minneapolis, Minn.: Picture Window Books, 2004. 24p.

The Town Mouse and the Country Mouse. Retold and illustrated by Lorinda Bryan Cauley. New York: Putnam, 1984. 30p.

The Town Mouse and the Country Mouse. Retold and illustrated by Helen Craig. Cambridge, Mass.: Candlewick Press, 1995.

The Town Mouse and the Country Mouse: An Aesop Fable. Retold and illustrated by Janet Stevens. New York: Holiday House, 1987. 32p.

Town Mouse, Country Mouse. Retold and illustrated by Jan Brett. New York: Putnam, 1994. 32p.

This is also a good time to talk about retelling stories and the choices illustrators make when illustrating the retellings. There are videocassettes and DVDs of many of the versions.

Set up a simple puppet theater. Use two spring-loaded curtain rods. One rod should have a fabric curtain that can be considered a backdrop. This rod will be placed at one edge of the doorframe. The second rod will have two pieces of fabric that can be parted. This rod will be placed at the other edge of the doorframe. There should be two to four inches between the two curtain rods. The rods can be taken down and put up easily in any doorway.

The mice paper dolls will be pulled back and forth between the sides of the door, using one of these two methods:

1. Attach a strong string to each side of one mouse paper doll. As the mouse is pulled to one side, an outfit can be placed on the doll while it is behind the curtain and then be pulled to the center of the stage. The student will describe the character being portrayed in this outfit. What is the character like? The paper doll is pulled to the other side behind the curtain, the outfit is changed, and then the puppet goes back to the center of the stage. The student talks discusses the character being portrayed in this outfit. A summary is made to highlight the differences between the two and how they came out in the characters and books being shared.

2. The second option is to have two paper dolls. A string or cord is placed on each doll. Both dolls are dressed. The first character is pulled out to the center of the stage, discussed, and then pulled back behind the curtain on one side. The second dressed doll is then pulled to the center, discussed, and pulled back. Both dressed dolls are pulled to the center, and a summary is made.

Evaluation:

Each student will read at least two mice books and select one or two main characters. Two outfits will be made or selected that show at least one difference between the mice. The difference may be physical or mental.

Follow-Up:

The student may transfer the activity to an animated version. The change in outfits to show the differences may be done using software for simple movement. Show the mouse as a character change artist.

Use these techniques with other kinds of paper dolls to show a change or difference in the character or the character's behavior. For example, a character might dress in one way to impress schoolmates as opposed to parents.

Paper Dolls:
Mice

These mice love to read. When they are wearing certain costumes, they are reminded of authors who have written terrific mouse character books.

Instructions: Name the mice, color their clothes, and read the books by the authors listed on pages 215–216.

When Mouse puts on the helmet, he imagines himself on the toy motorcycle!

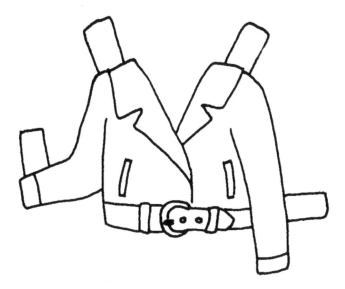

Mouse pretends she is Mariel of Redwall, a very brave female mouse, indeed.

When Mouse puts on this outfit, he thinks about the sailboat race in *Stuart Little*.

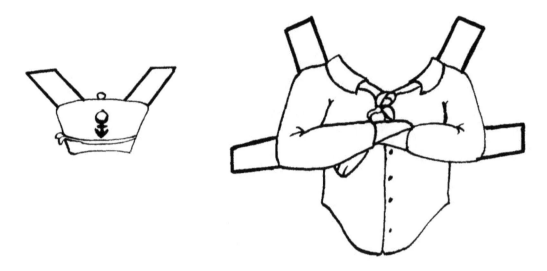

Mouse imagines herself as one of her favorite Henkes characters: Lilly and her purple purse!

Who can Mouse be?

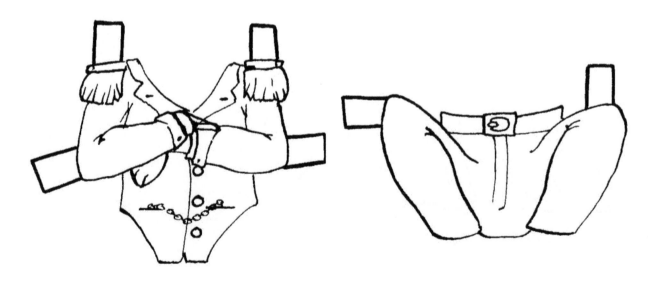

Gary Soto lives in Fresno, California. He says that he has known many cats like the ones in *Chato's Kitchen*. Do you suppose he knows Chato's mice neighbors, too?

Mouse pretends to be one of the mouse family guests in *Chato's Kitchen*. What will she take to the dinner?

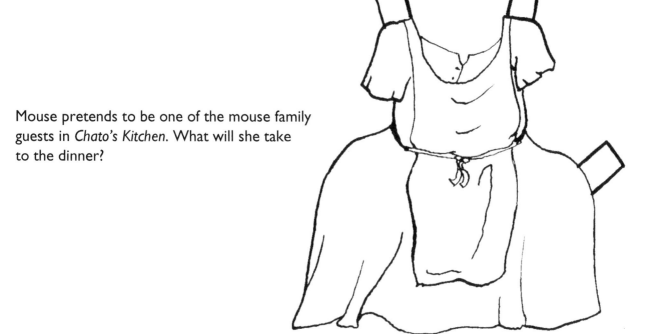

The mice can be many other characters.

When Mouse thinks about Dr. Desoto, the dentist, he likes to think about being a doctor.

Mouse loves to pretend that she is Katherine Holabird's *Angelina Ballerina*.

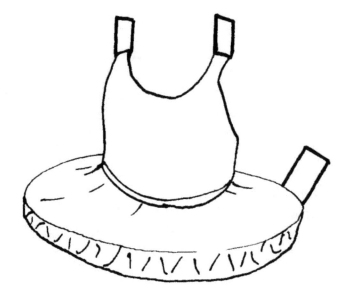

Who wouldn't have fun as Norman the Doorman at the Art Museum! He has read Don Freeman's story many times.

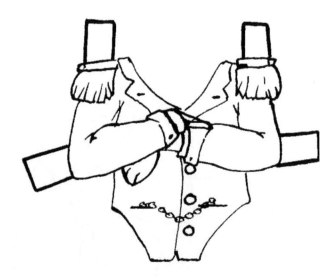

Chapter 12

Monkey Business! Monkey Books!

Who's the Main Monkey?

"Five Little Monkeys Jumping on the Bed" is a song many learn in kindergarten. Children chant the rhyme about "Five Little Monkeys Sitting in a Tree" who tease Mr. Crocodile. They clap their hands and yell, "Snap!" when the crocodile comes. Monkey characters can be tricky or full of mischief. Sometimes the characters may even remind us of ourselves.

Monkey book characters are found in many places besides the jungle. There are monkeys on parade, monkeys in trees, and monkeys to count. One monkey tricks a big, stingy buzzard, while another monkey is tricked by a wise old turtle. You can find a funny book that tells about a giant ape who wants to sell "Ape-on" cosmetics door-to-door, called *Ding Dong Ding Dong*, by Margie Palatini. A favorite monkey story, which has been around since 1947, is *Caps for Sale* by Esphyr Slobodkina. The peddler learns firsthand the meaning of the saying "Monkey see, monkey do!"

Not All Apes Are Monkeys

Many stories include monkeys as human's best friends or "sidekicks." Tarzan and Aladdin both had monkey friends, and the Kratt brothers in the PBS show *Zaboomafoo* have Zabu the lemur to help move their show along. (Lemurs are relatives of monkeys and part of the ape family.) In times past, organ grinders and street musicians used trained monkeys to attract an audience and collect donations from the crowd as they listened and watched. Today, people who are disabled can have monkeys who are trained to help them with the tasks of daily living. These monkeys can fetch, turn on computers and lights, open books and containers, and do all sorts of things for a person with limited abilities.

One of the most famous "monkey" book characters is Curious George. A closer look tells us he is a chimpanzee, but he seems to fall into the monkey category in library catalogs. Hans Augusto Rey and Margaret Rey originally called the little ape Zozo, probably because they didn't want to offend King

George of England. The little fellow made it big in many books and television programs and can be found in stores as a stuffed toy.

Perhaps what attracts us to monkeys and apes is the fact that they seem to look and act so much like human beings. We are related to them because we are all members of the primate family. In the wild, monkeys live in ordered societies with rules and behaviors much like our own. Monkeys can use tools, solve problems, and even be trained to communicate by using sign language.

Name That Monkey!

These teasers are easily used in a booktalk with youngsters to judge their knowledge of "Monkey Business." Books can be on display or used for further introduction and discussions.

1. I am a monkey (No, I'm not an aardvark!). I have a little sister named Violet (Not D. W.) Some of the stories you can read about me tell about my "pen pal," my "loose tooth," and my "first day back at school." Who am I? (Hint: The author who created me is Lillian Hoban.)

    Did you guess that my name is Arthur? You're right! I hope you'll take me home sometime, to see if you can read about me all by yourself. I like to wear overalls and play and read and do all of the things that many kids like to do. Sometimes I get mad and frustrated about the way things happen, but you can read about how I learn to make decisions and solve my growing-up problems. Happy reading!

2. Hi! I'm another monkey or chimp you might know. I am very, very curious, and I often get myself into lots of trouble. Does your curiosity get you into trouble sometimes, too? I live with my friend, who likes to wear a yellow hat. Can you guess my name?

    Right! I am Curious George. The author who created me is H. A. Rey. Sometimes he is helped by Margaret Rey. I have been learning so many things! I learned my "alphabet," how to "ride a bicycle," how to "fly a kite," and how to "feed the animals." I've been around in the children's book sections of libraries since about 1941! I'll bet your parents, and even some of your grandparents, have read my books. I hope you'll look for my books and read about all of my adventures.

3. Jambo! That's how some people in Africa say hello. I'm the best animal friend of a man who was raised in the jungle by apes. He likes to swing on vines and protect animals that are in danger from hunters. Edgar Rice Burroughs created his story a long time ago, but that was only the beginning. His story and adventures have been retold in several books, movies, a television series, and now in a new film version by Walt Disney Productions. Do you know me? In the older versions of the movie, my name was Cheetah. In the new Disney version, my name is Terk. Can you guess the name of my famous friend?

    You got it! Tarzan. If you want to read a great version of his story, with beautiful pictures, check out *Tarzan*, retold by Robert D. San Souci and illustrated by Michael McCurdy. You can find it in the picture book sections of many libraries.

4. Hi. I'm a chimpanzee, and my adventures take place in a city. I dress and act pretty much like most kids. I have good days and not so good days; I face problems and find solutions. I've been known as "a wimp," "a champ," "a wizard," and "a dreamer." My author, Anthony Browne, paints lovely pictures with interesting details. Some of his pictures remind people of the great artists whose paintings hang in museums. Have you met me yet?

    My name is Willy. Look for me where the picture books are shelved in your library. Usually you can find me with books by authors whose last name begins with "B."

5. Here's an easy one for you. I am mischievous, and I often get my master into trouble. He's the star of a Disney movie. We live on the streets, so sometimes we snitch food and other things in order to live. My master fell in love with the daughter of the Rajah. He also found a magic lamp with a genie in it, who grants him three wishes. Just look for stories named after my master, Aladdin. Have you remembered my name?

Yes! It's Abu. This whole story originated a long time ago as one of the tales of *The Arabian Nights*. You won't find me in all of the versions of the Aladdin story, but I am in the Disney movie. Even though I'm not the star of the show, I show up in a lot of the scenes that keep the story moving, especially when mischief is involved!

Sayings Give Monkeys a Bad Rap!

Another way of introducing monkey and ape books can be through sayings. There are many. Give students the following test and match the sayings with books they are associated with. Can they match the "monkey" saying with its meaning?

1. Monkey business.

2. Monkey-ing around.

3. A monkey in silk is a monkey no less.

4. Make monkey-shines.

5. Going ape.

6. Monkey see, monkey do.

7. Throw a monkey wrench into the works.

8. More fun than a barrel of monkeys

9. Well, I'll be a monkey's uncle!

A. Losing control or going crazy

B. Copying someone or doing something just because someone else does.

C. Something silly and hilarious or really fun.

D. I am really surprised.

E. Something against the "rules" (illegal, immoral etc.) but not too serious.

F. Fooling around or killing time.

G. No matter how you dress something up, it is still the same underneath.

H. Do something to stop a plan or a process—jam up the works.

I. Make faces or act silly.

Answers: 1 = E; 2 = F; 3 = G; 4 = I; 5 = A; 6 = B; 7 = H; 8 = C; 9 = D

Monkeys and Apes in the Movies

Most movies that include monkeys can easily be classified as comedy, with some exceptions. Monkeys provide comedic relief. It is surprising how many ape family members can be found. A more comprehensive listing of characters can be found at:

List of Fictional Apes—http://en.wikipedia.org/wiki/List_of_fictional_apes (accessed June 30, 2008).

Mr. Monkey's Index of Famous Movie Monkeys—http://www.citizenlunchbox.com/monkey/famous/ (accessed June 30, 2008).

Some of the more enjoyable movies that can be seen by a wide audience are discussed below.

Bonzo

Bedtime for Bonzo. Los Angeles: Universal Studios, 1951. 84 min.

A psychology professor who has been bad mouthed because his father is a convict tests his theory that environment rather than heredity dictates a person's personality on Bonzo the chimp . Bonzo responds to the kindness he is shown but is accused of robbery, and the professor almost goes to jail. Former president Ronald Reagan starred in the film. A sequel was *Bonzo Goes to College*.

Casey

A Summer to Remember. Universal City, Calif.: MCA Home Video, 1984. 94 min.

Casey, a trained orangutan, is thrown from a truck near Toby Wyler's home. Toby, who has been deaf since he had meningitis, becomes friends with Casey, and they begin to communicate. The orangutan has been taught sign language by trainer and scientist Dr. Dolly McKeever.

Curious George

Curious George. Los Angeles: Universal Studios, 2006. 88 min. Rated G.

Whether in the full or wide screen version, on DVD or downloaded, this animated version of *Curious George*, directed by Matthew O'Callaghan and with the voices of Will Ferrell, Drew Barrymore, Eugene Levy, Dick Van Dyke, David Cross, and Joan Plowright, will keep viewers who love the monkey/chimp entranced. Ted, dressed head-to-toe in yellow, returns from Africa with a lonely monkey, George, who gets into mischief. Ted must help save the museum from destruction, with some help from George.

Dodger

Monkey Trouble. New York: New Line Home Video, 1994. 87 min. Rated PG.

A monkey named Dodger runs away from his organ grinder owner when a mob boss wants to use him in a crime. Eva wants a pet and finds one in Dodger. She gets into trouble when Dodger starts bringing her valuables! Ellen Leroe wrote a book based on the movie screenplay, called *Monkey Trouble* (New York: Minstrel/Pocket Books, 1994. 150p.).

Dunston

Dunstan Checks In. Los Angeles: 20th Century Fox, 2002. 99 min. Rated PG.

An orangutan named Dunston is owned by a jewel thief. Dunston escapes from his owner while they are staying in a five-star hotel in New York and is found by ten-year-old Kyle, son of the hotel manager. Dunston turns the hotel event of the season into a riot.

King Kong

King Kong. Los Angeles: Universal Studio, 2006. 188 min. Rated PG-13.

King Kong. Los Angeles: Paramount Home Video, 1976. 134 min. Rated PG.

King Kong, the Eighth Wonder of the World. Los Angeles: Universal Studio, 1933. 105 min. Rated PG.

King Kong, the eighteen-foot-tall ape (forty feet in the 1976 movie remake and twenty-five feet in the 2005 movie remake), was conceived by filmmaker Merian C. Cooper. Kong, as hew was originally named, lived on Skull Island with dinosaur beasts. He is captured and taken to New York for display, where he escapes and is eventually killed. King Kong has become an icon and is the subject of many movie remakes and sequels. Ian Thorne wrote *King Kong* (Crestwood House, 1977. 47p.), in which he provides synopses of several films whose plots revolve around the escapades of the giant ape. It contains some great scenes and stills from the older movies.

Sequels include *Son of Kong* (1933), *King Kong vs. Godzilla* (1962), *King Kong Escapes* (1967), and *King Kong Lives* (1986).

Mighty Joe

Mighty Joe Young. Burbank, Calif: Walt Disney Home Video/Buena Vista Home Entertainment, 1999. 114 min. Rated PG.

Joe, a fifteen-foot-tall gorilla, and his lifelong best friend, Jill Young, leave the remote mountains of Central Africa for California when Joe is endangered by poachers. He ends up in an animal conservancy in California.

Raffles

The Barefoot Executive. Burbank, Calif.: Walt Disney, 1971. 96 min. Rated G.

Steven Post is a pageboy at a television network who discovers his girlfriend's chimpanzee, Raffles, is amazing at rating programs. Steven is picked to be the head of programming, until his former boss finds out what is going on.

Rusty, Poppy, and Teeger

Going Ape. Los Angeles: Paramount, 1981. Rated PG.

Oscar's rich circus-owning father dies and leaves him a $5 million estate, on the condition that he keep his dad's three pet orangutans safe and sound for the next three years.

Space Chimps (Ham, Luna, and Titan)

Space Chimps. Los Angeles: 20th Century Fox, 2008. 81 min. Rated G.

Three chimps are sent into space. Lt. Luna and Commander Titan, along with Ham III, the grandson of the first chimp astronaut, must help find the planet of an evil leader Zartog.

Chimps in the Summer of the Monkeys

Summer of Monkeys. Burbank, Calif.: Walt Disney Home Video /Buena Vista Home Video, 1998. 101 min. Rated G.

Bored farm boy Jay learns there is a great reward for the return of four trained circus chimps who escaped when a train was derailed. Jay researches chimp behavior in the library and sets out to capture the animals. He must fight local bullies and use creativity to pursue the reward. Based on the book by Wilson Rawls.

Zira and Galen

Planet of the Apes. Beverly Hills, Calif.: 20th Century Fox Home Videos, 1967. 112 min. Rated G.

Colonel George Taylor crashes his spacecraft on what seems to be an unfamiliar planet. He is captured and held prisoner by a race of apes. Chimpanzees Zira and Galen are liberal scientists who befriend Taylor and help him escape, to find a dreadful truth.

Sequels include *Beneath the Planet of the Apes* (1970), *Escape from the Planet of the Apes* (1971), *Conquest of the Planet of the Apes* (1972), and *Battle for the Planet of the Apes* (1973). Television programs also followed: *Planet of the Apes* (1974*)* and *Return to the Planet of the Ape*s (1975).

Monkey Stories on the Internet

Chunky Monkey's Rainforest Friends—http://www.chunkymonkey.com/rainforest/rainforest.htm (accessed June 30, 2008).

Find lots to do here at this site created by cartoonist Paula Comanor. Learn to draw and download pictures to color Chunky Monkey and all his friends. Read some Chunky Monkey stories and print and color a map of South America with great but simple topographical features.

The World of Curious George's—http://www.georgeworld.com or http://www.houghtonmifflinbooks. com/features/cgsite/ (accessed March 21, 2009).

Join his fan club, send a greeting card, and go on a mini-adventure with Curious George. Try playing a hat-switching game or find out more about Curious George software and products.

Stories about Monkeys and Other Members of the Ape Family

Books about the scientific order of primates range widely. For clarification, the order follows:

Order: Primate

Suborder Strepsirrhini: non-tarsier prosimians
    Infraorder Lemuriformes
        Superfamily Cheirogaleoidea
            Family Cheirogaleidae: dwarf lemurs and mouse-lemurs
        Superfamily Lemuroidea
            Family Lemuridae: lemurs
            Family Lepilemuridae: sportive lemurs
            Family Indriidae: woolly lemurs and allies
    Infraorder Chiromyiformes
        Family Daubentoniidae: Aye-aye
    Infraorder Lorisiformes
        Family Lorisidae: lorises, pottos and allies
        Family Galagidae: galagos

Suborder Haplorrhini: tarsiers, monkeys and apes
    Infraorder Tarsiiformes
        Family Tarsiidae: tarsiers
    Infraorder Simiiformes
Parvorder Platyrrhini: New World monkeys
        Family Cebidae: marmosets, tamarins, capuchins and squirrel monkeys
        Family Aotidae: night or owl monkeys
        Family Pitheciidae: titis, sakis and uakaris
        Family Atelidae: howler, spider and woolly monkeys
Parvorder Catarrhini
    Superfamily Cercopithecoidea
        Family Cercopithecidae: Old World monkeys
    Superfamily Hominoidea
        Family Hylobatidae: gibbons or "lesser apes"
        Family Hominidae: humans and other "great apes" as gorillas and chimpanzees

Authors have gravitated toward old and new world monkeys, lemurs, chimpanzees, gorillas, and orangutans.

Monkeys (Old and New World)

Ahlberg, Allan. *Monkey Do*. Illustrated by Andre Amstutz. Cambridge, Mass.: Candlewick Press, 1998. 32p. ISBN 10: 0763604666; ISBN 13: 978-0763604660.
    This rhyming story follows a mischievous little monkey from his escape from the zoo through all the other animal friends he meets during the day until he begins to miss his mother. Grades K–2.

Aylesworth, Jim. *Naughty Little Monkeys*. Illustrated by Henry Cole. New York: Dutton Children's Books, 2004. 32p. ISBN 10: 0525469400; ISBN 13: 978-0525469407.
    When the humans leave the monkeys alone for the evening, the monkeys romp through the letters of the alphabet, making mischief. Grades K–3.

Banks, Kate. *The Bird, the Monkey, and the Snake in the Jungle*. Illustrated by Tomek Bogacki. New York: Farrar, Straus & Giroux, 1999. 32p. ISBN 10: 0374307296; ISBN 13: 978-0374307295.
    When a bird, a monkey, and a snake lose their home in a tree, they look for a new home and encounter jungle animals on the way. Solve the rebuses, which are identified with labels in the margins of the pages. Grades K–2.

Barber, Antonia. *The Monkey and the Panda*. Illustrated by Meilo So. New York: Macmillan Books for Young Readers, 1995. 32p. ISBN 10: 0711209014; ISBN 13: 978-0711209015.
    Why would a monkey be jealous of a panda? Celebrate differences in this fable. Grades K–3.

Blos, Joan W. *Nellie Bly's Monkey: His Remarkable Story in His Own Words*. Illustrated by Catherine Stock. New York: Morrow Junior Books, 1996. 37p. ISBN 10: 0688126774; ISBN 13: 978-0688126773.
    McGinty the monkey and his new owner, a woman journalist, travel from Singapore to New York, where he finally takes up residence at the Menagerie. Grades 1–3.

Bunting, Eve. *Monkey in the Middle*. Illustrated by Lynn Munsinger. New York: Harcourt Brace Jovanovich, 1984. 36p. ISBN 10: 0152553169; ISBN 13: 978-0152553166.

Mohammed's monkey finds a way to make peace when coconut pickers Mohammed and Hashim fight over a bicycle. Grades K–3.

Cassidy, Anne. *The Sassy Monkey*. Illustrated by Lisa Smith. Minneapolis, Minn.: Picture Window Books, 2000. 32p. ISBN 10: 1404800581; ISBN 13: 978-1404800588.

Wendy doesn't know how to get the monkey out of her tree house. Grades K–2.

Christelow, Eileen. *Five Little Monkeys Bake a Birthday Cake*. Boston: Houghton Mifflin, 2005. 32p. ISBN 10: 0618496475; ISBN 13: 978-0618496471.

The five little monkeys are up with the sun to bake a cake for their mama's birthday. (Former title was *Don't Wake Mama!*) Grades K–3.

Christelow, Eileen. *Five Little Monkeys Go Shopping*. New York: Clarion, 2005. 32p. ISBN 10: 0618821619; ISBN 13: 978-0618821617.

When Mama takes the five little monkeys shopping, they all disobey and go separate ways. Grades K–3.

Christelow, Eileen. *Five Little Monkeys Jumping on the Bed*. New York: Clarion Books, 1989. 32p. ISBN 10: 0899197698; ISBN 13: 978-0899197692.

The monkeys in this favorite nursery rhyme are serious bed jumpers. (An audio version is available, as are finger puppets.) Grades K–3.

Christelow, Eileen. *Five Little Monkeys Play Hide-and-Seek*. New York: Clarion, 2004. 32p. ISBN 10: 0618409491; ISBN 13: 978-0618409495.

The babysitter agrees to play hide-and-seek with the monkeys and ends up finding more monkeys than there are. Grades K–3.

Christelow, Eileen. *Five Little Monkeys Sitting in a Tree*. New York: Clarion, 1991. 32p. ISBN 10: 0395544343; ISBN 13: 978-0395544341.

Five silly monkeys tease a crocodile, with serious consequences. (An audio version is available, as are finger puppets.) Grades K–3.

Christelow, Eileen. *Five Little Monkeys Wash the Car*. Boston: Houghton Mifflin, 2000. 32p. ISBN 10: 0395925665; ISBN 13: 978-0395925669.

The five little monkeys want to help mama spiff up her car, but it ends up in the swamp. (A sound recording is available.) Grades K–3.

Christelow, Eileen. *Five Little Monkeys with Nothing to Do*. New York: Clarion Books, 1996. 32p. ISBN 10: 0395758300; ISBN 13: 978-0395758304.

Five little monkeys are bored, so their mother has them clean up the house for Grandma Bessie's visit!

Clifford, Eth. *Harvey's Marvelous Monkey Mystery*. Boston: Houghton Mifflin, 1987. 119p. ISBN 10: 0395426227; ISBN 13: 978-0395426227.

What kind of mystery involves a monkey that appears in Harvey's bedroom window in the middle of the night? Grades 3–6.

Dodds, Dayle Ann. *The Color Box*. Illustrated by Giles Laroche. Boston: Little, Brown, 1992. 32p. ISBN 10: 0316188204; ISBN 13: 978-0316188203.

Alexander the monkey finds an ordinary-looking box with spots of color inside, through which he journeys to many bright landscapes of different colors. Each page has a hole in it revealing the next color he will find. Grades K–2.

Drescher, Henrik. *The Yellow Umbrella*. New York: Bradbury Press, 1987. 32p. ISBN 10: 0027332403; ISBN 13: 978-0027332407.

Make up your own story with this wordless picture book, in which two monkeys and one yellow umbrella can go anywhere. Grades K–2.

Faulkner, Keith. *Ten Little Monkeys: A Counting Storybook*. Illustrated by Jonathan Lambet. Toronto: Scholastic Inc., 2001. 16p. ISBN 10: 0756782031; ISBN 13: 978-1855650992.

One by one the little monkeys are reduced in number as they visit the watering hole and experience one calamity after another. Grades K–1.

Franklin, Kristine L. *When the Monkeys Came Back*. Illustrated by Robert Roth. New York: Atheneum; Maxwell Macmillan, 1994. 32p. ISBN 10: 0689318073; ISBN 13: 978-0689318078.

Marta remembers that the howler monkeys in her Costa Rican valley disappeared when all the trees were cut down. How does Marta bring the monkeys back? Grades K–4.

Gage, Amy Glaser. *Pascual's Magic Pictures*. Illustrated by Karen Dugan. New York: Carolrhoda Books, 1996. 32p. ISBN 10: 0876148771; ISBN 13: 978-0876148778.

After he saved enough money to buy a disposable camera, Pascual goes into the Guatemalan jungle to take pictures of howler monkeys, with unexpected results. Grades K–3.

Gave, Marc. *Monkey See, Monkey Do*. Illustrated by Jacqueline Rogers. New York: Scholastic, 1993. 32p. ISBN 10: 0606027572; ISBN 13: 978-0606027571.

Follow the play of monkeys through the day while you read the rhymes. Grades K–3.

Gelman, Rita Golden. *More Spaghetti, I Say!* New York: Scholastic, 1993. 32p. ISBN 10: 0606036210; ISBN 13: 978-0758714695.

Minnie the monkey can't play with his friend Freddie because he is too busy eating spaghetti. (A sound recording is available.) Grades K–3.

Goldsmith, Howard. *The Twiddle Twins' Music Box Mystery*. Illustrations by Charles Jordan. New York: Mondo, 1997. 40p. ISBN 10: 0613089693; ISBN 13: 978-0613089692.

Who stole their music box? The Twiddle twins find clues such as banana peels, a coconut shell, and a chocolate bar wrapper. Grades 2–4.

Goode, Diane. *Monkey Mo Goes to the Sea*. New York: Blue Sky Press, 2002. 40p. ISBN 10: 0439266815; ISBN 13: 978-0439266819.

When Bertie and his pet, Mo, lunch aboard the *Blue Star*, the luxury liner captained by Bertie's grandfather, monkey Mo mimics a gentleman even when the gentleman falls overboard. Grades K–3.

Henderson, Aileen. *The Monkey Thief*. Illustrated by Paul Mirocha. Minneapolis, Minn.: Milkweed Editions, 1996. 157p. ISBN 10: 1571316124; ISBN 13: 978-157131612.

Steve visits his uncle in a Costa Rican rain forest and meets a monkey and a smuggler. Grades 3–6.

Koller, Jackie French. *One Monkey Too Many*. Illustrated by Lynn Munsinger. New York: Harcourt Brace, 1999. 32p. ISBN 10: 0152000062; ISBN 13: 978-0152000066.

Mischievous monkeys have a series of escapades in which a bike, a canoe, a restaurant, and a hotel figure. Grades K–3.

Kurtz, Jane, and Christopher Kurtz. *Water Hole Waiting*. Illustrated by Lee Christiansen. New York: Greenwillow Books, 2001. 32p. ISBN 10: 0060298502; ISBN 13: 978-0060298500.

A young vervet monkey comes with the troop to the water hole, but mother is very protective. Grades K–3.

McAllister, Angela. *Matepo*. Illustrated by Jill Newton. New York: Dial Books for Young Readers, 1991. 32p. ISBN 10: 0803708386; ISBN 13: 978-0803708389.

Matepo meets many animals in the jungle before he finds the perfect gift for his mother. Grades K–3.

McKissack, Pat, and Robert L. Hillerich. *Who Is Coming?* Illustrated by Clovis Martin. New York: Children's Press, 1986. 32p. ISBN 10: 0516020730; ISBN 13: 978-051602073.

An African monkey is not afraid of one of the most dangerous animals. Grades K–2.

Moncure, Jane Belk. *What Do You Say When a Monkey Acts This Way?* Mankato, Minn.: Child's World, 1988. 32p. ISBN 10: 0895656892; ISBN 13: 978-0895656896.

Each day of the week, monkey learns another way to behave in a given situation, such as meeting someone new. Grades K–2.

Murphy, Stuart J. *Spunky Monkeys on Parade*. Illustrated by Lynne Cravath. New York: HarperCollins, 1999. 32p. ISBN 10: 006028014X; ISBN 13: 978-0060280147.

In the Monkey Day Parade, monkey majorettes, cyclists, tumblers, and band members create a spectacle as they move along in groups of two, three, and four. Grades K–4.

Myers, Walter Dean. *How Mr. Monkey Saw the Whole World*. Illustrated by Synthia Saint James. Garden City, N.Y.: Doubleday Books for Young Readers, 1996. 32p. ISBN 10: 0385320574; ISBN 13: 978-0385320573.

Mr. Buzzard tricks other animals into working for his food. How does Mr. Monkey solve this problem?

Myers, Walter Dean. *Mr. Monkey and the Gotcha Bird: An Original Tale*. Illustrated by Leslie Morrill. New York: Delacorte Press, 1984. 32p. ISBN 10: 0385292929; ISBN 13: 978-0385292924.

Monkey must think fast to keep the Gotcha Bird from gobbling him up. Grades 1–4.

Nelson, Theresa. *The Empress of Elsewhere*. New York: DK Publishing, 1998. 278p. ISBN 10: 0789424983; ISBN 13: 978-0789424983.

Jimmy and his younger sister agree to help their wealthy, elderly neighbor care for the capuchin monkey that keeps getting away from her. Jimmy must deal with the woman's granddaughter and the family's past. Grades 3–6.

Regan, Dana. *Monkey See, Monkey Do*. New York: Penguin, 2000. 32p. ISBN 10: 0448422999; ISBN 13: 9780448422992.

Monkey children move through their activities from day to day. Grades K–2.

Santat, Dan. *The Guild of Geniuses.* New York: Arthur A. Levine Books, 2004. 32p. ISBN 10: 0439430968; ISBN 13: 978-0439430968.

    Mr. Pip, a monkey, gives his actor friend a special gift for his birthday. Grades K–3.

Sierra, Judy. *Counting Crocodiles.* Illustrated by Will Hillenbrand. San Diego: Harcourt Brace, 1997. 32p. ISBN 10: 0152001921; ISBN 13: 9780152001926.

    Because a clever monkey can count, she outwits ten hungry crocodiles that stand between her and a banana tree on another island across the sea. Grades K–3.

Sierra, Judy. *What Time Is It, Mr. Crocodile?* Illustrated by Doug Cushman. Orlando, Fla.: Gulliver Books, 2004. 32p. ISBN 10: 0152164456; ISBN 13: 978-0152164454.

    Mr. Crocodile has a schedule to keep, but the monkeys come and make a mess of his time. Grades K–3.

Slobodkina, Esphyr. *Caps for Sale.* New York: HarperTrophy, 1947. 48p.

    Naughty monkeys steal the peddler's hats when he takes a nap under their tree. (A sound recording is available. Also try *Circus Caps for Sale.*) Grades K–3.

Chimpanzees

Alborough, Jez. *Hug.* Cambridge, Mass.: Candlewick Press, 2001. 32p. ISBN 10: 0763615765; ISBN 13: 978-0763615765.

    There are no hugs for Bobo the chimp until he finds his mother. Grades K–2.

Alborough, Jez. *Tall.* Cambridge, Mass.: Candlewick Press, 2005. 32p. ISBN 10: 0763627844; ISBN 13: 978-0763627843.

    Little Bobo wanders through the forest feeling very small as he has different animals lift him onto their heads, but a tumble brings him back to feeling large, with his mother. Grades K–2.

Alborough, Jez. *Yes.* Cambridge, Mass.: Candlewick Press, 2006. 32p.

    Bobo the chimp doesn't want to go to bed, but he learns how to say yes. Grades K–1.

Anholt, Catherine, and Laurence Anholt. *Chimp and Zee and the Big Storm.* New York: Phyllis Fogelman Books, 2002. 32p. ISBN 10: 0803727003; ISBN 13: 978-0803727007.

    A storm blows Chimp and Zee out of their coconut tree house over the cliffs and into the sea; they are rescued by Mumkey and Papakey. The British authors have created many other Chimp and Zee titles, including *Chimp and Zee, Chimp and Zee's First Words and Pictures, Chimp and Zee's Noisy Book, Happy Birthday Chimp and Zee,* and *Monkey about with Chimp and Zee.* Grades K–2.

Browne, Anthony. *Things I Like.* New York: Knopf, 1989. 32p. ISBN 10: 0394941926; ISBN 13: 978-0394941929.

    A little chimp tells about all of the many day-to-day activities he likes. Grades K–2.

Browne, Anthony. *Willy and Hugh.* New York: Knopf, 1991. 26p. ISBN 10: 0679814469; ISBN 13: 978-0679814467.

    Willy the chimpanzee is lonely until he meets Hugh Jape, a gorilla, in the park. The two become friends when Hugh frightens off a bully, and Willy assures Hugh that a spider is nothing frightening. Grades K–2.

Browne, Anthony. *Willy the Dreamer*. Cambridge, Mass.: Candlewick Press, 1997. 26p. ISBN 10: 0763603783; ISBN 13: 978-0763603786.

Willy dozes in his chair and imagines himself an actor who combines Mary Poppins, Dracula, and Charlie Chaplin; as Elvis; as a ballet dancer; and as a famous writer, surrounded by Sir John Tenniel's Cheshire Cat, Mad Hatter, and other residents of Wonderland. Grades K–2.

Browne, Anthony. *Willy the Whimp*. Cambridge, Mass.: Candlewick Press, 2002. 32p. ISBN 10: 0394870611; ISBN 13: 978-0394870618.

Willy encounters a bullying gang. He finds a book ad and sends away for a muscle-building program. Grades K–3.

Browne, Anthony. *Willy the Wizard*. New York: Knopf, 1995. 32p. ISBN 10: 0679876448; ISBN 13: 978-0679876441.

Willy is given a pair of shoes that he thinks are magic and that somehow allow him to be picked for the soccer team. Grades K–3.

Browne, Anthony. *Willy's Pictures*. Cambridge, Mass.: Candlewick, 2000. 28p. ISBN 10: 0763609625; ISBN 13: 978-0763609627.

Willy becomes a painter with his own copies or renditions of art masterpieces, including *American Gothic*, *The Birth of Venus*, and *Mona Lisa*.

Dickinson, Peter. *Eva*. New York: Delacorte Books for Young Readers, 1989. 219p.

A young girl who has been in an accident wakes up to find that she has been given the body of a chimp. (A sound recording is available.) Grades 4–7.

Durango, Julia. *Cha-Cha Chimps*. Illustrated by Eleanor Taylor. New York: Simon & Schuster, 2006. 32p. ISBN 10: 0689864566.

Mama catches up with five chimps who snuck out of bed to dance their way to the watering hole. Grades K–2.

Hoban, Lillian. *Arthur's Back to School Day*. New York: HarperCollins, 1996. 45p. ISBN 10: 0060249552; ISBN 13: 978-0060249557.

Arthur and his friend accidentally switch lunches and are in for surprises. Grades K–3.

Hoban, Lillian. *Arthur's Birthday Party*. New York: HarperTrophy, 2000. 64p. ISBN 10: 006027798X; ISBN 13: 978-0060277987.

Arthur is having a gymnastics birthday party and wants to be the best, but he may be in for a surprise. Grades K–3.

Hoban, Lillian. *Arthur's Camp-out*. New York: HarperCollins, 1993. 63p. ISBN 10: 0060205253; ISBN 13: 978-0060205256.

Arthur goes on his own overnight field trip in the woods behind his house, but it doesn't go as he planned until he meets up with the girls, who are roasting hot dogs and singing camp songs. (An audio version is available.) Grades K–3.

Hoban, Lillian. *Arthur's Christmas Cookies*. New York: HarperCollins, 1972. 63p. ISBN 10: 0060223677; ISBN 13: 978-0060223670.

Violet lets Arthur use her "Bake-E-Z" oven to make Christmas cookies, but fighting and dropping dough cause the cookies to be less than perfect. (An audio version is available.) Grades K–3.

Hoban, Lillian. *Arthur's Funny Money*. New York: Harper & Row, 1981. 64p. ISBN 10: 006022343X; ISBN 13: 978-0060223434.

Arthur and Violet solve their money problems by going into business together. (An audio version is available.) Grades K–3.

Hoban, Lillian. *Arthur's Great Big Valentine*. New York: Harper & Row, 1981. 64p. ISBN 10: 0060224061; ISBN 13: 978-0060224066.

Arthur and his friend Norman are having a fight, and Arthur won't send a valentine to his friend until he learns that Norman might send him one. Grades K–3.

Hoban, Lillian. *Arthur's Halloween costume: Story and Pictures*. New York: Harper & Row, 1984. 64p. ISBN 10: 0060223871; ISBN 13: 978-0060223878.

Arthur ends up winning the most original costume in school. Grades K–3.

Hoban, Lillian. *Arthur's Honey Bear*. New York: HarperCollins, 1990. 64p. ISBN 10: 0064440338; ISBN 13: 978-0064440332.

Arthur doesn't want to sell his honey bear and puts a high price on him at the yard sale. Who buys the bear? (An audio version is available.) Grades K–3.

Hoban, Lillian. *Arthur's Loose Tooth: Story and Pictures*. New York: Harper & Row, 1985. 63p. ISBN 10: 084466555X; ISBN 13: 978-0844665559.

Violet and the babysitter teach Arthur the meaning of bravery when he loses his tooth. (An audio version is available.) Grades K–3.

Hoban, Lillian. *Arthur's Pen Pal*. Harper & Row, 1976. 62p. ISBN 10: 0060223723; ISBN 13: 978-0060223724.

Arthur thinks his pen pal, Sandy, sounds like much more fun than his sister, Violet. Wait until you find out about Sandy! (An audio version is available.) Grades K–3.

Ives, David. *Monsieur Eek*. New York: HarperCollins, 2001. 179p. ISBN 10: 0060295295; ISBN 13: 978-0060295295.

A chimpanzee who is visiting MacOongafoondsen is put on trial for being a thief and a spy, but wise Emmaline and her friend Young Flurp the Town Fool are determined that justice will be served. Grades 4–6.

Mallat, Kathy. *Mama Love*. New York: Walker, 2004. 24p. ISBN 10: 0802789021; ISBN 13: 978-0802789020.

A little chimp tells how his mother shows her love for him. Grades K–1.

Mundis, Hester. *My Chimp Friday: The Nana Banana Chronicles*. New York: Simon & Schuster Books for Young Readers, 2002. 168p. ISBN 10: 0689838379; ISBN 13: 978-0689838378.

Rachel is dying to know the mystery behind the chimp who is dropped off at the family apartment in the middle of the night. Grades 3–6.

Napoli, Donna, and Eva Furrow. *Bobby the Bold*. Illustrated by Ard Hoyt. New York: Dial Books for Young Readers, 2006. 32p. ISBN 10: 0803729901; ISBN 13: 978-0803729902.

Bobby isn't really a chimp, he is a bonobo, who is befriended by the zookeeper and taught to communicate. Grades K–2.

Ostrow, Kim. *Darwin's Family Tree*. Illustrated by the Thompson Bros. (Wild Thornberry's Series). New York: Simon Spotlight/Nickelodeon, 2001. 32p. ISBN 10: 0613356020; ISBN 13: 978-0613356022.

Eliza and chimp Darwin meet a lemur in Madagascar, and Darwin feels he has met his long-lost cousin. Grades K–3.

Parish, Peggy. *Mr. Adams's Mistake*. Illustrated by Gail Owens. New York: Macmillan, 1982. 61p. ISBN 10: 0027698009; ISBN 13: 9780027698008.

Truant officer Mr. Adams is near-sighted and accidentally takes a chimp to school. Grades 1–4.

Rawls, Wilson. *Summer of the Monkeys*. New York: Bantam Doubleday Dell Books for Young Readers, 1999. 280p. ISBN 10: 0385114508; ISBN 13: 978-0385114509.

In the late 1800s, a fourteen-year-old Ozark mountain boy spends the summer trying to recapture twenty-nine monkeys that escaped from a traveling circus.

Rey, H. A. *Curious George*. New York: Houghton Mifflin, 1941. 64p. ISBN 10: 0395159938; ISBN 13: 9780395159934.

A monkey (chimp) is captured and gets himself into mischief. (Audio and video versions are available.) Grades K–3.

Many titles have been written with George as the main character. The original books by H. A. Rey and Margret Rey are *Curious George* (1941); *Curious George Takes a Job* (1947); *Curious George Rides a Bike* (1952); *Curious George Gets a Medal* (1957); *Curious George Flies a Kite* (1958); *Curious George Learns the Alphabet* (1963); and *Curious George Goes to the Hospital* (1966).

Books based on the television program include *Curious George Goes to the Aquarium* (1984); *Curious George Visits the Zoo* (1985); *Curious George and the Pizza* (1985); *Curious George Plays Baseball* (1986); *Curious George Walks the Pets* (1986); *Curious George at the Airport* (1987); *Curious George and the Dump Truck* (1988); *Curious George Goes Fishing* (1988); *Curious George at the Fire Station* (1988); *Curious George at the Ballet* (1988); *Curious George Goes Sledding* (1988); *Curious George at the Beach* (1988); *Curious George at the Laundromat* (1988); *Curious George Goes to a Restaurant* (1988); *Curious George Goes to the Circus* (1988); *Curious George Visits a Police Station* (1988); *Curious George at the Railroad Station* (1988); *Curious George Goes Hiking* (1988); *Curious George Visits an Amusement Park* (1988); *Curious George Goes to the Dentist* (1989); *Curious George Goes to an Ice Cream Shop* (1989); *Curious George Goes to School* (1989); *Curious George and the Dinosaur* (1989); *Curious George Goes to a Toy Store* (1989); *Curious George Goes Camping* (1990); *Curious George Goes to an Air Show* (1991); and *Curious George Bakes a Cake* (1993).

The style used by the Reys is still being used to by other authors of Curious George titles. Those illustrated by Vipah Interactive include *Curious George Goes to a Chocolate Factory* (1998); *Curious George and the Puppies* (1998); *Curious George Makes Pancakes* (1998); *Curious George Feeds the Animals* (1998); *Curious George Goes to a Movie* (1998); *Curious George and the Hot Air Balloon* (1998); *Curious George in the Snow* (1998); *Curious George's Dream* (1998); *Curious George Goes to the Beach* (1999); *Curious George and the Dump Truck* (1999); *Curious George Goes Camping* (1999); and *Curious George at the Parade* (1999) . Titles illustrated by Martha Weston include: *Curious George Goes to a Costume Party* (2001); *Curious George in the Big City* (2001); *Curious George Takes a Train* (2002); *Curious George Visits a Toy Store* (2002); *Curious George and the Birthday Surprise* (2003); *Curious George Visits the Library* (2003). Books illustrated by Anna Grossnickle Hines include: *Curious George and the Firefighters* (2004); *Curious George's First Day of School* (2005); *Curious George's Dinosaur Discovery* (2006); *Curious George at the Baseball Game* (2006); and *Curious George at the Aquarium* (2007).

Mary O'Keefe Young and Cathy Hapka wrote *Merry Christmas, Curious George* (2006). There are toys, interactive media and games, and other sound and video versions of the stories.

Rorby, Ginny. *Hurt Goes Happy*. New York: Tom Doherty Associates, 2006. 267p. ISBN 10: 0765314428; ISBN 13: 978-0765314420.

Joey, a deaf girl, learns to sign, and Dr. Charles Mansell and his chimp use signs to communicate. Grades 4–7.

Yolen, Jane. *The Boy who Spoke Chimp*. Illustrated by David Wiesner. New York: Knopf, 1981. 120p. ISBN 10: 0394944674; ISBN 13: 978-0394944678.

A boy rescues a chimp from a wrecked van, and they communicate through sign language when they are stranded in a California earthquake. Grades 3–6.

Gorillas

Bornstein, Ruth. *Little Gorilla*. New York: Clarion Books, 1976. 32p. ISBN 10: 0395287731; ISBN 13: 978-0395287736.

Little Gorilla grows and grows with the love of his family and friends. (A sound recording is available.) Grades K–2.

Boston, Lucy Maria. *A Stranger at Green Knowe*. Illustrated by Peter Boston. New York: Harcourt, Brace, 1961. 208p. ISBN 10: 0152025839; ISBN 13: 978-0152025830.

Ping, the Chinese boy who has come to Green Knowe, loves and helps Hanno, the giant gorilla who escapes from the zoo. (Carnegie Award Winner). Grades 3–6.

Browne, Anthony. *Gorilla*. New York: Candlewick Press, 2002. 40p. ISBN 10: 0763618136; ISBN 13: 978-0763618131.

A toy gorilla comes to life on the eve of Hannah's birthday. Grades K–3.

Conaway, Judith. *King Kong*. Written by Delos W. Lovelace and adapted by Judith Conaway. New York: Random 1983. 207p. ISBN 10: 0448439131; ISBN 13: 978-0448439136.

Carl Denham and Ann Darrow journey to Skull Island and discover King Kong. Grades 5–8.

Hazen, Barbara Shook. *The Gorilla Did It*. Illustrated by Ray Cruz. New York: Scholastic Inc., 1974. 32p. ISBN 10: 0689301383; ISBN 13: 978-0689301384.

Amazingly, a gorilla is blamed for waking up a little boy and messing up his room. Grades K–1.

Howe, James. *The Day the Teacher Went Bananas*. Illustrated by Lillian Hoban. New York: Dutton Children's Books, 1984. 32p. ISBN 10: 0525441077; ISBN 13: 978-0525441076.

The classroom teacher turns out to be a gorilla. Grades K–2.

Mauser, Pat Rhoads. *Patti's Pet Gorilla*. Illustrated by Diane Palmisciano. New York: Atheneum, 1987. 45p. ISBN 10: 0689312792; ISBN 13: 978-0689312793.

Patti invents a pet gorilla for show-and-tell, and the children want to meet him. Grades K–3.

Osborne, Mary Pope. *Good Morning, Gorillas*. Illustrated by Sal Murdocca. New York: Random House, 2002. 96p. ISBN 10: 0375806148; ISBN 13: 978-0375806148.

Jack and Annie are sent by the Magic Tree House to Africa, where they meet a huge gorilla. Grades 2–4.

Paulsen, Gary. *Amos Goes Bananas*. New York: Bantam Doubleday Dell Books for Young Readers, 1996. 59p. ISBN 10: 0440410088; ISBN 13: 978-0440410089.

  Because Amos and the gorilla named Lousie can communicate, Dunc thinks that the gorilla can help them solve a crime. Grades 3–5.

Willis, Jeanne. *Gorilla! Gorilla!* Illustrated by Tony Ross. New York: Atheneum Books for Young Readers, 2006. 32p. ISBN 10: 1416914900; ISBN 13: 978-1416914907.

  A mouse is trying to find her baby and is chased by a seemingly fierce gorilla. Grades K–3.

Orangutans

Grindley, Sally. *Little Sibu: An Orangutan Tale*. Illustrated by John Butler. Atlanta, Ga.: Peachtree, 1999. 32p. ISBN 10: 1561451967; ISBN 13: 978-1561451968.

  Seven-year-old Sibu's mother begins to help him go out on his own in the rain forest. Grades K–4.

Tarcher, Mallory. *Keep Your Hands Off My Orangutan!* Mahwah, N.J.: Troll Communications L.L.C., 1997. 96p. ISBN 10: 0816744262; ISBN 13: 978-0816744268.

  One-year-old orangutan Zoey is going to a faraway zoo, but sister Molly gets the feeling that the nasty woman who has come to pick up her sister does not like animals. Grades 2–4.

Folktales about Monkeys

Monkeys appear in many folktales around the world. Stories may be found in single volumes like those listed here, or in collections of tales.

Chen, Debby. *Monkey King Wreaks Havoc in Heaven*. Illustrated by Wenhai Ma. Union City, Calif.: Pan Asian Publications, 2001. 32p. ISBN 10: 1572270683; ISBN 13: 978-1572270688.

  Monkey King tries to prove to the emperor of Heaven that he is a match for the celestial warriors. Grades 1–5.

Cleveland, Rob. *The Clever Monkey: A Folktale from West Africa*. Illustrated by Baird Hoffmire. Atlanta, Ga.: August House Story Cove, 2006. 32p. ISBN 10: 1435207297; ISBN 13: 978-1435207295.

  A clever monkey solves the problem of how to divide cheese between two greedy jungle cats. Grades K–4.

Climo, Shirley. *Monkey Business: Stories from Around the World*. Illustrated by Erik Brooks. New York: H. Holt, 2005. 128p. ISBN 10: 0805063927; ISBN 13: 978-0805063929.

  Thirteen stories of old and new world monkeys are arranged by continent, interspersed with sayings and information about monkeys. Grades K–8.

Diakité, Baba Wagué. *The Hatseller and the Monkeys: A West African Folktale*. New York: Scholastic Press, 1999. 32p. ISBN 10: 0590960695; ISBN 13: 978-0590960694.

  A hat seller falls asleep under a mango tree. Monkeys steal his hats and then shower him with fruit, which he eats, allowing him to find a solution. Grades K–4.

Galdone, Paul. *The Monkey and the Crocodile: A Jataka Tale from India*. New York: Clarion Books, 1997. 32p. ISBN 10: 9990800863; ISBN 13: 978-9990800869.

  Who is trickier than whom in this tale of jungle creatures? Grades K–3.

Galdone, Paul. *The Turtle and the Monkey: A Philippine Tale*. New York: Clarion Books, 1983. 32p. ISBN 10: 0899191452; ISBN 13: 978-0899191454.

Greedy Monkey tries to cheat Turtle out of her bananas. Grades K–5.

Jiang, Ji-li. *The Magical Monkey King: Mischief in Heaven: Classic Chinese Tales*. Illustrated by You-Shan Tang. New York: HarperCollins, 2002. 124p. ISBN 10: 1885008244; ISBN 13: 978-1885008244.

Monkey is a trickster, and the stories dealing with his birth and dealings with the Jade Emperor show him in this way, until he is stopped by the Buddha. Grades 2–6.

McKissack, Pat, and Robert L. McKissack. *Itching and Twitching: A Nigerian Folktale*. Illustrated by Laura Freeman. New York: Scholastic, 2003. 40p. ISBN 10: 0606274456; ISBN 13: 978-0606274456.

Rabbit twitches and Monkey itches; they drive each other crazy at a dinner party. Grades K–4.

McKissack, Patricia, and Robert L. McKissack. *Monkey-Monkey's Trick: Based on an African Folktale*. Illustrated by Paul Meisel. New York: Random House, 1988. 48p. ISBN 10: 0394991737; ISBN 13: 978-0394991733.

How does Monkey-Monkey find out about greedy hyena's mean tricks? Grades K–4.

Metaxas, Eric. *The Monkey People*. Illustrated by Diana Bryan. New York: Simon & Schuster, 1995. 32p. ISBN 10: 0689801912; ISBN 13: 978-0689801914. 32p.

Monkey-Monkey manages to trick Hyena after being tricked himself. (Audio and video recordings are available.) Grades K–4.

Reddy, Kumuda, and John Emory Pruitt. *The Monkey and the Crocodile*. Illustrated by Vasu. Schenectady, N.Y.: Samhita Productions, 1997. 31p. ISBN 10: 1929297084; ISBN 13: 978-1929297085.

Monkey wants to get across the stream and seems to fall for crocodile's scam. Grades 1–3.

San Souci, Robert D. *Pedro and the Monkey*. Illustrated by Michael Hays. New York: Morrow Junior Books, 1996. 28p. ISBN 10: 0688137431; ISBN 13: 978-0688137434.

Pedro shows mercy to a monkey who is caught stealing from his field, and the monkey does him a good turn. Grades K–4.

Shepard, Aaron. *Monkey: A Superhero Tale of China*. Los Angeles: Skyhook Press, 2005. 45p. ISBN 10: 0938497251; ISBN 13: 978-0938497257.

This superhero does his best to outdo all other heroes. Grades K–5.

Van Laan, Nancy. *So Say the Little Monkeys*. Orlando, Fla.: Harcourt, 1998. 64p. ISBN 10: 0689810385; ISBN 13: 978-0689810381.

Monkeys have no home in this rhyming retelling of an Indian rhyming folktale from Brazil. Grades K–5.

Wriggins, Sally Hovey. *White Monkey King: A Chinese Fable*. Illustrated by Ronni Solbert. New York: Pantheon Books, 1977. 113p. ISBN 10: 0394934504; ISBN 13: 978-0394934501.

Monkey is a super power and creates havoc throughout the heavens. Grades 2–6.

Wu, Cheng'en. *Adventures of Monkey King*. Illustrated by Marlys Johnson-Barton. Monterey, Calif.: Victory Press, 1989. 128p. ISBN 10: 0962076511; ISBN 13: 978-0962076510.

Stories of the Monkey King tell all, from his birth to his submission to the Buddha. Grades 3–6.

Published Monkey Paper Dolls

Few monkey paper dolls appear in print, but early issues of *Circus Day* included "Muggins the Monkey" to dress. *The Original Monchhichi Paper Doll Play Book* (New York: Golden, 1983) can be found on Ebay from time to time. It includes the characters, ten outfits, and tree house and playroom settings.

Several printed monkey paper dolls are available.

Rey, H. A., and Kathy Allert. *Curious George Paper Dolls in Full Color.* Mineola, N.Y.: Dover, 1983. 32p. ISBN 10: 0486243869; ISBN 13: 978-0486243863.

> Two views of the character plus 48 outfits allow for many hours of recreating George in his many book roles. Grades K–5.

Sarnat, Marjorie. *Monkey Family Sticker Paper Dolls.* Mineola, N.Y.: Dover, 1998. 4p. ISBN 10: 0486405796; ISBN 13: 978-0486405797

On the Internet, one set can be downloaded and copied from *Chimpanzee Paper Dolls* (http://www.billybear4kids.com/PrimateRescue/PaperDoll/Chimp.html; accessed March 21, 2009).

Lesson Plan:
Monkeys Were Seen Where?

Library Media Skills Objective:

The student will identify the setting of a book or movie and re-create it as a backdrop for a character in the book or movie.

Curriculum (Subject Areas) Objectives:

The activity may be incorporated into a reading/language arts unit on setting or into a drama and art unit focusing on landscape or painting.

Grade Level: 2–5

Resources:

Paper doll handouts

Paper sheets (larger size, about 11-by-14 inches or more)

Books

Paints and pencils

Scissors

Instructional Roles:

The library media specialist or teacher may complete this activity. It will take approximately 1 hour to introduce the activity and prepare the students. Student reading and designing may take 1 to 3 hours, depending on students' ability and the scene selected. Time for discussion will vary but should take about an hour.

Activity and Procedures for Completion:

Display a set of books that are about the same character, such as Curious George or Arthur. Explain that each of the books in the series has the same main character. One of the things besides the plot that distinguishes each book from the others is the setting. Discuss what setting is and how it is related to the plot. Students may help select one of the stories to be shared aloud.

When the story is done, explain that students are going to be stagehands, set directors, and fashion coordinators for a monkey film or a book ad shoot. Each student or student pair will select a book and read it or select a movie and view it. Provide book lists or pull suitable books. Videos or DVDs may be displayed or set up for viewing if students are interested. (Share the movie list with parents so that they can obtain the movies from outside sources if desired. Contact the public library and discuss showings or borrowing.)

After reading the books or viewing the movies, students will discuss the book or movie with the teacher or partner. Next they will design at least one background set for a scene in the book or movie. It must be in the proper scale for the monkey characters in the scene. Discuss scale and provide examples. Students will draw the scene and paint it. They will cut out and color the paper dolls to be shown in the scene. They may use the paper dolls provided or draw and make their own if they are able. It may be useful to set up a few easels and paints in an area for student use during the process. This will allow for discussion.

Students will also make the costumes for the scene or use the costumes provided. When finished, they can use the paper doll to act out or role play the scene. They may also use the scene and doll to discuss what happened in the book. This can become a book report or review prop.

In a group follow-up or discussion about how difficult or easy it was to make the scene, discuss how easy it is to do a scene when the original book is a picture book rather than a novel or folktale with no illustrations. What must one do?

Evaluation:

After selecting and reading a book or movie about a monkey or ape, each student will identify the setting or one of the scenes in the book or movie and re-create it as a backdrop for a paper doll character in the book or movie.

Follow-Up:

The student may design and complete a set for a story or a short drama that can be videotaped.

Paper Dolls: Monkeys

Instructions: Dress the monkey or chimp characters on pages 237 and 240 like some of the many book characters that you have read about. Color and cut out the figures.

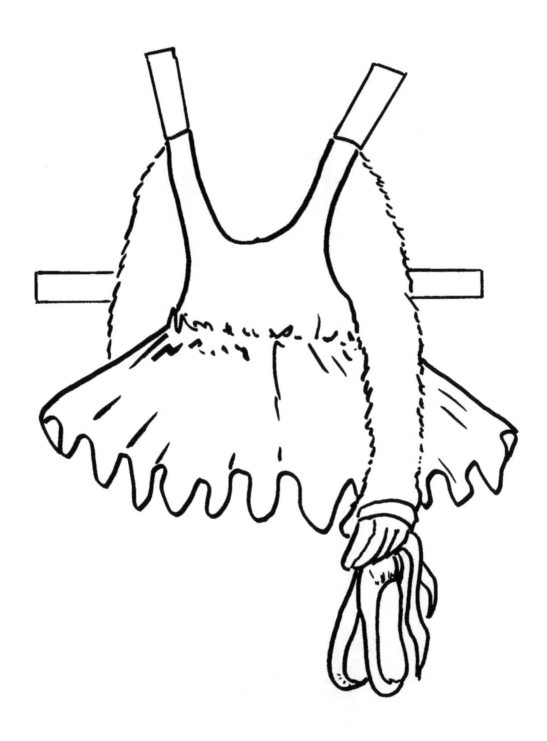

From *Paper Action Figures of the Imagination: Clip, Color and Create* by Paula K. Montgomery.
Santa Barbara, CA: Libraries Unlimited. Copyright © 2009.

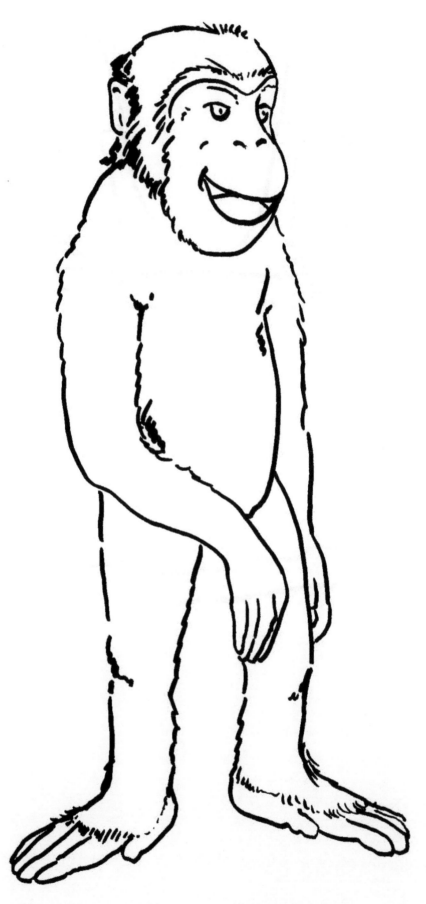

From *Paper Action Figures of the Imagination: Clip, Color and Create* by Paula K. Montgomery.
Santa Barbara, CA: Libraries Unlimited. Copyright © 2009.

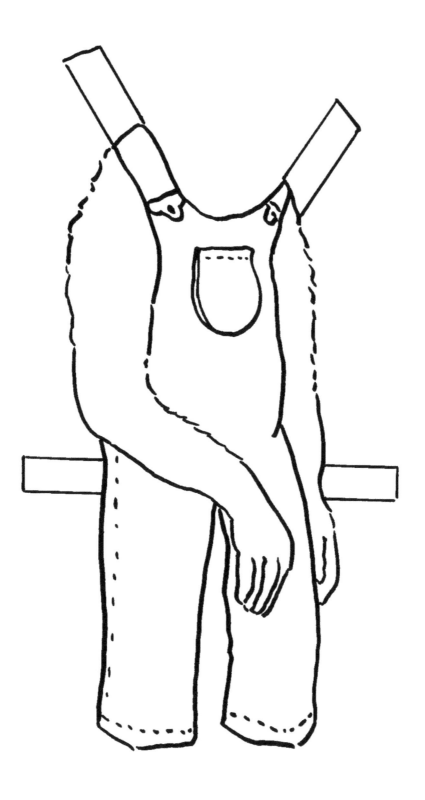

Chapter 13

Those Trickster Rabbits!

Rabbits can be tricky! In fact, storytellers share their secrets about trickster rabbits from all over the world. Brer Rabbit is outwitted by Brer Bear in the southern United States. In the American southwest, rabbit tricks coyote. No one can forget Zomo, the wildly dressed African rabbit who uses his wits to gain wisdom. These folktale rabbits have something in common. They can be tricky, and can be tricked by other animals! Bugs Bunny, Roger Rabbit, and even the Easter Bunny have their wily ways. It doesn't matter; we love them anyway. Rabbits are small, furry creatures with many predators who would love to have them for lunch. People enjoy stories in which small creatures can outwit bigger ones.

Rabbits in Fiction

One might say that books about rabbits have multiplied like—rabbits! For those who want longer reads with many chapters (long eared) there are Deborah Howe's and James Howe's *Bunnicula: A Rabbit-tale Mystery* (Atheneum, 1979); Richard Adams's *Watership Down* (Macmillan, 1972); or Margery Williams' *Velveteen Rabbit; or How Toys Become Real* (Doubleday, 1988). For shorter reads (short eared), usually illustrated, look for versions of short fables such as "The Tortoise and the Hare."

Rabbits: Long-Eared Tricks

Good for a long read!

Adams, Richard. *Watership Down*. New York: Scribner, 1991. 448p. ISBN 10: 068483605X; ISBN 13: 978-0684836058.
     A warren of rabbits must flee from the destruction of their homes because of land development. (Audio and video versions are available.) Grades 5+.

Borgenicht, David. *Brer Rabbit: From the Collected Tales of Joel Chandler Harris*. Illustrated by Don Dailey. Philadelphia: Running Press Kids, 2008. 56p. ISBN 10: 0762432195; ISBN 13: 978-0762432196.
     Seven tales about Brer Rabbit and his fellow animal friends. Grades 3–6.

Carroll, Lewis. *Alice in Wonderland*. Illustrated by Ralph Steadman. Buffalo, N.Y.: Firefly Books, 2003. 132p.

    It begins when Alice falls down a rabbit hole. Grades 3–7.

Doucet, Sharon Arms. *Why Lapin's Ears Are Long and Other Stories of the Louisiana Bayou*. Illustrated by David Catrow. New York: Orchard Books, 1997. 57p. ISBN 10: 0531330419; ISBN 13: 978-0531330418.

    Compere Lapin tricks Cajuns and Creoles. Grades 3–6.

Harris, Joel Chandler. *The Favorite Uncle Remus*. Illustrated by A. B. Frost. Boston: Houghton Mifflin, 1975. 310p. ISBN 10: 0395068002; ISBN 13: 978-0395068007.

    This large collection includes some favorite stories and songs. Grades 4+.

Howe, Deborah, and James Howe. *Bunnicula: A Rabbit-tale of Mystery*. Illustrated by Alan Daniel. New York: Atheneum, 1979. 112p. ISBN 10: 0689307004; ISBN 13: 978-0689307003.

    Chester the Cat tries to warn the family that their baby rabbit is a vampire. (An audio recording is available.) Grades 2–4.

    Other titles are *Bunnicula Strikes Again!*; *The Celery Stalks at Midnight*; *Howliday Inn*; *Return to Howliday Inn*; *Rabbit-Cadabra!*; *Scared Silly*; *The Vampire Bunny*; *Creepy-Crawley Birthday*; *It Came from Beneath the Bed*; *The Fright Before Christmas*; and *Bunnicula Meets Edgar Allan Crow*.) Grades 2–5.

Jaquith, Priscilla. *Bo Rabbit Smart for True: Folktales from the Gullah*. Illustrated by Ed Young. New York: Philomel Books, 1981. 55p. ISBN 10: 0399226680; ISBN 13: 978-0399226687.

    These four stories were collected from Savannah, Georgia. Grades 3–6.

Lester, Julius. *Further Tales of Uncle Remus: The Misadventures of Brer Rabbit, Brer Fox, Brer Wolf, the Doodang, and Other Creatures*. Illustrated by Jerry Pinkney. New York: Dial, 1990. 148p. ISBN 10: 0803706103; ISBN 13: 978-0803706101.

    Brer Rabbit usually shows his clever side with his friends in these tales. Grades 2–5.

Lester, Julius. *The Last Tales of Uncle Remus*. Illustrated by Jerry Pinkney. New York: Dial, 1994. 156p. ISBN 10: 0803713037; ISBN 13: 978-0803713031.

    These are the final stories about Brer Rabbit and his misdeeds, as well as other stories from Uncle Remus. Grades 3–7.

Lester, Julius. *More Tales of Uncle Remus: Further Adventures of Brer Rabbit, His Friends, Enemies, and Others*. Illustrated by Jerry Pinkney. New York: Dial, 1988. 143p. ISBN 10: 0803704194; ISBN 13: 978-0803704190.

    Don't miss the stories about how the rabbit is tricked in some of these tales. Grades 3–7.

Lester, Julius. *The Tales of Uncle Remus and the Adventures of Brer Rabbit*. Illustrated by Jerry Pinkney. New York: Dial, 1987. 151p. ISBN 10: 080370271X; ISBN 13: 978-0803702714.

    The author retells the stories of Joel Chandler Harris, retaining much of the original flavor. Grades 3–7.

Mayo, Gretchen. *Here Comes Tricky Rabbit!* New York: Puffin, 1994. 75p. ISBN 10: 0140377808; ISBN 13: 978-0140377804.

    These tales are credited to Native American tellers from specific tribes. Grades 2–5.

Potter, Beatrix. *The Tale of Peter Rabbit: The Commemorative Edition*. New York: Warne, 2006. 80p. ISBN-10: 0723258732; ISBN 13: 978-0723258735.

> There are many editions of this volume, originally published in 1902. Movies, dolls and stuffed toys, sound and video recordings, musicals, and more have been produced. Peter manages to disobey his mother's warnings and still escape with only the loss of his jacket. (See http://www.peterrabbit.com/ and <http://wiredforbooks.org/kids/beatrix/p1.htm; accessed August 30, 2008.) Grades K–4.

Ross, Gayle. *How Rabbit Tricked Otter and Other Cherokee Trickster Stories*. Illustrated by Mury Jacob. New York: HarperCollins, 1994. 79p. ISBN 10: 0060212853; ISBN 13: 978-0060212858.

> Fifteen tales relate Rabbit's adventures as he plots and schemes against others. Grades 2–5.

Weiss, Jaqueline Shachter. *Young Brer Rabbit, and Other Trickster Tales from the Americas*. Illustrated by Clinton Arrowood. Owings Mills, Md.: Stemmer House, 1985. 65p. ISBN 10: 0880450371; ISBN 13: 978-0880450379.

> These fifteen tales about Brer Rabbit come from Central and South America and the Caribbean. (An audio recording is available.)

Williams, Margery. *The Velveteen Rabbit, or How toys Become Real*. Illustrated by William Nicholson. New York: Avon Books, 1922. 40p.

> This is the original version. Many versions with other illustrators have been published. Audio and video versions are available, and there are soft toys on the market. A boy is given a soft rabbit that is snubbed at first in favor of other toys. It becomes the boy's companion while the boy is sick with scarlet fever. When the boy recovers, the toy is considered germ-ridden and is sent to be burned, but something happens to change that. (Full text is available at http://digital. library.upenn.edu/women/williams/rabbit/rabbit.html; accessed August 30, 2008). Grades 1–6.

Rabbits: Short-Eared Tricks

Davies, Mark. *Brer Rabbit*. Illustrated by Arthur Suydam. New York: Kipling Press, 1988. 32p. ISBN 10: 0943718163; ISBN 13: 978-0943718163.

> Four stories are adapted from the Uncle Remus stories. Grades 1–4.

Duvall, Deborah L. *How Rabbit Lost His Tail: A Traditional Cherokee Legend*. (The Grandmother Stories, vol. 3). Illustrated by Murv Jacob. Albuquerque: University of New Mexico Press, 2003. 32p. ISBN-10: 082633010X; ISBN 13: 978-0826330109.

Han, Suzanne Crowder. *The Rabbit's Escape = Kusa Ilsaenghan Tokki*. Illustrated by Yumi Heo. New York: H. Holt, 1995. 32p. ISBN 10: 0805026754; ISBN 13: 978-0805026757.

> The dragon King wants rabbit's liver, but rabbit is too tricky. (English and Korean). Grades K–3.

Han, Suzanne Crowder. *The Rabbit's Judgment*. Illustrated by Yumi Heo. New York: H. Holt, 1994. 32p. ISBN 10: 0805026746; ISBN 13: 978-0805026740.

> In a tricky situation, the reader learns whether tiger is allowed to eat a man after being freed from a trap. (English and Korean). Grades K–3.

Hayward, Linda. *Hello, House!* Illustrated by Lynn Munsinger. New York: Random House, 1988. 32p. ISBN 10: 0394988647; ISBN 13: 978-0394988641.

> Brer Wolf hides in Brer Rabbit's house in order to catch him. Grades K–2.

Ho, Minfong, and Saphan Ros. *Brother Rabbit: A Cambodian Tale*. Illustrated by Jennifer Hewitson. New York: Lothrop, Lee & Shepard, 1997. 32p. ISBN 10: 0688125530; ISBN 13: 978-0688125530.

Brother Rabbit tricks a crocodile, two elephants, and a woman. Grades K–4.

Johnston, Tony. *The Tale of Rabbit and Coyote*. Illustrated by Tomie dePaola. New York: Putnam, 1994. 32p. ISBN 10: 0399222588; ISBN 13: 978-0399222580.

Rabbit manages to fool coyote in Southwestern twists. (An audio version is available.) Grades 1–4.

Mayo, Gretchen. *Big Trouble for Tricky Rabbit!* New York: Walker, 1994. 37p. ISBN 10: 0802782760; ISBN 13: 978-0802782762.

This collection contains many stories about trickster Native American rabbits.

McDermott, Gerald. *Zomo the Rabbit: A Trickster Tale from West Africa*. San Diego: Harcourt Brace Jovanovich, 1992. 32p. ISBN 10: 0152010106; ISBN 13: 978-0152010102.

Zomo the trickster wants wisdom. Grades K–4.

Mora, Francisco X. *The Tiger and the Rabbit: A Puerto Rican Tale*. New York: Children's Press, 1991. 32p. ISBN 10: 051607105X; ISBN 13: 978-0516071053.

How does tiny rabbit outwit tiger? (An audio version is available.) Grades K–3.

Parks, Van Dyke, and Malcome Jones. *Jump!: The Adventures of Brer Rabbit*. Illustrated by Barry Moser. San Diego: Harcourt Brace, 1997. 40p. ISBN 10: 0606115269; ISBN 13: 978-0606115261.

Brer Rabbit tries his best to outsmart the other animals in these five stories.

Other titles are *Jump Again! More Adventures of Brer Rabbit* and *Jump on Over! The Adventures of Brer Rabbit and His Family*. Grades 1–5.

Shute, Linda. *Rabbit Wishes: A Cuban Folktale*. New York: Lothrop, Lee & Shepard, 1994. 32p. ISBN 10: 0688131808; ISBN 13: 978-0688131807.

This folktale shares why the rabbit has long ears. Grades 1–5.

Stevens, Janet. *Tops and Bottoms*. San Diego: Harcourt Brace, 1995. 36p. ISBN 10: 0152928510; ISBN 13: 978-0152928513.

Rabbit makes a deal with a lazy bear. (Caldecott Honor Book). Grades K–4.

Tchin. *Rabbit's Wish for Snow: A Native American*. Illustrated by Carolyn Ewing. New York: Scholastic, 1997. 32p. ISBN 10: 0613086090; ISBN 13: 978-0613086097.

This is the Native American version of why rabbits look the way they do. Grades 1–4.

Tompert, Ann. *How Rabbit Lost His Tail*. Illustrated by Jacqueline Chwast. Boston: Houghton Mifflin, 1997. 32p. ISBN 10: 0395822815; ISBN 13: 978-0395822814.

In this Seneca tribal tale, Rabbit follows Squirrel's advice in order to get himself out of a tree, Grades K–4.

Rather than provide a list of all the books available on rabbits, students might be given the names of authors and illustrators who have been "taken" with this character. For those who want to help younger children find the authors arranged alphabetically on shelves, try a quiet bunny hop relay race. Write the name of each "rabbit writing" author on a 3-by-5-inch card. Shuffle the cards and place them on a small table or chair equidistant from two or more teams of five to seven children each. This is a quiet and quick relay. The object is for each team to send the players one at a time to hop to the stack of cards, pick up one card, and find the name of the author on the appropriate shelf. The library media special begins the game with the words, "Hop, Bunny, Hop!" The first player from each relay team hops to the cards, takes one, reads the name, and hops to the correct spot by a shelf. The player holds the card above his or her head like wiggling rabbit ears. The library media specialist will be checking to see that the finds are correct and nod so the player can hop back to the team and the next player can hop to the card stack. The team that finishes first wins.

Here are some additional authors for consideration:

Verna Aardema	Margaret Read MacDonald
Jim Arnosky	David McPhail
Marc Tolan Brown	Deanna Medearis
Margaret Wise Brown	Clare Turlay Newberry
Dick Bruna	Dav Pilkey
Nancy Carlson	Andrea Posner
Stephen Cosgrove	Tim Preston
Tomie dePaola	Cynthia Rylant
Kate DiCamillo	Richard Scarry
Marjorie Flack	Paul Stewart
Candace Fleming	Cyndy Szekeres
Kevin Henkes	Nancy Tafuri
Du Bose Heyward	Elizabeth Wallace
Donna Kosow	Nancy Wallace
Kathryn Lasky	Rick Walton
Theo LeSieg	Rosemary Wells
Wendy Lewison	Harriet Ziefert
Christine Loomis	

Published Rabbit Paper Dolls

Rabbits fare well in the paper doll arena. There are several choices on the market; these are some of the more popular ones.

Allert, Kathy. *Peter Rabbit Paper Dolls in Full Color*. Mineola, N.Y.: Dover, 1982. ISBN 10: 0486242811; ISBN 13: 978-0486242811.

> Peter Rabbit has twenty-eight full-color wardrobes to display and cut out, including policeman, archaeologist, football player, rock star, backpacker, magician, and space bunny.

Hopper Family Paper Dolls—http://www.chinaberry.com/prod.cfm/pgc/30000/sbc/30014/inv/10295 (accessed March 21, 2009).

> These replicas of Victorian dolls include Mama Rose, Papa Fred, and the children, Bobby and Bunny Hopper, each with about four outfits.

King, Elizabeth. *Bunny Rabbit Family Sticker Paper Dolls*. Mineola, N.Y.: Dover, 1990. ISBN 10: 048626503X; ISBN 13: 978-0486265032.

> Each member of the Bunny Rabbit Family has five to seven lovely peel-and-apply, reusable outfits.

Lesson Plan:
Who Will Bunny Be Today?

Library Media Skills Objective:

The student will identify physical characteristics such as clothing and how they help form a given literary figure.

Curriculum (Subject Areas) Objectives:

This activity may be incorporated into a study in reading and language arts on characterization.

Grade Level: 1–3

Resources:

>   Paper doll handouts
>
>   Rabbit books in which rabbits are wearing clothes
>
>   Scissors
>
>   Crayons, paints, and colored markers

Instructional Roles:

The teacher or library media specialist may introduce and complete this activity. The introduction will take 30–45 minutes. Students' selecting books, completing their paper dolls, and retelling the story will take 2 hours.

Activity and Procedures for Completion:

Do clothes make the man? Or bunny? Select a rabbit book such as *Peter Rabbit* for a read-aloud. After reading the story, show a paper doll of Peter Rabbit and add his jacket. This jacket can be shown without a button and a button can be put on during the discussion of the story. The discussion of the story should highlight the role of the jacket and its importance to Peter and the tale. Change Peter's outfit to a sweater, fireman's coat, T-shirt, or some other kind of clothing. Discuss how it would change the story or not fit at all. Begin to discuss how clothes make a difference in stories and in behavior.

Following the discussion, students will have a chance to find books about rabbits. Explain that they should look for books in which the rabbits seem to act like people and wear clothes. They may think about the rabbits in the book in the following ways:

>   Are they dressed or not?
>
>   How are they dressed? (Regional type of outfit, historic period, stylishly?)
>
>   Are they dressed for characteristics expressed in the story?

Their assignment is to read the book and then dress a paper doll in the way the character in the book is. When the students have finished, they will share the story and the character in the book. They should be prepared to explain why the costume was important to the story.

Evaluation:

The student will select a book with a rabbit as the main character, identify physical characteristics such as clothing, re-create the character in an outfit as a paper doll, and tell how the outfit contributed to the character in the story.

Follow-Up:

The students may redesign outfits for a rabbit character in a story they have read.

Paper Dolls: Rabbits

Meet Gen, short for Genevieve, and Eric (on the next page). They are generic rabbits who love to dress in costumes. They could be rabbits or hares in many different regions or countries. When they get dressed up, they can be the characters who wear those particular clothes.

Instructions: Read about rabbit folk characters in the books listed on the following pages and decide how you would like your rabbits to look. Then color their clothes and cut them out. Help Gen and Eric pretend to be other rabbit characters.

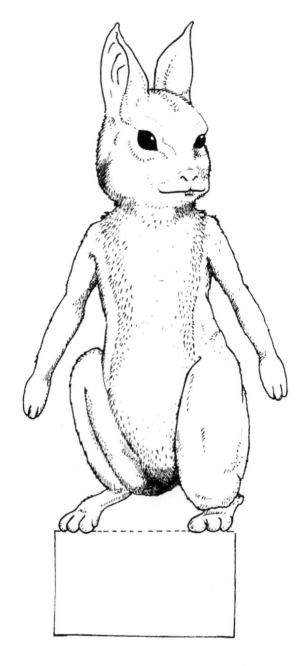

Jacket with waistcoat: When Eric puts on the jacket and waistcoat with the pocket watch, he becomes the white rabbit who keeps running to Alice. He is always late! Read Lewis Carroll's *Alice's Adventures in Wonderland* (Morrow, 1992) to find out about White Rabbit and all the other characters Alice meets when she falls down the rabbit hole.

Jacket: Put Peter Rabbit's blue jacket on him and feel the relief of escaping from Mr. Macgregor's garden with only a missing button. Read about Peter and his other bunny friends. You can find many books, audio recordings, video recordings, and CD-ROM programs about Peter Rabbit if you look for the author's name, Beatrix Potter, in library catalogs. The Peter Rabbit Internet site is http://www.peterrabbit.com/ (accessed March 21, 2009).

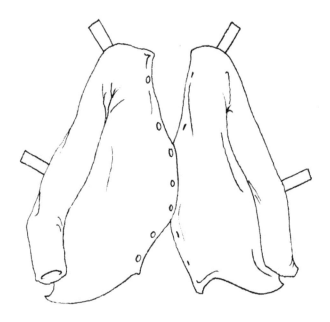

Dress: The dress makes Gen feel like Harriet, a character created by Nancy Carlson. *Harriet's Recital* is Gen's favorite story about Harriet and Loudmouth George. Gen can also be a bunny in Kathryn Lasky's *Lunch Bunnies,* illustrated by Marilin Hafner (Little, 1996); Tomie dePaola's *Too Many Bunnies* (Troll, 1997); or Du Bose Heyward's *Country Bunny and the Little Gold Shoes,* illustrated by Marjory Flack (Houghton Mifflin, 1949).

Tie: The tie can serve as P. J. Funnybunny's bow tie or Honeybunny's hair bow. Marilyn Sadler writes many stories like *Honey Bunny Funnybunny,* illustrated by Roger Bollen (Random House, 1997).

Award of Laurel Leaves: When the laurel leaf wreath is slipped around the neck, a rabbit feels like a winner! It's the way Harold must have felt when he became a champion in Bill Peet's *Huge Harold* (Houghton Mifflin, 1974).

Native American blanket: When Eric is wrapped in the blanket, he can feel right at home in front of the Native American fires, in Virginia Grossman's *Ten Little Rabbits,* illustrated by Sylvia Long (Chronicle, 1991).

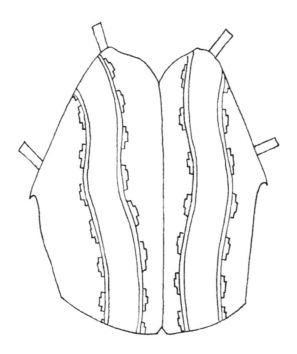

Overalls: Many rabbits wear overalls. A favorite is Max. Rosemary Wells writes about Max and his sister Ruby in many adventures. Read *Bunny Money* (Dial, 1997), *Max's Chocolate Chicken* (Dial, 1989), or *Max and Ruby's Midas: Another Greek Myth* (Dial, 1995).

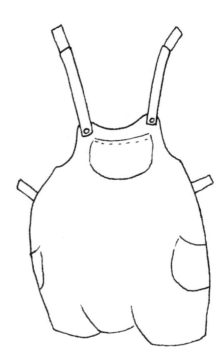

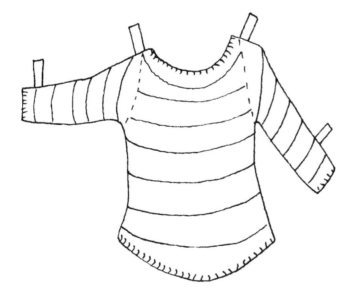

Sweater/shirt: Put on the shirt on the paper doll and color it like Solomon's, the rabbit who can change into a nail in William Steig's *Solomon the Rusty Nail* (Farrar, 1987). Make your own clothes for Gen and Eric. Change the shirt to Zomo's wild shirt, with geometric designs! Add suspenders to the pants for another version of Brer Rabbit.

Pants: The dumbest bunny is baby bunny in Sue Denim's *The Dumb Bunnies*, illustrated by Dave Pilkey (Scholastic, 1994). There are many other dumb bunny books in which rabbit might feel zany! Use pants and a shirt to dress the doll as Brer Rabbit in Van Dyke Parks' and Malcolm Jones's *Jump! The Adventures of Brer Rabbit*, illustrated by Barry Moser.

Chapter 14

Santa Claus by Many Names

Kris Kringle
St. Nickolas
Santa Claus
Christkindel
Belsnickel St. Aclaus
St. Iclaus
Santeclaw

St. Claus
Knecht Ruprecht
Sancte Klaas
Sinterklaas
Father Christmas
San Nicola

He is Saint Nicholas in Turkey, Sinter Claes in the Netherlands, Father Christmas in England, Weihnachtsmann in Germany, and San Nicola in Italy. These are only a few of the names by which the generous gift giver is known. Santa Claus is known in countries around the world by many names.

The First Santa

According to legend, Santa Claus's history reaches back to the third century AD in what is now Turkey. A boy was born to parents who were afraid that they would never have a child. They named this miracle baby Nicholas, which means "hero of the people" in Greek. Nicholas was twelve when his parents died, but this did not make him selfish or bitter. He became even more devoted to his religion and gave much of the money he inherited from his parents to the poor.

In one story about Nicholas's generosity, he anonymously tossed a bag of gold in the window of a poor man's home for his daughter's dowry. In those days, a young girl took a certain amount of property or money with her as a gift to her husband when they were married. The man had two other daughters who could not marry and would be forced into a life of poverty without a dowry. Nicholas secretly left gold in their stockings, which were drying by the fireplace overnight. News of Nicholas's kindness spread to other countries, and he became known and celebrated in many different ways.

Santa in the Netherlands

In the Netherlands, St. Nicholas became known as Sinter Claes. Churches started a tradition of placing three wooden shoes beside the front door of each church, filled with coins collected for the poor. This tradition was based on the three bags of gold Nicholas had given to the three poor maidens. Soon Dutch children began to leave their empty wooden shoes by the fireside on St. Nicholas Eve, December 5, in hopes that the kindly saint would fill them with small gifts.

Santa in Sweden

In Sweden the gift giver was known as Jultomten. He came with gifts on December 24, Christmas Eve. Jultomten was an elf who wore a red cap and had a long white beard. He road in a sleigh pulled by a Julbock (Christmas goat). Children would leave a plate of porridge for Jultomten and some carrots and hay for Julbock.

Santa in England

In England, Father Christmas, a gigantic figure dressed in a red robe lined with fur and wearing a crown of holly, ivy, or mistletoe, was the gift giver.

Santa in the United States

In the New World the European settlers shared their traditions, and soon the gift giver in America became known as Santa Claus. American Clement C. Moore wrote a poem for his children in 1823, "A Visit from Saint Nicholas." He described the jolly old elf in detail and named the eight reindeer. (It was not until 1939 that Rudolph came along.) Today we know Clement C. Moore's poem as "The Night before Christmas." Each year versions of the poem are published in print and on the Internet. Artists and cartoonists such as Arthur Rackham, John Steven Gurney, Tomie dePaola, Tasha Tudor, Jan Brett, Hilary Knight, Denys Cazet, Mary Engelbreit, Susan Perl, Gennady Spirin, Mercer Mayer, James Marshall, Lisbeth Zwerger, Ruth Sanderson, Leonard Weisgard, Jim Davis, James Rice, and many more have depicted Santa Claus. You'll have a wide selection from which to choose based on students' preferences.

Authors have also portrayed Santa in many ways. Hundreds of stories and books feature the yuletide character. Listing them all would require an entire book. These "biographical" versions focusing on Santa's character and life may be helpful for use with children or as adult reference.

Baum, Frank L. *The Life and Adventures of Santa Claus*. New York: Mass Market Paperback, 1994. 151p. ISBN 10: 0805038221; ISBN 13: 978-0805038224.

> This holiday classic was written by the author of *The Wizard of Oz* and relates the tale of a baby raised in an enchanted forest who grew up to be a maker of toys. Also available at www. gutenberg.org/etext/520 (accessed March 22, 2009).

Bonnice, Sherry. *Christmas and Santa Claus Folklore.* Broomall, Pa.: Mason Crest, 2003. 101p. ISBN-10: 1590843304; ISBN-13: 978-1590843307.

The book describes both the religious and secular customs of Christmas, including the story of Jesus's birth and the origins of Santa.

Church, Francis Pharcellus. *Yes, Virginia, There Is a Santa Claus.* Illustrated by Thomas Nast. New York: Delacorte Press, 1992. 32p. ISBN-10: 038530854X; ISBN 13: 978-0385308540.

Based on a letter sent to the *New York Sun* in 1897, the text is the editorial response explaining that Santa Claus does exist.

Crichton, Robin. *Who Is Santa Claus? The True Story Behind a Living legend.* Illustrated by Margaret Nisbet. Edinburgh: Canongate, 1987. 104 p. ISBN 10: 0862411602; ISBN 13: 978-0862411602.

This true story is based on the movie *The Curious Case of Santa Claus.*

Federer, William J. *There Really Is a Santa Claus: The History of Saint Nicholas and Christmas Holiday Traditions.* St. Louis, Mo.: Ameriserch, 2002. 341p. ISBN 10: 0965355748; ISBN 13: 978-0965355742.

This thorough history discusses Santa Claus across the world and provides historical perspective.

Gibbons, Gail. *Santa Who?* New York: Morrow Junior Books, 1999. 28p. ISBN 10: 0688155286; ISBN 13: 978-0688155285.

Traces Santa's history.

Giblin, James Cross. *The Truth about Santa Claus.* New York: Thomas Y. Crowell, 1985. 86p. ISBN 10: 0690044844; ISBN 13: 978-0690044843.

Santa Claus has been known by many names throughout the centuries. This book traces his history.

Jeffers, H. Paul. *Legends of Santa Claus.* New York: Lerner, 2001. 112p. ISBN 10: 0822549832; ISBN 13: 9780822549833.

Learn about Santa throughout history in paintings and songs.

Jones, E. Willis. *The Santa Claus Book.* New York: Walker, 1976. 127p. ISBN 10: 0802705413; ISBN 13: 978-0802705419.

The biography of the miracle worker explains how the early deeds were expanded into the mythical being he has become today.

Kalman, Bobbie. *Santa Claus from A to Z.* Illustrated by Barbara Bedell. New York: Crabtree, 2000. 32p. ISBN 10: 0613223284. ISBN 13: 978-0613223287.

Each letter of the alphabet provides some new fact about Santa.

Litak, Robert E. *101 Questions about Santa Claus.* St. Paul, Minn.: Blue Sky Marketing, 1998. 112p. ISBN 10: 0911493239; ISBN 13: 978-0911493238.

Everything you wanted to know about Santa as told by Santa himself.

Mayer, Marianna. *The Real Santa Claus: Legends of Saint Nicholas.* New York: Phyllis Fogelman Books, 2001. 32p. ISBN 10: 9780803726246; ISBN 13: 978-0803726246.

Historical overview of St. Nicholas through painting masterpieces provides a greater understanding of his role in various parts of the world.

Myra, Harold. *Santa, Are You for Real?* Illustrated by Dwight Walles. New York: T. Nelson, 1977. 32p. ISBN 10: 1400306299; ISBN 13: 9781400306299.
   Children discover Santa's origins in St. Nicolas.

Ouwendijk, George. *Santas from around the World.* New York: Chelsea House, 1997. 64p. ISBN 10: 0791046788; ISBN 13: 978-0791046784.
   Find out how Santa is perceived in cultures and countries around the world.

Paton, Kathleen. *Santa.* New York: Smithmark Publishers, 1998. 72p. ISBN 10: 0765108682; ISBN 13: 978-0765108685.
   The book includes many interesting facts about the commercialization of Santa.

Siefker, Phyllis. *Santa Claus, Last of the Wild Men: The Origins and Evolution of Saint Nicholas, Spanning 50,000 Years.* Jefferson, N.C.: McFarland, 1997. 219p. ISBN 10: 0786402466; ISBN 13: 978-0786402465.
   The history includes rare and old illustrations of St. Nick.

Stiegemeyer, Julie. *Saint Nicholas: The Real Story of the Christmas Legend.* Illustrated by Chris Ellison. St. Louis, Mo.: Concordia, 2003. 28p. ISBN-10: 0758603762; ISBN-13: 978-0758603760.
   The biography features the story of the Bishop of Myra, who became known as Santa.

Tolkien, J. R. R. *The Father Christmas Letters.* Boston: Houghton Mifflin, 1999. 160p. ISBN 10: 061800937X; ISBN 13: 978-0618009374.
   J. R. R. Tolkien, author of *The Lord of the Rings* and other tales, wrote letters to his children in response to their letters to Father Christmas. The letters span more than twenty years and tell many tales of the North Pole and events that took place there.

Tompert, Ann. *Saint Nicholas.* Illustrated by Michael Garland. Honesdale, Pa.: Boyds Mills Press, 2000. 32p. ISBN 10: 156397844X; ISBN 13: 978-1563978449.
   Read the biography of Saint Nicholas, believed to be the origin of the story of Santa.

Santa's Story in Video

Santa appears in many videos and television specials. This details the life of Santa in a documentary style.

Santa Claus. New York: A&E Television Networks, 2005. 50 min.
   Originally produced for *Biography*, the program follows the life of Santa.

Published Santa Paper Dolls

For those wanting to purchase paper dolls, the most commonly available product in many bookstores is by Tom Tierney's *Santa Claus Paper Dolls in Full Color* (Mineola, N.Y.: Dover, 1983. 32p. ISBN 10: 0486245462; ISBN 13: 978-0486245461).

Paper doll figures can be found on the Internet. Examples include the following:

   Christmas "Friends"—http://www.makingfriends.com/friends/f+christmas.htm (accessed March 22, 2009).

The Paper Doll Café The Legend of Santa Claus—http://www.paperdollcafe.dk/Santa2005/santa2005.htm (accessed March 22, 2009).

Santa Paper Doll—http://www.zoofun4u.com/christmas/games/santa_paperdoll/santa_Paper_Doll.htm (accessed March 22, 2009).

Santa Paper Doll PC Game—http://www.billybear4kids.com/paperdoll/SantaPaperDoll.html (accessed March 22, 2009).

Santa Paper Doll (Stitcherey) by Irene's Designs—<http://www.stitcherymall.com/display1.cfm?set_id=137 (accessed March 22, 2009).

Santa Paper Doll Set. Peachy Keen Stamps—http://peachykeenstamps.com/mm5/merchant.mvc?Screen=PROD&Store_Code=SpinAGrin&Product_Code=PK-315&Category_Code=xmas (accessed March 22, 2009).

Lesson Plan:
Off to the Rooftops!

Library Media Skills Objective:

The student will locate countries on a world map.

The student will locate illustrations and information in a reference source.

Curriculum (Subject Areas) Objectives:

This activity may be part of a reading/language arts lesson on letter writing or a geography lesson on map reading and countries of the world.

Grade Level: 2–5

Resources:

Maps of the world

Reference collection (countries of the world, costume, Santa)

Santa paper doll handouts

Crayons and paints

Scissors

Paper and pencils

Envelopes

Instructional Roles:

The teacher may introduce and execute the lesson with assistance from the library media specialist, who may help students find references for making their appropriate Santa costume. The introduction will take about 45 minutes. Allow an hour or more for students to select and research their Santas and locations. Preparation of the costumes and writing letters will take approximately an hour. The entire swapping of Santa will occur over a month's time as students pass the Santa along.

Activity and Procedures for Completion:

In this activity, the teacher and library media specialist will use the model of Flat Stanley with a Santa substitute.

Most students have heard of Flat Stanley. He is the character who was created by the author Jeff Brown. Stanley Lambchop is an ordinary kid who is flattened one night when a bulletin board over his bed falls on him. It could have been a disaster, but Stanley finds the positive. He can slide under doors and hide in places that people with mass can't get into. What turns out to be the biggest advantage is that he can be folded and mailed, thus making travel easy. Jeff Brown created a number of adventures for Stanley.

Brown, Jeff. *Flat Stanley*. Illustrated by Steve Björkman. New York: HarperTrophy, 2003. 57p.

Brown, Jeff. *Flat Stanley*. Illustrated by Scott Nash. New York: HarperTrophy, 2003. 64p.

Brown, Jeff. *Flat Stanley*. Illustrated by Tomi Ungerer. New York: HarperCollins, 1964. 48p. (Original).

Brown, Jeff. *Invisible Stanley*. Illustrated by Scott Nash. New York: HarperTrophy, 2003.

Brown, Jeff. *Stanley and the Magic Lamp*. Illustrated by Macky Pamintuan. New York: HarperTrophy, 2003. 112p.

Brown, Jeff. *Stanley, Flat Again!* Illustrated by Scott Nash. New York: HarperTrophy, 2003. 87p.

Brown, Jeff. *Stanley in Space*. Illustrated by Philippe Dupasquier. New York: Metheun, 1990. 64p.

Brown, Jeff. *Stanley's Christmas Adventures*. Illustrated by Scott Nash. 96p.

Brown, Jeff. *Flat Stanley*. Read by Daniel Pinkwater. Harper Children's Audio, 2003. 2 cassettes. 3 hrs. Includes *Flat Stanley*, *Invisible Stanley*, *Stanley in Space*, and *Stanley, Flat Again!*

For more information see:

"Flat Stanley" (http://en.wikipedia.org/wiki/Flat_Stanley; accessed March 22, 2009).

Flat Stanley Goes Hi-Tech—http://www.chesterfield.k12.sc.us/Jefferson%20Elementary/FlatStanley/stanleypage_3.htm (accessed March 22, 2009).

In the education world, Flat Stanley has become a boon to reading. A third-grade teacher in London, Ontario, Dale Hubert, invited other teachers to help him begin the Flat Stanley Project. The teachers could host flat visitors to their classroom and be part of a pen-pal exchange. Students make Flat Stanleys and write in journals that can be sent to other places. When Flat Stanley gets to the place, he is treated like a guest, and the journal is completed and returned to the sender. His journey is plotted on a map. The official site provides a list for signing up, templates for making Stanley, and many other curriculum activities. See *The Official Flat Stanley Project* (http://www.flatstanleyproject.com/; accessed August 30, 2008).

For more information about activities and results from more than 6,000 schools that have participated in the project, these articles may be useful:

Bacque, Peter. "Bundle Up, *Flat Stanley*: It's Cold in Antarctica: A Navy Lieutenant from Va. Brings Him along on a Mission." *Richmond Times-Dispatch*, February 2, 2008.

Bunge, Kayla. " 'Flat Stanley' Embarks on Global Adventure." *Janesville Gazette,* February 2, 2008.

"Enlist *Flat Stanley* to Help Students Learn Geography." *Curriculum Review* 41, no. 9 (May 2002): 7–9.

Hoewisch, Allison. "Creating Well-Rounded Curriculum with Flat Stanley. A School-University Project." *Reading Teacher* 55, no. 2 (October 2001): 154–169.

Johnston, Robert C. "Around the World—In No time flat." *Education Week* 23, no. 41 (June 2004): 35–37.

Johnston, Robert C. "Paper Trail". *Teacher Magazine* 16, no. 3 (November/December 2004): 20–23.

Osterheldt, Jenee. "Stanley Is Just Flat-out Popular." *The Kansas City Star,* May 3, 2008.

In this paper doll project, the teacher introduces the lessons by sharing *Flat Stanley*. Read aloud parts of the book or all of it over a few days after lunch. Follow up with a discussion of the book and the advantages of being flat, as paper dolls are. Explain that students will have a chance to do some mailing projects of their own. Introduce the Santa paper dolls. Students will be working in pairs. Each pair will have a Santa paper doll. The pair will sign up with the teacher in secret for a place in the world for the Santa t visit. The teacher will maintain the master list so that no pairs are going to the same country. The list will also help keep the places as secret as possible.

Each pair will research the country Santa will be visiting. The teacher may identify what specific items the class is to investigate. For example, a long list of food, customs, or dress, or one of two things. Students will work in the library media center to find out more about the place of interest. The pair will prepare journal entries about the place. There should be enough information in the journal entry for the next group to know where it is. The pair must also identify the costume for Santa in the country being visited. Paper dolls will be colored and the costume decorated with crayons or paint and mixed media (beads, fur, feathers, etc.) if desired.

The teacher may set up a bulletin board with a large world map on it. Each student pair should have a folder "mail box" by the bulletin board. These may be made from old large mailing envelopes. Students may decorate their mail folders. Each student pair should also decide on a mail folder address. When students have finished, they will be ready to write a short letter about their Santa and the place where he is. The letter should be written in proper form. The teacher should review or introduce this format. The teacher may write the mail folder addresses on small pieces of paper for a drawing. Each student pair will draw an address from the "hat" so they can address the letter and envelope.

Each pair will fold their letter, journal pages, Santa, and costume, and place them in the envelope with the return name and address. On a specific day, the teacher may serve as mail deliverer and collect the envelopes. After the mail is delivered, the student pairs may read and examine what they have received. After they have read the letters, they will identify where the Santa came from and locate it on the world map. Next they will add to the journal and tell about their own place, add a costume from their country, and write a letter in return. This process may be repeated as time allows.

Review map location skills and post pins on small flags on the map to show the countries and locations the Santas are visiting.

Evaluation:

Each student will work as part of a pair to locate information about a country, find out about the costume for the Santa visiting that country, and use the information to write a journal entry and prepare a paper doll costume. Each student will locate at least two countries on a world map.

Follow-Up:

Expand the project to an exchange between classes.

Paper Dolls:
Dress Your Own Santa!

Instructions: Read more about Santa and decide how you would like to illustrate him. Color the figures and cut them out. Use them for decorations.

Belgium

Sweden

Germany

Russia

You will find hundreds of picture and fiction books, audiotapes, and videotapes in which Santa appears. Look for him in your local library or library media center. Find the subject SANTA CLAUS. How many stories are waiting for you to read?

Chapter 15

Who Guards the Sheep?

How long have there been shepherds and flocks of sheep? An old profession, sheepherding or shepherding probably began about 6,000 years ago in Asia Minor. Both the meat and wool of the sheep were prized and became necessary for families' survival. The practice spread. Because sheep need to graze, someone had to watch over them when they moved from pasture to pasture. The job of the shepherd was to keep watch over the sheep, keep the flock together, and protect the flock from wolves and other predators. The shepherd sold the sheep for shearing and, later, for butchering. This job could be lonely, because the shepherd had to stay with the animals. Sometimes shepherds would band together and merge their herds so they could have company and help with responsibilities. Sheep were marked so they would know their own.

Sheep grazed on land that was not usually as good for farming. Early shepherds could be found in Greece, Israel, and Jordan, and in the Carpathian Mountains, Scotland. Today large sheep ranches are found in New Zealand and Australia, parts of the United States like Wyoming and Montana, and Africa. In many of these areas, wolves have almost been eradicated, and so there is less need for shepherds. Sheep are left alone in the fields.

Stories about shepherds guarding and caring for their sheep have been told for hundreds of years. Many of our stories are found as fables. One of the most famous tellers of fables was Aesop. Scholars believe that Aesop was born a Greek slave sometime during the sixth century BC. Some say he was owned by two masters and was finally given his freedom. As a freeman, he was an adviser to King Croesus of Lydia. He met his death at Delphi.

Implicit or Explicit: You Judge the Lesson

A fable is usually a very short tale that often features animals that behave like human beings. The tale is told to teach a moral or a lesson. Sometimes the moral or lesson of a fable is stated at the end. It is explicit. The following fables that include sheep or shepherds do not have the lesson written at the end. Their lesson is implicit. Challenge children to understand the lessons and match them with the fable.

The Wolf and the Lamb

Wolf met a lamb that had wandered from the flock. Wolf was hungry and wanted to eat Lamb, but he wanted Lamb to think that it was a fine idea to be eaten by Wolf.

Wolf said to Lamb, "You insulted me the last time we met." But Lamb replied, "I have never met you before."

Then Wolf said, "You are eating grass in my pasture." But Lamb replied, "I have not eaten any grass yet."

The Wolf said, "You drank water from my well." Lamb replied, "Oh no! I still drink my mother's milk."

Wolf was angry and grabbed Lamb and ate him up, saying, "I am still going to eat you, even if you disagree with everything I say."

The Wolf in Sheep's Clothing

Wolf was hungry. He dressed himself in a sheepskin and went out into the pasture with the sheep. The shepherd was fooled by the wolf's costume. The shepherd decided to kill one of the sheep for food. He caught Wolf dressed in a sheep costume and killed him instantly.

The Shepherd Boy Who Cried Wolf

A young shepherd boy who tended his sheep near a forest was bored and lonely. He wanted excitement, so he rushed to the village and called, "Wolf! Wolf!" The villagers grabbed their sticks and pitchforks and ran out to help the shepherd boy. They stayed with the boy for a while, which pleased the shepherd boy, but no wolf came. The boy tried the same thing the next day. The villagers came again, but again there was no wolf. The next day, a wolf came out of the forest and began to chase the sheep. The shepherd boy ran toward the village, calling, "Wolf! Wolf!" The villagers had been fooled twice and did not believe the boy. The wolf ate up many of the shepherd boy's sheep.

The Wolf and the Shepherd

Wolf followed Shepherd and his flock for many days. Shepherd was very watchful, but Wolf never tried to hurt the sheep. When Shepherd saw that Wolf made no move to grab his sheep, he let down his guard. One day he had to go into the village and he left the flock with Wolf. Now Wolf saw his chance and gobbled up half the flock.

The Pig, the Sheep, and the Goat

Pig, Goat, and Sheep were left together in a fold. Shepherd came out and grabbed Pig. Pig squealed and squealed while he tried to get away. Sheep and Goat complained, "Stop that racket. Shepherd grabs us, too." Pig cried, "When he grabs you it is for your wool and milk. When he grabs me, it is for my life."

Answers

"The Wolf and the Lamb" lesson: A bully or tyrant can always find a reason for his or her actions.

"The Wolf in Sheep's Clothing" lesson: It does not pay to pretend to be what you are not.

"The Shepherd Boy Who Cried Wolf" lesson: A liar is not believed, even when telling the truth.

"The Wolf and the Shepherd" lesson: You can't change the nature of a wolf.

"The Pig, the Sheep, and the Goat" lesson: It is easy to criticize others when you are not in their situation.

There are hundreds of books that retell the stories of Aesop. The following list represents the range that can be found. Favorites abound.

Aesop: Five Centuries of Illustrated Fables. New York: New York Graphic Society, 1964. 95p. ISBN 10: 0870990292: ISBN 13: 9780870990298.

The Aesop for Children: A Classic Collection of Children's Fables. Illustrated by Milo Winter. New York: Barnes & Noble, 2005. 112p. ISBN 10: 1566192927; ISBN 13: 978-1566192927

Aesop's Fables. Retold by Fiona Black. Illustrated by Richard Bernal. Kansas City, Mo.: Andrews and McMeel, 1991. 32p. ISBN 10: 0836249143; ISBN 13: 978-0836249149.

Aesop's Fables. Selected and illustrated by Michael Hague. New York: Holt, Rinehart & Winston, 1985. 27p. ISBN-10: 0805063153; ISBN: 9780805063158.

Aesop's Fables. Illustrated by Jerry Pinkney. San Francisco: Chronicle Books, 2000. 96p. ISBN 10: 1587170000; ISBN 13: 978-1587170003.

Aesop's Fables. Illustrated by Arthur Rackham. New York: Barnes & Noble, 2005. 269p. ISBN: 1593083300; ISBN 13: 9781593083304.

Aesop's Fables. Retold by Werner Thuswaldner. Translated by Anthea Bell. Illustrated by Gisela Durr. New York: North-South Books,1994. 32p. ISBN 10: 0517169878; ISBN 13: 9780517169872.

Aesop's Fables. Illustrated by Lisbeth Zwerger. New York: North-South Books, 2006. 26 p. ISBN-10: 0735820686; ISBN-13: 978-0735820685.

Aesop's Fables: Retold in Verse by Tom Paxton. Illustrated by Robert Rayevsky, New York: Morrow Junior Books, 1988. 40p. ISBN 10: 0688073603; ISBN 13: 9780688073602.

Animal Fables from Aesop. Adapted and illustrated by Barbara McClintock. Boston: D. R. Godine, 2000. 48p. ISBN 10: 0879239131; ISBN 13: 978-0879239138

Anno's Aesop: A Book of Fables. New York: Orchard Books, 1989. 63p. ISBN 10: 0531083748; ISBN 13: 9780531083741.

The Boy Who Cried Wolf: A Retelling of Aesop's Fable. Retold by Eric Blair. Illustrated by Dianne Silverman. Minneapolis, Minn.: Picture Window Books, 2004. 24p. ISBN 10: 140480319X; ISBN 13: 9781404803190.

The Caldecott Aesop: Twenty Fables: A Facsimile of the 1883 Edition. Illustrated by Randolph Caldecott. New York: Doubleday, 1978. 79p. ISBN 10: 0385126549; ISBN 13: 9780385126540.

Fables from Aesop. Adapted and illustrated by Tom Lynch. New York: Viking, 2002. 32p. ISBN 10: 0670889482; ISBN 13: 978-0670889488.

Fables from Aesop. Retold by James Reeves. Illustrated by Maurice Wilson. London: Bedrick/Blackie, 1985. 123p. ISBN 10: 0872260275; ISBN 13: 978-0872260276.

The Illustrated Book of Aesop's Fables. Illustrated by Germano Ovani, Simona Bucan, Daniela Pellegrini, and Manuela Cenci. Hauppauge, NY: Barron's, 2005. 128p. ISBN-10: 0764159305; ISBN-13: 978-0764159305.

The McElderry Book of Aesop's Fables. Adapted by Michael Morpurgo. Illustrated by Emma Chichester Clark. New York: Margaret K. McElderry Books, 2005. 96p. ISBN 10: 1416902902; ISBN 13: 9781416902904.

The Wolf in Sheep's Clothing: A Retelling of Aesop's Fable. Retold by Mark White. Illustrated by Sara Rojo. Minneapolis, Minn.: Picture Window Books, 2004. 24p. ISBN 10: 1404802207; ISBN 13: 978-1404802209.

The Wolf in Sheep's Clothing and Other Fables from Aesop. Illustrated by Gavin Bishop. Denver: Shortland Publications, 2000. 24p. ISBN 10: 0790119668; ISBN 13: 978-0790119663

The Wolf in Sheep's Clothing: A Tale about Appearances. Retold by Susan Kueffner. Illustrated by Artful Doodlers. Pleasantville, N.Y.: Reader's Digest Young Families, 2006. 32p. ISBN 10: 1599390868; ISBN 13: 9781599390864

Fractured Fairy Tales

Levine, Gail Carson. *Betsy Who Cried Wolf.* Illustrated by Scott Nash. New York: HarperCollins, 2002. 34p. ISBN 10: 0060287632; ISBN 13: 978-0060287634.
    After graduating from Shepherd School and taking the shepherd's oath, eight-year-old Betsy goes off to guard her sheep and meets up with a hungry wolf named Zimmo. Grades 2–5.

Audio Versions—Just for the Voices!

Aesop's Fables. Read by Boris Karloff. New York: Caedmon, 1989/1967.

The Children's Aesop. Read by Stephanie Calmenson. Soundelux Audio Publishing, 1992. 60 min.

Fables from Aesop. Read by Ennis Rees. New Rochelle, N.Y.: Spoken Arts, 1967. 80 min.

Video Versions

Aesop's Fables, I. Universal City, Calif.: MCA Home Video, 1986. 30 min.

Aesop's Fables, II. Universal city, Calif.: MCA Home video, 1986. 30 min.

The Boy Who Cried Wolf. Pine Plains, N.Y.: Live Oak, 1992. 13 min.

The Wolf and the Lamb and The Boy Who Cried Wolf. New York: Golden Book Video, 1986. 25 min.

Internet

Aesop's Fables—http://www.aesops-fables.org.uk/ (accessed March 22, 2009).

Sheep and Shepherds in Folklore and Fiction around the World

Those living in the city may have a stereotypic or iconic view of shepherds. Images from religion and folk stories mingle with a few images on travel programs of shepherds with their staffs, long cloaks, and perhaps faithful sheep dogs. Other names for this job are herder, mutton puncher, and sheepherder. One need only look on the Internet for sample job descriptions:

Job Title: Sheepherder

Salary: $775.00–$800.00 Monthly

Location: Wellington, Utah

Description: Tends flock of sheep on range or pasture; moves sheep from grazing area to grazing area to prevent over-grazing; checks grazing areas for poisonous plants; rounds up strays with trained dogs; keeps track of animals and checks count to prevent loss; and docks and shears animals.

Open Date: 09/24/2009

Education: None

Shifts: Day

Terms: Full

Days Off: 0

Openings: 1

Sheepherders can be found in many parts of the world today who have these very responsibilities. Sheepherders are found in the Basque area of Spain, Greece, Mongolia, Iraq, Iran, Jordan, Israel, New Zealand and Australia, and the American Southwest, including on the Navajo reservation. One can find evidence of the Basque and Peruvian shepherds who came to the Southwest and left arborglyphs, dendroglyphs, or aspen art in what is now Great Basin National Park, Nevada (http://www.nps.gov/grba/historyculture/basque-sheepherder-aspen-carvings.htm; accessed June 30, 2008).

Books and films set in various countries give some idea of the sheepherding life.

Europe

England

Kennard, David. *The Dogs of Windcutter Down*. New York: St. Martin's Press/Macmillan, 2007. 288p. ISBN 10: 0312362005; ISBN 13: 978-0312362003.

> David worries about how to save his way of life as a sheepherder, and his dogs prove to be saviors. (An audio version is available.) Grades 6+.

Kennard, David. *A Shepherd's Watch: Through the Seasons with One Man and His Dogs*. New York: St. Martin's Press, 2005. 192p. ISBN: 0312332661; ISBN 13: 9780312332662.

> The author paints a picture of the difficulty of being a shepherd of 850 sheep in North Devon. Grades 6+.

Mist: The Tale of a Sheepdog Puppy. Written, directed, and edited by Richard Overall. Woodland Hills, Calif.: Distributed by Allumination FilmWorks, 2008. 75 min.

> Mist is born on the Borough Farm in North Devon, and it seems that she dreams of being a sheep dog from the moment she opens her eyes. Grades 4+.

Snyder, Zilpha Keatley. *The Changing Maze*. Illustrated by Charles Mikolaycak. New York: Macmillan, 1985. 32p. ISBN-10: 0689716184; ISBN-13: 978-0689716188.

> A shepherd boy faces an evil wizard to save his lamb. Grades 1–4.

Year of the Working Sheep Dog. Contender Entertainment Group, 2002. 85 min.

> Narrated by Christopher Timothy from BBC TV's *All Creatures Great and Small*, this story tells of the hard-working dogs that help the shepherd. "There is no good flock without a good shepherd, and there is no good shepherd without good dogs." Grades 5+.

France

Jennings, Patrick. *The Wolving Time*. New York: Scholastic Press, 2003. 197p. ISBN 10: 0439395550; ISBN 13: 978-0439395557.

> In sixteenth-century France, thirteen-year-old Laszlo Emberek tends his werewolf parents' flock. Laszlo is enamored with Muno, an orphaned Basque girl whose parents were executed as witches, and learns that she has seen his mother as she changed. He worries if she can keep the secret. Grades 5–8.

Greece

Hoyt, Lenny. *Goatherd and the Shepherdess: A Tale from Ancient Greece*. Illustrated by Lloyd Bloom. New York: Dial Books Young Readers, 1995. 32p. ISBN 10: 0803713525; ISBN 13: 978-7777047445.

> In this retelling of a Greek legend, a baby is found, adopted, and named Cloe. She becomes a shepherdess. In her youth she develops a friendship with a goatherd, Daphnis. A young cowherd, Dorcon, vies with Daphnis for Cloe, but gives his life for the two when pirates abduct Cloe. Grades 2–5.

Italy

Guarnieri, Paolo. *A Boy Named Giotto*. Illustrated by Bimba Landmann. New York: Farrar, Straus & Giroux, 1999. 32p. ISBN 10: 0374309310; ISBN 13: 978-0374309312.

> Giotto is not a very good shepherd, because he spends his time sketching instead of minding the sheep. He becomes the protégé of Florence, Italy's Cimabue (1266–1337). Grades 2–5.

Scotland

Shepherd on the Rocks. Written by Paul Adam. Directed by Bob Keen. Salt Lake City, Utah: BWE Video, 1999. 97 min.

Originally broadcast on television as part of the *Wonderworks series*, the story tells how a Scottish shepherd, Tam Ferrier, fights to preserve his sheep and livelihood and keep developers out. Grades 3–7.

North America

Mexico

Aardema, Verna. *Borreguita and the Coyote: A Tale from Ayutla, Mexico*. Illustrated by Petra Mathers. New York: Knopf, 1991. 32 p. ISBN 10: 0679909214; ISBN 13: 978-0679909217.

A lamb uses her brain to keep the coyote from eating her. Grades K–2.

United States—Southwest

Baylor, Byrd. *Coyote Cry*. Illustrated by Symeon Shimin. New York: Lothrop, Lee & Shepard, 1972. 39p. ISBN 10: 0688516246; ISBN 13: 978-0688516246.

A young shepherd learns a lesson when one of his collie's pups is stolen by a coyote. Grades 1–4.

Eversole, Robyn Harbert. *Red Berry Wool*. Illustrated by Tim Coffey. Morton Grove, Ill.: Albert Whitman, 1999. 32p. ISBN 10: 0807506540; ISBN 13: 978-0807506547.

Lalo the lamb loves the bright wool sweater that his shepherd wears and wants one, too, but he can't seem to figure out how to wash, spin, and dye his own wool. (Note: The setting could be any number of places.) Grades K–3.

Franklin, Kristin L. *The Shepherd Boy*. Illustrated by Jill Kastner. New York: Macmillan, 1994. 32p. ISBN 10: 068931809X; ISBN 13: 978-0689318092.

A Navajo boy and his two dogs go out to rescue a lost sheep before nightfall. Grades K–4.

Patent, Dorothy Hinshaw. *Maggie, a Sheep Dog*. Photographed by William Muñoz. New York: Dodd, Mead, 1986. 47p. ISBN 10: 0396086179; ISBN 13: 978-0396086178.

Maggie, a Hungarian sheep dog known as a Kuvasz, works with Ralph to protect the sheep on a Montana ranch. Grades 2–4.

Perrine, Mary. *Nannabah's Friend*. Illustrated by Leonard Weisgard. Boston: Houghton Mifflin, 1989. 23p. ISBN 10, 0395520207. ISBN 13: 978-0395520208.

A lonely young Navajo shepherd girl makes dolls to keep her company while she tends the sheep. Grades K–3.

Schaefer, Jack. *Old Ramon*. Illustrated by Harold West. Boston: Houghton Mifflin, 1960. 112p. ISBN 10: 0395070872; ISBN 13: 978-0395070871.

Old Ramon is the wise old shepherd who teaches a young boy how to care for a flock of sheep in the Mojave Desert, as well as some more intrinsic ideals. (An audio recording is available.) (Newbery Honor Book). Grades 3–6.

Thomson, Peggy. *Katie Henio: Navajo Sheepherder*. Photographed by Paul Conklin. New York: Dutton, 1995. 64p. ISBN 10: 0525651608; ISBN 13: 978-0525651604.

> Katie Henio is a Navajo sheepherder and weaver on the Ramah Navajo Reservation in New Mexico, where she tends 150 sheep with her horse, Dakota, and her dog, Ma'ii. Grades K–5.

Tripp, Valerie. *Josefina's Song*. Illustrated by Jean-Paul Tibbles. (American Girl Series). Middleton, Wis.: Pleasant Company Publications, 2001. 48p. ISBN 10: 1584852720; ISBN 13: 978-1584852728.

> When Josephina's father has an accident on the way up into the New Mexican Mountains to help an elderly shepherd, Josephina proves herself, in this story set in the early 1800s. Grades 2–5.

Urbigkit, Cat. *A Young Shepherd*. Honesdale, Pa.: Boyds Mills Press, 2006. 32p. ISBN 10: 1590783646; ISBN 13: 978-1590783641.

> Cass is a twelve-year-old shepherd who shares his daily tasks on a ranch in Wyoming. Grades K–4.

West Africa

Nigeria

Bryan, Ashley. *The Story of Lightning and Thunder, a West African Tale*. New York: Aladdin Paperbacks, 1999. 28p. ISBN 10: 0613121597; ISBN 13: 978-0613121590.

> Mother sheep Ma Sheep Thunder and her impulsive son, Ram Lightning, persuade their friend Rain to shower the earth with water for thirsty crops. However, the mother sheep and her son are forced to leave their earthly home because of troubles Ram causes. Grades K–4.

Middle East

Ben-Ezer, Ehud. *Hosni, the Dreamer*. Illustated by Uri Shulevitz. New York: Farrar, Straus & Giroux, 1997. 32p. ISBN 10: 0374333408 ISBN 13: 9780374333409.

> Hosni the shepherd spends his dinar and changes his life. Grades 2–5.

Brown, Margaret Wise. *Little Lost Lamb*. Illustrated by Leonard Weisgard. Garden City, N.Y.: Doubleday, 1945. 40p. ISBN 10: 0385077505; ISBN 13: 978-0385077507.

> A shepherd boy climbs the highest dark mountain peak to find his lost lamb. Grades K–3.

Calhoun, Mary. *A Shepherd's Gift*. Illustrated by Raul Colon. New York: HarperCollins, 2001. 32p. ISBN 10: 0688151760 ISBN 13: 9780688151768.

> A shepherd looks for his sheep and finds Mary, Joseph, and the baby Jesus. Grades K–2.

Flinn, Lisa, and Barbara Younger. *The Christmas Garland*. Illustrated by Lucy Corvino. Nashville, Tenn.: Ideals Children's Books, 2003. 32p. ISBN-10: 0824954602; ISBN-13: 978-0824954604.

> The shepherd's daughter gives her garland to Mary after seeing the baby Jesus. Grades K–3.

Mills, Claudia. *One Small Lost Sheep*. Illustrated by Walter Lyon Krudop. New York: Farrar, Straus & Giroux, 1997. 32p. ISBN10: 0374356491. ISBN13: 9780374356491.

> Benjamin looks for his sheep, Kivsa, who leads him to the babe born in Bethlehem on Christmas eve. Grades K–2.

Scheidl, Gerda Marie. *Four Candles for Simon: A Christmas Story*. Illustrated by Marcus Pfister. New York: North-South Books, 1987. 25p. ISBN-10: 1558580654 ISBN-13: 978-1558580657.

> A nine-year-old shepherd searches for his lost lamb and comes upon a baby born in a stable manager. Grades K–3.

Tharlet, Eve. *Simon and the Holy Night*. Saxonville, Mass.: Picture Book Studio, 1991. 32p. ISBN 10: 0887081851; ISBN 13: 978-0887081859.

> A young shepherd witnesses the events of the birth of Jesus. Grades K–3.

General Books about Shepherds

Ada, Alma Flor. *Jordi's Star*. Illustrated by Susan Gaber. New York : Putnam, 1996. 32p. ISBN 10: 039-9228322 ISBN 13: 9780399228322.

> Jordi thinks a star seen reflected on the water of a pond is in the water and tries to make the star feel at home. Grades K–3.

Gantschev, Ivan. *Moon Lake*. New York: North-South Books, 1996. 32p. ISBN 10: 1558585990. ISBN 13: 978-1558585997.

> A shepherd boy finds a lake encrusted with silver, gold, and precious gems when looking for his lost sheep. Grades K–3.

Lewis, Kim. *The Shepherd Boy*. New York: Four Winds Press, 1990. 26p. ISBN 10: 0744517621; ISBN 13: 978-0744517620.

> James wants to be a shepherd just like his father, but he isn't old enough yet.

Shepherds and Sheep as Symbols in Art, Literature, and Religion

The ubiquitous sheep can be found throughout the pages of art and religious books. Perhaps because shepherding is such an old profession and sheep are the main part of many people's diets worldwide, the shepherd, sheep, and lamb are symbols of caretaking, watchfulness, protection, and following. Other religions include the idea of the shepherd. For example, Lord Krishna was a shepherd, as was Islam's Prophet Muhammad.

Published Shepherd Paper Dolls

The shepherd as a paper doll is part of religious literature. Two Web sites where dolls may be found are:

> *King David: The Shepherd and the Prince*—http://www.paperdolls.com/dolls/kingdavid01.htm (accessed March 22, 2009).

> *Shepherd Paper Doll*—http://www.paperdali.com/dalis.html (accessed March 22, 2009).

Lesson Plan:
Which Shepherd Are You?

Library Media Skills Objective:

The student will use clues from resources to locate places on maps.

Curriculum (subject areas) Objectives:

The activity may be incorporated into a geography unit or a set of units on multicultural topics featuring people's work in various parts of the world.

Grade Level: 2–4

Resources:

> Paper doll handouts
>
> Crayons, paints, and scissors
>
> Geography reference sources
>
> Maps

Instructional Roles:

The classroom teacher may introduce and monitor student progress. The library media specialist may help students research sheep and shepherds. The introduction will take about 45 minutes. Students will work with the library media specialist and on their own for 2 or more hours. The teacher will use an hour or more on follow-up and discussion.

Activity and Procedures for Completion:

In this lesson, the teacher may wish to introduce or review jobs that people have now compared to jobs in the past. Select examples might be used along with pictures. For example, pictures of Basque shepherds in the Southwest might be used to show how shepherds came to the United States and continued to do the jobs that they knew. Share pictures of shepherds in other parts of the world. Ask students to make comparisons between the kinds of sheep or goats herded. Compare the differences in dress. Discuss what customs the shepherds might have had. Read aloud a story or stories about shepherds. Aesop's fables might be shared for student practice in explaining the lessons to be learned. Follow up with a discussion of why shepherds might have figured so prominently in the stories.

Students will have an opportunity to learn more about shepherds around the world. Explain that they will be playing "Stump the Jury: Which Shepherd Are You? Which sheep are you guarding or herding?" In order to prepare for the game, the students will read about a shepherd in another part of the world. Then they will select that shepherd or another and research what breed of sheep the shepherd might be herding. They will also research costumes from that part of the world and identify what the shepherd might be wearing. This may be expanded to food, stories, and music if time permits. The

From Paper Action Figures of the Imagination: Clip, Color and Create by Paula K. Montgomery.
Santa Barbara, CA: Libraries Unlimited. Copyright © 2009.

students will find a picture of the sheep breed and prepare paper dolls complete with appropriate costumes.

Students should meet with the library media specialist either as a class for an overview of resources available or in small groups to review sources and strategies for research. Students should come prepared with an area where they think shepherds might exist. Or, the library media specialist may want to show them statistical information about sheepherding today and in the past. Students might also look at art books to find pictures of shepherds.

The library media specialist and teacher may introduce students to Web sites and nonfiction books about sheep that provide information about the origins of different breeds of sheep. Examples of Web sites that may be helpful are:

> *Breeds of Livestock—Sheep Breeds*—http://www.ansi.okstate.edu/breeds/sheep/ (accessed March 22, 2009).

> *Sheep 101—Breeds of Sheep A–Z*—http://www.sheep101.info/breeds.html (accessed March 22, 2009).

Each student may look for a sheep breed and locate pictures of shepherds, farmers, and people from that area. When they have collected their information, students may prepare paper dolls in appropriate costumes. Paper dolls should be colored and displayed. The students may print a copy of the sheep to display behind the paper doll or cut out a picture in the correct size to place with the paper doll, as if it were one of the herd. Each paper doll should then be matched to a place on the world map to show origin or locale. The teacher may review map skills for finding locations on a large world map. Ask students to display their dolls. Gather the class and have them play "Stump the Jury." In one version, three of the students display their paper dolls in front of a panel of four or five other students. A description or picture of the sheep is shown. Each of the three students holds his or her paper doll for scrutiny. The jury must decide which paper doll matches the sheep. Ask students to follow up with a written account of what they learned from their research.

Evaluation:

Each student will read at least one story about shepherds; will identify an area of the world and a type of sheep originating in that part of the world, and will make and dress a paper doll as a shepherd from that part of the world to accompany that sheep, based on information from reference sources. Each student will locate the part of the world from which the shepherd and sheep come.

Follow-Up:

The students may try other variation with the paper dolls. For example, the pictures of different sheep breeds might be displayed and students might use clues from descriptions to match dressed paper dolls to the right sheep.

Paper Dolls:
Shepherds

Instructions: Make your own shepherd. Color the dolls and outfits. Cut them out. Which characters or shepherds do they represent?

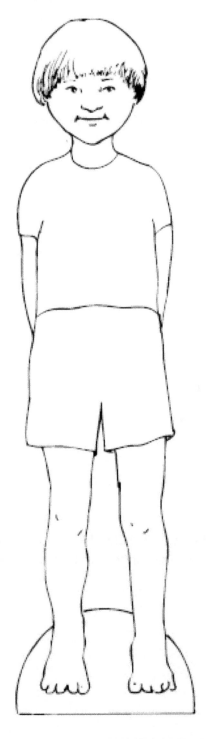 

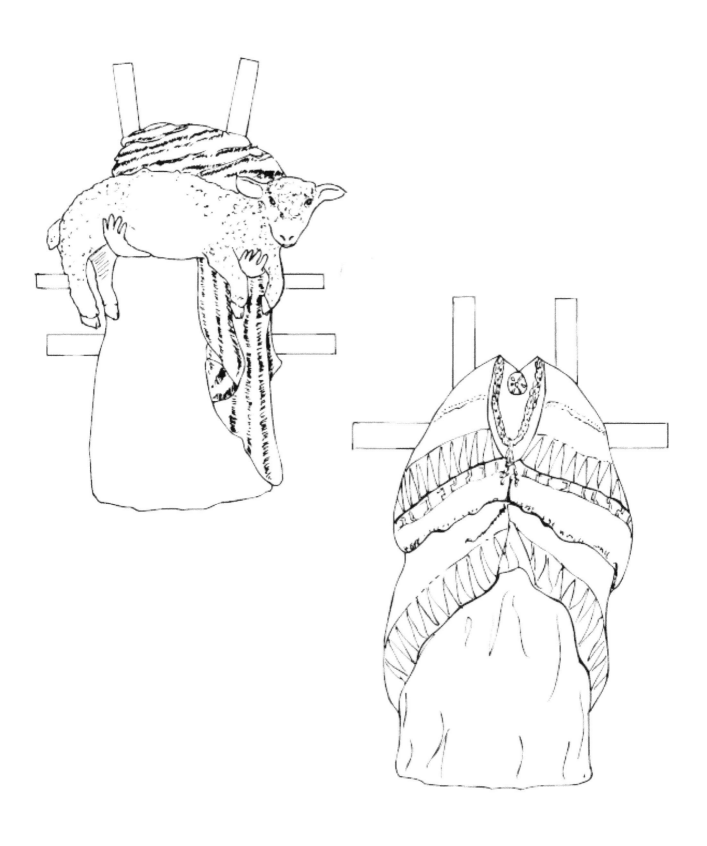

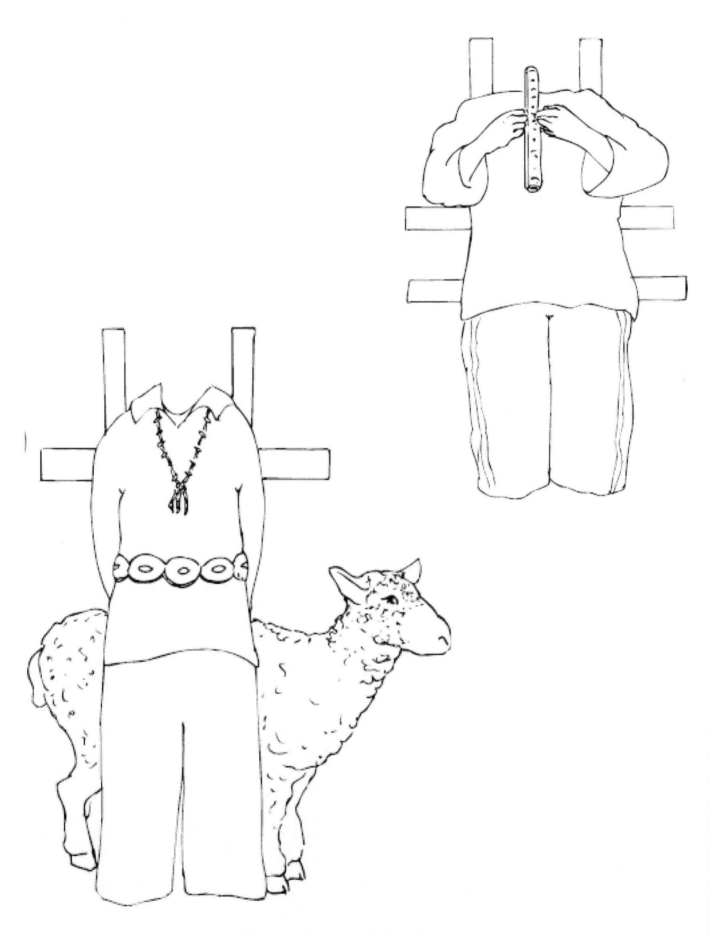

From *Paper Action Figures of the Imagination: Clip, Color and Create* by Paula K. Montgomery.
Santa Barbara, CA: Libraries Unlimited. Copyright © 2009.

Chapter 16

Icy Maidens in the North Lands

Once upon a time, there was a lonely young man who boasted that he did not need any one. His home was in the far northern coast of Japan. In the winter the icy winds blew the icy waters and snow against the walls of his house. It was a bitter cold.

One night he heard knocking at his door. When he opened it, he found a young woman shivering in the deep snow. He picked her up and brought her inside. He slowly helped bring the young girl back to health. When she was well and strong, he could see how lovely she was. They were married and spent the rest of the winter together. Even though the wind continued to blow and the snow piled up high above the roof, they were warm.

Time passed. The closer it came to spring, the more the young bride became ill. Soon she could not rise from the bed. Nothing the young man did could bring health to his bride. Neither broth nor medicine seemed to help. Even the laughter of friends in the village couldn't help.

One warm evening, the man went out to collect some herbs. When he returned to his wife, he called out to her, but could hear nothing. He went in to her bed but found her gone. On her bed were her kimono and a pool of water.

The first day of spring had come.

This is one of many versions of a story about snow maidens that can be found in Russia, Japan, Finland, Denmark, Iceland, and Sweden. The snowy creature motifs of winter, transformation, and supernatural rebirth can be read about in many of the folktale collections of countries in or near the Arctic Circle. What makes these creatures so fascinating? If you have ever built a snowman or snow woman, you know how much fun it is mold and dress them. How do you feel when the sun comes out and soon the creation is gone? In the Japanese story, the theme is complex. Not only is there the ice and cold in transformation, but the problem of broken promises.

Versions of the story can be found in several collections and illustrated titles, including the following:

Bamberger, Richard. *My First Big Story-Book*. Illustrated by Emanuela Wallenta. Irvington-on-Hudson, N.Y.: Harvey House, 1960. Pages 188–193. ISBN: 0140304053.

San Souci, Robert D. *The Snow Wife*. Illustrated by Stephen Johnson. New York: Dial Books for Young Readers, 1993. 32p. ISBN 10: 0803714106; ISBN 13: 978-0803714106.

Seki, Keigo. *Folktales of Japan*. Chicago: University of Chicago Press, 1963. Pages 81–82. ISBN 10: 0226746143; ISBN 13: 978-0226746142.

The Snow Wife—http://www.angelfire.com/hi/herdreaming/snowwife.html (accessed March 22, 2009).

A related telling of the story in which the promise is broken is:

Bodkin, Odds. *The Crane Wife*. San Diego: Harcourt Brace, 1998. 32p. ISBN 10: 0152014071; ISBN 13: 978-0152014070.

The snowy ice maidens appear in other countries, such as Russia, with slightly different messages. In some cases, childless couples make a sow child or maid, and love makes it come to life. Some snow creatures have icy hearts, which raises the question, what does it take to melt the heart of such creatures? In some stories, she is the daughter of Spring and Frost. She craves human companionship and is attracted to a shepherd, but her heart is unable to know love. Spring takes pity and gives her this ability, but as soon as she falls in love, her heart warms up and she melts.

Each of the following versions deals with similar themes: loss and subsequent return; love bringing life and the ice melting for the coming of spring. In Russia, the ice maiden character is known as Snegurochka or the Snow Maiden. In this role during the Communist era, she became the granddaughter and helper of Dyed Moroz (Grandfather Frost or Russia's Santa), who brings gifts on New Year's Eve. In modern Russia, the snow maiden is young with long golden braids. She wears a light blue robe with white fur. In Russia at the Kremlin, a giant party is given for New Year's. The white-bearded Grandfather Frost in his red robe trimmed in white fur arrives. Among his attendants are clowns, snow bunnies, and a snow maiden.

Afanasyev, Aleksandr. *Russian Fairy Tales*. New York: Random House, 1976. 661p. ISBN 10: 039449914X; ISBN 13: 978-0394499147.
> This is one of the largest folklore collections completed by one individual and includes Snegurochka and Jack Frost.

Buyske, Gail. *How the Russian Snow Maiden Helped Santa Claus*. Illustrated by Natasha Voronina. Boulder, Colo.: Vernissage Press, 2005. 32p. ISBN 10: 0972502742; ISBN 13: 978-0972502740.
> Santa Claus asks for help from his friend Father Frost, and the Snow Maiden goes to the North Pole. (Comes with a set of matching five-piece Matroyshka nesting dolls.) Grades K–3.

Cech, John. *First Snow, Magic Snow*. Illustrated by Sharon McGinley-Nally. New York: Simon & Schuster, 1992. 32p. ISBN 10: 0027179710; ISBN 13: 9780027179712.
> An elderly couple searches for their lost snow child at the home of Grandfather Frost. Grades K–5.

Fregosi, Claudia. *Snow Maiden*. Englewood Cliffs, N.J.: Prentice-Hall, 1979. 36p. ISBN 10: 013815340X; ISBN 13: 978-0138153403.
> The Snow Maiden is treated like the Greek myth of Persephone. Grades 2–4.

Lang, Andrew. *The Pink Fairy Book*. New York: Peter Smith, 1966. 360p. ISBN 10: 084460755X; ISBN 13: 978-0844607559.

"Snowflake is the story of the little snow girl made by a childless couple." (Various versions are available, for example at http://www.mythfolklore.net/andrewlang/413.htm; accessed March 22, 2009.) Grades 2–5.

Littledale, Freya. *The Snow Child*. Illustrated by Barbara Lavallee. New York: Scholastic, 189. 32p. ISBN 10: 0590421417; ISBN 13: 978-0590421416.

A childless couple make a child out of snow, but she leaves when it gets warm. (An audio version is available.) Grades K–4.

Marshall, Bonnie C. *The Snow Maiden and Other Russian Tales*. Westport, Conn.: Libraries Unlimited, 2004. 176p. ISBN 10: 1563089998; ISBN 13: 978-1563089992.

The Snow Maiden (story on pages 59–60) must leave when the warmth of spring comes.

Ransome, Arthur. *Old Peter's Russian Tales*. Illustrated by Dmitri Mitrokhin. New York: Peter Stokes, 2005. 172p. ISBN 10: 1557424659; ISBN 13: 978-1557424655.

Originally published in Russia in 1914, "Little Daughter of the Snow" (on pages 57–64) tells about the couple and the daughter made from snow, with the addition of the daughter being lost and after returning, melting by the fire in the hearth. (Available online at http://www.gutenberg.org/etext/16981; accessed March 22, 2009).

Riordan, John. *Russian Folk-Tales*. Illustrated by Andrew Breakspeare. New York: Oxford University Press, 2000. 96p. ISBN 10: 0192745360; ISBN 13: 978-0192745361.

In "The Snow Maiden" (page 33), the daughter of Spring and Frost is entrusted to a peasant couple. Grades 3–6.

Sanderson, Ruth. *The Snow Princess*. Boston: Little, Brown, 2004. 32p. ISBN 10: 0316779822; ISBN 13: 978-0316779821.

Father Frost and Mother Spring warn the Snow Princess when she sets out to see the world that she should never fall in love. Grades K–4.

Ziefert, Harriet. *The Snow Child*. Illustrated by Julia Zanes. New York: Viking, 2000. 32p. ISBN 10: 067088748X; ISBN 13: 978-0670887484.

A childless couple creates a snow child to love, but what will happen when spring comes? Grades K–4.

Web Sites

Variations of the story may be found at several Web sites.

Little Snow Girl—http://russian-crafts.com/tales/lit_snow.html (accessed March 22, 2009).

The Little Snow Girl by Sunitichandra Mishra—http://www.bolokids.com/2006/0199.htm (accessed March 22, 2009).

Russian Fairy Tales—http://www.geocities.com/Athens/Delphi/6422/tale.html (accessed March 22, 2009). Includes the poem, "The Snow Maiden."

Russian Fairy Tales, Spring 1998: Snow Maiden—http://clover.slavic.pitt.edu/~tales/snow_maiden.html (accessed March 22, 2009).

Russian Folktale Snow Maiden—http://www.geocities.com/Athens/Delphi/6422/snow.html (accessed March 22, 2009).

The Snow Maiden—http://www.information-resources.com/Library/library149a.html (accessed March 22, 2009).

Finland, Sweden, and Denmark—Snow Queen

It is from Denmark that we get Hans Christian Andersen's version of the Snow Queen story, which is the best known. It is considered one of Andersen's best stories. He wrote it in seven stories: 1) About the Mirror and Its Pieces; 2) A Little Boy and a Little Girl; 3) The Flower Garden of the Woman Who Knew Magic; 4) The Prince and Princess; 5) The Little Robber Girl; 6) The Lapp Woman and the Finn Woman; and 7) What Happened at the Snow Queen's Palace and What Happened Afterward. Andersen focused on a struggle between good and evil. The Snow Queen takes a young lad, Kay, to her palace, and Gerda, the heroine, must save him. Andersen's version was translated and became popular in America. An annotated version can be found at http://www.surlalunefairytales.com/snowqueen/index.html (accessed June 30, 2008). An excellent summary, bibliography, and list of modern tales based on the story are also found there.

For children, the following are examples of the many versions of the story from various retellers, translators, publishers, and illustrators.

Dulac's The Snow Queen, *and Other Stories from Hans Andersen*. New York: Doubleday, 1981. 143p. ISBN 10: 0385116780; ISBN 13: 978-0385116787.

Hans Christian Andersen's The Snow Queen. Translated by Eva Le Gallienne. Illustrated by Arieh Zeldich. New York: Harper & Row, 1985. 117p. ISBN 10: 0060236949; ISBN 13: 978-0060236946.

Hans Christian Andersen's The Snow Queen. Translated by Naomi Lewis. Illustrated by Angela Barrett. Cambridge, Mass.: Candlewick Press, 1968. 42p. ISBN 10: 1564022153; ISBN 13: 978-1564022158.

Hans Christian Andersen's The Snow Queen: *A Fairy Tale Told in Seven Stories*. Retold by Ken Setterington. Illustrated by Nelly and Ernst Hofer. Toronto: Tundra Books, 2000. 47p. ISBN 10: 0887764975; ISBN 13: 978-0887764974.

Kate Greenaway's Original Drawings for The Snow Queen. Translated by Charles Boner. New York: Schocken Books, 1981. 58p. ISBN 10: 0805237763; ISBN 13: 9780805237764.

Mary Engelbreit's The Snow Queen. New York: Workman, 1993. 48p. ISBN 10: 1563054388; ISBN 13: 978-1563054389

The Snow Queen. Illustrated by Stasys Eidrigevicius. Mankato, Minn.: Creative Education, 1984. 48p. ISBN 10: 0871919508; ISBN 13: 9780871919502.

The Snow Queen. Translated from the original Danish text by Marlee Alex. Illustrated by Uwe Häntsch. New York: Barron's, 1984. 41p. ISBN-10: 289088242X; ISBN 13: 9780849985393.

The Snow Queen. Retold and illustrated by Richard Hess. New York: Macmillan, 1985. 59p. ISBN-10: 0375415122; ISBN-13: 9780375415128

The Snow Queen. Retold by Amy Ehrlich. Illustrated by Susan Jeffers. Dial Press, 1982. 32p. ISBN 10: 0525476946; ISBN 13: 978-0525476948.

The Snow Queen. Translated by Naomi Lewis. Illustrated by Errol Le Cain. New York: Penguin/Puffin, 1968. 32p. ISBN 10: 0722654871; ISBN-13: 9780670653782.

The Snow Queen. Retold from the original English version by Caroline Peachey. Illustrated by P. J. Lynch. New York: Gulliver/Harcourt Brace, 1994. 48p. ISBN 10: 0152008748; ISBN 13: 978-0152008741.

The Snow Queen. Illustrated by Pavel Tatarnikov. New York: Purple Bear Books, 2006. 48p. ISBN 10: 1933327235; ISBN-13: 978-1933327235.

The Snow Queen. Illustrated by Vladyslav Yerko. Slovakia/New York: A-BA-BA-HA-LA-MA-HA Publishers, 2000/2006. 32p. ISBN 10: 966704758X; ISBN 13: 978-9667047580.

The Snow Queen: A Fairy Tale. Translated by Anthea Bell. Illustrated by Bernadette Watts. New York: North-South Books, 1987. 32p. ISBN 10: 1558580530; ISBN 13: 978-1558580534.

Audio Versions

The Snow Queen. Narrated by Natalia Makarova; Tchaikovsky, *Album for the Young*, op. 39. Delos/A & M Records, 1990.

The Snow Queen & Other Tales. Chatham River Press; distributed by Crown Publishers, 1985.

Video Versions of Snow Maiden Films

The Snow Queen. BBC Enterprises Ltd./BFS Video, 1992. 90 min.

The Snow Queen. Universal International/Walterscheid Productions, 1990. 180 min.

The Snow Queen. Narrated by Sigourney Weaver. New York: Lightyear Video, 1996. 106 min.

Web Sites

Gerta and the Reindeer—http://childhoodreading.com/Edmund_Dulac_and_Gus/Snow_Queen.01.html (accessed March 22, 2009).

Hans Christian Andersen. The Snow Queen—http://hca.gilead.org.il/snow_que.html (accessed March 22, 2009).

The Snow Queen—http://www.angelfire.com/hi/FaerieGodmother/ (accessed March 22, 2009).

The Snow Queen—http://aesopfables.com/cgi/aesop1.cgi?hca&a97 (accessed March 22, 2009).

The Play Is the Thing

Traditional fairy tales lend themselves to plays and role playing. These written versions may be adapted and performed by children's groups.

Hans Christian Andersen's The Snow Queen: *A Christmas Pageant.* Adapted by Richard Kennedy. Music by Mark Lambert. Illustrated by Edward S. Gazsi. New York: Laura Geringer Book, 1996. 88p. ISBN 10: 0060271159; ISBN 13: 978-0060271152.

Peaslee, Richard. *The Snow Queen: A Play with Songs.* London: Oberon Books, 1997. 52p. ISBN 10: 0769220096; ISBN 13: 978-0769220093, (An audio recording is available.)

The Snow Maiden and Snow Queen in Opera and Ballet

In 1882 at the Mariinsky Theatre in St. Petersburg, Russia, *Snegurochka* or *The Snow Maiden* was first performed. The composer, Nikolay Andreyevich Rimsky-Korsakov, considered it one of his best works. He based his opera on the story of the snow maiden who must be kept away from the sun god, Yarilo. A rich young man loves her and wants her, but the sun god sees her and warms her heart. She melts away.

Many artists and musicians have recorded the opera and ballet. Listen to the CD *Rimsky-Korskov: Greatest Hits* (Sony Classics, 69250). Pyotr Ilyich Tchaikovsky also wrote ballet music for *The Snow Maiden*, in March and April 1873. He incorporated many Russian folk tunes. Read more about it at *The Snow Maiden* (http://www.tchaikovsky.host.sk/work/snowmaiden.htm). Listen to it on the CD *The Snow Maiden* (NAXOS, 8.553856).

Published Snow Maiden Paper Dolls

Outfits that might be used for the snow queen could be found in sets of storybook paper dolls or actresses and stars. An actual paper doll of the Snow Maiden can be found at:

Wilks, Patricia. "The Snow Maiden." *The Doll Reader* (February/March 1987): 234–235. (Madavor Media, LLC; 420 Boylston Street, 5th Floor, Boston, MA 02116).

Lesson Plan:
What Is Your Message, Maid of the Snow?

Library Media Skills Objective:

The student will identify the theme of a story and design a collage to illustrate it.

Curriculum (subject areas) Objectives:

This activity may be used in reading/language arts or art to teach the concept of theme.

Grade Level: 3–6

Resources:

> Paper dolls handouts
>
> Crayons and paints
>
> Scissors
>
> Glue
>
> Confetti and paper cutters
>
> Glitter
>
> Art paper (11-by-14 inch)
>
> Magazines for cutting
>
> Scrap construction paper
>
> Scrap fabric or other found materials

Instructional Roles:

The library media specialist or classroom teacher may introduce the topic with a story about ice maidens. The classroom teacher, with backup from the art teacher, may work with the students on their collages and the follow-up. The introduction will take about 45 minutes. Paper dolls and collages and follow-up will take 2 or more hours.

Activity and Procedures for Completion:

Introduce the idea of snow maidens with one or more stories about the snow maiden or snow queen. Videos or audio presentations may be used. Following the story, discuss the plot and what themes might be found in the story. Tell about ice maidens and snow queens in folklore and literature. Share information about the Snow Maiden in Russia at Christmas. The concept of theme or motifs may be reviewed or introduced. The following themes or motifs are usually found in these stories: return, loss, promises, rejuvenation, seasons, winter, transformation, and supernatural rebirth.

Display some of the titles related to the Snow Queen. This is an excellent time to discuss translations and illustrator interpretations of a subject. Allow time for students to browse books before regrouping to discuss how illustrators portrayed their subjects. What colors did they use? How did they portray the background? What kind of media did they use? Discuss how translators might also modify or change a story. Compare two translations of the story.

Explain that students will also have an opportunity to prepare their own ideas about snow queens or ice maidens. Students may work with a partner or on their own. They will select a book and read it. After they read the story, they will identify one or more themes and share them with the teacher or library media specialist. Based on the theme, they will cut out and color a snow maiden paper doll and outfit. They will also make a background collage for displaying the paper doll. This collage will show the theme they found in the story. Discuss how to show this theme. For example, they might select cooler colors. Review or introduce this art concept. They might use blue because it is a color of the snow maiden. How might they show the cold or winter as a theme? Cut-out snowflakes? White torn scrap paper? How might they show rebirth from winter to spring? Cut out pictures showing winter and spring from magazines? An ice cube beside a pool of water?

Allow students to brainstorm and provide them with space and supplies to begin working on the paper dolls and collages. When students have finished their paper dolls and collages, they may display them.

For sharing, arrange for half of the groups or individuals to stand by their displays. They must be prepared to explain what story they read and what theme they chose to represent. The other half of the groups and individuals will rotate in three- to five-minute intervals from display to display to see what has been done. When all have rotated, switch groups so the ones who were explaining can now see others' work. At the end, have a general discussion on what the students saw in others' works. How did others represent themes? How did others display their dolls? What did they see in common?

Evaluation:

Each student will select and read one story about an ice maiden, identify one theme, and prepare one paper doll and collage to display representing the theme.

Follow-Up:

Students may design a collage slide show (in PowerPoint) of the dolls and the collage-themed background, with musical themes from Rimsky-Korsakov.

Paper Dolls:
Snow Maiden

Instruction: Dress the snow maiden in one of the costumes. Color the costumes for the story that you like best. Cut them out and use them to retell the story.

Japan:
Snow Wife Costumes

Russia:
Maiden Costumes

Chapter 17

Troll Tales

In the old days, when only narrow, twisting paths wound their way through the moss-grown mountains of Norway, few human beings ever set foot there. The mountains belonged to the trolls, who were as old and moss-grown as the mountains themselves.—*D'Aulaires' Trolls* (Doubleday, 1972)

Trolls are not humans; trolls are not animals. These gruesome critters are just trolls. Trolls appear frequently in Norwegian fairy tales. They play the greatest role in stories about the origin of geological sites in Norway. Because it is thought that sunlight turns a troll to stone, Norwegians believe many rock formations in their country are actually trolls turned to stone long ago.

How to Recognize a Troll

According to folktales and myths, trolls lived throughout Scandinavia, deep in forests or in caves under waterfalls, far away from people. They had a frightening appearance and were misshapen, but very powerful. These mischievous beings could be small and wizened or as tall as giants. Some were simply human sized. They were thought to have big noses, big pointed ears, big hands and feet, and small eyes. They had long, wild, woolly hair and potbellies. They were occasionally helpful to humans, but for the most part trolls were mean and grumpy. They also tended to be a bit stupid. In some folktales, such as *The Three Billy Goats Gruff,* trolls were outwitted by the cleverness of other characters. Multiple versions of the tale exist for read-aloud.

The Language of Trolls

Like prehistoric man, trolls were thought to have a simple language to share information. Communication between trolls would usually be in short, simple sentences, such as, "Look—bad snake on the path" or "See that bird." Trolls were not very good storytellers. They didn't see themselves as very important, so they never liked to talk about themselves.

Power of Trolls

Did trolls have magical powers? The answer depends on the meaning of "magical." To a troll, preserving life is magical. Trolls knew the cure for any disease with which they were familiar, and they had very good memories for anything unusual. They were probably able to communicate with more intelligent mammals, such as bears and moose. To humans, communication with animals would be considered a magical power.

The main focus for trolls was taking care of their family group. They liked company and lived together in groups. A female troll was called a troll hag. Troll hags were a little different from male trolls. They were usually smaller and could be out in the sun without bursting.

Troll Beliefs

Helping other creatures and taking good care of the land were characteristics of trolls. They lived for the sake of living and accepted life as it is. They needed no reason for why they existed or why they would die.

Trolls had no gods or devils. Interestingly, trolls hated everything to do with Christianity. (A word of advice: A church is a good place to hide if you ever run into an angry troll!)

What did trolls love? They loved early November mornings when the sun shone from a clear blue sky, and the ground was covered with frost. They also loved late summer evenings, when they met up with trolls from other tribes on the shores of a small forest lake.

Trolls usually roamed about at night. According to troll myths, the two greatest weaknesses of trolls were that they could not stand noise and that sunlight turned them to stone. Because they could not stand the light of day, trolls were careful not to be out and about after the sun came up.

Trolls loved beautiful things. They often guarded a dazzling treasure, which a hero could bring back to his family after defeating the trolls. Trolls were also known to swap human babies for their own newborns, as they considered human babies quite beautiful. These swapped babies were called changelings.

Troll Types

In Norway, there were many different types of trolls: mountain trolls, forest trolls, water trolls, trolls with one head, trolls with three heads, trolls with twelve heads. There were even troll-steeds (troll horses), which lived in stables deep in the mountains. These creatures were huge and so fierce that flames spurted from their nostrils.

The *Tan-Verk-Trollet* was a tiny toothache troll. This troll would creep into the bedrooms of sleeping children by sneaking under a closed door. Once in the bedroom, this troll would look for a child who hadn't brushed his or her teeth. Once he found a victim, he would dig a hole in a tooth and live there.

The *Norwegian Mountain Troll* lived in caves near the top of mountains. These trolls had a wonderful view of the sea from their caves.

Good-Luck Trolls

In the 1950s trolls made their first commercial appearance. As the story goes, a man named Thomas Dam didn't have enough money to buy his daughter a birthday present. So he carved a little troll doll for her, based on legendary trolls that were thought to have lived in the forests of Norway. The little girl showed off her new toy around her village. Soon a local toy store owner took an interest in the little troll doll.

Thomas Dam's woodcarvings became so popular that by the late 1950s the "Dam Things Establishment" company (yes, that's the actual company name!) began producing molded plastic trolls. By the mid-1960s troll dolls were selling like crazy. For a couple of years, trolls ranked number two in toy sales in America. The troll doll was only one spot behind the number one selling toy, Barbie dolls!

It didn't take long for other toy companies to join the troll train. Companies such as Hasbro, Mattel, and Trollkins began producing different sized trolls, with all sorts of costumes and clothing offered as accessories. It was common to see trolls made into cowboys, rock stars, athletes and superheroes, vampires, bride and groom couples, and animals. Thanks to toy collectors, trolls are still popping up around the world in the most unlikely places!

Troll Descriptions

Jack Prelutsky has a wonderful description of trolls in his poem, "Monday's Troll." The poem can be helpful in describing mood or different characters of trolls. The poem is easily read aloud, and students can fill in the blanks about what trolls are like on each day of the week. Poetry indexes include many other examples of trolls in verse.

Poetry too good to miss!

Evans, Dilys. *Fairies, Trolls & Goblins: Poems About Fantastic Creatures*. Illustrated by Jacqueline Rogers. New York: Simon & Schuster Books for Young Readers, 2000. 36p.

Prelutsky, Jack. *Monday's Troll*. New York: Greenwillow Books, 1996. 40p.

Did You Know?

"According to legend, trolls can live to be 500 years old. In fact, it is almost impossible to kill a troll because it has the ability to regenerate, or re-grow, a lost or severed body part in a matter of days. This ability makes trolls excellent warriors" (Shari Cohen, *Draw Fantasy*). For teaching children how to draw trolls or make their own troll paper dolls, *Draw Fantasy* has six easy steps that are sketched with directions for drawing a gruesome-looking troll. As you draw, you can also read the Scandinavian story, "The Trolls of Dovrafell," which tells about a pack of unruly trolls who come down from the mountains every Christmas Eve to wreak havoc on the tiny home of a man named Halvor.

Cohen, Shari. *Draw Fantasy: Dragons, Centaurs & Other Mythological Characters*. New York: Contemporary Books, 1997, 18–19.

Trolls for the Holidays

Author and illustrator Jan Brett, in *Who's That Knocking on Christmas Eve?* (G. P. Putnam, 2002), has retold this Norwegian story in a fresh, exciting Christmas tale. Every year trolls knock down Kyri's door and gobble up her Christmas feast. This year the trolls are in for a surprise. A boy and his pet ice bear, on their way to Oslo, have come in from the cold. What happens when these visitors unexpectedly burst in on the trolls' feast? Jan Brett will captivate you with this folktale, beautifully illustrated with borders, detailed illustrations, and a stunning display of Northern Lights. A Jan Brett teacher resource is available at http://falcon.jmu.edu/~ramseyil/brett.htm (accessed on June 30, 2008).

Troll for these great, shorter picture books!

Bollinger, Max. *The Happy Troll.* Illustrated by Peter Sis. New York: H. Holt, 2005. 32p. ISBN 10: 0805069828; ISBN 13: 978-0805069822.

  Gus the troll has a beautiful voice, and others come from afar to hear him sing and bring him gifts. Gus wants one glittering ring that leads him to a hard lesson. Grades K–3.

Brett, Jan. *Christmas Trolls.* New York: G. P. Putnam's Sons, 1993. 32p. ISBN 10: 0399225072; ISBN 13: 978-0399225079.

  Teva's family Christmas items are disappearing. She soon learns that two mischievous trolls are the culprits. (A sound recording is available.) Grades K–4.

Brett, Jan. *Hedgie's Surprise.* New York: G. P. Putnam's Sons, 2000. 32 p. ISBN 10: 0399234772; ISBN 13: 978-0399234774.

  When Henry, the speckled hen, needs help, Hedgie, a hedgehog, helps trick the troll who has been taking Henry's eggs! (Sound and video recordings are available.) Grades K–4.

Brett, Jan. *Trouble with Trolls.* New York: G. P. Putnam's Sons, 1992. 32p. ISBN 10: 0399223363; ISBN 13: 978-0399223365.

  Trolls try to take Teva's dog while she is climbing Mt. Baldy, but Teva outsmarts them. (An audio recording is available.) Grades K–4.

Brett, Jan. *Who's That Knocking on Christmas Eve?* New York: G. P. Putnam, 2002. 32p. ISBN 10: 0399238735; ISBN 13: 978-0399238734.

  Kyri and her father want to enjoy their Christmas Eve meal. How can they, when hungry trolls keep bothering them? How do a boy from Finnmark and his ice bear help? (Audio and video versions are available.) Grades K–4.

Christiana, David. *White Nineteens.* New York: Farrar, Straus & Giroux, 1992. 32p. ISBN 10: 0374383901; ISBN 13: 978-0374383909.

  A fairy named Buttercup fearlessly tracks down a fat troll who stole her favorite wings. Grades K–4.

Dunrea, Olivier. *The Trow-Wife's Treasure.* New York: Farrar, Straus & Giroux, 1998. 32p. ISBN 10: 0374377928; ISBN 13: 978-0374377922.

  Bracken Van Eyck and his dog Caleb show kindness by helping a mother troll find her missing baby. Grades K–4.

Havill, Juanita. *Kentucky Troll*. Illustrated by Bert Dodson. New York: Lothrop, Lee & Shepard Books, 1993. 32p. ISBN 10: 0688104576; ISBN 13: 978-0688104573.
> A Swedish troll comes to live in Kentucky. He does his best to disguise himself from humans to make his way in the world. Grades K–4.

Hawkes, Kevin. *Then the Troll Heard the Squeak*. New York: Lothrop, Lee & Shepard Books, 1991. 22p. ISBN 10: 0688097588; ISBN 13: 9780688097585.
> A troll comes along to clean up after Little Miss Terry jumps on the bedsprings at night. Grades K–3.

Heller, Nicholas. *A Troll Story*. New York: Greenwillow Books, 1990. 24p. ISBN 10: 0688089704; ISBN 13: 978-0688089702.
> Lewis is special because he can turn into a troll whenever he wishes. Grades K–3.

Hilcox, Rebecca. *Per and the Dala Horse*. Illustrated by Yvonne Gilbert. New York: Doubleday Books for Young Readers, 1995. 32p. ISBN 10: 0385320752; ISBN 13: 978-0385320757.
> After his brothers fail, a young boy and his toy horse outwit a troll. Grades K–3.

Jewell, Nancy. *Silly Times with Two Silly Trolls*. New York: HarperCollins, 1996. 48p. ISBN 10: 1587170345; ISBN 13: 9781587170348.
> Nip and Tuck, two trolls, find a clock that has stopped at 5:00, which forms the basis for their silly adventures. Grades K–3.

Johnston, Tony. *Happy Birthday, Mole & Troll*. Illustrated by Cyndy Szekeres. New York: G. P. Putnam's Sons, 1979. 64p. ISBN 10: 0399611371; ISBN 13: 978-0399611377.
> Check out the four stories that show the great friendship between Mole and Troll. Grades K–3.

Lagerlof, Selma. *The Changeling*. Illustrated by Susanna Stevens. New York: Alfred A. Knopf, 1992. 42p. ISBN 10: 0679810358; ISBN 13: 978-0679810353.
> Trolls capture a farm wife's son and leave their own child. Her kindness causes the trolls to return her son. Grades K–4.

Le Guin, Ursula K. *A Ride on the Red Mare's Back*. Illustrated by Julie Downing. New York: Orchard Books, 1992. 48p. ISBN 10: 053105991X; ISBN 13: 978-0531059913.
> Imagine the bravery shown by a young girl who rides to the High House in the mountains to rescue her brother from trolls. Grades K–3.

Lindgren, Astrid. *The Tomtem*. Illustrated by Harald Wiberg. New York: Penguin Putnam Books for Young Readers, 1997. 32p. ISBN 10: 0698201477; ISBN 13: 978-0698201477.
> The author adapted the story from a poem by Viktor Rydberg in which a friendly troll or Tomtem visits a Swedish farm. Grades K–3.

Lobel, Anita. *Troll Music*. New York: HarperCollins, 1966. 32p. ISBN 10: 0060239301; ISBN 13: 978-0060239305.
> A troll puts a spell on musicians, whose instruments then only make the sounds of animals. Grades K–4.

Marshall, Edward. *Troll Country*. Illustrated by James Marshall. New York: Dial Books for Young Readers, 1980. 56p. ISBN 10: 0803762119; ISBN 13: 978-0803762114.
> Elsie Faye tries to outsmart a troll that she meets in the deep, dark woods. (An audio version is available.) Grades K–3.

McMullan, Kate. *Hey, Pipsqueak!* Illustrated by Jim McMullan. New York: HarperCollins, 1995. 30p. ISBN: 0062051008; ISBN 13: 9780062051004.

> A young boy makes his way to a party by going over a bridge. He must outsmart a troll to get across. Grades K–3.

Mills, Lauren. *Tatterhood and the Hobgoblins: A Norwegian Folktale*. Boston: Little, Brown, 1993. 32p. ISBN 10: 0316574066; ISBN 13: 978-0316574068.

> Princess Tatterhood rescues her sister from the trolls' curse. Grades K–3.

Minters, Frances. *Princess Fishtail*. Illustrated G. Brian Karas. New York: Viking, 2002. 32p. ISBN 10: 0670035297; ISBN 13: 978-0670035298.

> A Mer-King's daughter trades her mermaid tail to a troll for legs, but she gets homesick for her underwater world. Grades K–3.

Myers, Tim. *Good Babies: A Tale of Trolls, Humans, a Witch, and a Switch*. Illustrated by Kelly Murphy. Cambridge, Mass.: Candlewick Press, 2005. 32p. ISBN 10: 0763622273; ISBN 13: 9780763622275.

> A witch swaps human and troll babies, but her intentions are subverted. Grades 1–5.

Peet, Bill. *Jethro and Joel Were a Troll*. New York: Houghton Mifflin, 1987. 32p. ISBN 10: 0833549189; ISBN 13: 978-0833549181.

> Jethro and Joel, a two-headed troll, have a bad day and go off wreaking havoc throughout the countryside. Grades K–3.

Thiessen, Brad. *Orso: The Troll Who Couldn't Scare*. Illustrated by Jeremy Balzer. New York: CDS Books, 2005. 32p. ISBN 10: 159315142X; ISBN 13: 978-1593151423.

> Orso lives under a bridge with his father and doesn't want to scare people like his dad does. Grades K–2.

Vande Velde, Vivian. *Troll Teacher*. Illustrated by Mary Jane Auch. New York: Holiday House, 2000. 32p. ISBN 10: 0823415031; ISBN 13: 9780823415038.

> Elizabeth's new teacher has orange eyes, eats desks, and throws fruit at the students, but no one but Elizabeth seems to notice! Grades K–3.

Wolff, Patricia Rae. *The Toll-Bridge Troll*. Illustrated by Kimberly Bulcken Root. Orlando, Fla.: Harcourt Brace, 1995. 28p. ISBN 10: 0152776656; ISBN 13: 978-0152776657.

> A young boy use riddles to outwit a troll who tries to keep him from crossing a bridge on his way to school. Grades K–3.

Longer Reads for Troll Collectors

Trolls show up in adult fiction. In J. R. R. Tolkien's world of Middle-earth, trolls are very large evil, crude, and barely intelligent enough to communicate. In *The Hobbit* they speak with Cockney accents and enjoy eating meat and drinking beer. J. K. Rowling includes trolls in the Harry Potter series. The following titles feature trolls in longer reads for older children.

Ferris, Jean. *Once Upon a Marigold*. Orlando, Fla.: Harcourt, , 2002. 266p. ISBN 10: 0152167919; ISBN 13: 978-0152167912.

> A young man is raised by a troll. He leaves his home and meets an unhappy princess whom he has loved from afar. Grades 3–6.

Helgerson, Joseph. *Horns and Wrinkles*. Illustrated by Nicoletta Ceccoli. New York: Houghton Mifflin, 2006. 386p. ISBN 10: 0618616799; ISBN 13: 978-0618616794.

> Claire and Duke join a group of river trolls on a quest to learn about the magic along the Mississippi River. Grades 4–7.

Horvath, Polly. *The Trolls*. New York: Farrar, Straus & Giroux, 1999. 136p. ISBN 10: 0374479917; ISBN 13: 978-0374479916.

> The Anderson children's parents go on a trip to Paris and leave them with Aunt Sally. Each night at bedtime, Aunt Sally reveals another strange part of their family history.

Langrish, Katherine. *Troll Fell*. New York: HarperCollins, c2004. 272p. ISBN 10: 0060583045; ISBN 13: 978-0060583040.

> Peer is forced to live with his two greedy uncles, who are going to sell him to the Troll King. Grades 4–7.

McKenzie, Ellen Kindt. *Under the Bridge*. New York: HarperTrophy, 1994. 140p. ISBN 10: 080503398X; ISBN 13: 978-0805033984.

> Rosie receives letters from a troll when she is sick in bed. These letters help her get over her loneliness and problems with a class bully. Grades 3–6.

Stewart, Paul, and Chris Riddell. *Beyond the Deepwoods*. (The Edge Chronicles). New York: David Fickling Books, 1998. 288p. ISBN 10: 0385750684; ISBN 13: 978-0385750684.

> This first book in the series tells about a human who is being raised by wood trolls. (An audio recording is available.) Grades 5–8.

Vornholt, John. *The Troll King*. New York: Aladdin Paperbacks, 2001. 216p. ISBN 10: 0743424123; ISBN 13: 978-0743424127.

> Enter the land of Bonespittle and learn the "true" history of trolls, the underclass ruled by an evil sorcerer. Grades 4–7.

Yolen, Jane. *Boots and the Seven Leaguers: A Rock-and-Troll Novel*. San Diego: Harcourt, 2000. 192p. ISBN 10: 015202557X; ISBN 13: 978-0152025571.

> Troll Gog and his best friend Pook work for a troll rock and roll band. What happens when Gog's troll brother gets kidnapped? Grades 4–7.

Troll Story Collections

Trolls appear in many collections of folk and fairy tales. Troll stories can be found in these collections. Skim the table of contents to find something appealing. Norwegian folktales and legends by Peter Christen Asbjørnsen and Jørgen Moe include stories such as "The Three Princesses of Whiteland," "Soria Moria Castle," "Dapplegrim," "Tatterhood," and "The Cat on the Dovrefell," among many others. A good index to folk and fairy tales will reveal options. These collections offer easy access.

D'Aulaire, Ingri, and Edgar D'Aulaire. *D'Aulaires' Trolls*. New York: Doubleday, 1972. 72p. ISBN 10: 1590172175; ISBN 13: 978-1590172179. Grades 2–6.

Jonsen, George. *Favorite Tales of Monsters and Trolls*. New York: Random House, 1986. 32p. ISBN 10: 0394934776; ISBN 13: 978-0394934778. (A sound recording is available.)

Lunge-Larsen, Lise. *The Troll with No Heart in His Body and Other Tales of Trolls from Norway.* Boston: Houghton Mifflin, 1999. 92p. ISBN 10: 0395913713; ISBN 13: 978-0395913710. Grades 3–6.

Velde, Vivian Vande. *Tales from the Brothers Grimm and the Sisters Weird.* San Diego: Harcourt Brace, 1995. 128p. ISBN-10: 0152002200; ISBN 13: 978-0152002206. (A twisted version.) Grades 3–6.

Troll Web Sites

Troll Company—http://www.troll-company.dk/ (accessed March 22, 2009).
Play a fun Troll Memory Game at this troll Web site.

Trolls—http://library.thinkquest.org/12924/nortroll.htm (accessed March 22, 2009).
Symbols and traditions of trolls.

Welcome to the Troll Collectors Corner—http://www.trollshop.net/trolls/ (accessed June 30, 2008).
Everything troll!

Published Troll Paper Dolls

During the period when trolls were popular, several companies made troll paper dolls. In addition to Wishniks (Wishnik Trolls. Whitman, 1965) and Dam Things, you can also find trolls made in the 1970s, 1980s, and 1990s by Hasbro, Mattel, Russ Berry, Nyform, Trollkins, and Ace Novelty.

Troll Baby Paper Doll—http://www.daniellesplace.com/html/paper_dolls.html and http://www.daniellesplace.com/images/trollpat.gif (accessed March 22, 2009).
This make-it-your-self pattern can be copied to make clothes for different occasions.

Jan Brett's Troll Pencil Toppers—http://www.janbrett.com/make_a_pencil_topper.htm (accessed March 22, 2009).
Although these are not paper dolls, the patterns for the pencil toppers could be used for paper dolls, for which students could make clothes.

Lesson Plan:
Trolls in the Mood

Library Media Skills Objective:

The students will identify the mood of a story and the characters in a story.

Curriculum (subject areas) Objectives:

This activity may be part of a music appreciation class on classical music (Grieg, etc.) or a reading/language arts unit on mood in literature.

Grade Level: 1–3

Resources:

Paper doll handouts

Crayons or paints

Scissors

Paper

Music

Charts with pictures of happy faces, etc.

Musical recordings

Instructional Roles:

The classroom teacher, with assistance from the library media specialist and music teacher, may complete this activity. An introduction will require about 30 minutes. Students should be given at least an hour spaced out over time to read troll books. Once the students have read their books, they will need an hour or more to make their paper dolls and the appropriate clothes. Allow 45 minutes to an hour for sharing the results of the books and the mood of the characters.

Activity and Procedures for Completion:

Introduce troll books and read two of them. One should contrast with the other, for example, a book about a fierce or scary troll and another about a happy one.

Prepare several 11-by-14-inch charts with simple faces (happy faces, etc.). Include such troll face emotions as happy, grumpy, mad, fierce, sad, and surprised. The faces may be simple circles with eyes, nose, and mouth in the appropriate form. Smiley faces like those found on the Internet might also be used. Set up the charts and ask students what the faces show in terms of emotion or mood. Discuss what causes these moods. Ask students to classify the two stories read in terms of the troll character's mood. Explain that in literature, "mood" is the emotion that you feel while you are reading. Some literature

From *Paper Action Figures of the Imagination: Clip, Color and Create* by Paula K. Montgomery. Santa Barbara, CA: Libraries Unlimited. Copyright © 2009.

makes you feel sad, others joyful, still others, angry. Mood can be reflected in the character, the setting, and the words used to tell the story.

Following the discussion, explain that students will work in small groups of three to read at least two books about trolls. They will be reading for story as well as the mood of the characters or story. For each book, students will prepare a troll paper doll with clothes that help reflect the mood of the story. They will dress the paper dolls and display them with the book that they read beside the face chart.

For this activity, pull the books about trolls so that students can focus on selecting among similar topics. Set up groups of three. If students need help, outline the steps on a worksheet or a large chart paper sign in the work area. Include the following steps:

Meet with your group.

Select two books about trolls from the group provided.

Read the books aloud to each other.

Talk about each book. What happened in the story? (plot) What kind of troll was in the story? (characterization) Where did the story occur? (setting) What did you feel about the character and the story? (mood)

When you have finished your discussion, decide within the group about coloring or painting a troll paper doll. What will its face look like? How will the paper doll be dressed to match the feeling of each of the stories read?

Color and cut out the paper dolls and outfits. Be prepared to display the dressed dolls and book by the appropriate face chart. Be prepared to explain why you matched the doll and book to the face chart.

Before students begin working, read *Troll Music* by Anita Lobel. Explain that composers also capture mood in their works. Introduce some of the composers who have featured trolls. Examples are:

Edvard Grieg. "In the Hall of the Mountain King," "Wedding Day at Trolldhaugen," and "March of the Trolls" from *Peer Gynt*.

Johan Halvorsen. "The Princess and the Giant Troll," "The Trolls Enter the Blue Mountain," and "Dance of the Little Trolls."

Geirr Tveitt. "Troll-Tuned Hardanger Fiddle," and "The Boy with the Troll-Treasure" from *Troll Tunes*.

Students will play the sound recordings at the work area.

On the day of sharing, each group may place the dressed paper dolls and books beside the faces. They will explain to other groups why they dressed the dolls the way they did and what it was about the characters and story that helped them make their match. Follow up with one or more of the musical recordings and discuss the mood of the selections.

Evaluation:

Each student will work in a group to select two stories, read them, make a paper doll and dress it to match the mood of each story, and display the dressed doll with a face that symbolizes the mood of a story or character.

Follow-Up:

The students may look for Scandinavian motifs and design outfits that match the motifs. The students may read and learn more about the composers of troll music.

Paper Dolls:
Trolls

Instructions: Decorate these trolls by coloring or painting them. When you are finished, cut them out.

From Paper Action Figures of the Imagination: Clip, Color and Create by Paula K. Montgomery.
Santa Barbara, CA: Libraries Unlimited. Copyright © 2009.

303

Copyright Acknowledgments

All chapters are adapted from original *Crinkles* publications listed below.

Chapter 2: "Cat Tales" by Pamela B. Lichty and Cat Figure Paper Dolls by Vicky Weeks Elliott. *Crinkles* 4, no.5 (May/June 2002): 42–46.

Chapter 3: "Who Goes Moo?" by Jennifer Galvin and Cow Figure Paper Dolls by Vicki Weeks Elliott. *Crinkles* 4, no.1 (September/October 2001): 27–32.

Chapter 4: "Dinosaurs Everywhere! by Pamela Lichty and Dinosaur Figure Paper Dolls by Tami Ferraro. *Crinkles* 6, no. 1 (September/October 2003): 46–50.

Chapter 5: "Elephants on Parade!" by Denice L. Baldetti and Elephant Doll Figures by Gayle Travis-Keene. *Crinkles* 3, no.2 (November/December 2000): 12–17.

Chapter 6: "Kiss a Frog? Frogs in Fiction and Folklore" by Jennifer Galvin and Frog Figures by Gayle Travis-Keene. *Crinkles* 4, no. 2 (November/December 2001): 30–34.

Chapter 7: "The Big Ones: Giants Around the World" by Denice L. Baldetti and Giant Figures by Gayle Travis-Keene. *Crinkles* 3, no. 3 (January/February 2001): 40–45.

Chapter 8: "Judgment of Paris" by Paula Montgomery and Greek Figures by Debra Goodrich. *Crinkles* 1, no. 1 (September/October 1998): 18–21.

Chapter 9: "Guiding Us Along: Characters as Guides by Jennifer Galvin and Characters as Guides Figures by GayleTravis-Keene. *Crinkles* 3, no. 4 (March/April 2001): 4–7.

Chapter 10: "Checking Out Some RRRRoarin' Good Reads!" by Barbara Campbell and Lion Figures by Taliesyn Gallett. *Crinkles* 2, no. 3 (January/February 2000): 4–7.

Chapter 11: "Books about Mice Are Twice as Nice" by Annette Marie Bailey and Mice Figures by Taliesyn Gallett. *Crinkles* 2, no. 1 (September/October 1999): 4–7.

Chapter 12: "Monkey Business! Monkey Books!" by Barbara Campbell and Monkey Figures by Gayle Travis-Keene. *Crinkles* 2, no. 5 (May/June 2000): 40–45.

Chapter 13: "Mirror, Mirror on the Wall" by Lori Kebetz and Princess Figures by Gayle Travis-Keene. *Crinkles* 3, no. 1 (September/October 2000): 27–32.

Chapter 14: "Those Trickster Rabbits" by Paula Montgomery and Rabbit Figures by Taliesyn Gallett. *Crinkles* 1, no. 3 (January/February 1999): 4–8.

Chapter 15: "Santa Claus by Many Names" by Diana Erbio and Santa Figures by Vicky Weeks Elliott. *Crinkles* 5, no. 2 (November/December 2002): 38–41.

Chapter 16: "Who Guards the Sheep?" by Paula Montgomery and Shepherd Figures by Gayle Travis-Keene. *Crinkles* 3, no. 5 (May/June 2001): 41–44.

Chapter 17: "Icy Maidens in the North Lands" by Pamela Lichty and Snow Maiden Figures by Vicky Weeks Elliott. *Crinkles* 4, no. 4 (March/April 2002): 4–7.

Chapter 18: "Troll Tales" by Denice Baldetti and Troll Figures by Tami Ferraro. *Crinkles* 5, no. 3 (January/February 2003): 4–7.

About the Author

PAULA MONTGOMERY is the founder and former publisher of *School Library Media Activities Monthly* and *Crinkles*.

www.ingramcontent.com/pod-product-compliance
Ingram Content Group UK Ltd.
Pitfield, Milton Keynes, MK11 3LW, UK
UKHW050147280225
455689UK00007B/87